Encyclopedia of
KNITTING
&
CROCHET

Encyclopedia of
KNITTING
&
CROCHET

CAVENDISH HOUSE

Published by
Marshall Cavendish Books Limited
58 Old Compton Street
London W1V 5PA

© Marshall Cavendish Limited 1972 – 84

ISBN 0 86307 178 3

Printed and bound in Italy by L.E.G.O.

CONTENTS

Knitting Know-how

Basic Wardrobe

CONTENTS (continued)

Crochet Know-how

Basic Wardrobe

Collector's Pieces

ACKNOWLEDGEMENTS

Photographers:
John Adriaan, Malcolm Aird, Adèle Baker, Michael Barrington-Martin, Stephen Bicknell, Clive Boursnell, John Carter, Clive Corless, Bob Croxford, Richard Dormer, Leslie Emms, Michael Harvey, Michael Harwood, Chris Lewis, Patrick Lichfield, Dawn Marsden, David Newsome, Peter Rand, Paul Redman, Bruce Scott, M. Stuart, Chris Thomson, Peter Watkins, Jim Williams

Illustrators:
Annette Critten, H. Edwards, Elizabeth Embleton, Barbara Firth, Sally Foy, Susan France, Diane Groves, Isobel Hollowood, Andrei Pearman, Margaret Power, Renée Robinson, Posy Simmonds, Paul Williams

Designers:
Diana Chabot, Rae Compton, Marjorie Finbow, Bairnswear, J. & P. Coats Ltd, Jaegar Hand Knitting Ltd, Lister & Co. Ltd, Martin Mahony Ltd, R. V. Marriner Ltd, Patons & Baldwins Ltd, Pingouin yarns, Robin yarns, Sirdar Ltd, J. Templeton & Son Ltd, H. G. Twilley Ltd, Wendy yarns

Text:
Rae Compton, Pam Dawson, Marjorie Finbow; Ena Milton

Credits:
W. Bill Ltd; Camera Press, London: GMN

We would like to thank the following for their help and co-operation:
Abel Morrall Ltd; Mary Coleman; Dixon & Partners Ltd; The Felt and Hessian Shop, London; Highland Home Industries, Edinburgh; Patons & Baldwins Ltd

Introduction

Knitting and crochet are still as popular as ever and the increasing range of yarns and designs means endless possibilities for making beautiful garments and household articles. So whether you are keen to experiment with new ideas or whether you are a traditionalist at heart, the Golden Hands Encyclopedia of Knitting and Crochet has something for you.

The step-by-step instructions, clearly illustrated with diagrams and colour photographs at each stage, could not be simpler to follow, and beginners will be encouraged to find that they can create garments right from the start—from a cosy knitted scarf to a multi-coloured waistcoat in crocheted squares.

A professional-looking finish is vital to the success of a piece of work, and this book is full of tips to help you achieve this, covering such techniques as buttonholes, hems, pockets and necklines.

For all those who have a favourite pattern but would like to experiment with different effects, Golden Hands include a wide variety of stitch patterns from the most delicate of lacy looks to the chunkiest of fabric weaves, and from the boldest of jacquard motifs to the most subtle of toning stripes. As you become more skilful, try the superb traditional designs of Aran and Shetland knitting or Irish crochet lace.

The Basic Wardrobe patterns after each section are related closely to the techniques described in the Know-how chapters, and are the ideal way of putting your newly-acquired skills into practice. There are garments for the whole family—pretty, practical play clothes for children, chunky casuals for men and boys and a whole range of fashion garments for yourself, including sweaters, shawls, dresses and trousers for every occasion from a country weekend to a special evening out.

Once you have mastered the techniques and experimented with the stitches, you can learn to create designs of your own, combining new styles, colours and patterns to make truly original garments.

Anyone excited by all the possibilities of hand knitting and crochet today will find this book a constant source of inspiration so begin right away. You will be delighted by the results.

Chapter 1

Knitting Know-how

Introduction to fashion knitting

Hand knitting is one of the most exciting fashion crafts these days. New dyes, fibres, metallic yarns, mixed yarns and beautifully nubbly textures all combine happily with the fluid, flexible quality of hand knitting. What is more, the techniques from different countries are now circulating internationally, so that there is a wealth of new information to draw on. For beginners, these Knitting Know-how chapters give a clear guide to the basic techniques. For the more experienced knitter there are many clever, little-known techniques, like the invisible casting on in Knitting Know-how 3, a range of garments in the Basic Wardrobe chapters, and hints on how to do your own designing.

The tools of the trade

- [ ] A rigid metal or wooden inch/centimetre rule
- [ ] Scissors
- [ ] Sewing-up needles with blunt points
- [ ] Rustless steel pins
- [ ] Stitch holder or a large safety pin, to hold stitches not in use
- [ ] Knitting register for counting rows
- [ ] Knitting needle gauge to check correct needle size
- [ ] Cloth or polythene bag in which to keep knitting clean
- [ ] Iron and ironing surface with felt pad or blanket
- [ ] Cotton cloths suitable for use when pressing

Know your needles

Modern knitting needles are usually made of lightweight coated metal or of plastic, and should always be kept in good condition. Bent, scratched or uneven needles will spoil the evenness of your knitting, and should be discarded.

For 'flat' knitting—that is, knitting worked backwards and forwards on two needles—needles with knobs at one end are advisable as they lessen the possibility of dropped stitches, which is frustrating to the most even-tempered knitter.

For socks, gloves, certain types of sweaters, and any garment which is knitted 'in the round'—that is, in a circle instead of 'flat' —a set of four needles, pointed at both ends, is used. A flexible circular needle is used for some designs for seamless circular garments like skirts. The effect is the same as dividing the work between three needles, but a greater number of stitches can be used, and the danger of loose stitches where the needles join is avoided.

Needle sizes

Here is a chart of the British, American and French needle sizes. As you can see, with British sizes the higher the number, the smaller the diameter of the needle, whereas the French and American system is the reverse. Much larger needles can be obtained, which are in sizes 0, 00 and 000 or $\frac{1}{2}$in, $\frac{3}{4}$in and

Knitting Needle Sizes

British	French	American
14	2	00
13	2.25	0
12	2.50	1
11	3.00	2
10	3.25	3
–	3.50	4
9	4.00	5
8	4.50	6
7	4.75	7
6	5.00	8
5	5.50	9
4	6.00	10
3	7.00	$10\frac{1}{2}$
2	8.00	11
1	9.25	13

Yarns and ply

Yarn is the word used to describe any spun thread, whether it is fine or thick. It may be a natural fibre like wool, cotton, linen, silk, angora, or mohair—or a man-made fibre like Acrilan, Orlon, Nylon or Courtelle.

When choosing a yarn, you will come across the word ply. This indicates the number of spun single threads that have been twisted together. Each single thread can be spun to any thickness so that a simple reference to the ply does not necessarily determine the thickness of the finished yarn, although the terms 2-ply, 3-ply and 4-ply are often used to mean yarn of a recognised thickness. The following ply classification is broadly applicable to the majority of hand-knitting yarns whether made from wool, man-made fibres or blends of both.

Baby yarns are usually made from the higher quality yarns, and are available in 3-ply and 4-ply, also Quickerknit yarns which are equivalent to a 4-ply yarn but are light in weight due to their being softly twisted.

2, 3 and 4-ply yarns may be wool, wool and man-made fibre blends, or 100% man-made fibre.

Double Knitting yarns are the most widely used of all yarns, and are usually made from four spun single threads (although there are exceptions to this) twisted together to produce hardwearing yarns, virtually double the thickness of 4-ply yarns.

Chunky yarns and Double-Double Knitting yarns are extra thick yarns which knit up more quickly than finer yarns.

Crepe yarns are usually available in 4-ply (sometimes called single crepe) and double knitting (sometimes called double crepe). They are more tightly twisted than 4-ply and double knitting and so produce a smooth firm fabric which is particularly hardwearing and resistant to pilling.

Very important!

Since there is no official standardisation, yarns marketed by different firms often vary in thickness and in yardage.

If you cannot obtain the yarn quoted in the instructions, or have set your heart on something else, it is possible to use other yarn provided you can obtain the same tension as given in the pattern. The Great Yarn Chart on pages 10 and 11 will enable you to find an equivalent yarn from a wide range of those on the market which will knit up to the appropriate tension.

Always buy sufficient yarn at one time so that all the yarn used is from the same dye lot. Yarn from a different dye lot may vary very slightly, but even the slightest difference can cause an unsightly line across your work, spoiling the whole effect.

Yarns and metrication

When purchasing yarns it is advisable to check with your stockist as to the weight of the balls, since they now vary due to the introduction of the metric system. Metrication has been adopted by some manufacturers already, while others are in the process of changeover. Also large stocks of wool in standard ounces will take time to run out, so this confused situation will be with us for some time. In our Basic Wardrobe patterns we have specified the number of balls required and whether they are sold in ounces or grammes at the time of publication, but to help you further we have included a conversion table to accustom you to the new system. If you are at all worried, remember, it is wiser to overbuy than run short.

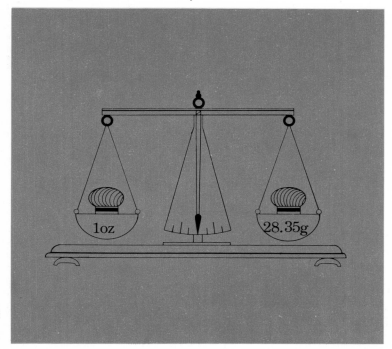

A 1 oz ball of wool weighs just a little more than a 25g ball.

Useful weights—in grammes (g) and kilogrammes (kg)

1oz	= 28·35g
4oz	= 113·4g
8oz	= 226·8g
1lb	= 454g
25g	= 0·9oz
50g	= 1·8oz
1kg/1000g	= 2·2lb

Knitting yarn quantities (to convert either way)

1oz=25g+3·35g
For 3oz buy 4 balls of 25g

7oz buy 8 balls of 25g	16oz buy 18 balls of 25g
12oz buy 14 balls of 25g	20oz buy 23 balls of 25g

Your success depends on tension

To make any design successfully it is absolutely vital that you obtain the tension stated in the pattern.

This means that you must obtain the same number of stitches to the inch and *also* the same number of rows to the inch as the designer obtained.

As a beginner, it is advisable when you first begin knitting to keep on practising, trying to obtain the correct tension. If however you cannot hold yarn and needles comfortably and at the same time obtain the correct tension, then change the size of needles you are using. If you are making too many stitches to the inch try using a larger size needle; if you are making too few stitches to the inch try a size finer needle.

This applies not only to the beginner but to all knitters beginning a new design. Always test that you have the correct tension by knitting a minimum of a 2 inch square. However, if you use a 4 inch square, it will be easier to measure exactly.

A few minutes spent on this preparation lays the foundation for a successful garment. If it is overlooked, a great deal of work may be undertaken before the error in size is realised. Even half a stitch too many or too few, although seemingly little, amounts to nine stitches too many or too few on the back of a 34in sweater. This can mean the completed sweater is 2 inches too large or small.

Once you have worked your tension square, lay it on a flat surface and pin it down. Place a measure on your knitting and mark out one inch with pins. Count the number of stitches between the two pins very carefully.

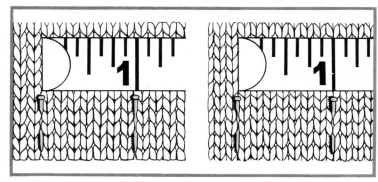

▲ *The inches are marked out with pins, left, showing 7 stitches to the inch: right, measuring between the pins gives 7½ stitches to the inch*

▼ *The tension square is pinned into a perfect square, ready to measure*

The Great Yarn Chart

How to use your favourite yarns for all the garments in the Golden Hands Encyclopedia of Knitting and Crochet

We're going to let you into a trade secret. If you've fallen in love with a particular colour or yarn, or find it impossible to obtain the yarn featured in any of the photographs, it is possible to use an equivalent yarn.

This does not mean that you will automatically be able to substitute one for another, but if you test carefully, you should be able to use an alternative. It may not necessarily look quite the same, but it will knit up to the same size in your hands as the original yarn would have.

Start by knitting a small square, for example 4 in by 4 in, in the yarn of your choice, to see that you can get the same number of stitches and rows to the inch as given in the pattern. Every yarn on these two pages has been tested and the chart is based on the results. To make your number of stitches to the inch equal those in the chart, you may need to use a size smaller or larger needle. Don't worry. Some people knit very loosely, others very tightly. The important point is for you

to have exactly the same number of stitches and rows to 1 inch as given in the pattern.

This chart shows the yarns listed under the number of stitches to 1 inch worked on a given needle size and measured over stocking stitch.

However, it is difficult to judge how to count, say, $3\frac{1}{2}$ stitches or $4\frac{1}{4}$ stitches to the inch! Therefore it is always wise to count stitches over 4 inches and then divide by four. (For example, $3\frac{1}{2}$ sts x 4=14 sts over 4 in.) If however the tension reference includes a $\frac{1}{3}$ in, measure over 3 inches to get a whole number of stitches, then divide by 3.

Never believe that a $\frac{1}{4}$ of a stitch in an inch is too little to consider. If a 36 in sweater in double knitting yarn has either $\frac{1}{4}$ stitch to the inch too few or too many, the finished garment will be almost 2 inches too tight or too wide.

Those of you who have had problems of conversion for crochet yarn will be happy to know that these yarn equivalents apply also to crochet.

$8\frac{1}{2}$ sts and $10\frac{1}{2}$ rows on No.10 needles
Jaeger
Faerie-spun 2 ply
Ladyship
3 ply Newtimer
3 ply Babyship

$8\frac{1}{2}$ sts and 11 rows on No.11 needles
Wendy
Peter Pan 3 ply yarns

8 sts and 10 rows on No.10 needles
Sirdar
All 3 ply yarns
Coats
Carefree Bri-nylon 3 ply

8 sts and 10 rows on No.11 needles
Patons
Fuzzy Wuzzy
Beehive Baby Wool 3 ply
Nylox 3 ply
Limelight Courtelle Baby 3 ply
Brilliante 3 ply

$7\frac{1}{2}$ sts and $9\frac{1}{2}$ rows on No.10 needles
Emu
All 4 ply yarns (including Super Crepe and Tweed)
Robin
Baby Nylon 3 ply
Sirdar
All 4 ply yarns
Ladyship
Siesta
Renown
Countryman

$7\frac{1}{2}$ sts and $9\frac{1}{2}$ rows on No.11 needles
Robin
Baby soft Bri-nylon 3 ply
Vogue 3 ply

$7\frac{1}{2}$ sts and 10 rows on No.10 needles
Lister
Lavenda 3 ply
Baby Bel 3 ply Courtelle
Nursery Time 3 ply Nylon
Twilleys
Goldfingering
Lyscordet
Wendy
Invitation cotton
Ladyship
4 ply Newtimer

Lee Target
Cherub Baby 3 ply Nylon
Lullaby Baby 3 ply Courtelle

7 sts and 9 rows on No.9 needles
Martin Mahony
Blarney Berella
Baby Quickerknit
Coats
Carefree Bri-nylon 4 ply

7 sts and 9 rows on No.10 needles
Pingouin
Age d'or
Coton
Perle 4 ply
Mademoiselle Pingouin
Coats
Cadenza Crepe 4 ply
Lee Target
All 4 ply yarns
Lister
All 4 ply yarns (including Bel Air Starspun and Cashmere)
Robin
All 4 ply yarns (including Vogue and Tricel Nylon Perle Casino Crepe, Soft Bri-nylon)
Hayfield
All 4 ply yarns including Baby Courtier Bri-nylon
Patons
Cameo Crepe
Kingfisher
Limelight Courtelle
Crepe-knits as 4 ply
All 4 ply yarns (including Baby Quickerknit
Brilliante Quickerknit
Limelight Courtelle Quickerknit
Beehive Baby Wool 4 ply
Purple Heather 4 ply
Nylox 4 ply)
Wendy
All 4 ply yarns (including Peter Pan 4 ply—Courtelle
Peter Pan 4 ply—Bri-nylon)
Jaeger
Dappelwul 4 ply
Dappelwul Courtelle Crepe
Gaelic-spun
Marriner
All 4 ply yarns
Twilleys
Stalite

7 sts and 10 rows on No.10 needles

Twilleys
Crysette
Cortina

6½ sts and 8½ rows on No.8 needles

Coats
Baby Quick-knit

6½ sts and 8½ rows on No.9 needles

Coats
Carefree Bri-nylon 4 ply

6½ sts and 8½ rows on No.10 needles

Templetons
H & O Fleece

6 sts and 8 rows on No.8 needles

Pingouin
Madame Pingouin
Super Jaspee

Lee Target
Lullaby Baby Quick Knit
Courtelle
Cherub Baby Quick Knitting

Lister
Nursery Time Baby Quick Knit
Baby Bel Quick Knit
Courtelle

Robin
All Double Knitting yarns (including
Vogue
Inspiration
Specklespun
Bri-nylon and
Soft Bri-nylon Baby Quicker Crepe)
Tricel Nylon and
Tricel Nylon Perle

Sirdar
All Double Knitting yarns (including Double Crepe)

Patons
Promise

Wendy
Double Knit Nylonised
Peter Pan Bri-nylon
New Tricel Nylon
Double Knit
Tricel Nylon Double Crepe

Ladyship
Safari
County
Chubby Tweeds
Creation Double Knit
Newtimer Double Knit
Tricel Double Knit

6 sts and 8 rows on No.9 needles

Wendy
Courtelle Double Crepe
Peter Pan Courtelle Double Knitting

Jaeger
Celtic-spun
Astral-spun
Shadow-spun
Donegal

Lister
All Double knitting yarns

Lee Target
All Double knitting yarns

Martin Mahony
Blarney Berella Double Knitting
Killowen Double Knitting
Killowen Extra Double Knitting
Killowen Quartet Double Knitting

Templetons
Antler Double Crepe
H & O Charm

5½ sts and 7 rows on No.8 needles

Hayfield
All Double Knitting yarns

5½ sts and 7½ rows on No.7 needles

Coats
Carefree Bri-nylon Double Knitting

Wendy
Peter Pan Bri-nylon Baby Quick

5¾ sts and 7½ rows on No.8 needles

Patons
Fiona

5½ sts and 7½ rows on No.8 needles

Patons
Double Knitting Wool
Totem Double Crepe
Four Seasons
Moorland Double Knitting
Limelight Courtelle Double Knitting and Double Crepe
Brilliante Double Knitting
Term Time Double Knitting

Jaeger
Spiral-spun
Spiral-spun Courtelle

Wendy
Peter Pan Courtelle
Baby Quick

Coats
Cadenza Courtelle Double Crepe

5½ sts and 7½ rows on No.9 needles

Coats
Cadenza Courtelle Double Knitting
Cadenza Courtelle Double Crepe

Pingouin
Classique Crylor
Multipingouin

Twilleys
Knitcot

5½ sts and 8 rows on No.8 needles

Emu
All Double Knitting yarns
Crochet wool

5½ sts and 8 rows on No.9 needles

Emu
Baby Quickerknit Courtelle
Baby Quickerknit Bri-nylon

5 sts and 6½ rows on No.8 needles

Patons
Capstan

Jaeger
Chenille

Wendy
Kinvara

5 sts and 7 rows on No.8 needles

Jaeger
Mohair-spun

5 sts and 7 rows on No.9 needles

Jaeger
Sunlin

5 sts and 9 rows on No.10 needles

Twilleys
Mohair

4¾ sts and 7½ rows on No.8 needles

Patons
Camelot

4½ sts and 5½ rows on No.6 needles

Lee Target
Special Quality for Aran Knitting
Motoravia Triple Knitting

Hayfield
Croft Thickerknit

4½ sts and 6 rows on No.7 needles

Robin
Aran Pure New Wool

Martin Mahony
Blarney Bainin
Blarney Heatherspun

4½ sts and 6½ rows on No.7 needles

Jaeger
Pebble-spun
Double Double Crepe

4¼ sts and 5¼ rows on No.5 needles

Patons
Doublet

Wendy
Diabolo Double Double Knit

Coats
Crescendo Double Double Knitting

4 sts and 5 rows on No.5 needles

Robin
Vogue Double Double
Chunky Knit

3½ sts and 5 rows on No.3 needles

Lee Target
Super Fleetknit

Lister
Prema Bulky Knitting

Information in this table has been checked at the time of publishing, but brands and standards can change. To avoid disappointment, we suggest you take particular care to knit up a tension square before you begin.

When you use a different yarn you may find that the number of ounces or balls is slightly different.

11

Yarn manufacturers' addresses

(U.K., Australia, New Zealand, South Africa).

Coats yarns

J. & P. Coats (U.K.) Ltd., Central Office, 12 Seedhill Road, Paisley, Scotland.

Emu yarns

Emu Wools Ltd., Low Street, Keighley, Yorks,

Hayfield yarns

John C. Horsfall & Sons Ltd., Hayfield Mills, Glusburn, Nr. Keighley, Yorks. BD20 8QP.
Mail order stockists—Messrs. Abbey Dale, 8 Ilkley Road, Addingham, Uttley, Yorks.

Jaegar yarns

Jaegar Hand Knitting, PO Box 5, Suttingham Road, Shepshed, Loughborough, Leics., LE12 5BR.

Ladyship yarns

Baldwin & Walker, Westcroft Mills, Halifax, Yorks.
Overseas mail orders can be sent to Campbell (Wools) Ltd., 199 King Cross Road, Halifax, Yorks.

Lee Target yarns

George Lee & Sons Ltd., PO Box 37, Wakefield, Yorks.

Lister yarns

Lister & Co. (Knitting Wools) Ltd., PO Box 37, Providence Mills, Wakefield, Yorks.

Mahony yarns

Martin Mahony (Great Britain) Ltd., The Coal Road, Seacroft, Leeds, Yorks., LS14 2AQ.

Marriner yarns

R. V. Marriner Ltd., Greengate Mills, Keighley, Yorks. BD21 5LN.
Villawool Head Office (Australia), 255 George Street, Sydney, N.S.W. 2000, Australia.

Patons yarns

Patons & Baldwins (Sales) Ltd., PO Box 22, Darlington, Co. Durham.
Coats Patons (Australia) Ltd., PO Box 110, Mount Waverley, Melbourne, Australia.
Coats Patons (New Zealand) Ltd., PO Box 6149, Auckland, New Zealand.
Patons & Baldwins South Africa (PTY) Ltd., PO Box 33, Desert Street, Randfontein, Transvaal, South Africa.

Pingouin yarns

French Wools Ltd., 7 Lexington Street, London W1R 4BJ.

Raffene yarns

Atlas Handicrafts, 27 Laurel Street, Preston, PR1 3XS.

Robin yarns

Robert Glew & Co. Ltd., Robin Mills, Idle, Bradford, Yorks., BD10 9TE.

Sirdar yarns

Sirdar Ltd., PO Box 31, Bective Mills, Alversthorpe, Wakefield, Yorks.
Sirdar Wools (Australia) PTY Ltd., PO Box 472, Goulburn, New South Wales 2580, Australia.
Sirdar Wools (New Zealand) Ltd., PO Box 4199, Auckland, New Zealand.
Sirdar Wools (PTY) Ltd., PO Box 49072, Rosettenville, Johannesburg, South Africa.

Twilley yarns

H. G. Twilley Ltd., Roman Mills, Stamford, Lincs. PE9 1BG.
Panda Yarns Ltd., 69 Cremorne Street, Richmond, Victoria 3121, Australia.
Mosgiel Woollens Ltd., Roslyn Mills, Kai Korai, Valley, Dunedin, New Zealand.
Sinclair & Robinson Ltd., PO Box 2644, Johannesburg, South Africa.

Wendy and Peter Pan yarns

Carter & Parker Ltd., Gordon Mills, Netherfield Road, Guiseley, Yorks., LS20 9PD.

Abbreviations

Here is a list of knitting terms which are usually printed in a shortened form.
In some designs it is necessary to use a special abbreviation applicable to that design only. In such a case the abbreviation will be explained at the point where it is first used, or placed in a clear note before the beginning of the instructions.

alt	=alternate(ly)		No	=number
approx	=approximate(ly)			
			P	=purl
beg	=begin(ning)		patt	=pattern
			PB	=purl into back of stitch
			psso	=pass slip stitch over
cm	=centimetre		P up	=pick up and purl
cont	=continu(e)(ing)		P-wise	=purlwise
dble	=double		rem	=remain(ing)
dec	=decreas(e)(ing)		rep	=repeat
			RH	=right hand
			RS	=right side
foll	=follow(ing)			
			sl 1	=slip 1 knitwise
g st	=garter stitch (every row knit)		sl 1P	=slip 1 purlwise
			st(s)	=stitch(es)
			st st	=stocking stitch (one row knit, one row purl)
in	=inch(es)			
inc	=increas(e)(ing)		tbl	=through back of loop
			tog	=together
K	=knit		TW2B	=twist 2 back by knitting into back of 2nd stitch then back of first stitch on left hand needle and slipping 2 stitches off needle together
KB	=knit into back of stitch			
K1B	=knit one through loop below next stitch			
K up	=pick up and knit			
K-wise	=knitwise			
			TW2F	=twist 2 front by knitting into front of 2nd stitch then front of first stitch on left hand needle and slipping 2 stitches off needle together
LH	=left hand			
M1K	=make one knitwise by picking up loop that lies between stitch just worked and following stitch, and knitting into back of it		WS	=wrong side
			ybk	=yarn back
			yfwd	=yarn forward
M1P	=make one purlwise by picking up loop that lies between stitch just worked and following stitch, and purling into back of it		yon	=yarn over needle
			yrn	=yarn round needle

Symbols

An asterisk, (*), shown in a pattern row denotes that the stitches shown after this sign must be repeated from that point. Unless otherwise stated, square brackets, [ ], denote instructions for larger sizes in the pattern. Round brackets, (), denote that this section of the pattern is to be worked for all sizes.

Chapter 2

The secret of knitting success

Your finished garment should look just as attractive and well fitting as in the pattern photograph but the secret lies in reading right through all the instructions before ever you put needle to wool. Otherwise it is all too easy to end up with a garment which is too small to squeeze into or so enormous that there is room to spare. Do not allow yourself to be carried away by that first rush of enthusiasm to cast on and start knitting. Make sure first that you completely understand from buying the yarn right through to the final pressing. Publication styles vary but basically instructions fall into three sections:
1. Materials required and finished sizes
2. Working instructions
3. Making up details
The first section is often the most neglected but all three are of vital importance to the success of your garment.

Sizes

Check that the pattern actually provides you with the sizes you want. If it is one size smaller or larger than required the results will be unsatisfactory. If the skirt or sleeve length needs alteration read through the working instructions to see if the design allows for this adjustment. It is usually only where a large, intricate repeat is used that alterations in length may be difficult to adjust.

After the actual measurements of the design are given it is often mentioned that the smallest size is given first throughout the instructions and that any alterations for other sizes follow in order or in brackets. If, after giving several sets of figures for more than one size, you find only one figure is given then you can be sure that this applies to all sizes.

Tension

Although it is often ignored completely, this section is the key to your success. If you don't get the same number of stitches and rows to the inch as the designer did, then no amount of careful knitting and making up will give you a perfect garment.

In order to do this you may have to alter the size of needles that you use. If you have too many stitches to the inch you will need to try a size larger needle. If on the other hand you have too few stitches to the inch you will need to use a size smaller needle. The fact that you may have to use a different needle size is of no importance at all. What is of the greatest importance is that you obtain the same number of stitches and rows as the designer. When knitting a tension square never try to measure over one inch only. It is much easier to measure over not less than 4 inches. If there is even a quarter of a stitch too many or too few it will begin to show over 4 inches whereas over an inch it is too easy to feel that it is not enough of a difference to matter. Measure on a flat surface and don't be tempted to push or pull the sample to the right size!

Ignoring notes on tension or yarn may lead to garments like these!

Materials

Each design has been worked out for the knitting yarn which is stated and you should always try to use this yarn if you want your garment to look like the picture. If for any reason it is quite impossible for you to obtain it then you can substitute something else, but only if you make absolutely sure that you can achieve the tension stated. Even if the pattern is for a simple double knitting yarn don't be fooled into believing that any other double knitting yarn will automatically knit up to the same tension. You can find a substitute yarn by referring to the Great Yarn Chart on pages 10 and 11, or by working sample squares until you find a yarn which works up identically.

If you use a different yarn from the make given you may well find that you use a slightly different quantity. The quantity given only applies to the make stated.

Always buy or reserve enough yarn to complete the garment. If you fail to do this you may have to buy extra balls of a different dye lot. This means that it will be the same yarn but it will have been dyed at a different time. It can vary sufficiently to cause a nasty stripe across your work where the two different dyes meet. Each ball of yarn is not only marked with the shade number but with a dye lot number so that you can always tell whether all the balls are the same or not.

Do not overlook the fact that needle and stitch holders should be in good condition. Bent, twisted or roughened needles or holders will spoil the yarn and make the best of knitting irregular. If it is many years since you bought new needles perhaps now is the time to treat yourself to some new tools.

Measuring knitting

When measuring knitting, it is necessary to lay it on a flat surface. It is very tempting to try and measure it lying along your knee or on the arm of your chair but you must be accurate and not just hope that it is correct. Always measure with a rigid rule and not a tape, and of course don't be tempted to stretch it 'just a little' so that you can avoid having to work those extra few rows before reaching the next stage. If you do this it will take you longer to finish because you will find that the sections will not fit together when it comes to making up. Also never measure round a curve. If you want to measure an armhole, then you must measure the depth on a straight line. To measure a sleeve, don't measure up the sloping side but up the centre of the work (unless stated).

Points to note

The main sections of a garment are usually given first in the instructions, although sometimes a small section such as a pocket lining must be worked before beginning the main section, so that it is ready to join in when required. Where an asterisk* is used it means repeat and is used in two different ways. It may be used during the instructions for one particular row, when it means repeat from that point as directed. It is also used before the beginning of a sentence, and sometimes after a paragraph, to show a part which is repeated later on in the instructions. This will always be made clear in the instructions.

In certain designs, the rows which form the pattern to be repeated throughout the garment are given in a note on their own before the instructions begin. If you have read through the instructions you will have noticed them and will know to refer back to them when you read 'continue in pattern'.

Where there is only brief mention about casting on and off or increasing and decreasing, you may find it helpful to look at the specific chapters for detailed instructions on these points.

Marker threads

Occasionally you are asked in a design to place marker threads at one or both ends of a row. This is only to act as a visual guide so that this point will be easily identified later on in the instructions, either as a point for measuring to or from, or in order to assist when it comes to making up. All that is required is that a short length of any contrasting yarn is threaded through the stitch and tied in place so that it does not accidentally come out while you are working. It is always removed after it has served its purpose.

Making up

Details are always given in the order in which the sections are to be assembled together with instructions for edges and finishing. Also in this part of the instructions you will find a guide to whether or not you will need to press the yarn. Again remember that the instructions refer to the most suitable yarn for the particular pattern. It is most important to make certain whether or not the yarn requires pressing. Some man-made fibres can be completely spoilt by pressing.

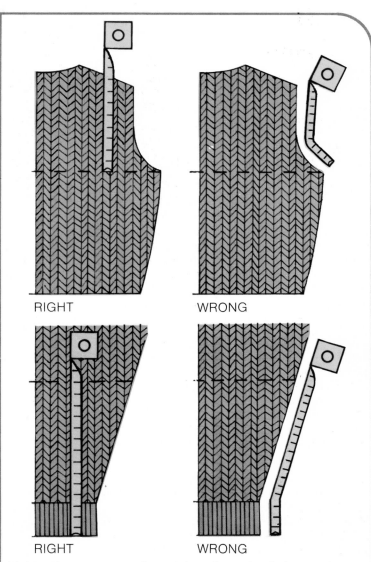

RIGHT   WRONG

RIGHT   WRONG

Right and wrong ways of measuring. A metal rule is most accurate

The marker thread

Chapter 3

Casting on methods

Casting on is the first step in knitting, because it provides the first row of loops, or stitches, on the needle. There are various ways of casting on, each with its own appropriate use, and here we outline the two most popular methods. Also we introduce the intriguing 'invisible' European method, which may be new to many experienced knitters.

The Thumb method (using only one needle) is an excellent way to begin most garments since it gives an elastic and therefore hard wearing edge. On the other hand, the Two needle (or English cable) version is necessary when you want to cast on extra stitches during the knitting itself, for instance for a buttonhole or pocket.

The 'invisible' European method of casting on gives the fashionably flat-hemmed effect of a machine-made garment. It is a flexible strong finish which can hold ribbon or elastic and is very useful for designs which need casings.

The scarf on this page uses the Thumb method and in Knitting Know-how Chapters 4 and 5 are further instructions for completing your scarf.

Pick your own scarf colour, then follow instructions on the facing page

Thumb method— using one needle

To cast on make a slip loop in the yarn about a yard from the end. (This length varies with the number of stitches to be cast on—1 yard will cast on about one hundred stitches. A guide to the length required is—the width of the piece of knitting to be cast on, multiplied by three.)

1. Slip loop on to needle which should be held in the right hand.

Two needle method— or English cable

To cast on make a slip loop in the yarn as given for the Thumb method, at least three inches from the end. It is not necessary to try and gauge the length of yarn required to cast on the number of stitches with this method, as you will be working from the ball of yarn. Slip this loop on to the left hand knitting needle.

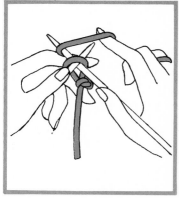

1. Insert right hand needle into loop holding yarn in right hand and wind yarn under and over the needle.

Invisible casting on

Even if you are an experienced knitter, you'll be delighted to discover the many uses to which this marvellous new technique lends itself.

1. Using a contrast yarn, which is later removed, and the Thumb method, cast on half the number of stitches required, plus one. Now using the correct yarn for the garment, begin the ribbing.

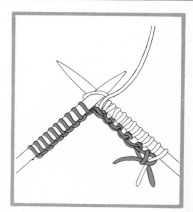

1st row. K1, *yfwd, K1, rep from * to end.
2nd row. K1, *yfwd, sl 1, ybk, K1, rep from * to end.
3rd row. Sl 1, *ybk, K1, yfwd, sl 1, rep from * to end.

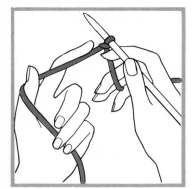

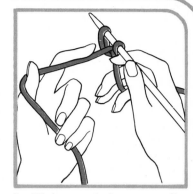

2. Working with the short length of yarn in the left hand, pass this round the left thumb.

3. Insert the point of the needle under the loop on the thumb, and hook forward the long end of yarn from the ball.

4. Wind yarn under and over the needle and draw through loop, leaving stitch on needle.

5. Tighten stitch on needle, noting that yarn is round thumb ready for next stitch.
6. Repeat action 3-5 for required number of stitches.

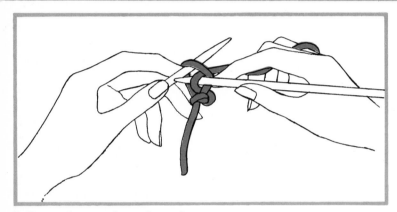
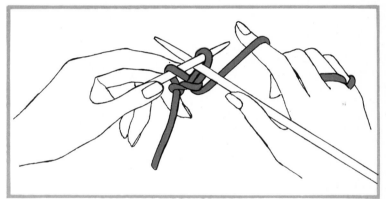

2. Draw the new loop through the first loop on left hand needle thus forming a second loop. Pass newly made loop onto the left hand needle.

3. Place point of right hand needle between two loops on left hand needle and wind yarn under and over the right hand needles as in diag. 1. Draw this new loop through between the two stitches on the left hand needle. Slip this loop on to left hand needle.

4. Repeat action described in paragraph 3 between last 2 stitches on left hand needle until the required number of stitches have been cast on.

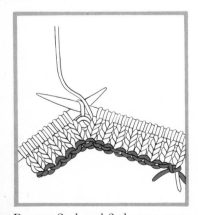
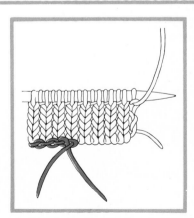

Repeat 2nd and 3rd rows once more.
6th row. K1, *P1, K1, rep from * to end.
7th row. P1, *K1, P1, rep from * to end.

2. Continue in rib for the required length. Unpick contrast yarn. The ribs should appear to run right round the edge.

Beginners—knit a super scarf

If you have never knitted before start with one of the scarves on the opposite page. After Chapter 5 it will be ready to wear.

What you need: Mother's Scarf—5 50g balls plus 2 50g balls for the fringe if required. Child's Scarf—3 50g balls plus 1 50g ball for the fringe.
Yarn: Patons Totem Double Crepe.
Needles: One pair of 0 size.
Measurements: Mother's Scarf— Length 70in Width 12½ in. Child's Scarf— Length 50in Width 7½in.
Tension: 4 stitches = 1in.

Casting on: Using the Thumb method, cast on 50 stitches for the Mother's Scarf, or 30 stitches for the Child's Scarf. **(For how to work, see Knitting Know-how Chapter 4)**

Chapter 4

The basic stitches

In knitting, there are only two basic stitches—knit or purl. The pattern you make by using either one or a combination of both of these stitches may be smooth or textured, chunky and heavy like a rope, or light as lace.

How to join yarn

Always join yarn at the beginning of a row, never in the centre, or it will spoil the continuity of the stitches. The only exception is in tubular or round knitting, which is featured in Chapter 19. Leave a short length of yarn, enough to darn into the edge of the work, at the end of the row. Begin the next row with the new yarn, again leaving a short end for darning in. You can then darn these ends neatly into the edge when your knitting is finished.

How to measure

Never try to lay the work to be measured over your knee or along the arm of a chair. Be certain that you lay the knitting on a flat surface and that you measure with a non-stretch rule rather than a tape. Do not include the cast-on edge in your measurement, but begin with the base of the first row. When measuring an armhole or sleeve, do not measure around the curve or up the sloping edge (unless stated) but up the centre of the fabric.

Every time you meet a new stitch, it's wise to make a 4in tension square. When you've enough squares, sew them up into a bright patchwork quilt!

Knit stitch

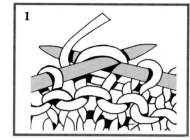

1. Take the needle with the cast-on stitches in your left hand, and the other needle in your right hand. Insert the right-hand needle point through the first stitch on the left-hand needle from front to back.
Keeping the yarn away from you behind the needles, pass the yarn round the point of the right-hand needle so that you form a loop.

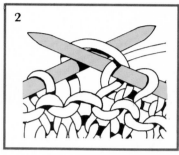

2. Draw this loop through the stitch on the left-hand needle, so forming a new loop on the right-hand needle.
3. Allow the stitch on the left-hand needle to slip off.
Repeat this action until you have drawn loops through all the stitches on the left-hand to the right-hand needle.

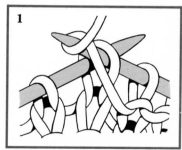

You have now knitted one row. To work the next row, change the needle holding the stitches to your left hand and the free needle to your right hand, and work this row exactly the same way as the first one.

Purl stitch

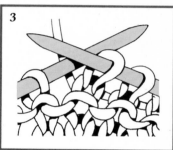

1. Take the needle with the cast-on stitches in your left hand, and the other needle in your right hand. Insert the right-hand needle point through the first stitch on the left-hand needle from back to front.
Keeping the yarn towards you in front of the needles, pass yarn round point of right-hand needle to form a loop.

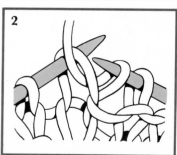

2. Draw this loop through the stitch on the left-hand needle, thus forming a new loop on the right-hand needle.
3. Allow the stitch on the left-hand needle to slip off.
Repeat this action, with the next stitch, until you have drawn loops through all the stitches on the left-hand needle and passed them on to the right-hand needle.

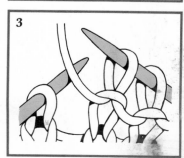

You have now purled one row. Change the needles, and work other rows in the same way. If you practise knitting and purling, you will find that you become faster and that your work becomes much more even.

Garter stitch

This is the simplest of all the knitting patterns formed by working every row in the same stitch, either knit or purl.

If you purl every row, however, you don't get such a smooth, even fabric as when you knit every row. This is because all knitters knit more regularly than they purl. So, whenever you come across instructions referring to garter stitch it is intended that you should knit every row.

▲ *Knitted garter stitch*

Stocking stitch

This is the smoothest of all the patterns in knitting and is made by knitting one row and purling the next, alternately. The knit side of the work in stocking stitch is usually called the right side. If the pattern uses the purl side as the right side it is then called reversed stocking stitch.

▲ *Stocking stitch*

▼ *Reversed stocking stitch*

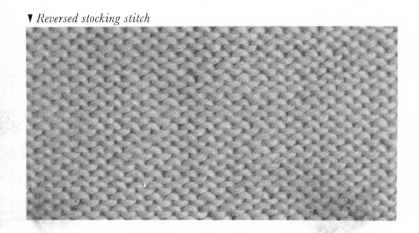

When the scarf is completed, you can muffle up and laugh at the cold

Beginners—continuing your scarves

Having cast on 50 sts for the Mother's Scarf or 30 sts for the Child's Scarf you are now ready to start knitting.

To make: work in garter stitch (knit every row) for 70in for Mother's Scarf or 50in for Child's Scarf.

You can, of course, make either scarf shorter or longer if you like. Remember, you will need to buy more yarn if you want to make the scarf longer.

Don't be tempted to press your scarf at any stage. Garter stitch should always be treated like velvet—never pressed or flattened. If by any chance this warning is too late and the harm is already done, it can quite easily be repaired. Hold the scarf in the steam from a steadily boiling kettle, and the damp heat will rapidly raise the flattened wool fibres back to their original springiness.

Chapter 5

Casting off and the slipped stitch

This chapter starts with casting off. Tension control is very important for this, as it must be exactly the same as the tension of the knitting. If it is not, the edge will be too tight or too loose, and either would spoil the effect of the garment. Slipped stitch is so called because it is slipped from the left-hand to the right-hand needle without being worked, the yarn being carried either behind or in front of the stitch. Slipped stitches can be used in several different ways—in forming part of a pattern, in decreasing and shaping, in producing a neat edge for making up a garment, or in making a fold for a pleat or facing.

If you are working a pattern and the strand is passed behind the work, the stitch itself forms the pattern. If the strand is carried across the front of the stitch, then it can be used to build up the design, in much the same way as a woven design is made. You can also make fascinating herringbone textured effects as well.

Casting off

To cast off on a knit row, knit the first two stitches. Then * with the left-hand needle point, lift the first stitch over the second stitch, leaving one stitch on right-hand needle. Knit the next stitch, repeat from * until all but one stitch have been worked off. Cut the yarn, draw through the last stitch and pull the stitch tight.

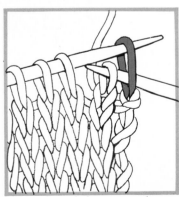

Lifting first stitch over second

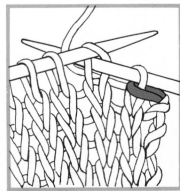

Knitting the next stitch

In the case of a purl row, each stitch is purled before it is cast off. To cast off patterned or ribbed work, lift each stitch over the next stitch following the pattern of the knitting.

Care should always be taken that the casting off is not too tight or too slack, but is similar to the tension of the work itself. If you always cast off too tightly, then use a needle one size larger for casting off. If, on the other hand, you cast off too loosely, use a needle one size smaller to obtain the best results.

Slip stitch purlwise on a knit row

Slipped stitches

Slip stitch knitwise on a knit row
Hold the yarn behind the work as if to knit the stitch. Insert the right-hand needle point into the stitch from front to back, as you would to knit, and slip it on to the right-hand needle.

Slip stitch purlwise on a knit row
Hold the yarn behind the work as if to knit the stitch. Insert the right-hand needle point into the stitch from back to front, as you would to purl, and slip it on to the right-hand needle.

Slip stitch purlwise on a purl row
Hold the yarn at the front of the work as if to purl the stitch. Insert the right-hand needle point from back to front as you would to purl, and slip it on to the right-hand needle.

It is most important to remember that when a slip stitch forms part of a decrease on a knit row, the stitch must be slipped knitwise, otherwise it will become crossed. On a purl row, make sure you slip the stitch purlwise.

In working a pattern, however, where the slip stitch is not part of a decrease it must be slipped purlwise on a knit row, to prevent it becoming crossed when purled in the following row. Don't forget to check which you need for the best results.

Slip stitch purlwise on a purl row

Fringe making

Take six strands of yarn and fold them in half. Draw the loop through the edge of the knitting, then draw the ends of yarn through the loop and pull tight. Repeat evenly all the way along the cast-on and cast-off edges of the scarf.

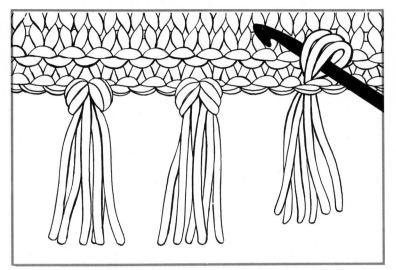

Drawing the loop through the edge of the knitting

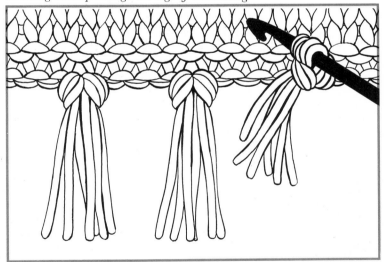

Drawing the ends of yarn through the loop

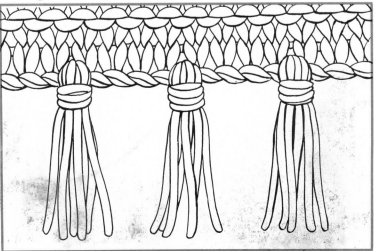

The fringe seen from the other side (usually called the right side)

The fringed scarves when they are finished

Scarves for mother and child (continued)

You've just learned how to cast off—so now you can put it into practice. When you have finished casting off your scarf you are ready to start working the fringe.

The garter stitch scarf in itself has no right or wrong side, but the first tassel dictates the pattern the rest must follow. Continue to work on the same side along the first end, and make sure that the other end matches the first.

To make the fringe: cut lengths of yarn 20in long for the Mother's Scarf, or 16in long for the Child's Scarf. You will need six strands for each tassel, and 16 tassels at each end of the Mother's Scarf, or 10 tassels at each end of the Child's Scarf. Use a crochet hook to pull the tassel loops through the edge of the scarf.

Chapter 6

Casting off invisibly

Experienced knitters and beginners alike have experimented with the special invisible casting on method shown in Knitting Know-how Chapter 3. Here, Golden Hands introduces you to another marvellous technique—invisible casting off. You will also see how to work double casting on, and both of these methods provide a ready-made hem with built-in casing for elastic or cords. The depth of the hems can be varied by the number of rows worked.

It may be a little slower than the normal method you use, but once you have mastered this new technique you will find that the results look most professional.

The drawing on the opposite page shows some of the uses for which these invisible casting off methods are most appropriate. For example, you can use them for neck edging, belts and hems; for rib collars, V-necks and round necks; for cuffs, pocket trims and edgings.

Invisible casting off

Instructions are given for casting off when K1, P1 rib over an odd number of stitches has been used, the first row beginning with K1.

Work the ribbing normally until only two more rows are required to give the finished depth or, if a hem casing is required, less the depth of this hem, ending with a wrong side row.

1st row. K1, *yfwd, sl 1, ybk, K1, rep from * to end.
2nd row. Sl 1, *ybk, K1, yfwd, sl 1, rep from * to end.
Repeat these 2 rows once more, or required number of times to give correct depth of hem.

Break yarn, leaving a length at least three times the length of the edge to be cast off and thread this into a bodkin or wool needle. Hold the bodkin in the right hand and the needle with the stitches in the left hand, working throughout from right to left along the stitches on the needle.

1. Insert the bodkin in the first knit stitch as if to purl it and pull the yarn through, then into the next purl stitch as if to knit it and pull the yarn through, leaving both of these stitches on the left-hand needle.

2. *First work 2 of the knit stitches.
Insert the bodkin into the first knit stitch as if to knit it, pull the yarn through it and slip off the needle.
Pass the bodkin in front of the next purl stitch and into the following knit stitch as if to purl it. Pull the yarn through.

3. Now work 2 of the purl stitches.
Insert the bodkin into the purl stitch at the end of the row as if to purl and slip it off the needle.
Pass the bodkin behind the next stitch and into the following purl stitch as if to knit it. Pull yarn through.
Repeat from * until all stitches have been worked off. Fasten off.

1. *Invisible casting off, working the first two stitches on the row*

2. *Invisible casting off, working the 2nd knit stitch*

3. *Invisible casting off, working the 2nd purl stitch*

Double casting on

When a less elastic cast-on edge is required at the lower edge of a jacket or sweater, the double casting on method is more suitable. Use a short length of contrasting yarn for casting on. This does not become part of the finished work. Using the one needle method, cast on half the number of stitches required.

Using the yarn in which the garment is to be made, begin with a knit row and work 6 rows of stocking stitch, or the required number of rows to give correct depth of hem casing.

1. Slip the first row of loops which show in the contrast yarn on to a spare needle and unpick the contrast yarn because it is no longer required.

2. Fold the work in half, holding the spare needle behind the other needle and work both sets of stitches on to one needle in the following way: *K1 from front needle, P1 from back needle, rep from * until all stitches are on one needle.

Continue in rib for required length. If you want to use this edge for a pattern which does not give detailed instructions, simply cast on half number of stitches given. Total number of stitches will be made up when the stitches are worked on to one needle.

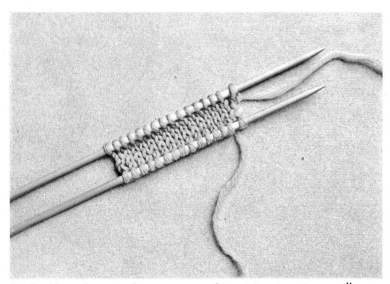

1. *Double casting on—the garment yarn loops put on to a spare needle*

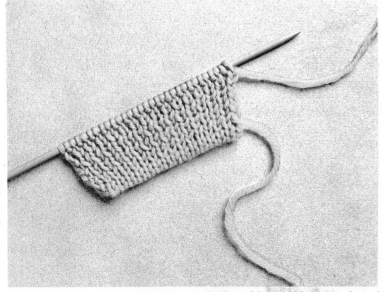

2. *Double casting on, showing the smooth edge with its hidden inner channel*

Chapter 7

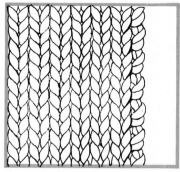

Knitting Know-how

Patterns from purl and knit

Once you have learnt to knit and purl, both stitches can be combined to make a wide variety of decorative patterns, as you can see from the illustrations on the opposite page. The best way to try out these simple stitches is by knitting squares. If you have no left-over scraps of wool, buy several toning colours all the same ply—double knitting is best. A good size for the squares is 4 inches, but they can be made larger or smaller, as long as they are all the same size. As well as giving you practice, these squares can be put to a very good use—you can eventually sew them up into a cushion cover or even a coverlet—and then it acquires the grand name of an afghan.

This chapter also shows how to give a neat edge to a piece of knitting, so your squares will be easier to make up.

1. Edge stitch
You'll find that the edges of your work are neater and therefore more easily made up, if you slip the first stitch and knit the last stitch of each row. This is particularly the case with stocking stitch where the row ends tend to be slack. Knitting the last stitch of every row tightens this edge and gives a neat finish.

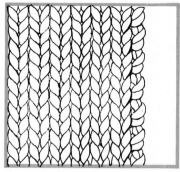

▲ Sl st edge at the end of row

Another means of making a neat edge for stocking stitch is by knitting the first and last stitch on every purl row. This is particularly good for making up using back stitch or invisible seaming (see Knitting Know-how Chapter 11).

K st edge at the end of row ►

2. Rib (1 and 1 rib, or single rib)
Cast on an even number of stitches.
1st row. *K1, P1, rep from * to end
Rep this row for length required.

3. Rib (2 and 2 rib, or double rib)
Cast on a number of stitches divisible by 4.
1st row. *K2, P2, rep from * to end.
Rep this row for length required.

4. Moss stitch
Cast on an odd number of stitches.
1st row. K1, *P1, K1, rep from * to end.
Rep this row for length required.

5. Twisted stocking stitch
This looks very like stocking stitch, but has an added twist, made by knitting into the back of the stitch on all K rows.
Cast on any number of stitches.
1st row. K into back of all stitches.
2nd row. P.
Rep these 2 rows for length required.

6. Double moss stitch
Cast on a number of stitches divisible by 4, plus 2.
1st row. K2, *P2, K2, rep from * to end.
Rep this row for length required.

7. Basket stitch
Cast on a number of stitches divisible by 8.
1st row. *K4, P4, rep from * to end.
2nd, 3rd, and 4th rows. As first row.
5th row. *P4, K4, rep from * to end.
6th, 7th, and 8th rows. As 5th row.
These 8 rows form the pattern, and are repeated as required.

Single rib ▲

Moss stitch ▲

Double rib ▲   *Twisted stocking stitch* ▼

Double moss stitch ▲   *Basket stitch* ▼

Chapter 8

Knitting Know-how

Increasing step by step

Knitting can be straight or shapely and it is by increasing or decreasing that we give garments the shape they need. Putting it simply, knitting is made wider by increasing the number of stitches in a row and made narrower by reducing the number of stitches. Interest is added in more ambitious designs by using these two processes to form patterns in lace knitting. These step-by-step pictures show all the techniques from plain increasing to openwork lace effects.

How to increase

The simplest way is to make an extra stitch at the beginning or the end of a row depending on the shape you're making.
Do this by knitting or purling the stitch in the usual way, but do not slip it off the needle. Instead, place the point of the right-hand needle into the back of the stitch and knit or purl into the stitch again. Slip both these stitches on to your right-hand needle. You have now made two stitches out of one.

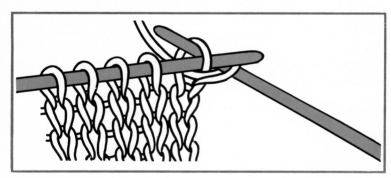

Invisible increasing

Insert the right-hand needle into the front of the stitch below that on the left-hand needle and knit a new stitch. If the increase is on purl work, then purl the new stitch. As it's almost invisible, this method is particularly good when the increase is not at the end of a row, or doesn't form part of a pattern.

Increasing between stitches knitwise (M1K)

1. With right-hand needle, pick up the yarn which lies between the stitch just worked and the next stitch, and place it on the left-hand needle.
2. Knit into back of this loop. This twists and tightens the loop so that no hole is formed.
3. Slip the loop off the left-hand needle, so making one stitch.

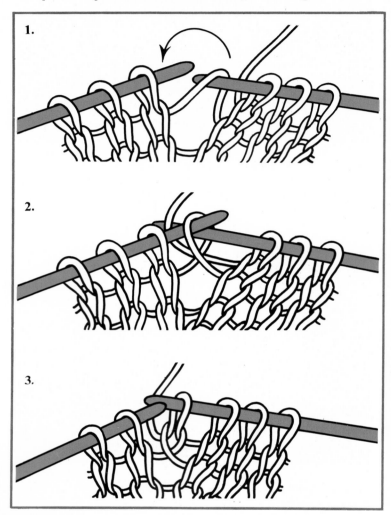

Increasing between stitches purlwise (M1P)

This is worked in the same way as for M1K, but the loop picked up is purled into from the back.

Multiple increasing

You will need this technique when you make a magyar sleeve. Cast on the required number of stitches at the beginning of the side edge, using the two needle method. At the end of the row, reverse the work and cast on.

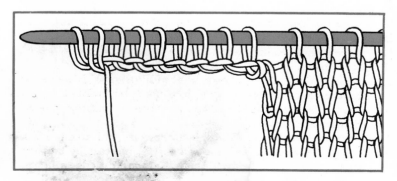

To make a stitch between two knit stitches
Bring the yarn forward (yfwd) as if to purl, then back over the right-hand needle ready to knit the next stitch.

To make a stitch between a purl and a knit stitch
The yarn is already in position to the front, and the next stitch is knitted in the usual way, the yarn taken over the needle (yon).

To make a stitch between two purl stitches
Take the yarn over and round the needle (yrn).

To make a stitch between a knit and a purl stitch
Bring the yarn forward and once round the needle (yrn).

Decorative increasing

Increasing can be used not only to shape a garment but to be decorative at the same time. This way of increasing is usually made one or more stitches in from the edge, the number of edge stitches being determined by the pattern you are using or by your own preference. In the illustrations, three stitches are used for the edge.

The simplest lace effect may be obtained by lifting the yarn immediately after the edge stitches and then knitting into it. The end of the row is worked in the same way, lifting the yarn before the edge stitches.

A more openwork effect, shown in the illustration, is made by knitting the edge stitches, knitting into the stitch below the next stitch on the left hand needle, then increasing by knitting into the stitch immediately above.

To reverse this for the left hand side of the work, knit to one stitch before the edge stitches. Knit the next stitch, increase by knitting into stitch immediately below this stitch, then knit edge stitches.

Increase at beginning of row ▼

Increase at end of row ▼

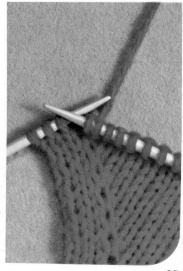

Chapter 9

Methods of decreasing

Passing a slipped stitch over a knitted stitch (Sl1, K1, psso)

Decreasing simply means shaping a piece of work to reduce the size, whether it is at the side-seams of a garment or for darts, tucks or forming gussets. It can be worked so that it is almost invisible and may be hidden by seaming when the finished garment is made up. Decreasing can be decorative as well as practical and a good example of this is when it is used on the raglan shaping of a sweater or cardigan. If the decreasing is worked on the end stitches a neat, hidden-shaping effect will be achieved when seamed or, alternatively, by working the decreasing inside, say, two or three stitches, a fully-fashioned effect is produced.

The way to make a simple decrease is by working two stitches together, either at the ends of the row or at any other given point.

To decrease one stitch knitwise (K2 tog)
Insert the right-hand needle point through two stitches instead of one, and knit together. This will slant to the right.

Knit two stitches together (K2 tog)

Purl two stitches together (P2 tog)

To decrease one stitch purlwise (P2 tog)
Insert right-hand needle point through two stitches, and purl together as if they were one stitch. This will slant to the left.
A simple decrease can also be made by knitting or purling through the backs of the stitches and is then referred to as K2 tog tbl, or P2 tog tbl. This reverses the slant of the stitches.

To decrease using a slipped stitch (sl 1, K1, psso)
This method is most commonly used where decreases are paired, one slanting left and one slanting right as on a raglan sleeve. Slip the first stitch from left to right-hand needle, knit the next stitch. With left-hand needle point, lift the slipped stitch over the knitted one and off the needle. This will slant to the left.
On a purl row the decrease, slanting to the right, is normally made by purling 2 together through the back of the stitch (P2

tog tbl). You can also achieve the same effect by purling one stitch and returning it to the left-hand needle. With the right-hand needle point lift the next stitch over and off the needle. Return the purled stitch to the right-hand needle.

Decreasing in pairs on alternate rows
When you are decreasing at both ends of a row and forming a line that will be seen in the finished garment, the lines should be paired so that they slant in opposite directions.
When decreasing on knit rows of stocking stitch on the right-hand side of the work slip 1, knit 1, pass slip stitch over (sl1, K1, psso). These stitches will slant to the left.
For the other end of the row use a knit 2 together (K2 tog) decrease. These stitches will slant to the right.
When used at opposite ends on alternate rows, they will then give you the inward sloping chain effect shown in the illustration.

Right hand side (Sl1, K1, psso) ▲ *Left hand side (K2 tog)* ▼

Lines formed by slanting decreases on alternative rows

Decreasing in pairs on every row

When decreasing on the purl side of the work as well as on the knit side, you should decrease in pairs to keep the slant correct. On the knit side use a slipped stitch at the beginning of the row and a knit 2 together (K2 tog) decrease at the end.

On the following row, use a purl 2 together (P2 tog) decrease at the beginning and purl 2 together through the back of the stitch (P2 tog tbl) at the end.

The alternative to purling 2 together through the back of the stitch (P2 tog tbl) is to purl the stitch and return it to the left-hand needle. With the right-hand needle point lift the second stitch on left-hand needle over the purled stitch. Return the purled stitch to right-hand needle.

To make use of the chain effect, and so that it is not lost in the seam when making up, the decreases are often worked inside two or more edge stitches, the number of which can vary.

Purling 2 tog on purl side ▲ *Lifting st over st already purled* ▼

Beginning to forget your abbreviations? Then look back to Knitting Know-how Chapter 1.

Twisted Decorative Decreasing

Sometimes the decorative use of decreasing is accentuated by twisting the stitches around the decrease to give them emphasis. This can also be given by incorporating a lace or eyelet effect into the decreasing.

The illustration below shows a decrease which is accentuated by having been twisted as well as lying in the opposite direction to the line of the seam.

This decrease is worked at the end of right side or knit rows for the left-hand side, and at the end of the wrong side or purl rows for the right-hand side.

Knit to last 6 stitches, pass right-hand needle behind first stitch on the left-hand needle and knit next 2 stitches together through the backs of the loops, then knit the first stitch and slip both stitches off left-hand needle. Knit the last 3 stitches in the usual way.

On the next row purl to the last 6 stitches, pass right-hand needle across front of first stitch on left-hand needle and purl the next 2 stitches together, then purl the first stitch and slip both stitches off left-hand needle. Purl the last 3 stitches as usual.

Left hand side decorative decrease ▲ *Right hand side decorative decrease* ▼

Chapter 10

Double increasing & decreasing

Knitting Know-how

Double increasing in knitting is where two stitches are made as a pair, usually at either side of a central point. Double decreasing is where two stitches are taken out of the work. Both double increasing and decreasing may be used for shaping only, although they can also have decorative uses, especially for lace pattern making and for zigzag designs and stripes which produce a chevron effect as shown here.

Double increasing

Purled double increase
This method uses a central stitch and is worked on stocking stitch. Knit up to one stitch before the centre stitch. Knit into that

Striped chevron pattern for a little girl's dress

stitch but before slipping it off the needle purl into the yarn in the row immediately below from the back of the work. Slip the original stitches off the left-hand needle. Knit the centre stitch. Knit the next stitch but again purl into the back of the stitch below before slipping the stitch off the needle. Purl all the stitches in the next row.

Twisted double increase
Again a central stitch is used and the increased stitches are on either side of it.
Work to one stitch before the centre stitch. Knit into the front and then into the back of this stitch. Knit the centre stitch. Knit into the front and then the back of the next stitch. Purl all stitches in the next row.

Crossed double increase
With this method, both stitches to be increased are worked into the centre stitch.
Knit to the centre stitch. Knit into the row below the centre stitch, knit the centre stitch and knit again into the row below the centre stitch. Purl all the stitches in the next row.

Double decreasing

The simple double decrease
Probably the most commonly used pair of double decreases are those made by working three stitches together.
Knitting three stitches together (K3tog) gives you a right-slanting decrease.
Knitting three stitches together through the back of the loops (K3tog tbl) gives you a left slanting decrease.
A neater form of this left slanting decrease is to slip the first stitch and then the second stitch from left to right-hand needles. Knit the next stitch. With the left-hand needle point, lift both slipped stitches over the knitted stitch.

The slipped decrease
This decrease is worked over three stitches. Slip the first stitch on to the right-hand needle. Knit the next two stitches together and, with the left-hand needle, lift the slipped stitch over the stitch made by knitting two together. This slants to the left.
The right-slanting version of this is not so often used and working instructions for it are usually given in full when it does occur.
Slip the first stitch on to the right-hand needle. Knit the next stitch and, with left-hand needle point, lift the slipped stitch over the knitted stitch and off the needle, put the knitted stitch back on to the left-hand needle, lift the next stitch over it with the right-hand needle point. Return the knitted stitch to the right-hand needle.

A double decrease worked on the purl side of the work
This decrease is worked on the purl, or wrong side, of stocking stitch and slants to the left, on the knit side of the work. Purl two together (P2tog) and return to the left-hand needle. With the right-hand needle point, lift the second stitch on the left-hand needle over the first and then return the first stitch to the right-hand needle.
The reverse of this (slanting to the right on the knit side of the work) is worked by slipping one stitch on to the right-hand needle. Knit the next stitch, then twist the following one by reversing it on the needle, leaving it on the left-hand needle. Return the knitted stitch to the left-hand needle with the right-hand needle point, lift the twisted stitch over it. Return the knitted stitch to the right-hand needle.

Purled double increase   *Twisted double increase*   *Crossed double increase*

Simple double decrease : K3tog ▲ K3 tog tbl ▼   *Slipped decrease : slip stitch over K2tog ▲ lift second slip stitch over ▼*

Chapter 11

Sewing up, blocking and pressing

Knitting Know-how

The finishing of a garment is very important. If you have followed the instructions and made each piece with great care it would be a great pity to spoil it all by being in too much of a hurry to give proper attention to the finishing.

First check whether or not the instructions tell you to press the pieces before you begin to make them up. It will be too late to read that you must not press after you have already begun and certain man-made fibres can be completely ruined by contact with heat.

Blocking

If, however, pressing is required prepare the pieces by neatening any yarn ends. To do this, darn the ends up the edges of the work which are to be seamed so that the ends are secure and cannot eventually work themselves loose.

Now, place each piece of knitting, right side down, on an ironing pad and pin evenly round the edges. It is better to use too many pins rather than too few for this and they should be steamproof like tailor's pins so that they do not rust. Never stretch the knitting or the pins will tend to make a fluted edge. The shape you obtain when pinning should be the perfect finished shape which you seam. Once the pieces are pinned, check with a rule that the width and length are the same as those given in the instructions.

Pressing

An ironing board is too narrow for most knitted pieces so the knitter who wants a perfectly finished garment would be well advised to make herself an ironing pad. This can easily be done. First decide on the size you want: it could be a square or an oblong, and should be large enough to take a dress length.

To back the ironing pad use felt or a piece of baize, lay three or four pieces of blanket on top (old blanket pieces are ideal), then two layers of white sheeting. Bind all the edges together with wide bias binding. You now have a pressing pad which can be used on an unpolished hard surface like a kitchen table or even on the floor.

Wring out a clean, white, cotton cloth or piece of old sheeting in warm water and place over the top of the knitted work to be pressed. Do not allow the damp cloth to extend over any of the ribbed edges: these require no pressing. With a warm iron, press evenly but not too heavily the surface of the knitting. You could spoil your work by pressing too heavily, such as flattening the stitches out of all recognition or leaving tell-tale iron marks. The iron must be pressed down and lifted up again without moving along the surface as you would do if you were actually ironing. If you do use an ordinary ironing method you are liable to stretch and crease the knitting and spoil the perfect shape you have

obtained by carefully pinning out the garment in the first place. If any garter stitch or ribbing becomes pressed in error, it can be steamed back into shape (this applies only to wool and not to man-made fibres), but take great care not to direct the steam on to yourself as you hold the knitting in the jet of steam from a boiling kettle. The damp and heat will soon make the over-flattened strands spring up into shape again.

Of course, this can prove a tedious job if the area to be revived is rather large, in which case lay the piece to be treated on your ironing pad. Do not pin, simply pat it flat. Wring out the damping cloth in warm water, place flat on the knitting and leave until the ribbing, garter stitch or pattern springs back into life.

Knitting pinned in place for pressing with warm iron through damp cloth

Seams

To stitch knitting, use a blunt-pointed needle as it is less likely to split the stitches and spoil the effect of a neat seam.

If the garment has been made in a fairly thick yarn it is best to split the yarn for seaming or buy a thinner one in the same shade. You will then find the stitching a lot easier and the result neater.

Back stitch seam

The back stitch seam is worked in very much the same way as in dressmaking except that it is important to keep looking at the other side of the seam to check that you are not splitting any of the stitches and are working along a straight line. Whether you work half or one stitch in from the edge is a matter of personal choice and may be determined by the thickness of the garment which is to be seamed.

Start seaming by working two small stitches, one on top of the other. *Now, with the needle at the back of the work, move along to the left, bringing the needle through to the front of the work the width of one stitch away from the last stitch. Take the needle back to the left-hand end of the last stitch and take it through to the back of the work. Repeat from * until the seam is complete. Care must be taken to pull the stitches firmly through the knitting so that they do not show like an untidy ladder on the right side when finished. Do not stretch the seam by pulling it over your fingers, or draw it too tight so that it becomes a different length to the knitting round about it.

Back stitch seaming

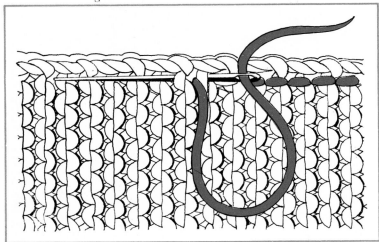

Invisible seam

The diagram shows the seam being worked on the right side of the work.

Begin by securing the sewing yarn to one side. Pass the needle directly across to the other side of the work, picking up one stitch. Pass the needle directly back to the first side of the work, picking up one loop. Continue working in this way as if you were making rungs of a ladder but pull the stitches tight so that they are not seen on the right side when finished.

All seams should be pressed on the wrong side after completion.

Invisible seaming

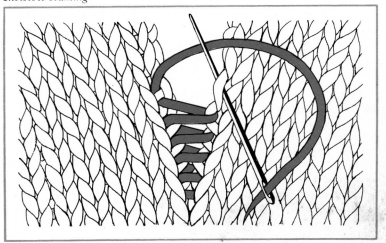

Flat seam

This is the best seam to use when two edges are to be drawn together such as in ribbing.

This method can also be worked on the wrong side working through the extreme edge stitches as seen in the diagram on the right. Pass the threaded wool needle through the edge stitch on the right-hand side directly across to the edge stitch on the left-hand side and pull the yarn through. Turn the needle and work through the next stitch on the left-hand side directly across to the edge stitch on the right-hand side, again pulling the yarn through. Continue up the seam in this manner.

Pockets

When sewing either patch or inserted pockets, they must be absolutely in line with the knitted stitches and rows. The best way is to run a fine knitting needle up the line of the stitches to be followed, picking up alternate loops; the edge is slip stitched to these loops. It is very important that the cast-on lower edge lies straight along a row.

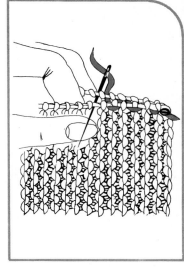

Flat seaming

Sewing in a pocket

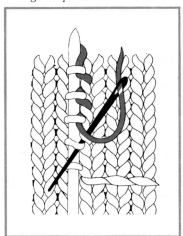

Casing stitch

Casing stitch is often referred to in making-up instructions where a waist edge requires a non-bulky hem to carry elastic, as on a skirt. This is usually worked like herringbone stitch, using a needle, but the strongest method of working is to crochet a zigzag chain using the same yarn as used for the garment. The number of chain used to form the sloping sides of the zigzag will depend on the width of the elastic which you plan to use for a particular garment.

Casing stitch

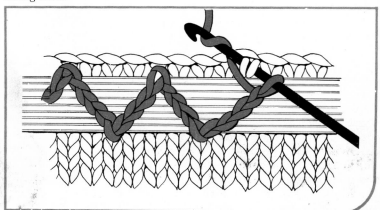

Chapter 12

Picking up stitches and grafting

The colour is right, the yarn and the needles are right, your tension is correct and the knitting looks immaculate. But still more care is required when you come to the final stages of making up your work if it is to look absolutely perfect. Knitted borders, collars, cuffs or contrasting edgings, for example, can be ruined if stitched on by hand with thick, lumpy seams which are impossible to press. To pick up the stitches instead is quite a simple job if done with care but it can completely mar the finished effect if it is worked carelessly or irregularly.

Grafting, too, is often overlooked as a method of finishing. The instructions on these pages give you grafting for stocking stitch (which is used fairly often) and also for joining purl fabrics, garter stitch and ribbing.

Picking up stitches

This method of finishing a neckline or other edge saves the trouble of casting on a separate collar, cuff, or edging and seaming it on when completing the garment. It is not difficult to pick up stitches but time can be saved, and disappointment avoided, if you tackle it carefully.

It is usual to begin to pick up stitches with the right side of the work facing you. If, however, this is not the case in a particular pattern, the instructions will always specify it.

Lifting stitches on to the needle with a crochet hook

Lifting stitches with a Cro-Pin—specially designed for this purpose

The most widely known method is to use the knitting needle which is going to be used to knit the edging. Hold the yarn behind the work and insert the tip of the needle through the stitch drawing through a loop of yarn to the right side and forming one loop on the needle. Continue until all the required stitches are on the needle.

Some knitters prefer to draw the loop of yarn through with a crochet hook then slip the loop on to the needle to be used. There is however a special tool on the market which makes the entire process much easier. It is an Aero Cro-Pin and it looks like a long slender knitting needle but with a hook on one end. The hook end is used as a crochet hook to draw through the loop which is then on the needle and does not need to be transferred to another needle. Once the stitches have been picked up you can knit them off the pointed end with the correct size of needle.

So that the yarn is already attached at the pointed end for knitting it is easier to measure in from the end of the ball about three times the length of the row to be picked up and then work from this point back towards the end as you pick up the loops. If you don't feel you can judge the length required, then use a separate length of yarn for picking up the stitches and join in the ball of yarn in the normal way when you begin to knit the stitches on to the correct size of needle.

You only need one size of Aero Cro-Pin. The fineness of the pin is a great help in drawing loops through firmer fabrics and there is no chance of the loop slipping off and staying on the wrong side as only too often happens when using a knitting needle. If you are picking up stitches round a neck, or on a long edge, it is always easier to mark the edge into sections than to attempt a trial and error method. Some instructions will give you detailed information as to just how many stitches should be on the back neck, side neck and the centre front of the neck; but sooner or later you will be confronted with a pattern which states that you have to pick up 124 stitches evenly round the neck. If you always make it a practice to divide the edge by putting in marker pins then you will have no trouble and will not have to try again and again to get the correct number of stitches. Mark the centre back and front with pins, then fold this in half again and insert two more pins. Now you will know that between pins you have a quarter of the total number of stitches to pick up. If you treat every edge in this way, dividing it as often as you like, it is easy to pick up the correct number of stitches first time.

Grafting

Grafting is a method of joining two rows of stitches invisibly. It is used in knitting mittens and at the toes of socks where the ridge formed by a seamed cast-off edge would be uncomfortable. It is also most useful for joining buttonhole and button strips where they are not continuous but meet at the centre back of the neck. The bulkiness of underarm seams can be completely avoided by leaving the stitches normally cast off at armholes and sleeve top shapings unworked and by grafting them together before the remainder of the sleeve and side-seams are worked. Grafting is usually worked on stocking stitch, purled or garter stitch fabrics, but, if worked with care, can also be used for joining ribbing.

Grafting off needles

When the edges are ready for grafting, cut off the ball of yarn leaving an end about three to four times the length of the row to be grafted and thread this into a blunt-ended wool needle. The illustrations below show a contrast coloured yarn being threaded through the stitches so that you can see it clearly. As the graft is to be invisible you would naturally use the same yarn as the garment. The illustrations also show the stitches slipped off the needles. Some knitters do graft in this way but there is always the danger of dropping one or more of the stitches.

Grafting on needles

To graft two stocking stitch edges together have the stitches on two knitting needles, one behind the other, length of yarn threaded into the wool needle and needle points, all at the right-hand side of the work with the wrong sides of work touching.

Insert the threaded wool needle into the first stitch on the front knitting needle as if to purl it and draw the yarn through, leaving the stitch on the knitting needle. *Insert the wool needle into the first stitch on the back knitting needle as if to purl it and slip it off the knitting needle, then insert the wool needle into the next stitch on the back needle as if to knit it and leave it on the knitting needle but draw the yarn through. Insert the wool needle into the first stitch on the front knitting needle as if to knit it and slip it off the knitting needle, then insert the wool needle into the next stitch on the front needle as if to purl it leaving it on the knitting needle, but pulling the yarn through. Now repeat from * until all the stitches have been worked off. When you draw the yarn through don't pull it too tight, or leave it too slack. The row of grafting stitches should be the same size as the knitted ones thus making them invisible. If they are not even, use the wool needle to work the yarn along the row before finishing off the end, pulling wide stitches smaller or working extra yarn along the row if the stitches are too tight. When you are grafting hold the needles, with the stitches on them, in your left hand keeping the stitches near the tips of the needles so that you do not need to tug at them to slip them off the points.

To join two edges of purl fabric together, work in the same way as for stocking stitch, reading knit for purl and purl for knit. It is, however, possible to turn the knitting to the wrong side and work as for stocking stitch, turning to the right side when the grafting is finished.

Grafting ribbing. If you learn both of these methods you will be able to graft any type of ribbed edges together because you simply use both methods. Join stocking stitch rib to stocking stitch rib with the stocking stitch method, and purl rib to purl rib using the purl method.

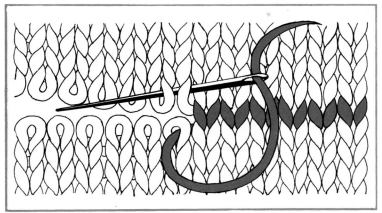

▲ *Grafting stocking stitch, knit side facing (contrast yarn only for clarity)*
▼ *Grafting stocking stitch with purl side facing is worked similarly*

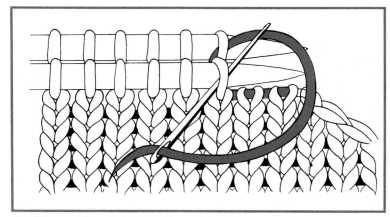

Grafting stocking stitch on needles which are held in the left hand

To graft garter stitch edges, you work as given for stocking stitch but you must first make certain that the last row knitted on the front needle left a ridge on the right side of the work and that the last row on the back needle formed a ridge on the wrong side or inside of the work. It may be necessary to add or take off a row on either side to obtain this before beginning to graft.

Grafting seems involved the first time you try but it is not difficult and there is one easy way to work it out. The yarn passes through each stitch twice. The first time it enters the stitch, it enters in the opposite way to the type of stitch. That is, into a knit stitch you must insert the needle purlwise and into a purl stitch you must insert the needle knitwise—the stitch is left on the knitting needle. The second time the stitch is slipped off the knitting needle after the wool needle has passed through it for the same type of stitch. This means that the second time you pass the wool needle knitwise into a knit stitch and purlwise into a purl stitch.

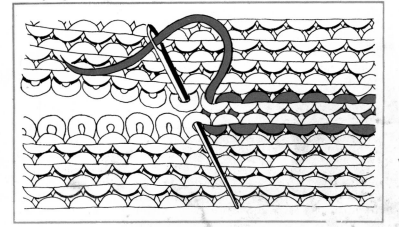

Chapter 13

'V' neckbands

A well-knitted garment can be spoiled by a badly finished 'V' neck. Either the neckband looks frilly or the 'V' doesn't lie flat. These simple variations will help you to achieve a professional-looking neck line every time.

These neckbands are added to a garment by picking up stitches around the neck as shown in Knitting Know-how Chapter 12. One shoulder should be left unseamed, so that the neckband can be worked in rows on two needles.

For an even more attractive finish on the single rib examples shown here, cast off by the invisible method, see Knitting Know-how Chapter 6.

Count the number of rows on the right and left fronts from the centre 'V' point and allow one stitch for every row and one stitch for every stitch of the back neck cast off stitches. Note the multiples of stitches, plus odd stitches, which are required to keep the rib correct on either side of the centre point. For example, the double rib neckband requires two centre stitches and multiples of four stitches plus two odd stitches.

Single rib neckband with centre stitch using slip stitch decreasing

With RS facing, pick up the required number of stitches noting that the centre stitch must be a knit stitch for the right side of the work. Mark the centre stitch with coloured thread. Rib 1 row.

1st row. (right side) Work in K1, P1 rib to within 2 sts of centre st ending with P1, K next 2 sts tog tbl, K centre st, K next 2 sts tog, beg with P1 rib to end.

2nd row. Rib to 2 sts before centre st, P2 tog, P centre st, P2 tog, beg with P1 rib to end.

Rep these 2 rows for required depth of neckband. Cast off in rib still decreasing at centre point, or cast off invisibly.

Single rib neckband with centre stitch combining 2 methods of decreasing

With RS facing, pick up the required number of stitches noting that the centre stitch must be a knit stitch for the right side of the work. Mark the centre stitch with coloured thread. Rib 1 row.

1st row. (right side) Work in K1, P1 rib to within 2 sts of centre st ending with P1, sl 1, K1, psso, K centre st, K2 tog, beg with P1 rib to end.

2nd row. Rib to 2 sts before centre st, sl 1, K1, psso, P centre st, K2 tog, beg with P1 rib to end.

Rep these 2 rows for required depth of neckband. Cast off in rib still decreasing at centre point, or cast off invisibly.

A 'V' neckband for a cricket sweater ▶

▲Single rib neckband with centre stitch using slip stitch decreasing method
▼Single rib neckband with centre stitch combining two methods of decreasing

▲Double rib neckband with two centre stitches combining two methods of decreasing
▼An example of a single rib neckband, the 'V' neck stitches picked up and cast off by the invisible method

Double rib neckband with 2 centre stitches combining 2 methods of decreasing

With RS facing, pick up the required number of stitches noting that the 2 centre stitches must be knit stitches for the right side of the work. Mark 2 centre stitches with coloured thread. Rib 1 row.

1st row. (right side) Work in K2, P2 rib to within 1 st of centre 2 sts ending P1, K tog next st and first of 2 centre sts, sl 2nd centre st, K next st, psso, beg with P1, rib to end.

2nd row. Rib to 1 st before 2 centre sts, P next st and replace it on left-hand needle, sl first of 2 centre sts over this st and replace st on right-hand needle, P tog 2nd centre st and next st, rib to end.

3rd row. Rib to 1 st before 2 centre sts, K tog next st and first of 2 centre sts, sl 2nd centre st, K next st, psso, rib to end.

Rep 2nd and 3rd rows for required depth of neckband. Cast off in rib still decreasing at centre point.

Chapter 14

Neat corners on borders

Where front and hem borders or collars are to be worked for a knitted garment, it is extremely effective to use a mitred corner to obtain a neat look. These edges can be worked separately from the outside edge and sewn on when the garment is completed, or stitches can be picked up for the required length of the border.

As an alternative, by the clever use of a contrasting stitch, a border can be easily worked at the same time as the main fabric of the garment. This method is particularly useful when making square or rectangular shawls and cot blankets.

The child's coat illustrated shows how a contrasting stitch can be used effectively as an edging. The hem and front borders are in moss stitch against a stocking stitch background. The collar is cleverly shaped inside the moss stitch edge to give a very neat fit and—to continue the theme—the sleeves are edged with a moss stitch cuff.

Moss stitch border

Cast on an odd number of sts, allowing 10 sts for each side border.
1st row. *K1, P1, rep from * to last st, K1.
Rep 1st row 9 times more for lower moss st edge.
11th row. (K1, P1) 5 times, K to last 10 sts, (P1, K1) 5 times.
12th row. (K1, P1) 5 times, P to last 10 sts, (P1, K1) 5 times. Rep 11th and 12th rows until work is required size, less 10 rows. Rep 1st row 10 times more for top moss stitch edge. Cast off.

Ribbed edge

Work collar or pocket over an odd number of sts with double pointed needles for required depth of K1, P1 rib ending with a right side row. Leave sts on holder. Break off yarn.
1st row. WS is reversed to become RS of work so that first st on needle is P1, use second needle and pick up required number of sts along one side edge ending with K1, (mark this corner st with coloured thread). Work in rib across sts on holder and beg with K1 pick up same number of sts along second side, (mark this corner with coloured thread).
2nd row. Work in K1, P1 rib to end, keeping corner sts correct.
3rd row. Work in K1, P1 rib to corner st, inc 1 by working into loop between sts, K corner st, inc 1 as before, work in rib to next corner st, inc 1 as before, K corner st, inc 1 as before, rib to end.
Rep 2nd and 3rd rows for required depth ending with a 3rd row. Cast off in rib.

Garter stitch edge—method 1

Cast on required number of sts and mark corner st with coloured thread.

1st row (right side) K to within 2 sts of corner st, K2 tog, K corner st, K2 tog tbl, K to end.
2nd row. K to corner st, P corner st, K to end.
Rep these 2 rows until edge is required depth. Cast off still decreasing on either side of corner st.

Garter stitch edge—method 2

Cast on as for first garter st edge.
1st row. (right side) K to within 2 sts of corner st, K2 tog, yfwd, K corner st, yfwd, K2 tog tbl, K to end.
2nd row. K to within 2 sts of corner st, K next st and made st tog, P corner st, K made st and next st tog, K to end.
Rep these 2 rows until edge is required depth ending with a 1st row. Cast off still decreasing on either side of corner st.

▼ *Contrasting stitch borders worked on the main fabric of a child's coat*

▲ *Garter stitch border worked from outside edge with simple decreasing at either side to achieve the mitre, method 1*

▲ *Moss stitch border worked with stocking stitch*

▲ *Garter stitch border worked from outside edge, method 2*

▲ *Rib border worked on collar edges or on a pocket*

Chapter 15

Neatly finished buttonholes

Unless buttonholes are worked very neatly they can spoil the appearance of an otherwise perfectly made garment.

Depending on the size of the button and the width of the buttonhole border, different methods can be applied. They can be worked horizontally when the buttonhole band is fairly wide but it is neater to work them vertically on a narrow band. Buttonholes on baby garments are worked as eyelet holes.

Horizontal buttonholes

Simple buttonhole

When the buttonhole is to be made as part of the main fabric of a cardigan, finish at the centre front edge. On the next row, work a few stitches to the position for the buttonhole, then cast off the number of stitches needed to take the button and work to the end of the row. On the following row, work to the cast off stitches in the previous row, turn the work and cast on the same number of stitches, turn the work again and continue to the end of the row. Always remember to work the stitch immediately after the last cast on stitch fairly tightly, to make the buttonhole look even.

A perfect buttonhole

Often a horizontal cast on and off buttonhole is spoilt by a loose loop of yarn across one end. To avoid this, work as follows.

Work the first row as given, casting off the full number of stitches. On the second row work to the last stitch before the cast off stitches and increase in this stitch by working into the front and back of it. Then cast on one stitch less than you cast off so that you retain the correct number of stitches.

Tailored buttonhole

When the position for the buttonhole is reached, work the stitches required to take the button in a different coloured yarn, then slip these stitches back on to the left-hand needle and work them again in the original yarn being used. When the work is finished, pull out the different coloured yarn, taking care not to drop the stitches. Now complete the buttonhole by threading a length of the correct yarn through these stitches. Oversew, or buttonhole stitch, round the edges to hold and neaten the buttonhole.

Vertical buttonholes

Work until the point for the buttonhole is reached. On the next row work a few stitches to the position for the buttonhole, then work the required number of rows over these stitches to take the button. Break off the yarn and return to the remaining stitches. Rejoin the yarn and work the same number of rows over these stitches, then continue across all the stitches in the usual way.

Layette buttonhole

Work until the point for the buttonhole is reached. On the next row work a few stitches in to the position for the buttonhole, pass the yarn over or round the needle to make an eyelet hole and work the next two stitches together. On the next row work across all the stitches in the usual way, including the made stitch.

Reinforcing buttonholes

All buttonholes, except possibly those on baby garments, require reinforcing before they are complete, to prevent wearing. Vertical and horizontal buttonholes require buttonhole stitching in matching silk along both edges with three straight stitches at each end. Small round eyelets require several evenly spaced buttonhole stitches around the hole, the loops lying towards the centre.

Take care not to work too many stitches around the hole so that the edges become stretched or too few stitches, which would make the hole smaller than intended.

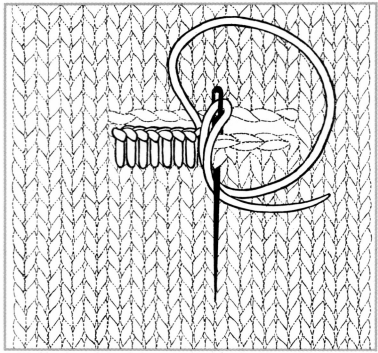

▲ *Working buttonhole stitch to strengthen a knitted buttonhole*
▼ *Correctly reinforced buttonhole with straight stitches at each end*

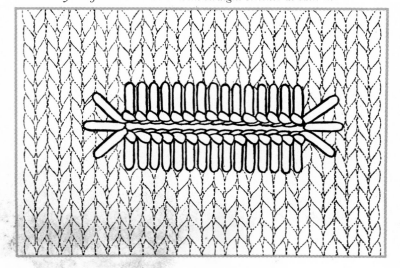

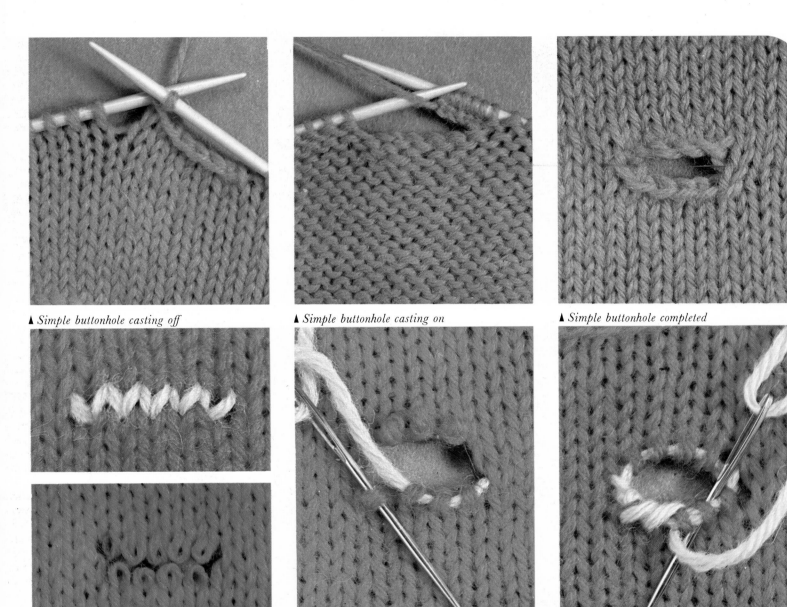

▲ *Simple buttonhole casting off*　　　▲ *Simple buttonhole casting on*　　　▲ *Simple buttonhole completed*

▲ *Method for tailored buttonhole, contrast yarn used for clarity throughout*

▲ *Tailored buttonhole completed*

▼ *Vertical buttonhole, one side completed*

▼ *Layette eyelet buttonhole*

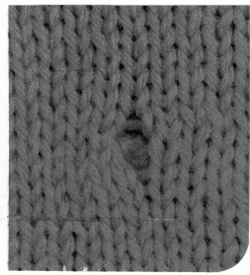

Chapter 16

Hem techniques

Most knitted garments look neater when finished with a knitted hem or border, rather than facing the edge with binding. The hem will have a better appearance if the rows which are to form the under layer are worked on one size smaller needle than the main part of the garment.

Stocking stitch hem for sweater hem

Cast on the required number of stitches and beginning with a knit row, work an odd number of rows. Knit the next row instead of purling it, to mark the fold line, then beginning with a knit row work the same number of rows as were worked initially to complete the hem. When the garment is finished, turn the hem to the wrong side of the work at the fold line and slip stitch in place. This hem is ideal for the bottom of a sweater where a certain amount of elasticity is needed.

Knitted-in hem for coats and jackets

Cast on and work as given for the stocking stitch hem, working one row less after the fold line to end with a purl row. Before continuing with the garment, pick up the stitches of the cast on row with an extra needle and hold these stitches behind the stitches already on the left-hand needle. Knit to the end of the next row by working one stitch from the left-hand needle together with one stitch from the extra needle. Beginning with a purl row continue

▲ *Stocking stitch hem* ▼ *Stocking stitch hem sewn up*

▲ *Knitted in hem* ▼ *Knitted in hem from right side*

in stocking stitch. This forms a very firm hem line and is excellent for use on a coat or jacket.

Picot hem for lacy patterns

Cast on an odd number of stitches and beginning with a knit row work an even number of rows in stocking stitch. On the next row, or right side of the work, make a row of picot eyelets by *K2 tog, yfwd, and repeat from * to last stitch, K1. Beginning with a purl row work the same number of rows as were worked initially to complete the hem. When the garment is finished, turn the hem to the wrong side of the work at the picot row and slip stitch in place. This method forms an attractive scalloped edge, suitable for baby garments, or to give a dainty edge to lace patterns.

Reversed stocking stitch hem for necklines and sleeve edges

When the garment is completed, leave the stitches on the needle instead of casting off and fold the required depth of hem on to the right side of the work, so that the purl fabric forms the hem. Sew along the edge taking one stitch from the needle, and one stitch from the fabric. This method is ideal for finishing necklines, or skirts which are worked from the waist down. It can also be made by folding the hem to the wrong side to form a plain stocking stitch edge.

Slip stitch vertical edge for jacket edges

Cast on the required number of stitches allowing six extra stitches for the border. Work in stocking stitch across the full width of stitches but on every knit row slip the 6th stitch in from the required edge of the row knitwise to form a foldline. When the garment is finished, turn the border to the wrong side at the foldline and slip stitch down. This edge is suitable for the fronts of a jacket or a coat which is unbuttoned.

◄ *Picot hem before sewing up*　▲ *Picot hem completed*
◄ *Slip stitch border for cardigans*
▼ *Reversed stocking stitch hem picking up one stitch from needle and one from fabric*

Chapter 17

Placing pockets

Most inserted pockets can be worked in one with the main fabric of a garment, and knitting patterns usually include directions for working pockets. This chapter includes the know-how for the placing of pockets, and by following these simple, step-by-step instructions you can quite easily add them to a plain dress, sweater or cardigan.

Patch pockets, as shown on the illustrated jacket, are made to the required size and then simply sewn on to the outside of the finished garment. They can be bulky and for details of applying them neatly see Knitting Know-how Chapter 11.

Inserted pocket with garter stitch edge

When working an inserted pocket, make the inside flap first and leave these stitches on a holder until they are required. Calculate the number of stitches you need to make the size of pocket and cast on this number plus an extra two stitches. Work in stocking stitch for the required length of pocket, knitting two stitches together at each end of last row and leave stitches for the time being. Now work the front of the sweater or cardigan in stocking stitch until the position for the pocket is reached, less four rows, ending with a right side row and making sure that you allow for the depth of the inside pocket flap. With the wrong side of the work facing, purl until the pocket opening stitches are reached, knit across these stitches, then purl to the end of the row. Work a further three rows, working in garter stitch across the pocket opening stitches, then cast off the pocket opening stitches knitwise. Place the needle holding the inside flap stitches behind the main fabric with the right side facing, knit to the cast off opening stitches then knit across inside flap stitches in place of those cast off and knit to the end of the row (see Figure 1). Continue in stocking stitch, working three more rows in garter stitch across pocket opening stitches (see Figure 2). When work is completed, stitch down inside flap neatly to wrong side of work (see Figure 3).

Flap pocket

Work inside pocket flap as given for garter stitch edged pocket but do not knit two together at each end of last row, and cast off stitches instead of leaving them on a holder. Work outside pocket flap in the size and pattern desired and leave these stitches on a holder. Now work in stocking stitch on the front of the sweater or cardigan until the position for the pocket is reached, ending with a right side row. On the next row, purl until the pocket opening stitches are reached, cast off the pocket opening stitches knitwise and purl to the end of the row. Place the needle holding the outside pocket flap stitches in front of the main fabric with the right side facing you, knit to the cast off opening stitches then knit across the pocket flap stitches in place of those cast off and knit to the end of the remaining stitches. Place the inside pocket flap behind the pocket opening on the wrong side and stitch neatly in place.

▲ **1.** *Inserting the inside of a pocket*
▼ **2.** *The completed garter stitch pocket opening*

▼ **3.** *Stitch down the inside of the pocket*

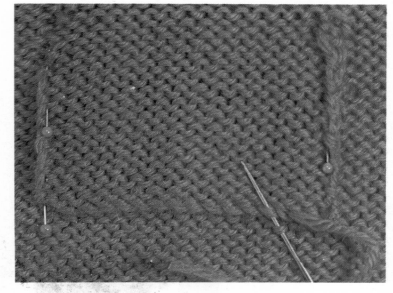

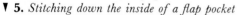

▲ **4.** *Pocket with an outside flap*
▼ **5.** *Stitching down the inside of a flap pocket*

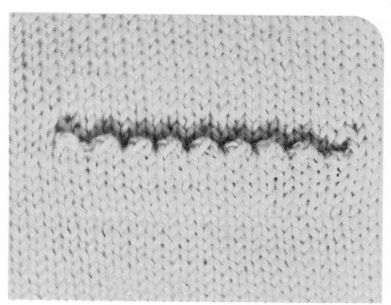

▲ **6.** *Pocket edge with picots*
▼ **7.** *Patch pockets on a smart jacket*

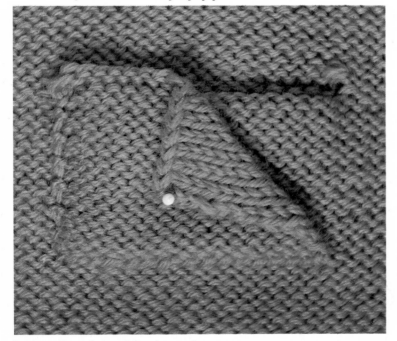

Inserted pocket with picot edge

Work inside pocket flap as given for garter stitch edged pocket. Now work the front of the sweater or cardigan in stocking stitch until the position for the pocket is reached, allowing an odd number of stitches for opening and ending with a wrong side row. With the right side of the work facing, knit until the pocket opening stitches are reached, then work across opening stitches as follows: K1, *yfwd, K2 tog, rep from * to the end of these stitches, then turn and work 5 more rows stocking stitch across pocket opening stitches only. Cast off these stitches knitwise. Break yarn and with right side of work facing, rejoin yarn to remaining stitches and knit to end. Place the needle holding the inside flap stitches in front of the main fabric, with purl side facing you, purl to the cast off opening stitches then purl across inside flap stitches in place of those cast off and purl to end of row. Continue in stocking stitch and when work is completed stitch down pocket opening stitches at picot row to wrong side. Stitch down inside pocket flap neatly to wrong side of work.

Chapter 18

Knitting Know-how

Knitted pleats

A knitted pleated skirt is a smart and useful addition to any wardrobe, and because it is casual and easy to wear also makes a useful garment for little girls. Made in pure wool, knitted skirts will hold their shape and the pleats will keep their swing. Pleats can be knitted on two needles, but for a woman's skirt requiring more stitches a circular needle is useful (see page 52).

Mock pleats

Decide on the full hem width required and use this measurement, plus the tension obtained to the inch in the yarn selected, to arrive at the number of stitches. Cast on a number of stitches divisible by 8, using two needles or a circular needle. For example: a hem width of 42 inches and a tension giving 7 stitches to the inch gives 294 stitches, so cast on either 288 or 296 stitches (both divisible by 8).

Two needle pattern
1st row. *K7, P1, rep from * to end.
2nd row. K4, *P1, K7, rep from * to last 4 sts, P1, K3. These two rows form pattern and are repeated for the required length.

Circular pattern
1st round. *K7, P1, rep from * to end of round.
2nd round. P3, K1, *P7, K1, rep from * to last 4 sts, P4. These 2 rounds form pattern and are repeated for required length.

To complete skirt
Join centre back seam if worked on two needles. Cut a waist length of 1in wide elastic and join into a circle. Sew inside waistband using casing stitch (see Knitting Know-how Chapter 11).

▲ *Finished effect of the full pleating stitch*
▼ *Dividing stitches to close a full pleat*

▼ *Finished effect of the mock pleating stitch*

▼ *Knitting stitches together to close a full pleat*

▲ *A full pleated skirt for a little girl*

Full pleats

Work out the full hem width as for mock pleating, based on 3 times the waist measurement required plus an extra 1½in. Cast on a number of stitches divisible by 12, plus 8, using two needles. This gives a pleat fold of 4 stitches.
1st row. *K8, P1, K2, sl 1P, rep from * to last 8 sts, K8.
2nd row. *P11, K1, rep from * to last 8 sts, P8.
These 2 rows form pattern and are repeated for the required length, less 1¼in for the waistband.

To close pleats

Two extra needles of the same gauge are required to close the pleats.
Next row. K4, * slip next 4 sts on to first extra needle, slip next 4 sts on to 2nd extra needle, place first extra needle behind 2nd extra needle and hold both extra needles behind left-hand needle,

(K tog one st from all 3 needles) 4 times, rep from * to last 4 sts, K4. Cast off.

To complete skirt

Join centre back seam and overlap 4 stitches at the beginning of the row over 4 stitches at the end of the row to complete pleating. Cast on required number of stitches for waistband, adding 2-3 inches extra for ease in dressing and undressing, and work 2½in in stocking stitch. Cast off.
With RS of waistband facing RS of top of skirt, sew band to skirt. Cut a waist length of 1in wide elastic and join into a circle. Fold waistband in half to WS and stitch down over elastic. This elasticated waistband means that a side opening is not necessary and does away with the need for an inserted zip fastener. The seam can be worn on either the side or back, thus minimising seating.

Chapter 19

Introduction to knitting in the round

Sweaters, socks, stockings, gloves, mittens, skirts and many other types of garment can all be worked on sets of needles, producing a tubular, seamless piece of work. This does not mean that there cannot be shaping, and with careful planning decreases or increases can be calculated to give the required shape.

Knitting in rounds has the added advantage for the knitter of always having the right side of the work facing, which is a great help when working complicated or multi-coloured patterns. It is, in fact, the method employed by Fair Isle knitters, even in sweaters with long sleeves. Instead of stopping at armhole level, a tube is worked the whole length of the sweater up to the shoulder. From the armhole level upwards the yarn is wound around the needle several times in a line where the armhole is required. On the next round, the previous loops are dropped and the process repeated. This gives a ladder of strands on either side which, when the work is completed, is cut and each end is darned back into the fabric. The stitches for the sleeves are then picked up around the armhole and the sleeves knitted in rounds down to the wrist. Not only is this a quick method but it is thrifty, particularly where children's sweaters are concerned, as it is a simple matter to add new cuffs or to lengthen old ones.

Casting on with more than two needles

The actual casting on of each stitch is exactly as normal, but because there are more needles to be considered there are two methods of working. When using a set of four needles, one is used for knitting and the total number of stitches is divided between the remaining three needles. You can either cast on the number of stitches required on the first needle, then proceed to the second and so on, or you can cast on the total number onto one needle and then slip them onto the other needles. The second method is perhaps the easier and is less likely to cause the cast on edge to become twisted. Form the needles into a circle and slip the spare needle into the first stitch on the first needle. If you now knit this stitch, taking the yarn directly to it from the last stitch, the circle you require is formed. Continue to knit all the stitches on the first needle. Once the needle is free of stitches, knit along the second needle. Continue in this way. This is all there is to round knitting. Because the right side of the work is always facing the knitter, every round produces stocking stitch and not garter stitch, as would be the case when working to and fro in rows. Garter stitch is made by working one round knit and one round purl alternately.

As it is easy to lose track of where a round begins, the simplest method of marking it is to slip a knotted loop of contrast yarn on to the needle before the first stitch of a round. Simply slip this loop on to the right hand needle, without knitting it, on every round, and the beginning of a round can be seen at a glance.

More than one marker may be required because the pattern may include shapings at either side of a point where a side seam would be placed, or down the back leg of a stocking. If a gored skirt is

being worked, it may be easier to mark each gore with a loop of one colour and use a second colour for the marker to the actual round beginning.

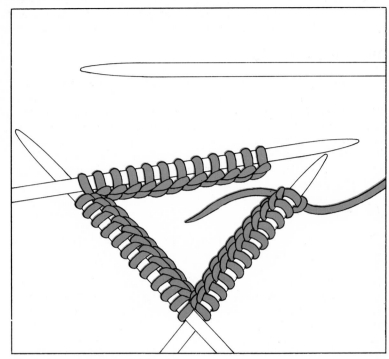

▲ *Casting on with four needles*

▼ *Joining casting on with 4 needles*

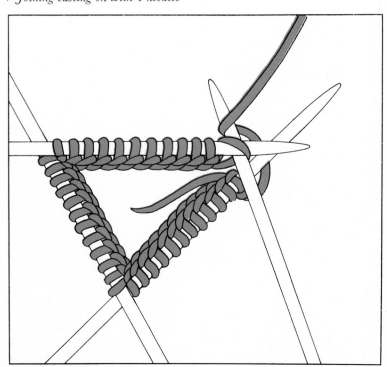

Socks and stockings

Socks and stockings, as well as being practical because of their longer life when handknitted, can be highly fashionable accessories if well made and well finished. The opposite page gives a few hints on the techniques involved—reinforcing, leg shaping, turning the heel and shaping the toe.

Shaping the leg

Leg shaping is necessary unless rib is used for the main part of the sock. Begin with 3 or 4 ins of ribbing reinforcing if necessary with shirring elastic at the back. Change to pattern and shape the leg either side of a centre st at the back forming a mock seam.

Dividing for the heel

On reaching the heel divide the sts into 2 sections, the instep and the heel itself. A well fitting sock has, if possible, an extra 2 sts in the instep section. The extra centre sts forming the back seam should be included in the instep sts as shown. The heel flap is worked in rows backwards and forwards and can be reinforced by knitting a fine matching sewing thread in with the yarn. Work in st st as this gives a flat comfortable fit. Work until the heel section is square.

Turning the heel

The French heel and the Dutch heel are the most common methods, the Dutch heel giving a squarer look.

French heel—Divide heel flap sts into 2 sections either side of a centre 2 or 3 sts. As the decs are worked on the side sections they must be divisible by 2. K across 1st section and centre sts, make 1st dec in side section thus—sl 1, K1, psso, turn, P dec st and centre sts, P tog first 2 sts of other side section, turn. Cont in this way until all heel flap sts have been worked.

Dutch heel—Divide heel flap sts into 3 sections. Work as for French heel but the decs should begin by using the last st of the centre section as the sl st plus 1 st from the side section and the same on the P 2 tog. Cont in this way until all heel flap sts have been worked.
Both heels should finish on a P row. Turn.

Forming the instep gusset

This is the triangle of decs either side of the instep and reduces the number of sts picked up for the heel. With 1st needle K half the heel sts, pick up and K sts evenly along side of heel flap, with 2nd needle K across all instep sts, with 3rd needle pick up and K same number of sts evenly along other side of heel flap. Work in rounds dec 1 st either side of instep sts, which would be at end of 1st needle and beginning of 3rd needle on alt rounds until heel sts are equal in number to instep sts. Continue in rounds for foot.

Shaping the toe

Begin about 2in before the end of the foot.

Flat toe—This is the most comfortable shape. Divide the sts equally onto 2 needles with sole sts on one needle and instep sts on the other. If the instep sts still include the extra st used for the back seam, dec by working 2 sts tog. Work across each needle as follows: K1, K2 tog, K to last 3 sts, K2 tog tbl, K1. Cont to dec on alternate rounds in this way until about half the sts have been decreased. Finish by casting 2 sets of sts off together or grafting together.

Round toe—Divide the sts into sections and work a dec in each section all round the toe ending with a few sts which are then pulled up on a thread, (see top of mittens, page 50).

▲ *Shaping for flat toe*

▲ *Dividing sts for heel showing centre back st*

▲ *French heel*

Knitting Know-how

Mittens and gloves

When gloves and mittens are worked on two needles side and finger seams must be completed, but worked on sets of double pointed needles they are smoothly seamless.

Choice of yarn

Select a yarn which is not too fine or too soft, and which will stand up to wear. Double Knitting and 4 ply yarns are suitable and a yarn with a crepe finish is a good choice. Needles should be finer than one might normally use for the yarn, so that the stitches are firm and do not snag. A tight-fitting, weatherproof wrist ribbing is made by using needles one size smaller than for the rest of the gloves or mittens. Remember that as well as fitting snugly, the wrist must be wide enough for the hand to be inserted easily.

▲ *Method of increasing for a thumb gusset, for both two and four needles*

▼ *Leaving the thumb gusset stitches on holder*

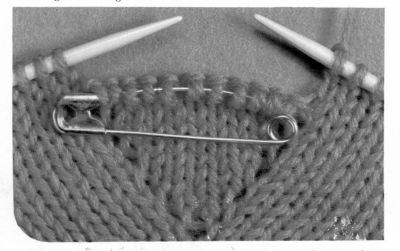

Calculating the number of stitches

As for any other garment, work a sample first so that you are satisfied that the pattern, the number of needles and the type of yarn together produce the fabric you want. Measure the sample carefully to check how many stitches there are to the inch. The circumference of the hand just above the thumb division determines the number of inches you require. Multiply the number of inches needed by the number of stitches in one inch. For example, if your hand measures 7 inches around and the test sample of knitting produces 6 stitches to the inch, multiply 7 by 6, making 42, and cast on 42 stitches. This number of stitches appears to gives a very loose wrist but ribbing will draw the extra width in to make the wrist fit neatly.

This number of stitches makes no allowance for the extra width below the thumb division but this is usually worked as extra increasing in a triangular area between the wrist and thumb division. When sufficient stitches have been increased, they are slipped onto a stitch holder while extra stitches, to take their place, are cast on and then the remainder of the palm is worked.

Mittens on four needles

Size

To fit an average adult hand, the length is adjustable

Basic yarn tension

5½ sts and 7½ rows to 1in over st st worked on No.8 needles

Materials shown here

1 50g ball Patons Double Knitting
One set of No.8 double pointed needles

Mittens

Begin at wrist edge. Cast on 40 sts. Work 2in K2, P2 rib. Continue in st st. Working every round K, work 6 rounds.

Shape for thumb

1st round K2, K up thread before next st to inc, K next st and mark with coloured thread as a guide to centre thumb st, K up thread before next st to inc, K to end of round.

K 1 round.

3rd round K2, K up 1, K3, K up 1, K to end.

K 1 round.

Continue in this way, inc at either side of thumb gusset until 5 sts at either side have been inc.

K 1 round.

Next round K2, sl 11 sts for thumb on to holder, turn work and using 2 needle method cast on to left hand needle 7 sts to replace thumb sts, turn and K to end of round.

Next round K1, sl 1 K-wise, K1, psso, K5, K2 tog, K to end.

K 1 round.

Next round K1, sl 1 K-wise, K1, psso, K3, K2 tog, K to end.

K 1 round.

Next round K1, sl 1 K-wise, K1, psso, K1, K2 tog, K to end.

Continue in st st until work measures 1in less than required length to finger tip or approximately 3½in from thumb division.

Shape top

Dec 5 sts evenly on next round. K 1 round.
Rep last 2 rounds once.
Dec 5 sts evenly on next 5 rounds.
Break yarn leaving an end long enough to thread through rem sts. Draw up and finish off.

Thumb

Rejoin yarn to thumb sts, K 6 sts from holder on to 1st needle, K rem 5 sts from holder on to 2nd needle and K up 7 sts along 7 cast on sts.
Work in rounds of st st until 2in long or 2 rounds less than required length.

Next round *K1, K2 tog,

rep from * to end.
Last round *K2 tog, rep from * to end.
Break off yarn and thread through rem sts. Draw up and finish off.
Make 2nd mitten in same way. This design is reversible and can be used for either hand.

Gloves on two needles

Size and Basic yarn tension
As given for mittens

Materials shown here
2 50g balls Patons Double Knitting
One pair No.8 needles

Right hand

Begin at wrist. Cast on 40 sts. Work 1¼in K1, P1 rib.
1st patt row (RS) P.
2nd patt row *K1, P1, rep from * to end.
These 2 rows form patt and are rep throughout.
Continue in patt until work measures 2½in from beg, ending with a WS row.

Shape thumb
1st row P21 sts, inc in next st by purling twice into same st, P1 marking this as centre thumb st with coloured thread, inc in next st, P rem 16 sts.
2nd row Patt to end.
3rd row P21 sts, inc 1, P3, inc 1, P to end.
4th row As 2nd.
Keeping patt correct, continue in this way inc one st on either side of centre thumb st on next and every alt row until 6 incs at either side have been worked. 52 sts.
Next row Patt to last 22 sts, turn and work on thumb sts only.
Continue in patt across thumb sts, inc one st at each end of 1st row, until work measures 2¼in, or required thumb length.
Last row *P2 tog, rep from * to end.
Break yarn and thread through rem sts. Draw up and seam side of thumb.
With WS facing, rejoin yarn

▲ *Simple and inexpensive accessories to make to team with an outfit*

to 22 sts, work to end of row.
Next row Patt to thumb, K up 4 sts from base of thumb, patt to end of row. 42 sts.
Continue in patt until work measures 5¼in from beg, or required length to division for 1st finger ending with WS row. Break yarn.
Rejoin yarn to 12 central sts, leaving 15 sts on either side on holders.

Work 1st finger
Continue in patt on 12 sts, inc one st at each end of 1st row, for 2½in or required length, ending with a WS row.

Last row *P2 tog, rep from * to end.
Draw thread through rem sts and seam finger.

Work 2nd finger
With RS facing work 5 sts from each holder and K up 4 sts along lower edge of 1st finger.
Continue in patt on 14 sts, inc one st at each end of 1st row, for 2¾in or required length, ending with a WS row. Complete as for 1st finger.

Work 3rd finger
Work as given for 2nd finger

until 2½in or required length. Complete as before.

Work little finger
Work 5 rem sts from each holder and K up 4 sts from 3rd finger. Work as before for 2¼in or required length. Complete as before.
Join little finger and side seam.

Left hand

Work as given for Right hand, reversing all shaping.
1st shaping row will read: P16, inc in next st, P1, inc in next st, P to end.

Bags in circular knitting

Circular knitting is a quick and simple way of making tubular, seamless fabrics. This method is used for the two handbags shown in the photograph, one a rather classic pocket bag, the other a pretty novelty shape. Either bag would make a useful fashion accessory.

Circular knitting

Knitting patterns often suggest using a circular needle for tubular work such as the lower part of a sweater. Circular needles have many advantages over pairs or sets of needles and they are made in the same sizes as ordinary needles in several different lengths. The two points of the circular needle are exactly like ordinary needles but they are joined together by a flexible nylon cord.

Using circular needles

A circular needle may be used to take the place of 4 needles to make a skirt or sweater in one piece without seams. The fact that there is only one needle in use naturally makes the knitting of a garment easier. The only type of garment where they cannot be used as substitutes for sets of needles is where there are only a small number of stitches, which would be insufficient to stretch around even the shortest needle length, such as gloves, mittens, socks or stockings. The use of circular needles is not limited, however, to working large tubular sections, because they can also be used as a pair of needles by working

along a row in the usual way, turning and working back again. This is an additional advantage when working a sweater which has to be divided at the armholes.

Even distribution of weight

Because the work is held by both hands evenly, shoulders do not become strained or tired, even after many hours of knitting. Many handicapped knitters find that this makes circular needles ideal for all types of work.

New circular needles

If you have just purchased a circular needle which has not been used before place it in hot water for a few seconds before use and then dry it. The heat will remove the twist which will have formed in the nylon cord during packing and storage.

Bellrope bag

Size

Approximately 11in by 11in

> **Basic yarn tension**
> 5 sts and 6½ rows to 1in over st st worked on No.8 needles

Materials shown here

Patons Capstan
3 50g balls of main shade, A
1 additional ball of contrast colour B for bell clappers
One No.7 Aero Twin-Pin
One No.4·00 (ISR) Aero crochet hook
Lengths of stiffening and lining material

Bag

Using No.7 Twin-Pin and A, cast on 216 sts. Join into a circle, making sure that the sts are not twisted, by bringing end with last cast on st round to join to first cast on st. Work in rounds.
1st round *P2, K7, P2, K1 tbl, rep from * to end.
2nd, 3rd and 4th rounds As 1st.
5th round *P2, sl 1, K1, psso, K3, K2 tog, P2, K1 tbl, rep from * to end.
6th round *P2, K5, P2, K1 tbl, rep from * to end.
7th round *P2, sl 1, K1, psso, K1, K2 tog, P2, K1 tbl, rep from * to end.
8th round *P2, K3, P2, K1 tbl, rep from * to end.
9th round *P2, sl 1, K2 tog, psso, P2, K1 tbl, rep from * to end.
10th round *P2, K1 tbl, rep from * to end.
11th round *P2, K1 tbl, P2, (K1, P1, K1, P1, K1) all into next st—called 1 bell—rep from * to end.
12th round *P2, K1 tbl, P2, K5, rep from * to end.
13th and 14th rounds As 12th.
15th round *P2, K1 tbl, P2, sl 1, K1, psso, K1, K2 tog, rep from * to end.
16th round *P2, K1 tbl, P2, K3, rep from * to end.
17th round *P2, K1 tbl, P2, sl 1, K2 tog, psso, rep from * to end.
18th round *P2, 1 bell, P2, K1 tbl, rep from * to end.
19th round *P2, K5, P2, K1 tbl, rep from * to end.
20th and 21st rounds As 19th.
22nd round *P2, sl 1, K1, psso, K1, K2 tog, P2, K1 tbl, rep from * to end.
23rd round *P2, K3, P2, K1 tbl, rep from * to end.
24th round *P2, sl 1, K2 tog, psso, P2, K1 tbl, rep from * to end.
Rep from 11th-24th rounds twice more, then 11th-19th rounds once more.
Next round *P2, K1, K up 1, K3, K up 1, K1, P2, K1 tbl, rep from * to end.
Next round *P2, K7, P2, K1

tbl, rep from * to end.
Rep last round twice more.
Cast off.

Bells

Using No.7 Twin-Pin and B, cast on 14 sts. Work in rows turning the work at the end of every row.
1st row K.
2nd row P.
Rep these 2 rows once more.
5th row *K1, sl 1, K1, psso, K1, K2 tog, K1, rep from * once more.
6th row P.
7th row *K1, sl 1, K2 tog, psso, K1, rep from * once more.
8th row P.
9th row *Sl 1, K2 tog, psso, rep from * once more.
Break yarn and draw through rem sts, then seam two edges on WS to form bell.
Make 3 more bells in same way.

Bell clapper

Using No.4·00 (ISR) hook and B make 4ch. Join into a circle with ss into first ch.
1st round 2ch, 3dc into circle. Join with ss to 2nd of first 2ch.
2nd round 2ch, 1dc into same st, 2dc into each of rem 3dc. Join with ss to 2nd of first 2ch.
3rd round 2ch, *miss 1dc, 1dc into next dc, rep from * to end. Join with ss to 2nd of first 2ch.
4th round 2ch, work 1dc into each st leaving last loop of each dc on hook, yrh and draw through all loops on hook, work 4ch.
Finish off.
Work 12 more bell clappers in same way.

To make up

Press bell sections lightly, if required.
Sew one bell clapper inside each bell flute along half of cast on edge. Fold work in half so that the other side of each bell flute along cast on edge completes the bells. Sew ribs together between bells. Join bottom of bag by sewing

▲ *On the right, the bellrope bag with drawstring handle. On the left, the pocket bag with a tab and buckle fastening*

firmly between stitches just above bells.

Cut stiffening and lining to fit bag and join side edges on WS. Place stiffening and lining inside bag and sl st in place around lower edge of bells at cast off edge.

Using 18 strands of yarn, allowing 6 strands for each section, make a plait the required handle length and sew to either side of cast off edge of bag.

Trim each end of plait with 2 bells on each side.

Pocketbook bag

Size
Approximately 9in by 7in

Basic yarn tension
6 sts and 8 rows to 1in over st st worked on No.8 needles

Materials shown here
Madame Pingouin
2 50g balls
One No.8 Aero-Twin Pin
One cable needle
Lengths of stiffening and lining material. One buckle

Bag

Using No.8 Twin-Pin cast on 53 sts for base of bag.

Beg with a P row work 7 rows st st, turning work at end of each row.

Turn so that K side is facing and cast on 67 sts.

With P side facing join for circular knitting as given for Bellrope bag.

1st round P53 sts for front, K1, (P1, K1) 3 times for side, P53 sts for back, K1, (P1,K1) 3 times for other side. Place marker after last st worked to mark beg of round.

Rep 1st round until circular section measures 7in, or required depth, ending last round 6 sts before marker.

Divide for flap
Next round Cast off 6 sts from side, cast off 53 sts from front, cast off 6 sts from other side, K1, P53 sts across back, K1. Continue for flap on these 55 sts, working in rows of cluster patt.

1st row K.

2nd row K1, *P1, P3, sl last 3 P sts on to cable needle and wind yarn round all 3 sts 6 times ending with yarn at front of work, sl 3 sts from cable needle to right hand needle—called cl 3—rep from * to last 2 sts, P1, K1.

3rd row K.

4th row K1, P3, *cl 3, P1, rep from * to last 3 sts, P2, K1.

Rep last 4 rows 3 time more.

Divide for tab fastening
Cast off 20 sts, K to last 20 sts, cast off 20 sts.

With RS facing, rejoin yarn to rem 15 centre sts and work in cluster patt for 11 rows. Cast off.

Strap

Using No.8 Twin-Pin cast on 16 sts.

Work to and fro in K1, P1 rib until strap measures 20in or required length. Cast off.

To make up

Do not press.

Cut stiffening and lining to fit bag, allowing turning on lining around flap and opening edges. Join side seams. Seam cast on edge of base to cast on edge of Back. Seam cast on edges of sides to sides of base.

Insert stiffening and sl st in place. Insert lining and sew around all edges, turning in hem.

Seam long side edges of strap and insert stiffening through centre of strap. Join short ends and stitch in place on side panels.

Sew buckle in position on front to take tab fastening.

Chapter 20

Introduction to lace stitches

Knitting lace patterns will bring you compliments because they look so difficult. But most of them are straight-forward. The designs often build up from an arrangement of open-work patterns made by increasing one stitch and decreasing another, either next to the increase or in another part of the design, so that the number of stitches is constant. If you are a beginner you can use these patterns to make squares for ponchos, strips for scarves and oblongs for shawls which will not involve the shaping needed for a garment.

Shawls, ponchos, cushions and scarves are easy ways to use lacy stitches

Open-work ladder stitch

Open-work ladder stitch

Worked over a number of stitches divisible by 10, plus 6 (eg 36, 46, 56 and so on).

1st row (wrong side). P6, *K2 tog tbl, wind yarn twice round needle, K2 tog, P6, rep from * to end.
2nd row. K6, *P1, P into first made st and K into the second st, P1, K6, rep from * to end.
These 2 rows form the pattern and are repeated throughout.

Oblique open-work stitch

Worked over a number of stitches divisible by 9.

1st row. *K4, K up horizontal thread before next st to inc 1 st, K2 tog, lift inc st over sts knitted tog, K up horizontal thread before next st, K3, rep from * to end.
2nd row. P.
3rd row. *K3, K up horizontal thread before next st, K2 tog, lift inc st over sts knitted tog, K up horizontal thread before next st, K4, rep from * to end.
4th row. P.
These rows are repeated working one stitch less at the beginning of each row to move the crossed stitches to the right and so maintain the diagonal line. The extra stitches at the end of the row are worked into the pattern when possible.

Oblique open-work stitch

Ridged lace stitch

Worked over a number of stitches divisible by 6 plus 1.
1st row. *P1, P2 tog, yon, K1, yrn, P2 tog, rep from * to last st, P1.
2nd row. P.
3rd row. K.
4th row. P.
These 4 rows form the pattern and are repeated throughout.

The yarn used in the photographs on these two pages is Patons Double Knitting

Ridged lace stitch ▲

Old shale stitch

Worked over a number of stitches divisible by 11 plus 2.
1st row. K.
2nd row. P.
3rd row. K1, *(P2 tog) twice, (yon, K1) 3 times, yrn, (P2 tog) twice, rep from * to last st, K1.
4th row. P.
These 4 rows form the pattern and are repeated throughout.

The yarn in the photographs on pages 56 and 57 is Patons Purple Heather 4 ply

▲ *Old shale stitch*   ▼ *Criss-cross ladder stitch*

Criss-cross ladder stitch

Worked over a number of stitches divisible by 8 plus 4.
1st row (wrong side). *P6, yrn, sl 1 purlwise, P1, psso, rep from * to last 4sts, P4.
2nd row. *K6, yfwd, sl 1 knitwise, K1, psso, rep from * to last 4 sts, K4.
These 2 rows form the pattern and are repeated throughout.

Forgotten the abbreviations? Refer to Knitting Know-how Chapter 1 for how to work 'yfwd', 'yon' and 'yrn'.

More lace stitches

Lace stitches have always been one of the most popular forms of knitting and some of the most beautiful examples originated in the north of Scotland more than one hundred years ago. Many of these old stitches have charming and evocative names and are known to knitters all over the world. Three of the most popular are given in this chapter and you can practice candlelight stitch by making a charming cravat.

These stitches are quite simple to work, but however complicated the pattern may look the principle is exactly the same as shown on pages 54 and 55. That is, making a stitch by means of a loop and compensating for the made stitch by working two stitches together somewhere in the pattern sequence. The decreased stitches may not necessarily be worked in the same row as the made stitches, which means that on subsequent rows you will have more stitches than you started with. By the end of the number of rows needed to complete one whole pattern, however, you will have reverted to the correct number of stitches and will be ready to start the next repeat.

Travelling vine stitch

Cast on a number of stitches divisible by 8, plus 4.
1st row. Sl 1, K1, *yfwd, K1 tbl, yfwd, sl 1, K1, psso, K5, rep from * to last 2 sts, K2.
2nd row. Sl 1, P1, *P4, P2 tog tbl, P3, rep from * to last 2 sts, P1, K1.
3rd row. Sl 1, K1, * yfwd, K1 tbl, yfwd, K2, sl 1, K1, psso, K3, rep from * to last 2 sts, K2.
4th row. Sl 1, P1, * P2, P2 tog tbl, P5, rep from * to last 2 sts, P1, K1.

▼ *Travelling vine knitted lace stitch*

5th row. Sl 1, K1, *K1 tbl, yfwd, K4, sl 1, K1, psso, K1, yfwd, rep from * to last 2 sts, K2.
6th row. Sl 1, P1, *P1, P2 tog tbl, P6, rep from * to last 2 sts, P1, K1.
7th row. Sl 1, K1, *K5, K2 tog, yfwd, K1 tbl, yfwd, rep from * to last 2 sts, K2.
8th row. Sl 1, P1, *P3, P2 tog, P4, rep from * to last 2 sts, P1, K1.
9th row. Sl 1, K1, *K3, K2 tog, K2, yfwd, K1 tbl, yfwd, rep from * to last 2 sts, K2.
10th row. Sl 1, P1, *P5, P2 tog, P2, rep from * to last 2 sts, P1, K1.
11th row. Sl 1, K1, *yfwd, K1, K2 tog, K4, yfwd, K1 tbl, rep from * to last 2 sts, K2.
12th row. Sl 1, P1, *P6, K2 tog, P1, rep from * to last 2 sts, P1, K1.
These 12 rows form pattern and are repeated throughout.

Fern stitch

Cast on a number of stitches divisible by 29, plus 2.
1st row. K1, *K1, sl 1, K2 tog, psso, K9, yfwd, K1, yrn, P2, yon, K1, yfwd, K9, sl 1, K2 tog, psso, rep from * to last st, K1.
2nd and every alt row. P1, *P13, K2, P14, rep from * to last st, P1.
3rd row. K1, *K1, sl 1, K2 tog, psso, K8, yfwd, K1, yfwd, K1, P2, K1, yfwd, K1, yfwd, K8, sl 1, K2 tog, psso, rep from * to last st, K1.
5th row. K1, *K1, sl 1, K2 tog, psso, K7, yfwd, K1, yfwd, K2, P2, K2, yfwd, K1, yfwd, K7, sl 1, K2 tog, psso, rep from * to last st, K1.
7th row. K1, *K1, sl 1, K2 tog, psso, K6, yfwd, K1, yfwd, K3, P2, K3, yfwd, K1, yfwd, K6, sl 1, K2 tog, psso, rep from * to last st, K1.
9th row. K1, *K1, sl 1, K2 tog, psso, K5, yfwd, K1, yfwd, K4, P2, K4, yfwd, K1, yfwd, K5, sl 1, K2 tog, psso, rep from * to last st, K1.
10th row. As 2nd.
These 10 rows form pattern and are repeated throughout. Note that when this pattern is completed it forms zigzag edges.

Candlelight stitch

Cast on a number of stitches divisible by 12, plus 1.
1st row. *K1, yfwd, sl 1, K1, psso, K7, K2 tog, yfwd, rep from * to last st, K1.
2nd and every alt row. P to end.
3rd row. *K1, yfwd, K1, sl 1, K1, psso, K5, K2 tog, K1, yfwd, rep from * to last st, K1.
5th row. *K1, yfwd, K2, sl 1, K1, psso, K3, K2 tog, K2, yfwd, rep from * to last st, K1.
7th row. *K1, yfwd, K3, sl 1, K1, psso, K1, K2 tog, K3, yfwd, rep from * to last st, K1.
9th row. *K1, yfwd, K4, sl 1, K2 tog, psso, K4, yfwd, rep from * to last st, K1.
11th row. *K4, K2 tog, yfwd, K1, yfwd, sl 1, K1, psso, K3, rep from * to last st, K1.
13th row. *K3, K2 tog, K1, yfwd, K1, yfwd, K1, sl 1, K1, psso, K2, rep from * to last st, K1.
15th row. *K2, K2 tog, K2, yfwd, K1, yfwd, K2, sl 1, K1, psso, K1, rep from * to last st, K1.
17th row. *K1, K2 tog, K3, yfwd, K1, yfwd, K3, sl 1, K1, psso, rep from * to last st, K1.
19th row. K2 tog, *K4, yfwd, K1, yfwd, K4, sl 1, K2 tog, psso, rep from * ending last rep sl 1, K1, psso.
20th row. As 2nd.
These 20 rows form pattern and are repeated throughout.

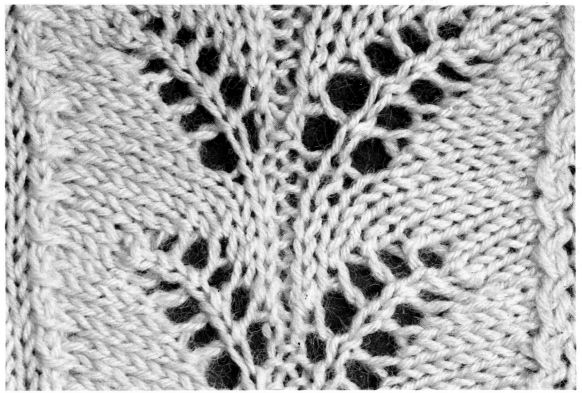

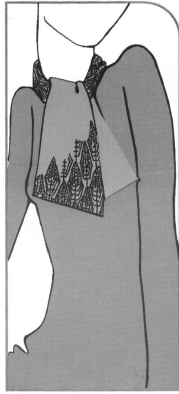

▲ *Lacy cravat lined for crispness*

▲ *Fern stitch with a leafy look*   ▼ *Candlelight stitch, used for the cravat*

Lace cravat in candlelight stitch

Size
8in wide by 30in long

Basic yarn tension
$8\frac{1}{2}$sts and $10\frac{1}{2}$ rows to 1in over st st worked on No.10 needles

Materials shown here
4 1oz balls Jaeger Fairie-spun
One pair No.10 needles
$\frac{1}{4}$yd 36in wide lining material

Cravat
Using No.10 needles cast on 73 sts.
Rep 20 patt rows given for Candlelight stitch 16 times in all.
Cast off.

To make up
Press lightly on WS under a damp cloth with a warm iron. Cut lining to fit cravat. With WS of cravat facing WS of lining, seam one short and 2 long ends. Turn to RS and sl st rem short end.

Lacy eyelet patterns

Most traditional lace patterns are based on the technique for making eyelets described in this chapter. The method consists of using the yarn over or round the needle to form the eyelet hole, then decreasing a stitch elsewhere in the pattern to compensate. The eyelet holes are worked in regular and repeating groups and produce a variety of patterns.

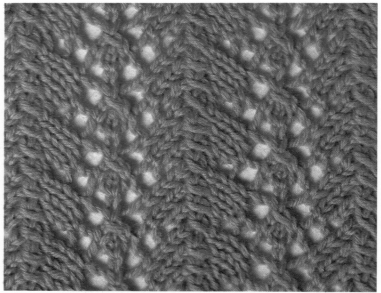

▲ *Spearhead lace rib pattern*

▲ *Diagonal eyelet rib (used above the ribbing on the jumper illustrated)*
▼ *Wavy eyelet rib pattern*

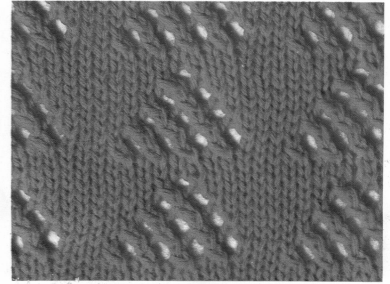

▲ *Arrowhead and diamond lace pattern*
▼ *Lace triangles pattern (used for a central panel on jumper illustrated)*

Diagonal eyelet rib

Cast on a number of stitches divisible by 5, plus 2. Example 27 stitches.

1st row. (RS) K1, *K3, K2 tog, yfwd, rep from * to last st, K1.
2nd and every alt row. P.
3rd row. K1, *K2, K2 tog, yfwd, K1, rep from * to last st, K1.
5th row. K1, *K1, K2 tog, yfwd, K2, rep from * to last st, K1.
7th row. K1, *K2 tog, yfwd, K3, rep from * to last st, K1.
9th row. K2 tog, *yfwd, K3, K2 tog, rep from * ending last rep K2.
10th row. P.
These 10 rows form pattern and are repeated throughout.

Wavy eyelet rib

Cast on a number of stitches divisible by 4, plus 2. Example 26 stitches.

1st row. (RS) K1, *K2, K2 tog, yfwd, rep from * to last st, K1.
2nd and every alt row. P.
3rd row. K1, *K1, K2 tog, yfwd, K1, rep from * to last st, K1.
5th row. K1, *K2 tog, yfwd, K2, rep from * to last st, K1.
7th row. K1, *K1, yfwd, K2 tog, K1, rep from * to last st, K1.
9th row. K1, *K2, yfwd, K2 tog, rep from * to last st, K1.
11th row. *K2 tog, K2, yfwd, rep from * to last 2 sts, K2.
12th row. P.
Rows 3–12 form pattern and are repeated throughout.

Spearhead lace rib

Cast on a number of stitches divisible by 12, plus 2. Example 38 stitches.

1st row. (RS) K1, *K3, yfwd, sl 1, K1, psso, K2, K2 tog, yfwd, K1, yfwd, sl 1, K1, psso, rep from * to last st, K1.
2nd and every alt row. P.
3rd row. K1, *K1, K2 tog, yfwd, K1, yfwd, sl 1, K1, psso, K1, K2 tog, yfwd, K1, yfwd, sl 1, K1, psso, rep from * to last st, K1.
5th row. K1, *K2 tog, yfwd, K3, yfwd, sl 1, K1, psso, K2 tog, yfwd, K1, yfwd, sl 1, K1, psso, rep from * to last st, K1.
6th row. P.
These 6 rows form pattern and are repeated throughout.

Arrowhead and diamond lace

Cast on a number of stitches divisible by 10, plus 2. Example 32 stitches.

1st row. (RS) K1, yfwd, *K3, sl 1, K2 tog, psso, K3, yfwd, K1, yfwd, rep from * to last 11 sts, K3, sl 1, K2 tog, psso, K3, yfwd, K2.
2nd and every alt row. P.
3rd row. K2, *yfwd, K2, sl 1, K2 tog, psso, K2, yfwd, K3, rep from * to end.
5th row. K2 tog, yfwd, *K1, yfwd, K1, sl 1, K2 tog, psso, K1, yfwd, K1, yfwd, sl 1, K2 tog, psso, yfwd, rep from * to last 10 sts, K1, yfwd, K1, sl 1, K2 tog, psso, K1, yfwd, K1, yfwd, sl 1, K1, psso, K1.
6th row. P.
These 6 rows form pattern and are repeated throughout.

Lace triangles

Cast on a number of stitches divisible by 11, plus 3. Example 36 stitches.

1st row. (RS) *K3, (yfwd, sl 1, K1, psso) 4 times, rep from * to last 3 sts, K3.
2nd and every alt row. P.
3rd row. *K4, (yfwd, sl 1, K1, psso) 3 times, K1, rep from * to last 3 sts, K3.
5th row. *K5, (yfwd, sl 1, K1, psso) twice, K2, rep from * to last 3 st, K3.
7th row. *K6, yfwd, sl 1, K1, psso, K3, rep from * to last 3 sts, K3.
8th row. P. *9th row.* K. *10th row.* P.
These 10 rows form pattern and are repeated throughout.

▲ *Diagonal eyelet rib used for a band above the ribbing, and lace triangles pattern used for a central panel, on a classic sleeveless jumper*

Adapting a pattern

It is not difficult to adapt a simple classic stocking stitch design to incorporate panels or bands of a patterned stitch which particularly appeals to you. Choose a stitch which is basically suitable. Don't select a pattern which has strong vertical lines, such as arrowhead and diamond or spearhead laces, for a horizontal band. Diagonal eyelet rib or wavy eyelet rib are much more suitable. Lace triangles would form an attractive border or panel, or are suitable to work as an all over pattern.

Remember that most patterns using eyelet stitches alter the tension slightly. This can usually be corrected by using one size smaller needles, provided the pattern is going to be used over a fairly large area, such as a border or as an all over fabric. Small inserted front panels are seldom large enough to affect the whole tension of the garment.

It is always easier to use a set of instructions which has the correct total number of stitches required for the repeating of the chosen pattern, but this is not always possible to find. Slight alterations can usually be made to overcome this point. For example, the lace stitches may require an even number of stitches, whereas the total number of stitches required for the jersey may be odd. If two lace panels were to be worked, one from each shoulder, the centre panel could be worked over an odd number of stitches in stocking stitch. If there is bust dart shaping, however, it is better to keep to one central panel, therefore one extra stitch should be decreased after the ribbing.

Where an alteration of this type is made it is important to remember that it may affect other parts of the pattern. In this case, it is necessary to leave one stitch less on the centre front stitches at the neck edge. If these are cast off instead of being slipped onto a holder, it will be simpler to pick up the correct total number of stitches required for the neckband.

Horizontal panel using diagonal eyelet rib

Work ribbing for Back and Front as given in your pattern. Work 8 rows stocking stitch, or required depth before beginning of band. Knit 2 rows. Change to one size finer needles. Work in pattern as given for stitch, including edge stitches, and K or P any extra stitches at beginning and end of each row. Work 2½in in pattern, or required depth. Change to former needles.
Knit 2 rows. Complete as given for pattern.

Chapter 21

Knitting Know-how

Techniques for looped effects

There are several different ways of working long looped stitches but usually their purpose is to form either an overlaid texture on a plain fabric background or to give a very lacy openwork appearance to the knitting.

Picking up a loop on the row below
This is a normal knitted stitch but the right-hand needle is inserted into the stitch directly below on the previous row, before the stitch is dropped from the left-hand needle. (figure 1).

Picking up a loop 4 rows below
This is similar to knitting into a stitch on the previous row and is used in patterns with a stocking stitch background. Insert the right-hand needle 4 or more rows below the stitch reached in the pattern, (figure 2), and knit one pulling up a long loop. Let the stitch drop from the left-hand needle until it reaches the row in which the loop stitch has been worked. (figure 3).

Knitting a stitch with 3 loops
This stitch can be combined with stocking stitch or garter stitch to form a band of lacy openwork but it can also be worked on its own to make soft, light stoles and evening tops. Begin with a knit row and wind the yarn 3 times round the right hand needle for

each stitch (figure 4). On the next row, knit or purl these stitches as required, unwinding the 3 loops of each stitch and letting them drop off the left-hand needle. (figure 5).

Picking up a loop with a crochet hook
Some novelty patterns require extra loops which are worked with the aid of a crochet hook.

These loops are picked up knitwise several rows below. Knit to the position where the loop is required, leaving the yarn at the back of the work. Insert the crochet hook from the front of the work 4 or more rows below and pull a long loop of yarn through to the right side of the work, making one extra long, loose stitch.

▲ 2. *Picking up a loop from 4 rows below*
▼ 3. *Pulling up long loop from 4 rows below*

▼ 1. *Picking up a loop from the row below*

(figure 6). Slip this extra stitch on to the left hand needle and knit into the back of it together with the next stitch on the left-hand needle.

To transfer this extra loop diagonally across the front of the work, leave it on the crochet hook and work 3 or more stitches on to the right-hand needle in the usual way. Then knit the extra loop together with the next stitch on the left-hand needle.

The yarn used in the photographs on these two pages is Patons Double Knitting

▲ **4.** *Winding yarn 3 times round needle*
▼ **5.** *Forming long openwork loops*

▲ **6.** *Dainty bedjacket with a looped effect*
▼ **7.** *Picking up a loop with a crochet hook*

Cap and collar set in loop stitch

Loop stitch knitting produces a warm-looking fabric which can be used to make fashion garments, accessories and pretty trims.

Working loop stitch

The loop lies on the right side, or outside, of the fabric but is formed when working a wrong side row. For a trial sample cast on 21 sts and K3 rows.

4th row (WS) K1, *insert needle into next st on left hand needle as if to knit it, wind yarn over needle point and round first and second fingers of left hand twice then over and round needle point once. Draw all 3 loops through stitch and slip onto the left hand needle, insert right hand needle through back of these 3 loops and through the original stitch and knit all together—called ML—, K1, rep from * to end of row.

5th row K.

6th row K2, *ML, K1, rep from * to last st, K1.

7th row K.

Rep the last 4 rows several times to see the effect of the loops. Cast off.

Variations of loop stitch

Loop stitch can be worked quickly if care is taken not to wind the yarn so tightly round the fingers that it becomes difficult to free the loops when the stitch is completed.

Different effects can be obtained by altering the number of stitches between loops and also by changing the number of rows between loop rows. The length of the loops can be varied by working over only two fingers for a short loop or

by working over 3 or even 4 fingers for a longer loop. Thick yarns, or two or more strands of yarn used together, worked over two fingers with loops close together and worked on alternate rows will give a close, deep, chunky pile. A dainty effect can be achieved on an evening stole or wrap by using a fine yarn wound round all 4 fingers and worked on every 4th stitch, with 3 plain rows between loops rows.

▲ *Cap and matching collar*

Caps and Collar

Size
Caps. To fit average adult head
Collar. Length 14in or as required

Tension for this design
4 sts and 7 rows to 1in over g st worked with double yarn on No.6 needles

Materials
Patons Fiona
Caps. 2 50g balls for one-colour version. 2 50g balls A, 2 50g balls B, for two-colour version
Collar. 2 50g balls A
One pair No.6 needles
Three buttons for collar
One No.4·00 (ISR) crochet hook

Caps
Using No.6 needles and A double, cast on 25 sts.
1st row (WS) K1, *insert needle into next st as if to K, wind yarn over needle point and first finger loosely 3 times then over and round needle point once, draw loops through st and return to left hand needle, insert right hand needle through back of loops and st and K tog—called ML—, K1, rep from * to end.

2nd row K.
3rd row K2, *ML, K1, rep from * to last 3 sts, yfwd to avoid making a hole, sl 1. Turn.
4th row Yfwd, sl 1, ybk, K to end.
5th row As 1st.
6th row Change to colour B if more than 1 colour is being used, K.
7th row K20, yfwd, sl 1. Turn.
8th row Yfwd, sl 1, ybk, K20.
9th row K18, yfwd, sl 1. Turn.
10th row Yfwd, sl 1, ybk, K18.
11th row K15, yfwd, sl 1. Turn.
12th row Yfwd, sl 1, ybk, K15.
13th row K12, yfwd, sl 1. Turn.
14th row Yfwd, sl 1, ybk, K12.
Work 11th, 12th, 9th, 10th, 7th and 8th rows once more.
21st row K all sts.
22nd row Change to colour A, K to end.
Rep 1st—22nd rows 4 times more, then 1st—21st rows once. Cast off.

To make up
Draw short top edge up and join back seam. Fasten off all ends.

Collar
Using No.6 needles and A double, cast on 15 sts.
Work first 2 rows as given for caps.
3rd row K2, *ML, K1, rep from * to last st, K1.
4th row K.
These 4 rows form patt. Continue in patt until work measures 14in, or required length. Cast off.

To make up
Using No.4·00 (ISR) hook and one strand of A, work in dc along one short end, work 2nd row dc, making 3 button loops at regular intervals by working 3ch and missing 2dc. Fasten off.
Sew on buttons to correspond.

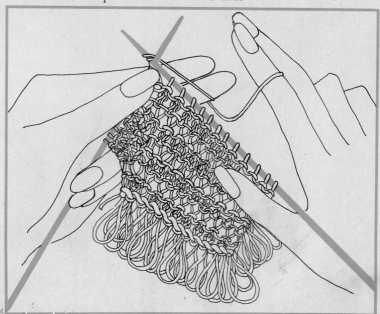

◄ *Winding yarn round two fingers*
One-colour version of looped cap ►

Chapter 22

Crochet look knitting stitches

There are many attractive knitting stitches which give a similar impression to lacy work done with a crochet hook. They are formed by using the same principle as for long loop stitches, shown in Knitting Know-how Chapter 21. These stitches are very quick and simple to knit, and in this chapter you can try patterns for two of the most attractive ones. If you work them in bands, alternating with stocking stitch or garter stitch, you will produce a firm but lacy finish which can be used for a variety of garments.

Dimple stitch and seashell stitch are effective in both 4 ply and double knitting yarn, although 4 ply may be more suitable for light summer garments. Try a lacy top or a little girl's party dress in 4 ply, or a delicate baby's jacket in a finer yarn. A double knitting yarn could make a pretty and unusual cot cover, or a dress with an openwork effect for summer or evening as shown in the illustration.

Dimple stitch
Cast on a number of stitches divisible by 3, plus 2.
1st row. P to end.
2nd row. P1, *yarn round right-hand needle twice—called y2rn—P1, rep from * to last st, P1.
3rd row. P1, *slip next 3 sts P-wise on to right-hand needle dropping extra loops, pull the loose loops gently upwards and slip back on to left-hand needle, K3 tog tbl, bring yarn forward over right-hand needle and back then K3 tog tbl again, rep from * to last st, P1.
4th row. P to end.
These 4 rows form pattern and are repeated throughout.

Seashell stitch
Cast on a number of stitches divisible by 6, plus 2.
1st row. K to end.
2nd row. P to end.
Rep 1st and 2nd rows once more.
5th row. K1, *y2rn, K1, rep from * to last st, K1.
6th row. P1, * holding yarn at back of work slip next 6 sts P-wise on to right-hand needle dropping extra loops, pull the loose stitches gently upwards and slip back on to left-hand needle, yrn and P6 tog without slipping them off left-hand needle, yon and K1 into these 6 sts, then P1, K1 into same 6 sts in usual way, rep from * to last st, P1.
These 6 rows form pattern and are repeated throughout.

The yarn used in the photographs on the opposite page is Patons Purple Heather 4 ply.

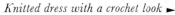

Knitted dress with a crochet look ▶

▲ *Dropping extra loops for dimple stitch*
▼ *Working loops together for dimple stitch*

▼ *Dropping extra loops for seashell stitch*

▼ *Working loops together for seashell stitch*

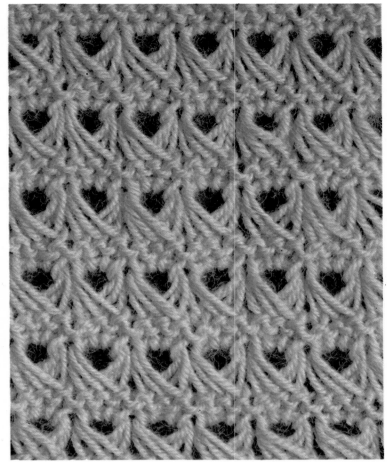

▼ *Seashell stitch*   ▲ *Dimple stitch*

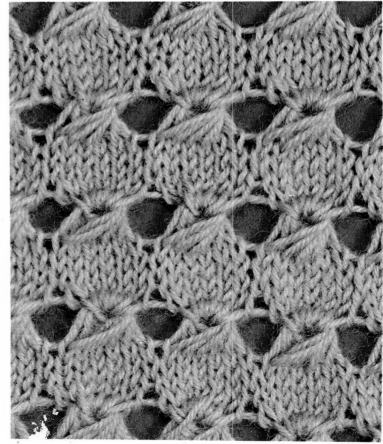

Chapter 23

Woven look stitches

Working with a favourite knitting pattern, interesting textures and a woven fabric effect can be achieved by substituting these simple 'woven knitting' stitches for stocking stitch and garter stitch. Because the stitches are based on multiples of two stitches, they are easily adapted to patterns based on an even number of stitches. The tension of these stitches is likely to be different from stocking or garter stitch and you should work a test sample and change the needle size if necessary until the tension quoted in the pattern is obtained. Both sides of these woven knitting stitches can be used as the pattern. An unusual and interesting effect could be achieved by using both sides of a stitch in one design, such as a panel down the front of a jersey.

Plain woven stitch
Worked over an even number of stitches, plus 2 edge stitches.
1st row. K.
2nd row. K1, *yfwd, sl 1 K-wise, rep from * to last st, K1.
3rd row. K1, *K2 tog tbl thus working together the slipped and the made stitch on previous row, rep from * to last st, K1.
The 2nd and 3rd rows form pattern and are repeated throughout.

Woven vertical rib stitch
Worked over an even number of stitches, plus 2 edge stitches.
1st row. K1, *yfwd, sl 1 K-wise, K1, rep from * to last st, K1.
2nd row. K1, *K1, K2 tog tbl thus working together the slipped and the made stitch on previous row, rep from * to last st, K1.
These 2 rows form the pattern and are repeated throughout.

Woven horizontal rib stitch
Worked over an even number of stitches, plus 2 edge stitches.
1st row. K.
2nd row. P.
3rd row. K1, *insert right-hand needle between next 2 sts on left-hand needle and draw stitch through, K first st on left-hand needle, rep from * to last st, K1.
4th row. K1, *P2 tog, rep from * to last st, K1.
These 4 rows form the pattern and are repeated throughout.

Woven herringbone stitch
Worked over an even number of stitches.
1st row. K2 tog tbl but drop only the 1st loop off the left-hand needle, *K the st rem on left-hand needle tog tbl with the next st on left-hand needle again dropping only the 1st loop off the needle, rep from * until 1 loop rem on left-hand needle, K1 tbl.
2nd row. P2 tog dropping only the 1st loop off the left-hand needle, *P the st rem on left-hand needle tog with the next st on left-hand needle again dropping only the 1st loop off the needle, rep from * until 1 loop rem on left-hand needle, P1.
These 2 rows form the pattern and are repeated throughout.

Pinafore dress with the woven look ►

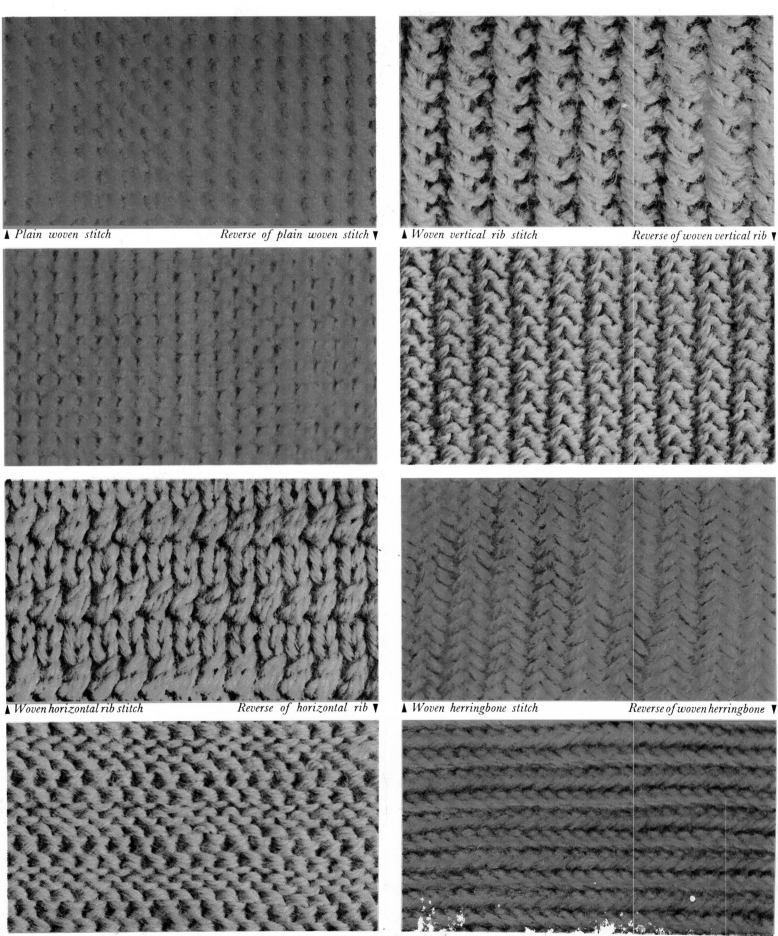

▲ *Plain woven stitch*   *Reverse of plain woven stitch* ▼

▲ *Woven vertical rib stitch*   *Reverse of woven vertical rib* ▼

▲ *Woven horizontal rib stitch*   *Reverse of horizontal rib* ▼

▲ *Woven herringbone stitch*   *Reverse of woven herringbone* ▼

Chapter 24

Knitting Know-how

Mock cable stitches

You have already seen how you can alter the appearance of knitted stitches by working into the back of the stitch to produce a twisted effect (Knitting Know-how Chapter 7).

To give an even more twisted appearance, the method is to actually cross two or more stitches. This means that the second stitch on the left-hand needle is worked before the first, so that the stitches change place, producing an attractive miniature cable or twisted rib effect.

There are countless variations of cable patterns, of which six are described in this chapter, together with their standard abbreviations.

Knitted crossed stitches with back twist. Tw2B

The twist lies to the left. Pass the right-hand needle behind the first stitch on the left-hand needle, knit into the back of the next stitch and leave on the needle. Then knit into the back of the first stitch and slip both stitches off the left-hand needle together. (Used in twisted rib pattern and mock cable.)

Knitted crossed stitches with front twist. Tw2F

The twist lies to the right. Pass the right-hand needle in front of the first stitch on the left-hand needle and knit the next stitch, leaving it on the needle. Then knit the first stitch and slip both stitches off the left-hand needle together.

Purled crossed stitches with front twist. Tw2PF

This is often used on a purl row when the purled side is the wrong side. It produces a crossed thread lying to the right on the knit side of the work. Pass the right-hand needle in front of the first stitch on the left-hand needle and purl the next stitch, leaving it on the needle. Then purl the first stitch and slip both stitches off the left-hand needle together.

Purled crossed stitch with back twist. Tw2PB

Because this is more difficult to work it is less often used. It forms a cross lying to the left on the knit side of the work. Pass the right-hand needle behind the first stitch on the left-hand needle, purl the next stitch through the back of the loop and leave it on the needle. Then purl the first stitch and slip both off the left-hand needle together.

It is sometimes easier to use a cable needle to help with this stitch. Slip the first stitch from the left-hand needle on to the cable needle and hold at the front of the work, purl the next stitch through the back of the loop and purl the stitch from the cable needle.

A slightly different, or mock, twist can be given to the stitches if each stitch is lifted over the first one before the first one is worked. This is not usually referred to by any standard abbreviation but will be described in detail in the instructions for knitting garments in which the stitch appears.

Knitted crossed stitch with back twist

Purled cross stitch with front twist

Crossing two stitches to the right

Crossing two stitches to the right. Cross 2R

Pass the right-hand needle in front of the first stitch on the left-hand needle and knit into the second stitch. Lift it over the first stitch and off the point of the needle. Knit the first stitch on the left-hand needle. (Used in crossed miniature cable.)

Crossing two stitches to the left

Slip the first stitch on the left-hand needle without knitting it. Knit the next stitch on the left-hand needle and slip it on to the right-hand needle. Using the left-hand needle point pass the slipped stitch over the newly knitted stitch, knitting into the slipped stitch at the same time.

Twisted rib pattern

Worked over a number of stitches divisible by 14, plus 2.

1st row. P2, *Tw2B, P2, K4 all tbl, P2, Tw2B, P2, rep from * to end.

2nd row. K2, *P2, K2, P4, K2, P2, K2, rep from * to end.

Rep 1st and 2nd rows once.

5th row. P2, *Tw2B, P2, into 4th and 3rd sts on left-hand needle work Tw2B leaving sts on left-hand needle,

work Tw2B into 2nd and 1st sts on left-hand needle and slip all 4 sts from left to right-hand needle,

P2, Tw2B, P2, rep from * to end.

6th row. As 2nd.

These 6 rows form the pattern and are repeated throughout.

Mock cable

Worked over a number of stitches divisible by 5, plus 3.

1st row. P3, *K2, P3, rep from * to end.

2nd row. K3, *P2, K3, rep from * to end.

Rep 1st and 2nd rows once.

5th row. P3, *Tw2B, P3, rep from * to end.

6th row. As 2nd.

These 6 rows form the pattern and are repeated throughout.

Crossed miniature cable

Worked over a number of stitches divisible by 7, plus 3.

1st row. P3, *K4, P3, rep from * to end.

2nd row. K3, *P4, K3, rep from * to end.

3rd row. P3, *(cross 2R) twice, P3, rep from * to end.

4th row. As 2nd.

These 4 rows form the pattern and are repeated throughout.

Right: twisted rib pattern ►
Below left: mock cable ▼
Below right: crossed miniature cable ►

Chapter 25

Chunky 'fabric' stitches

Here are four more patterns using twisted and crossed stitches. Basket weave may be worked using the yarn double throughout giving a very firm but light fabric which is suitable for jackets and clothes with a more tailored look.

Basket weave stitch
Worked over an even number of stitches.
1st row. *Tw2B, rep from * to end.
2nd row. P1, *Tw2PF, rep from * to last st, P1.
These 2 rows form the pattern and are repeated throughout.

Crossed basket weave stitch
Worked over an even number of stitches. This stitch is more easily and quickly worked than basket weave stitch but gives a similar effect.
1st row. *Holding yarn at back of work, sl 1 purlwise, K next st, yon, lift slipped stitch over both knitted stitch and yon, rep from * to end.
2nd row. P.
3rd row. K1, work from * as for 1st row to last st, K1.
4th row. P.
These 4 rows form the pattern and are repeated throughout.

Waffle stitch
Worked over a number of stitches divisible by 4.
1st row. *Tw2B, Tw2F, rep from * to end.
2nd row. P.
3rd row. *Tw2F, Tw2B, rep from * to end.
4th row. P.
These 4 rows form the pattern and are repeated throughout.

Twisted panel stitch
Worked over a number of stitches divisible by 8 plus 2.
1st row. K2, *(Tw2F) 3 times, K2, rep from * to end.
2nd row. P.
3rd row. K2, * (Tw3F) twice, K2, rep from * to end.
4th row. P.
These 4 rows form the pattern and are repeated throughout. Tw3F is worked in the same way as Tw2F, but is worked over 3 sts instead of 2. Work into the 3rd st on the left-hand needle, then into the 2nd and then into the 1st, slipping all 3 sts off the left-hand needle together.

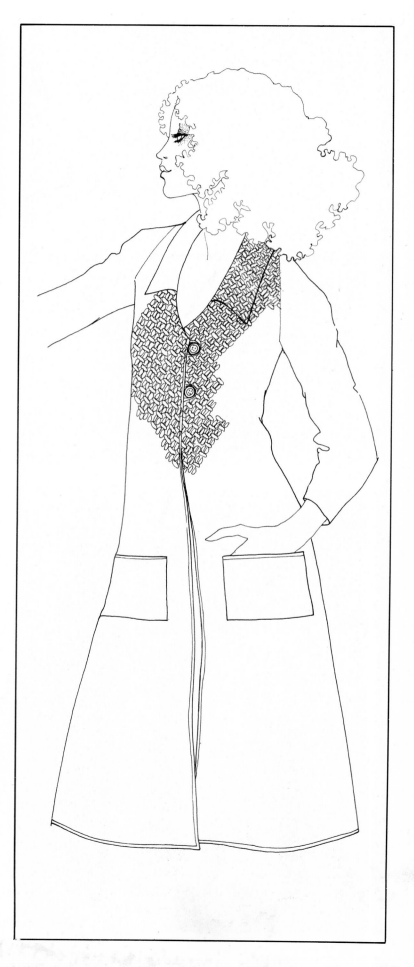

Coat in a firm fabric stitch ►

▲ *Basket weave stitch*   ▼ *Crossed basket weave stitch*   ▲ *Waffle stitch*   ▼ *Twisted panel stitch*

71

Introduction to cable stitch

Cable stitch patterns have many variations and because they are so easy to work they are very popular, either in a fine, lacy form or for giving texture to thicker fabrics for sportswear. Once you have mastered the principle of working cables, the possible variations are endless.

Panels of cables can give a special look to classic sweaters: for example, as two separate bands on the front and back of a plain stocking-stitch pattern, using the purl side of the fabric as the right side to give a more interesting finish. Test pieces of knitting are worth keeping and if you join them together they can make a very effective looking afghan. Or, more simply, use the test pieces described in this chapter as pockets on a button-through cardigan.

All cable designs are based on stitches being moved from one position to another by crossing over each other, which gives the effect of the twist you see in a rope.

In twisting two stitches it is possible to knit the second by passing the needle behind, or in front of the first, then working the first stitch. When altering the position of more than two stitches it is easier to do so by means of a third needle. For this purpose a cable needle is the best, although any double-pointed needle will do—a cable needle is very short and is less likely to get in the way while you are working the other stitches.

If the cable needle is not the same thickness as the needles being used for the garment, it should be finer, not thicker. A thicker needle is very difficult to use and it will stretch the stitches and spoil the appearance of the finished work.

Simple twist from right to left

Try a simple cable of six knit stitches against a background of purl fabric, as follows:
Cast on 24 sts.
1st row. P9, K6, P9.
2nd row. K9, P6, K9.
3rd row. As 1st.
4th row. As 2nd.
5th row. As 1st.
6th row. As 2nd.
7th row. P9, slip the next 3 knit stitches on to the cable needle and hold them at the front of the work; with the right-hand needle continue to knit the next 3 knit stitches from the left-hand needle, then knit the 3 stitches from the cable needle, P9.
8th row. As 2nd.
Repeat these 8 rows twice more. Cast off.
You will now have a sample with a rope-like pattern in the centre of the six knitted stitches, twisted three times. Each twist, or turn, lies in the same direction, from the right towards the left.

Simple twist from left to right

To twist the opposite way, that is from the left towards the right, the stitches on the cable needle are held behind the work instead of in front of it, as follows:
Cast on 24 sts.
1st row. P9, K6, P9.
2nd row. K9, P6, K9.
Rep 1st and 2nd rows twice more.
7th row. P9, slip the next 3 knit stitches on to the cable needle and hold them at the back of the work; with the right-hand needle continue to knit the next 3 knit stitches from the left-hand needle, then knit the 3 stitches from the cable needle, P9.
8th row. As 2nd.
Repeat these 8 rows twice more. Cast off.
This second sample will be similar to the first but the turns will lie in the opposite direction.

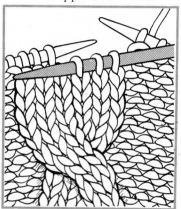

▲ *Cable six stitches to the front*   ▲ *Cable six stitches to the back*

Abbreviations

The abbreviations are usually given for cables in each set of instructions. The letter C often stands for a cable and is then followed by the number of stitches to be cabled. It is also necessary to show whether the stitches are to be held at the front or the back of the work, so that the number may be followed by the letter F or B. In this way the abbreviation for the first sample would read, C6F and for the second sample, C6B.

Remember that the number of stitches held on the cable needle is half the number given for the cable.

Cable rope with row variations

The appearance of the cable is altered very much by the number of rows worked between each twist. The illustration shows a sample worked in the same way as the first samples but merely altering the number of rows between each twist, as follows:
Cast on 24 sts.
1st row. P9, K6, P9.
2nd row. K9, P6, K9.
Rep 1st and 2nd rows once more.
5th row. P9, C6F, P9.
6th row. As 2nd.
Repeat 1st and 2nd rows twice, then 5th and 6th rows once.
Repeat 1st and 2nd rows 4 times, then 5th and 6th rows once.
Repeat 1st and 2nd rows 6 times, then 5th and 6th rows once.
Repeat 1st and 2nd rows once. Cast off.
Twisting on every alternate or even every 4th row gives the cable a very close, tight, rope look, whereas twisting every 8th or 12th row gives a much softer look.

an interesting ballooning out of the rope between the twists. Another simple variation is an alternating cable, as follows: Cast on 31 sts.

1st row. P1, *K4, P1, rep from * to end.
2nd row. K1, *P4, K1, rep from * to end.
3rd row. P1, *K4, P1, C4F, P1, rep from * to end.
4th row. As 2nd.
Repeat 1st and 2nd rows once more.
7th row. P1, *C4F, P1, K4, P1, rep from * to end.
8th row. As 2nd.
These 8 rows form the pattern and are repeated as required.

▲ *Alternating cables*
▼ *Pieces of test knitting joined together make multicoloured bedspreads*

▲ *Cable rope with row variation*

Alternating cables

The number of stitches over which the cable is worked also alters the appearance. A simple cable is usually worked over 4 or 6 stitches. Most attractive variations can be made, however, by working over 10 or 12 stitches, using thick needles and a bulky yarn. In this type of variation, more rows worked between the twists gives

73

Chapter 26 continued

Variations of cable stitch

Cables give an interesting texture to almost any simple or casual garment but the chunkiest patterns are perhaps shown to best effect on sports sweaters—men in particular admire heavily cabled cardigans and sweaters.

Here are some interesting variations of cable stitches to practise, which are made by combining twists to the right and to the left, forming more complicated-looking patterns, or interwoven fabrics.

Link cable

Dividing the number of stitches in a cabled panel and taking half to the right and half to the left gives the appearance of chain links, with each link appearing to come upwards out of the one below.
Cast on 24 sts.
1st row. P6, K12, P6.
2nd row. K6, P12, K6.
Repeat 1st and 2nd rows twice more.
7th row. P6, C6B (slip next 3 sts on to cable needle and hold at back of work, K next 3sts from left-hand needle, K3 sts from cable needle), C6F (slip next 3 sts on to cable needle and hold at front of work, K next 3 sts from left-hand needle, K3 sts from cable needle), P6.
8th row. As 2nd.
These 8 rows form the pattern and are repeated as required.

Link cable

Inverted link cable

The opposite effect of one link joining and passing under the link above is given by reversing the order of the cable on the previous pattern, as follows:
Cast on 24 sts.
1st row. P6, K12, P6.
2nd row. K6, P12, K6.
Repeat 1st and 2nd rows twice more.
7th row. P6, C6F, C6B, P6.
8th row. As 2nd.
These 8 rows form the pattern and are repeated as required.

Honeycomb cable

Both of the previous patterns worked alternately form a cable which appears to be superimposed on the fabric underneath. This is worked as follows:
Cast on 24 sts.
1st row. P6, K12, P6.
2nd row. K6, P12, K6.
Repeat 1st and 2nd rows once more.
5th row. P6, C6B, C6F, P6.
6th row. As 2nd.
Repeat 1st and 2nd rows twice more.
11th row. P6, C6F, C6B,.P6.
12th row. As 2nd.
These 12 rows form the pattern and are repeated as required.

Single plaited cable

A plaited effect can be achieved by dividing the group of stitches to be cabled into three instead of two and cabling each group alternately, as follows:
Cast on 30 sts or a number of sts divisible by 9, plus 3.
1st row. P3, *K6, P3, rep from * to end.
2nd row. K3, *P6, K3, rep from * to end.
3rd row. P3, *C4B (slip next 2 sts on to cable needle and hold at back of work, K2 sts from left-hand needle, K2 sts from cable needle), K rem 2 sts of K6 group, rep from * to end.
4th row. As 2nd.
5th row. P3, *K first 2 sts of K6 group, C4F (slip next 2 sts on to cable needle and hold at front of work, K2 sts from left-hand needle, K2 sts from cable needle), P3, rep from * to end.
6th row. As 2nd.
Repeat from 3rd-6th rows as required.

Double plaited cable

An even more textured and intricate appearance is given by a double plaited cable, as follows:
Cast on 30 sts or a number of sts divisible by 24, plus 6.
1st row. P6, *K18, P6, rep from * to end.
2nd row. K6, *P18, K6, rep from * to end.
3rd row. P6, *(C6B) 3 times, P6, rep from * to end.
4th row. As 2nd.
Repeat 1st and 2nd rows once more.
7th row. P6, *K3, (C6F) twice, K3, P6, rep from * to end.
8th row. As 2nd.
These 8 rows form the pattern and are repeated as required.

▲ *Inverted link cable*   ▼ *Single plaited cable*   ▲ *Honeycomb cable*   ▼ *Double plaited cable*

Chapter 27

Introduction to Aran knitting

The Aran islands of Inishmore, Inishmaan and Inisheer lie off the west coast of Ireland. Remote and weather-beaten, they are the home of the popular and richly textured knitting known as Aran. The Irish name for the thick, hard wearing homespun wool used for Aran knitting is bainin, pronounced 'bawneen', and means natural, or white. The traditional patterns show to their best advantage on this light-coloured wool, although it is sometimes tinted with seaweed or moss dyes to produce pale, subtle shades. Practise the stitches in this chapter (you can use double knitting yarn and No. 8 needles if bainin is difficult to obtain) by knitting panels which can then be joined together to make distinctive furnishings such as cushion covers, bedspreads, or rugs.

Like all folk crafts, the traditional Aran designs derive their inspiration from the daily life of the islanders. The rocks and cliff paths are remembered in stitches of zigzag patterns, and chunky bobbles and the fishermen's ropes are depicted by a vast number of cable variations which play a major part in most designs. The wealth of the sea around the islands is remembered in such designs as Lobster claw cable. Religious symbolism appears in stitches such as Tree of life. Trinity stitch and Ladder of life, and everyday life is depicted in the ups and downs of Marriage lines and in several different moss stitches (see single and double moss stitches, Knitting Know-how Chapter 7). Even the industrious bee is remembered in Honeycomb stitch.

Honeycomb stitch
Worked over a number of stitches divisible by 8.
1st row. *Sl 2 sts onto cable needle and hold at back of work, K2, K2 from cable needle—called C4B, sl 2 sts onto cable needle and hold at front of work, K2, K2 from cable needle—called C4F, rep from * to end.
2nd row. P to end.
3rd row. K to end.
4th row. P to end.
5th row. *C4F, C4B, rep from * to end.
6th row. P to end.
7th row. K to end.
8th row. P to end.
These 8 rows form the pattern and are repeated throughout. A variation of Honeycomb stitch is made by working extra rows in stocking stitch between the cable rows to elongate the design.

Ladder of life
This is a simple design, depicting man's desire to do better and climb upwards towards heaven. The rungs of the ladder are formed by purl rows worked on a stocking stitch background.
Worked over a number of stitches divisible by 6, plus 1, ie 37.
1st row. (RS) P1, *K5, P1, rep from * to end.

▲ *Honeycomb stitch*

▲ *Lobster claw cable*

2nd row. K1, *P5, K1, rep from * to end.
3rd row. P to end.
4th row. K1, *P5, K1, rep from * to end.
These 4 rows form the pattern and are repeated throughout. The number of stitches between the vertical purl lines may be altered to suit the area to be covered, as may the number of rows worked between the ladder rungs.

Trinity stitch
So called because the method of working is '3 in one and 1 in 3'. This stitch is also known as Blackberry stitch in England and Bramble stitch in Scotland.
Worked over a number of stitches divisible by 4.
1st row. P to end.
2nd row. *K1, P1, K1 all into same st making 3 sts from one st, P3 tog to make one st from 3 sts, rep from * to end.
3rd row. P to end.
4th row. *P3 tog, K1, P1, K1 all into one st, rep from * to end.
These 4 rows form the pattern and are repeated throughout.

▲ *Ladder of life*

▲ *Trinity stitch*

▲ *An unusual sampler of interlaced cable edged with a finishing panel of twisted stitches*

Lobster claw stitch

Worked over a number of stitches divisible by 9, ie 45.

1st row. *P1, K7, P1, rep from * to end.
2nd row. *K1, P7, K1, rep from * to end.
3rd row. *P1, sl 2 sts onto cable needle and hold at back of work, K1, K2 from cable needle, K1, sl 1 st onto cable needle and hold at front of work, K2, K1 from cable needle, P1, rep from * to end.
4th row. *K1, P7, K1, rep from * to end.

These 4 rows form the pattern and are repeated throughout. The number of stitches over which the claw is worked and the number of rows between the cable rows may be altered but too much alteration changes the appearance of the claw-like look.

Sample of cable stitches

This sample is worked over 64 sts and includes two types of cables, which depict the fisherman's ropes, and is edged with a twisted stitch often used in Aran patterns.

1st row. (RS) K1, P1, K1y2rn, K2, P3, (K6, P3) twice, K12, (P3, K6) twice, P3, K1y2rn, K2, P1, K1.

2nd row. K2, P2, sl 1 keeping yarn on WS, K3, (P6, K3) twice, P12, K3, (P6, K3) twice, P2, sl 1 keeping yarn on WS, K2.
3rd row. K1, P1, sl long st onto cable needle and hold at front of work, K1y2rn, K1, K1 from cable needle—called CTw3—, P3, (K6, P3) twice, K12, (P3, K6) twice, P3, CTw3, P1, K1.
4th row. As 2nd.
5th row. K1, P1, CTw3, P3, (sl next 3 sts onto cable needle and hold at front of work, K3, K3 from cable needle—called C6F—, P3) twice, C6F twice, P3, (C6F, P3) twice, CTw3, P1, K1.
6th row. As 2nd.
7th row. As 1st, keeping CTw3 at each end.
8th row. As 2nd.
9th row. As 7th.
10th row. As 2nd.
11th row. K1, P1, CTw3, P3, (C6F, P3) twice, K3, sl next 3 sts onto cable needle and hold at back of work, K3, K3 from cable needle—called C6B—, K3, P3, (C6F, P3) twice, CTw3, P1, K1.
12th row. As 2nd. *13th row.* As 7th.

Rows 2-13 form the pattern and are repeated throughout.

More Aran stitches

Stitches in cables and twisted panels which form many Aran patterns may change their position, but they usually return to their original place in the pattern sequence within a few rows. Travelling stitches, on the other hand, may move on every row or alternate row throughout the entire pattern repeat and form the basis of all trellis and lattice patterns, as well as being used in single motifs such as Tree of life pattern and Marriage lines pattern.

A simplified form of trellis stitch, where only one ridge travels in a zigzag pattern within a panel, symbolizes the ups and downs of married life. Using a double ridge a diamond pattern is formed (see the man's cardigan featured in Basic Wardrobe, page 178). This is often used as an all-over design and is reminiscent of the small walled fields of Ireland. The pattern also means 'wealth'. Extra texture may be added by filling the centre of each diamond with moss stitch, Trinity stitch, or rock-like bobbles.
Narrow lines of travelling stitches branching out from a central stem form the famous Tree of life design, sometimes used inverted, with the branches drooping instead of rising upwards.

Trellis sampler
The sampler is edged with a narrow panel of twisted stitches and is ideal for working in strips, which can then be joined together to make cushions, rugs or bedspreads.
Worked over 58 stitches.
1st row. K1, P1, K1 putting yarn twice round needle—called Kly2rn —, K2, P2, K1, P3, *(sl 2 sts on to cable needle and hold at back of work, K2, K2 from cable needle — called C4B —, P4) 4 times, C4B, P3, K1, P2, Kly2rn, K2, P1, K1.
2nd row. K2, P2, sl 1 dropping extra loop and keeping yarn on WS, K2, P1, K2, (P4, K4) 3 times, P4, K3, P1, K2, P2, sl 1 dropping extra loop and keeping yarn on WS, K2.
3rd row. K1, P1, sl next st on to cable needle and hold at front of work, Kly2rn, K1, K1 from cable needle—called CTw3 —, P2, K1, P2, (sl next st on to cable needle and hold at back of work, K2, P1 from cable needle—called C3PB —, sl next 2 sts on to cable needle and hold at front of work, P1, K2 from cable needle—called C3PF —, P2) 5 times, K1, P2, CTw3, P1, K1.
4th row. K2, P2, sl 1, K2, P1, K2, (P2, K2) 10 times, P1, K2, P2, sl 1, K2.
5th row. K1, P1, CTw3, P2, K1, P1, (C3PB, P2, C3PF) 5 times, P1, K1, P2, CTw3, P1, K1.
6th row. K2, P2, sl 1, K2, P1, K1, (P2, K4, P2) 5 times, K1, P1, K2, P2, sl 1, K2.
7th row. K1, P1, CTw3, P2, K1, P1, K2, P4, (sl next 2 sts on to cable needle and hold at front of work, K2, K2 from cable needle—called C4F—, P4) 4 times, K2, P1, K1, P2, CTw3, P1, K1.
8th row. K2, P2, sl 1, K2, P1, K1, (P2, K4, P2) 5 times, K1, P1, K2, P2, sl 1, K2.

9th row. K1, P1, CTw3, P2, K1, P1, (C3PF, P2, C3PB) 5 times, P1, K1, P2, CTw3, P1, K1.
10th row. K2, P2, sl 1, K2, P1, K1, (K1, P2, K1) 10 times, K1, P1, K2, P2, sl 1, K2.
11th row. K1, P1, CTw3, P2, K1, P2, (C3PF, C3PB, P2) 5 times, K1, P2, CTw3, P1, K1.
12th row. K2, P2, sl 1, K2, P1, K1, (K2, P4, K2) 5 times, K1, P1, K2, P2, sl 1, K2.
13th row. K1, P1, CTw3, P2, K1, P3, (C4B, P4) 4 times, C4B, P3, K1, P2, CTw3, K2, P1, K1.
Rows 2-13 form pattern and are repeated throughout.

Bobble sampler
This sampler is also edged and can be used in combination with the trellis sampler to produce a textured fabric.
Worked over 47 stitches.
1st row. (RS) K1, P1, Kly2rn, K2, P3, K1, P2, *into next st work K1, P1, K1, P1, K1 making 5 sts out of 1, turn and K these 5 sts, turn and P these 5 sts, lift 4th st over 5th and off needle and rep with 3rd, 2nd and 1st st until one st rems—called bobble 1—, P5, rep from * to last 12 sts, bobble 1, P2, K1, P3, Kly2rn, K2, P1, K1.
2nd row. K2, P2, sl 1 dropping extra loop and keeping yarn on WS, K3, P1, K29, P1, K3, P2, sl 1, K2.
3rd row. K1, P1, sl next st on to cable needle and hold at front of work, Kly2rn, K1, K1 from cable needle—called CTw3—, P3, K1, P29, K1, P3, CTw3, P1, K1.
4th row. As 2nd row.
5th row. K1, P1, CTw3, P3, K1, *P5, bobble 1, rep from * to last 14 sts, P5, K1, P3, CTw3, P1, K1.
6th row. As 2nd row.
7th row. As 3rd row.
8th row. As 2nd row.
9th row. K1, P1, CTw3, P3, K1, P2, *bobble 1, P5, rep from * to last 12 sts, bobble 1, P2, K1, P3, CTw3, P1, K1.
Rows 2-9 form pattern and are repeated throughout.

Tree of life
Worked over a number of stitches divisible by 15.
1st row. (RS) *P7, K1, P7, rep from * to end.
2nd row. *K7, P1, K7, rep from * to end.
3rd row. *P5, slip next st onto cable needle and hold at back, K1, P1 from cable needle—called C2F, K1, slip next st onto cable needle and hold at front, P1, K1, from cable needle—called C2B, P5, rep from * to end.
4th row. *K5, sl 1 keeping yarn on WS, K1, P1, K1, sl 1, K5, rep from * to end.
5th row. *P4, C2F, P1, K1, P1, C2B, P4, rep from * to end.
6th row. *K4, sl 1, K2, P1, K2, sl 1, K4, rep from * to end.
7th row. *P3, C2F, P2, K1, P2, C2B, P3, rep from * to end.
8th row. *K3, sl 1, K3, P1, K3, sl 1, K3, rep from * to end.
9th row. *P2, C2F, P3, K1, P3, C2B, P2, rep from * to end.
10th row. *K2, sl 1, K4, P1, K4, sl 1, K2, rep from * to end.
These 10 rows form pattern and are repeated throughout.

Marriage lines
Worked over a number of stitches divisible by 20.
1st row. *P1, Tw2F, P6, K2, P2, K2, P2, Tw2B, P1, rep from * to end.
2nd row. *K1, P2, K2, P2, K2, P2, K6, P2, K1, rep from * to end.
3rd row. *P1, Tw2F, P5, sl next st on to cable needle and hold at back of work, K2, P1 from cable needle—called T3R—, P1, T3R, P2, Tw2B, P1, rep from * to end.
4th row. *K1, P2, K3, P2, K2, P2, K5, P2, K1, rep from * to end.
5th row. *P1, Tw2F, P4, T3R, P1, T3R, P3, Tw2B, P1, rep from * to end.

▲ *Trellis sampler edged with twisted stitch panel*

▲ *Bobble sampler edged with twisted stitch panel*

▲ *Tree of life pattern*

▲ *Marriage lines pattern with twisted stitch panels*

6th row. *K1, P2, K4, P2, K2, P2, K4, P2, K1, rep from * to end.
7th row. *P1, Tw2F, P3, T3R, P1, T3R, P4, Tw2B, P1, rep from * to end.
8th row. *K1, P2, K5, P2, K2, P2, K3, P2, K1, rep from * to end.
9th row. *P1, Tw2F, P2, T3R, P1, T3R, P5, Tw2B, P1, rep from * to end.
10th row. *K1, P2, K6, P2, K2, P2, K2, P2, K1, rep from * to end.
11th row. *P1, Tw2F, P2, sl next 2 sts on to cable needle and hold at front of work, P1, K2 from cable needle—called T3L—, P1, T3L, P5, Tw2B, P1, rep from * to end.

12th row. As 8th row.
13th row. *P1, Tw2F, P3, T3L, P1, T3L, P4, Tw2B, P1, rep from * to end.
14th row. As 6th row.
15th row. *P1, Tw2F, P4, T3L, P1, T3L, P3, Tw2B, P1, rep from * to end.
16th row. As 4th row.
17th row. *P1, Tw2F, P5, T3L, P1, T3L, P2, Tw2B, P1, rep from * to end.
Rows 2-17 form pattern and are repeated throughout.

Traditional fisherman knitting

Fisherman knitting is the term used for seamless garments knitted in traditional closely-woven patterns.

Around the coast of England and Scotland, wherever there are fishing fleets and fishermen, there can still be found examples of the traditional seamless jersey correctly called guernsey. Whilst the guernseys are basically alike, each area has an individual style—some have distinctive yokes, others have vertical panel designs and some have horizontal patterns. Apart from regional styles each village, and even individual families, have their own designs. Some even have the initials of the owner worked into the pattern.

The designs are never haphazard, but use symbols to tell a story reflecting the fisherman's surroundings, family life and the tools of his trade.

Seamless knitting

The guernsey is knitted circularly, cast on with a set of four double pointed needles at the lower edge and worked up to the beginning of the armholes. The work then divides and the back and front are worked separately to the shoulders, which are cast off together. This line of casting off is often on the right side to give a decorative ridge. The neckband is then worked circularly again, although in Scotland buttons and buttonholes would be added at the shoulder to give a better fit.

To give greater ease of movement, a gusset is often made just before the armhole division

and carried on into the top of the sleeves, which are then picked up and knitted downwards to the cuff. Although entirely seamless, a mock seam is often worked at either side. The gusset is increased in the centre of the seam and the seam carried on down the sleeve once the gusset is completed.

Types of wool

The guernsey is not unlike a patterned brocade when finished and is always knitted on fine needles. The wool traditionally used is often as thick as double knitting, but it is made firm and weatherproof by the closeness of the stitches.

Anchor design

One of the many designs seen on guernseys on the coast of Fife in Scotland is the Anchor pattern, which can be worked as a repeat across the work or repeated upwards in a vertical panel. It repeats over a number of stitches divisible by 21.

1st row. *P2, K1, P2, K1, P2, K1, P2, rep from * to end.
2nd row. *K2, P1, K2, P11, K2, P1, K2, rep from * to end.
Rep 1st and 2nd rows once more.
5th row. *P2, K1, P2, K5, P1, K5, P2, K1, P2, rep from * to end.
6th row. *K2, P1, K2, P4, K1, P1, K1, P4, K2, P1, K2, rep from * to end.
7th row. *P2, K1, P2, K3, (P1, K1) twice, P1, K3, P2, K1, P2, rep from * to end.
8th row. *K2, P1, K2, P2, K1, P5, K1, P2, K2, P1, K2, rep from * to end.
9th row. *P2, K1, P2, K1, P1,

(K3, P1) twice, (K1, P2) twice, rep from * to end.
10th row. *(K2, P1) twice, K1, P7, K1, (P1, K2) twice, rep from * to end.
11th row. *P2, K1, P2, K5, P1, K5, P2, K1, P2, rep from * to end.
12th row. As 2nd.
13th row. As 11th.
14th row. As 2nd.
15th row. *P2, K1, P2, K3, P5, K3, P2, K1, P2, rep from * to end.
16th row. *K2, P1, K2, P3, K5, P3, K2, P1, K2, rep from * to end.
17th row. As 15th.
18th row. As 2nd.
19th row. As 11th.
20th row. As 2nd.
21st row. As 11th.
22nd row. *K2, P1, K2, P4, K1, P1, K1, P4, K2, P1, K2, rep from * to end.
23rd row. *P2, K1, P2, K3, (P1, K3) twice, P2, K1, P2, rep from * to end.
24th row. As 22nd.
25th row. As 11th.
26th row. As 2nd.

Sheringham design

This pattern was taken from a patterned yoke edged with ridged purl welts and shows patterning at its best. The pattern repeats over a number of stitches divisible by 24.
K2 rows. P2 rows.
Rep last 4 rows 3 times more.
Begin diamond pattern.
1st row. *K6, P1, K11, P1, K5, rep from * to end.
2nd row. *P4, K1, P1, K1, P9, K1, P1, K1, P5, rep from * to end.
3rd row. *K4, P1, K3, P1, K7, P1, (K1, P1) twice, K3, rep from * to end.
4th row. *P2, K1, (P1, K1) 3 times, (P5, K1) twice, P3, rep from * to end.
5th row. *K2, P1, K7, P1, K3, P1, (K1, P1) 4 times, K1, rep from * to end.
6th row. *K1, (P1, K1) 6 times, P9, K1, P1, rep from * to end.
7th row. *P1, K11, P12, rep from * to end.
8th row. *K11, P1, K1, P9, K1, P1, rep from * to end.
9th row. *K2, P1, K7, P1, K13, rep from * to end.

10th row. *P14, K1, P5, K1, P3, rep from * to end.
11th row. *K4, P1, K3, P1, K15, rep from * to end.
12th row. *P16, K1, P1, K1, P5, rep from * to end.
Rep 1st—12th rows as required.

Flag and cable design

This pattern is seen in designs from the Scottish and Yorkshire coastal areas, and can be used as an all over design or in narrow panels separated by moss stitch panels or cable panels.
Repeat the pattern over a number of stitches divisible by 26.
1st row (right side). *P2, K1, P2, slip next 3 sts onto cable needle and hold at back of work, K3, K3 from cable needle, P2, K1, P2, K2, P8, rep from * to end.
2nd row. *K7, P3, K5, P6, K5, rep from * to end.
3rd row. *P2, K1, P2, K6, P2, K1, P2, K4, P6, rep from * to end.
4th row. *K5, P5, K5, P6, K5, rep from * to end.
5th row. *P2, K1, P2, K6, P2, K1, P2, K6, P4, rep from * to end.
6th row. *K3, P7, K5, P6, K5, rep from * to end.
7th row. *P2, K1, P2, K6, P2, K1, P2, K8, P2, rep from * to end.
8th row. *K1, P9, K5, P6, K5, rep from * to end.
Rep 1st–8th rows as required.

Pine tree design

This design is found in many variations, usually on guernseys belonging to Scottish fishermen. It can be used separately as a motif or in conjunction with moss stitch borders and diamonds.
The pattern is worked over a number of stitches divisible by 15.
1st row (right side). K.
2nd row. P.
3rd row. *K7, P1, K7, rep from * to end.
4th row. *P6, K1, P1, K1, P6, rep from * to end.
5th row. *K5, P1, K3, P1, K5, rep from * to end.
6th row. *P4, (K1, P2) twice, K1, P4, rep from * to end.

7th row. *K3, P1, K2, P1, K1, P1, K2, P1, K3, rep from * to end.

8th row. *(P2, K1) twice, P3, (K1, P2) twice, rep from * to end.

9th row. *K1, (P1, K2) twice, P1, (K2, P1) twice, K1, rep from * to end.

10th row. *P3, K1, P2, K1, P1, K1, P2, K1, P3, rep from * to end.

11th row. *K2, P1, K2, P1, K3, P1, K2, P1, K2, rep from * to end.

12th row. *P4, K1, P2, K1, P2, K1, P4, rep from * to end.

13th row. *K3, P1, K2, P1, K1, P1, K2, P1, K3, rep from * to end.

14th row. *P5, K1, P3, K1, P5, rep from * to end.

15th row. *K4, P1, (K2, P1) twice, K4, rep from * to end.

16th row. *P6, K1, P1, K1, P6, rep from * to end.

17th row. *K5, P1, K3, P1, K5, rep from * to end.

18th row. *P7, K1, P7, rep from * to end.

19th row. *K6, P1, K1, P1, K6, rep from * to end.

20th row. P.

21st row. As 3rd.

22nd row. P.

▼ *Anchor design*

▼ *Pine tree design*

▲ *Sheringham design*

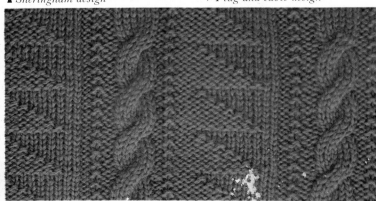

▼ *Flag and cable design*

Chapter 29

Shetland knitting

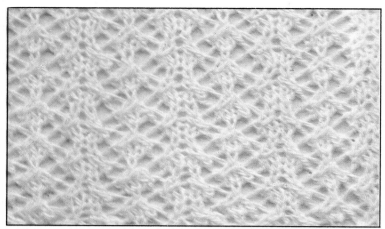

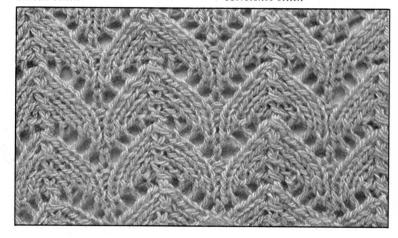

▲ *Bead stitch*   ▼ *Horseshoe stitch*

The most gossamer and the finest examples of lace knitting come from Unst, the most northerly of all the Shetland islands. In the early nineteenth century a visitor to the island brought with her a collection of fine Spanish lace, which inspired the islanders to create knitted lace of similar beauty using their single ply homespun yarn. Although single ply yarn is rarely used today, Shetland lace stitches can be used to make a variety of lovely garments.

Although Shetland lace stitches are adaptable they are seen at their best if worked with reasonably fine yarns and needles. No.10 needles and 2 ply yarn is recommended for the stitches in this chapter to produce a fine, knitted lace.

Casting on for lace should be kept as open as possible. Ideally use a simplified two-needle method. Cast on 2 stitches, insert the right-hand needle into the second stitch instead of between the stitches, draw one stitch through and transfer it to the left-hand needle. Wherever possible, graft edges together and cast off loosely so that there are no firm or hard edges.

Bead stitch

This is a simple lace to use for filling diamonds or hexagonal areas, or for working large areas such as shawl centres. The illustration uses it as an all over pattern. It can easily be adapted to have a more solid appearance by working 2, 3 or more knitted stitches between the panels.

It is worked over a number of stitches divisible by 7. For example, 28.

1st row. (RS) *K1, K2 tog, yfwd, K1, yfwd, sl 1 knitwise, K1, psso, K1, rep from * to end.
2nd row. *P2 tog tbl, yrn, P3, yrn, P2 tog, rep from * to end.
3rd row. *K1, yfwd, sl 1 knitwise, K1, psso, K1, K2 tog, yfwd, K1, rep from * to end.
4th row. *P2, yrn, P3 tog, yrn, P2, rep from * to end.
These 4 rows form the pattern and are repeated as required.

Crest of the wave stitch

Old shale stitch, reminiscent of the print left on sand by receding waves, is a simple design (see Knitting Know-how Chapter 20) which is also the basis for many equally simple but less often seen versions. Of these, crest of the wave stitch is perhaps the most effective.

It is worked over a number of stitches divisible by 12, plus 1. For example, 37.

1st, 2nd, 3rd and 4th rows. K.
5th row. K1, *(K2 tog) twice, (yfwd, K1) 3 times, yfwd, (sl 1 knitwise, K1, psso) twice, K1, rep from * to end.
6th row. P.
Rep 5th and 6th rows 3 times more.
These 12 rows form the pattern and are repeated as required.

Razor shell stitch

Another stitch which takes its name from a well known beach shell, this can be varied over 4, 6, 8, 10 or 12 stitches. Instructions are given for both 6 and 10 stitch variations.

The six stitch version is worked over a number of stitches divisible by 6, plus 1. For example, 25.
1st row. (WS) P.
2nd row. K1, *yfwd, K1, sl 1, K2 tog, psso, K1, yfwd, K1, rep from * to end.
Repeat 1st and 2nd rows as required.
The ten stitch version is worked over a number of stitches divisible by 10, plus 1. For example, 31.
1st row. (WS) P.
2nd row. K1, *yfwd, K3, sl 1, K2 tog, psso, K3, yfwd, K1, rep from * to end.
1st and 2nd rows are repeated as required.

Horseshoe stitch

The imprint of horseshoes on damp sand is a familiar sight to the islanders and is used in this stitch to create a lace which has innumerable uses.

It is worked over a number of stitches divisible by 10, plus 1. For example, 31.
1st row. (WS) P.
2nd row. K1, *yfwd, K3, sl 1, K2 tog, psso, K3, yfwd, K1, rep from * to end.
3rd row. As 1st.
4th row. P1, *K1, yfwd, K2, sl 1, K2 tog, psso, K2, yfwd, K1, P1, rep from * to end.
5th row. K1, *P9, K1, rep from * to end.
6th row. P1, *K2, yfwd, K1, sl 1, K2 tog, psso, K1, yfwd, K2, P1,

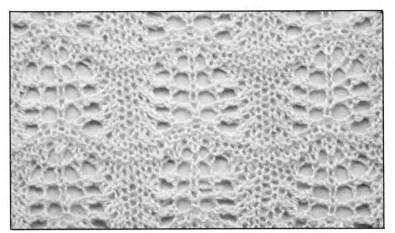

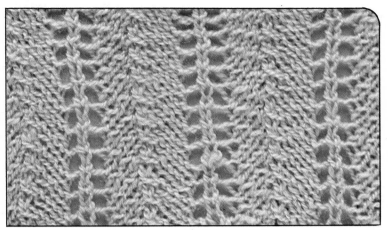

▲ *Crest of the wave stitch*   ▼ *Faggoting cable stitch*   ▲ *Razor shell stitch*   ▼ *Fern stitch*

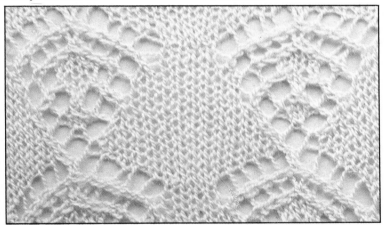

rep from * to end.

7th row. As 5th.

8th row. P1, *K3, yfwd, sl 1, K2 tog, psso, yfwd, K3, P1, rep from * to end of the row.

These 8 rows form the pattern and are repeated as required.

Faggoting cable stitch

Mainly a lace stitch, this gives an additional interest and texture to the lace by the introduction of the cable. The cable can be worked crossing in front or behind the work or can be alternated to incorporate both. It is often used as a single panel at either side of another motif or can form an all over pattern as illustrated. It is worked over a number of stitches divisible by 12, plus 8. For example, 32.

1st row. (WS) P2, *K2, yfwd, K2 tog, P2, rep from * to end.

2nd row. K2, *P2, yrn, P2 tog, K2, rep from * to end.

3rd and 4th rows. As 1st and 2nd.

5th and 6th rows. As 1st and 2nd.

7th row. P2, K2, yfwd, K2 tog, P2, *sl next 2 sts onto cable needle and hold at front of work, K2, K2 from cable needle—called C4F—, P2, K2, yfwd, K2 tog, P2, rep from * to end.

8th row. As 2nd.

9th and 10th rows. As 1st and 2nd.

11th and 12th rows. As 1st and 2nd.

13th and 14th rows. As 1st and 2nd.

15th row. P2, C4F, P2, *K2, yfwd, K2 tog, P2, C4F, P2, rep from * to end.

16th row. As 2nd.

These 16 rows form the pattern and are repeated as required.

Fern stitch

Often used as a shawl border, the shape of the motif allows for

easy corner shaping. The size of the motif can vary from a miniature fern to a very large shape but the method of working remains the same, extra stitches being worked in.

This is worked over a number of stitches divisible by 15. For example, 45.

1st row. (RS) *K7, yfwd, sl 1 knitwise, K1, psso, K6, rep from * to end.

2nd row. P.

3rd row. *K5, K2 tog, yfwd, K1, yfwd, sl 1 knitwise, K1, psso, K5.

4th row. P.

5th row. *K4, K2 tog, yfwd, K3, yfwd, sl 1 knitwise, K1, psso, K4, rep from * to end.

6th row. P.

7th row. *K4, yfwd, sl 1 knitwise, K1, psso, yfwd, sl 1, K2 tog, psso, yfwd, K2 tog, yfwd, K4, rep from * to end.

8th row. P.

9th row. *K2, K2 tog, yfwd, K1, yfwd, sl 1 knitwise, K1, psso, K1, K2 tog, yfwd, K1, yfwd, sl 1 knitwise, K1, psso, K2, rep from * to end.

10th row. P.

11th row. *K2, (yfwd, sl 1 knitwise, K1, psso) twice, K3, (K2 tog, yfwd) twice, K2, rep from * to end.

12th row. *P3, (yrn, P2 tog) twice, P1, (P2 tog tbl, yrn) twice, P3, rep from * to end.

13th row. *K4, yfwd, sl 1 knitwise, K1, psso, yfwd, sl 1, K2 tog, psso, yfwd, K2 tog, yfwd, K4, rep from * to end.

14th row. *P5, yrn, P2 tog, P1, P2 tog tbl, yrn, P5, rep from * to end.

15th row. *K6, yfwd, sl 1, K2 tog, psso, yfwd, K6, rep from * to end.

16th row. P.

These 16 rows form the pattern and are repeated as required.

Collector's Piece

Gossamer wool lace

This delicate wool lace shawl is probably one of the finest examples of handmade garments to be found in Britain today. Knitted by a few skilled Shetland Islanders in their own homes, these ring shawls, as they are called, are in great demand and worth twice their weight in gold. The designs have been passed on by word of mouth from one generation to the next, but the instructions have never been written down.

Lace knitting developed in the Shetlands on the island of Unst in the early nineteenth century after Mrs Jessie Scanlon had visited the island to show the inhabitants a collection of fine Spanish lace. The islanders, inspired by its beauty, developed a technique of knitting lace fabrics. The yarn used to knit ring shawls is woven from the fine wool which grows round the sheep's neck. After being knitted on fine, steel needles, the shawls are washed and then hung on frames by an open fire to dry to their correct shape.

All the patterns have colourful names and represent objects which the knitters see around them—Horseshoe, Cat's Paw, Bird's Eye, Print of the Wave. When complete, ring shawls measure about six feet by six feet, but weigh only three ounces. They are so gossamer-fine that the entire shawl can be drawn literally through a wedding ring, hence their name. Traditionally made as christening robes, ring shawls also make beautiful winter wedding veils.

A beautiful example of a Shetland ring shawl ►
◄ A tradition in knitting which still lives today
▼ Feather-light, a ring shawl slips through a ring

Chapter 30

Introduction to knitted lace

Knitted lace is both simple to do and lovely to look at. This chapter gives some tips for suitable yarns and casting on methods and two pretty edgings to work for handkerchief hems.

Suitable materials

The finer the thread used the daintier and more gossamer the lace will be. Some really beautiful shawls are made in one ply wool, but for household linens and fine edgings Coats Mercer-Crochet is one of the most successful yarns. It has a crisp neat finish and can be as dainty and fine as required.

Edgings are usually made on a pair of needles and worked across the edging so that the required length is obtained by repeating the pattern.

Table mats and larger areas of lace are usually worked on circular needles or sets of needles to avoid seams.

If a mat is worked from the centre outwards, it is neccesary to begin at the centre with only a few stitches on each needle. As the work progresses and the stitches increase, some workers may find it easier to transfer all the stitches onto a circular needle for the remainder of the work.

Needles must be fine. If too large a needle is used, perhaps in the mistaken hope of making the work grow more quickly, the solid areas will not be as regular as they should be and will not contrast as well against the openwork areas.

Casting on for lace

Hard, thick lines must be avoided whether cast e

seaming or by casting on or off as they immediately spoil the continuity of the lace.

The least noticeable cast on edge is a two-needle method in which the right-hand needle is inserted into the last stitch on the left-hand needle, the yarn passed round the needle point and drawn through to form the new stitch. This is similar to the two-needle method normally used, except that the new stitch is drawn through the stitch instead of between the stitches.

For edgings which are to be worked lengthwise, normal cast on and off edges will spoil the look of the work and it is best to

cast on using spare yarn which can later be withdrawn. This allows the casting on to be removed so that the first and last rows can be grafted together for an invisible finish (see Knitting Know-how Chapter 12).

Begin with these two simple designs for beautiful handkerchief edgings.

Bird's eye edging

Size

It is possible to work any length required.

> **Tension for this design**
> ¾in wide

Materials shown here

Coats Mercer-Crochet No.20
1 ball
One pair No.14 needles
One handkerchief

To make the edging

Using No.14 needles, cast on 7 sts.

1st row K1, K2 tog, y2rn, K2 tog, y2rn, K2.
2nd row Sl 1, K2, P1, K2, P1, K2.
3rd row K1, K2 tog, y2rn, K2 tog, K4.
4th row Cast off 2 sts, K3, P1, K2.
Repeat these 4 rows for length required, allowing a little fullness for corners. Cast off.

Leaf edging

Size

It is possible to work any length required

> **Tension for this design**
> 1in wide

Materials shown here

Coats Mercer-Crochet No.60
1 ball
One pair No.16 needles
One handkerchief

To make the edging

Using No.16 needles, cast on 10 sts.

1st row K3, (yfwd, K2 tog) twice, y2rn, K2 tog, K1.
2nd row K3, P1, K2, (yfwd, K2 tog) twice, K1.
3rd row K3, (yfwd, K2 tog) twice, K1, y2rn, K2 tog, K1.
4th row K3, P1, K3, (yfwd, K2 tog) twice, K1.
5th row K3, (yfwd, K2 tog) twice, K2, y2rn, K2 tog, K1.
6th row K3, P1, K4, (yfwd, K2 tog) twice, K1.
7th row K3, (yfwd, K2 tog) twice, K6.
8th row Cast off 3 sts, K4, (yfwd, K2 tog) twice, K1.
Repeat these 8 rows until required length. Cast off.

To make up

Pin edging out in perfect shape to correct measurements, wrong side up and press with a damp cloth and a warm iron.

Slip stitch, neatly and securely, to handkerchief hem using fine sewing cotton. Seam cast on and cast off edges as invisibly as possible. Re-press.

Bird's eye edging (left) and leaf edging for handkerchief hems ▶

▼ *Method of casting on with the same thread*

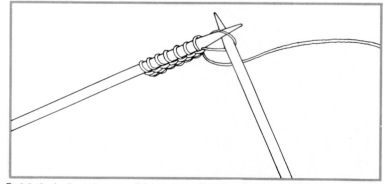

▼ *Method of casting on with separate thread to be removed later*

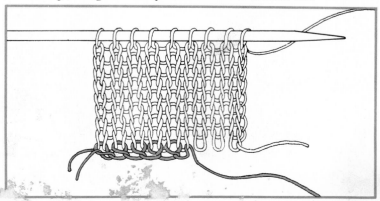

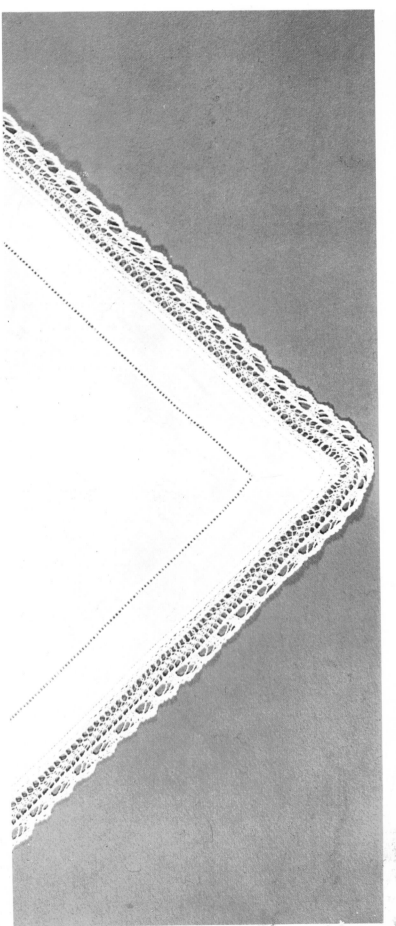

Knitting
Know-how

Lace edging for a pillowcase

Knitted lace can be used to give an individual finish to your household furnishings. This edging is not difficult to work and can be used to edge bed linen, table linen or lampshades.

The size is determined by the yarn and needles used. This table gives an approximate guide to the possibilities. Using Coats Mercer-Crochet No.5, work on No.11 needles. For No.10 use No.12 needles. For No.20 use No.14 needles. For No.40 use No.15 needles. For No.60 use No.16 needles. The pillowcase edging illustrated is worked on No.14 needles using No.20 cotton. Each repeat requires 16 stitches plus 5 extra stitches for the borders. The repeat measures about 18in by 2½in deep. For the border 5 repeats were worked, thus the required number to cast on was $5 \times 16 + 5 = 85$ sts.

Pillowcase edging

Length
18in

Tension
About 2½in deep

Materials shown here
Coats Mercer-Crochet No.20
One pair No.14 Aero needles
One No.1·00 (ISR) Aero crochet hook
One pillowcase

Edging
Using No.14 needles, cast on 85 sts.

1st row K2, *yfwd, K2 tog, yfwd, sl 1, K1, psso, K1, (K1, yfwd, K1, yfwd, K2) twice, K2 tog, yfwd, K1, rep from * to last 3 sts, yfwd, K2 tog, K1.
2nd row K1, P1, *yrn, P2 tog, P18, rep from * to last 3 sts, yrn, P2 tog, K1.
3rd row K2, *yfwd, K2 tog, yfwd, K1, (yfwd, sl 1, K2 tog, psso) 5 times, (yfwd, K1) twice, rep from * to last 3 sts, yfwd, K2 tog, K1.
4th row K1, P1, *yrn, P2 tog, P16, rep from * to last 3 sts, yrn, P2 tog, K1.
5th row K2,* yfwd, K2 tog, K1, yfwd, K2, yfwd, sl 1, K1, psso, K2, yfwd, K1, yfwd, K2, K2 tog, (yfwd, K2) twice, rep from * to last 3 sts, yfwd, K2 tog, K1
6th row K1, P1, *yrn, P2 tog, P20, rep from * to last 3 sts, yrn, P2 tog, K1.
7th row K2, *yfwd, K2 tog, K2, yfwd, K3, (yfwd, sl 1, K2 tog, psso) 3 times, (yfwd, K3) twice, rep from * to last 3 sts, yfwd, K2 tog, K1.
8th row K1, P1, *yrn, P2 tog, P20, rep from * to last 3 sts, yrn, P2 tog, K1.
9th row K2, *yfwd, K2 tog, K7, yfwd, sl 1, K1, psso, K1, K2 tog, yfwd, K8, rep from * to last 3 sts, yfwd, K2 tog, K1.
10th row K1, P1, *yrn, P2 tog, P20, rep from * to last 3 sts, yrn, P2 tog, K1.
11th row K2, *yfwd, K2 tog, K8, yfwd, sl 1, K2 tog, psso, yfwd, K9, rep from * to last 3 sts, yfwd, K2 tog, K1.
12th row As 10th.
13th row As 11th.
14th row As 10th.
15th row As 11th.

16th row As 10th.
17th row K2, *yfwd, K2 tog, K6, K2 tog, yfwd, K3, yfwd, sl 1, K1, psso, K7, rep from * to last 3 sts, yfwd, K2 tog, K1.
18th row As 10th.
19th row K2, *yfwd, K2 tog, K5, K2 tog, yfwd, K1, yfwd, sl 1, K2 tog, psso, yfwd, K1, yfwd, sl 1, K1, psso, K6, rep from * to last 3 sts, yfwd, K2 tog, K1.
20th row As 10th.
21st row K2, *yfwd, K2 tog, K4, K2 tog, yfwd, K3, yfwd, K1, yfwd, K3, yfwd, sl 1, K1, psso, K5, rep from * to last 3 sts, yfwd, K2 tog, K1.
22nd row K1, P1, *yrn, P2 tog, P22, rep from * to last 3 sts, yrn, P2 tog, K1.
23rd row K2, *yfwd, K2 tog, K3, K2 tog, yfwd, K1, (yfwd, sl 1, K2 tog, psso) 3 times, yfwd, K1, yfwd, sl 1, K1, psso, K4, rep from * to last 3 sts, yfwd, K2 tog, K1.
24th row As 10th.
25th row K2, *yfwd, K2 tog, K2, K2 tog, yfwd, K3, yfwd, (K1, yfwd, K3, yfwd) twice, sl 1, K1, psso, K3, rep from * to last 3 sts, yfwd, K2 tog, K1.
26th row K1, P1, *yrn, P2 tog, P24, rep from * to last 3 sts. yrn, P2 tog, K1.
27th row K2, *yfwd, K2 tog, K1, K2 tog, yfwd, K1, (yfwd, sl 1, K2 tog, psso) 5 times, yfwd, K1, yfwd, sl 1, K1, psso, K2, rep from * to last 3 sts, yfwd, K2 tog, K1.
28th row As 10th.
29th row K1, K3 tog, *K2 tog, yfwd, K3, (yfwd, K1, yfwd, K3) 3 times, yfwd, sl 1, K1, psso, K3 tog, rep from * to last st, K1.
30th row K1, P to last st, K1.
31st row K1, K2 tog, *yfwd, K1, (yfwd, sl 1, K2

tog, psso) 7 times, yfwd, K1, yfwd, sl 1, K2 tog, psso, rep from * to end.
Complete edging using crochet hook as follows:
Last row With WS of work facing, insert hook into first 2 sts and work 1dc, *7ch, 1dc into next st, 7ch, insert hook into next 3 sts and work 1dc, rep from * until all sts have been worked off. Finish off ends.

To make up
Block out to shape and press. Stitch securely to edge of pillowcase.

Finishing off lace
Lace is not usually starched, but hand knitted lace in cotton or linen thread is made for everyday use and is better lightly starched. Only table mats or articles which are to be fully supported by tray or table require stiff starching.

Washing lace
Wash lace when finished in warm mild suds, rinsing carefully until the water is clear. Starch as required and leave aside wet until ready for blocking out to size.

Blocking out
The exact size of the article should be drawn out on brown or white paper which will not stain when damp. Whatever the shape of the article, the method is the same. Pin out to the correct size working on opposite corners. If the mat is rectangular, pin each corner and half way along each side. Once the mat is positioned, divide each section by placing more pins to draw the mat to the required size. If the edging has tiny points of crochet or knitting, the final stage must be to pin each point separately so that the shape is perfect. Leave pinned until completely dry. Remove pins and press carefully without pulling out of shape to give the final smooth finish.

▼ *Pinning out a piece of lace*

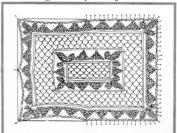

Knitted edging trims a pillowcase ►

Knitting lace in circles

This beautiful circular lace coffee table mat is achieved by graduating from a set of four needles to a slightly larger size and so on to a circular needle. In this way it is possible to cope with the ever increasing circumference.

Size
23in diameter

Tension for this design
8 sts and 9 rows to 1in over st st worked on No.11 needles

Materials shown here
Coats Mercer-Crochet No.20
3 balls
One No.1·25 (ISR) crochet hook
One No.11 circular needle 24in long
One set of 4 No.12 double pointed needles
One set of 4 No.11 double pointed needles

Using set of No.12 needles, cast on 10 sts, 3 sts on each of first and second needles and 4 sts on third needle.

1st round K.
2nd round *Yfwd, K1, rep from * to end. 20 sts.
3rd, 4th and 5th rounds K.
6th round *Yfwd, K2, rep from * to end. 30 sts.
7th round K.
8th round *Yfwd, K3, rep from * to end. 40 sts.
9th and following 5 alt rounds K.
10th round *Yfwd, K4, rep from * to end. 50 sts.
12th round *Yfwd, K5,

Knitting Know-how

rep from * to end. 60 sts.
14th round *Yfwd, K6, rep from * to end. 70 sts.
16th round *Yfwd, K7, rep from * to end. 80 sts.
18th round *Yfwd, K8, rep from * to end. 90 sts.
20th round *Yfwd, K9, rep from * to end. 100 sts.
21st round *Yfwd, K1, yfwd, K8, K2 tog, K9, rep from * to end. 105 sts.
22nd round *Yfwd, K3, yfwd, sl 1, K1, psso, K16, rep from * to end. 110 sts.
23rd round *Yfwd, K1, yfwd, sl 1, K2 tog, psso, yfwd, K1, yfwd, K15, K2 tog, rep from * to end. 115 sts.
24th round *Yfwd, K3, yfwd, K1, yfwd, K3, yfwd, sl 1, K1, psso, K14, rep from * to end. 130 sts.
25th round *Yfwd, sl 1, K1, psso, K1, K2 tog, yfwd, K1, yfwd, sl 1, K1, psso, K1, K2 tog, yfwd, K15, rep from * to end. 130 sts.
26th round *Yfwd, K1, yfwd, sl 1, K2 tog, psso, yfwd, K3, yfwd, sl 1, K2 tog, psso, yfwd, K1, yfwd, sl 1, K1, psso, K11, K2 tog, rep from * to end. 130 sts.
27th round *Yfwd, K3, yfwd, K1, yfwd, sl 1, K1, psso, K1, K2 tog, yfwd, K1, yfwd, K3, yfwd, K13, rep from * to end. 150 sts.
28th round *Yfwd, (sl 1, K1, psso, K1, K2 tog, yfwd, K1, yfwd) twice, sl 1, K1, psso, K1, K2 tog, yfwd, sl 1, K1, psso, K9, K2 tog, rep from * to end. 140 sts.
29th round *Yfwd, K1, (yfwd, sl 1, K2 tog, psso, yfwd, K3) twice, yfwd, sl 1,

K2 tog, psso, yfwd, K1, yfwd, K11, rep from * to end. 150 sts.
30th round *Yfwd, K3, (yfwd, K1, yfwd, sl 1, K1, psso, K1, K2 tog) twice, yfwd, K1, yfwd, K3, yfwd, sl 1, K1, psso, K7, K2 tog, rep from * to end. 160 sts.
31st round *Yfwd, K1, (yfwd, sl 1, K2 tog, psso, yfwd, K3) 3 times, yfwd, sl 1, K2 tog, psso, yfwd, K1, yfwd, sl 1, K1, psso, K5, K2 tog, rep from * to end. 160 sts.
32nd round *Yfwd, K3, (yfwd, K1, yfwd, sl 1, K1, psso, K1, K2 tog) 3 times, yfwd, K1, yfwd, K3, yfwd, sl 1, K1, psso, K3, K2 tog, rep from * to end. 170 sts.
33rd round *Yfwd, K1, (yfwd, sl 1, K2 tog, psso, yfwd, K3) 4 times, yfwd, sl 1, K2 tog, psso, yfwd, K1, yfwd, sl 1, K1, psso, K1, K2 tog, rep from * to end. 170 sts.
34th round *K3, (yfwd, K1, yfwd, sl 1, K1, psso, K1, K2 tog) 4 times, yfwd, K1, yfwd, K3, yfwd, sl 1, K2 tog, psso, yfwd, rep from * to end. 180 sts.
Change to set of No.11 needles.
35th round *Sl 1, K2 tog, psso, yfwd, K3, yfwd, rep from * to end.
36th round *Yfwd, K1, yfwd, sl 1, K1, psso, K1, K2 tog, rep from * to end.
37th round *Yfwd, K3,

K2 tog, psso, yfwd, K1, yfwd, K11, rep from * to end. 150 sts.
38th round *Sl 1, K1, psso, K1, K2 tog, yfwd, K1, yfwd, rep from * to end.
39th round As 35th.
40th round As 36th.
41st round As 37th. 180 sts.
42nd round *(K1 and P1 into each of next 2 sts, K1) twice, K1 and P1 into each of next 2 sts, K2, rep from * inc in last st. 289 sts.
Change to circular needle and place coloured marker loop before first st to mark round beginning.
43rd round *Yfwd, K15, K2 tog, rep from * to end.
44th round K.
Rep last 2 rounds 9 times more.
63rd round *Yfwd, K1, yfwd, sl 1, K1, psso, K12, K2 tog, rep from * to end.
64th round *Yfwd, K3, yfwd, sl 1, K1, psso, K10, K2 tog, rep from * to end.
65th round *Yfwd, sl 1, K1, psso, K1, K2 tog, yfwd, sl 1, K1, psso, K10, rep from * to end. 272 sts.
66th round *Yfwd, K1, yfwd, sl 1, K2 tog, psso, yfwd, K1, yfwd, sl 1, K1, psso, K7, K2 tog, rep from * to end.
67th round *Yfwd, K3, yfwd, K1, yfwd, K3, yfwd, sl 1, K1, psso, K7, rep from * to end. 323 sts.
68th round *Yfwd, sl 1, K1,

▼ *Close-up detail of the lace stitch*

▲ *Circular lace cloth gives elegance to a coffee table*

psso, K1, K2 tog, yfwd, K1, yfwd, sl 1, K1, psso, K1, K2 tog, yfwd, sl 1, K1, psso, K4, K2 tog, rep from * to end. 289 sts.

69th round *Yfwd, K1, yfwd, sl 1, K2 tog, psso, yfwd, K3, yfwd, sl 1, K2 tog, psso, yfwd, K1, yfwd, sl 1, K1, psso, K4, rep from * to end. 306 sts.

70th round *Yfwd, K3, yfwd, K1, yfwd, sl 1, K1, psso, K1, K2 tog, yfwd, K1, yfwd, K3, yfwd, sl 1, K1, psso, K1, K2 tog, rep from * to end. 340 sts.

71st round *(Sl 1, K1, psso, K1, K2 tog, yfwd, K1, yfwd) twice, sl 1, K1, psso, K1, K2 tog, yfwd, sl 1, K2 tog, psso, yfwd, rep from * to end. 306 sts.

72nd round *Sl 1, K2 tog, psso, yfwd, K3, yfwd, rep from * to end. 306 sts.

73rd round As 36th.

74th round As 37th.

75th round As 38th.

76th round As 35th.

77th–79th rounds As 36th to 38th. 306 sts.

80th round *K1, K1 and P1 into each of next 2 sts, rep from * to end. 510 sts.

81st round K inc 3 sts evenly in round. 513 sts.

82nd and 83rd rounds K.

84th round *Yfwd, sl 1, K1, psso, rep from * to last st, K1.

85th round K.

86th round *Yfwd, K7, K2 tog, rep from * to end.

87th round K.

88th round As 86th.

89th round K.

90th round As 86th.

91st round *Yfwd, K1, yfwd, sl 1, K1, psso, K4, K2 tog, rep from * to end.

92nd round *Yfwd, K3, yfwd, K6, rep from * to end. 627 sts.

93rd round *Yfwd, sl 1, K1, psso, K1, K2 tog, yfwd, sl 1, K1, psso, K2, K2 tog, rep from * to end. 513 sts.

94th round *Yfwd, K1, yfwd, sl 1, K2 tog, psso, yfwd, K1, yfwd, K4, rep from * to end. 627 sts.

95th round *Yfwd, K3, yfwd, K1, yfwd, K3, yfwd, sl 1, K1, psso, K2, rep from * to end. 798 sts.

96th round *Sl 1, K1, psso, K1, K2 tog, yfwd, K1, yfwd, sl 1, K1, psso, (K1, K2

tog, yfwd, K3, yfwd, rep from * to end. 798 sts.

97th round *Sl 1, K2 tog, psso, yfwd, K3, yfwd, sl 1, K2 tog, psso, yfwd, sl 1, K1, psso, K1, K2 tog, yfwd, rep from * to end. 684 sts.

98th round *Yfwd, K1, yfwd, sl 1, K1, psso, K1, K2 tog, rep from * to end. 684 sts.

Edging
Using No. 1·25 hook, *work 1dc into next 3 sts and slip off, 10ch, rep from * ending with 1ss into first dc. Fasten off.

To make up
Finish off ends.
Damp evenly and pin out to size. Leave to dry.

Chapter 31

Striped effects in knitting

Knitting Know-how

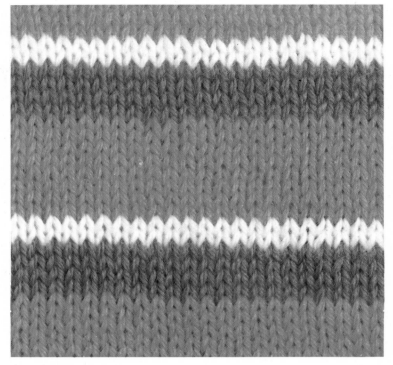

▲ *Horizontal striped pattern*

Stripes using one or more additional shades are the easiest way of achieving a colourful effect in knitting. As can be seen from the illustrations in this chapter, a wide variety of different results can be achieved by a simple change of colour or clever combination of colours while using the most ordinary of stitch patterns.

Horizontal stripes

These are usually worked on stocking stitch and are achieved by changing colour at the beginning of a row. This gives an unbroken line of colour on the RS of the fabric. Narrow stripes would need a colour change every second or third row but interest is added if the distance between the stripes is varied. The example shown is worked on a repeating sequence of 8 rows using A, 4 rows using B, 2 rows using C.

Ribbed stripes

Stripes on ribbing, if required to show an unbroken line, need to have the colour change row knitted throughout although the other rows are in ribbing, but an interesting effect is produced by working in rib or fancy rib irrespective of the colour change thus giving a broken, random type of line to the pattern. The sample given shows this and can be worked as follows:
Cast on a number of stitches divisible by 10 plus 5.
1st row P5, *K1, yfwd, sl 1P, ybk, K1, yfwd, sl 1P, ybk, K1, P5, rep from * to end.
2nd row K1, yfwd, sl 1P, ybk, K1, yfwd, sl 1P, ybk, K1, *P5, K1, yfwd, sl 1P, ybk, K1, yfwd, sl 1P, ybk, K1, rep from * to end.
These 2 rows form the pattern and should be repeated throughout. The colour sequence used is as follows:
2 rows using A, 10 rows using B, (2 rows using A, 6 rows using C) twice.

▲ *Ribbed striped pattern*

Chevron stripes

A zigzag striped effect can be made by the clever use of stitch added to colour changes. The illustration shows simple stripes of four rows of each colour, and the chevron shaping is formed by the vertical lines of increased and decreased stitches.
Cast on a number of stitches divisible by 14, using A.
1st row With A, *K1, inc by knitting into the loop below the next st on the left-hand needle and then K the stitch immediately above, K4, sl 1P, K2 tog, psso, K4, inc as before, rep from * to end.
2nd row With A, P.
3rd row With A, as 1st.
4th row With A, as 2nd.
Continue working four rows in this way in each of your chosen colours. A pretty effect can be achieved by using several shades of one or two colours, and graduating them from light to dark.

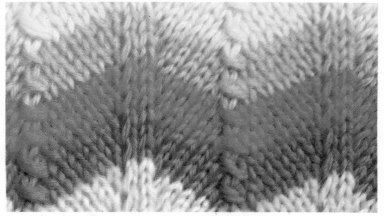

▲ *Chevron striped pattern*

Twisting yarns to change colour

When working any form of horizontal stripe, there is no problem about joining in a different coloured yarn, as one colour is finished at the end of a row and the new one is brought in at the beginning of the next row. Vertical or diagonal stripes, however, present a different problem, as the colours must be changed at several points within the same row.

When working narrow vertical or diagonal stripes it is quite simple to twist the yarn and carry it across the back of the work and this method can be used in the example of narrow diagonal stripes illustrated. For wider stripes it would be most unsatisfactory to use this means of carrying the yarn. Apart from the waste of material, there is the chance of pulling too tight resulting in unsightly bunching of the fabric and loss of tension. It is much better to divide the yarn into small quantities before beginning the pattern and this is done by winding the yarn into a small ball for each stripe and twisting the colours when the change is made. This is very simple to do as can be seen from the illustration.

When twisting the yarn, always cross it in the same direction, as this will prevent a gap appearing on the right side of the work, and will give a neat look at the back as shown.

It is important to remember that stripes worked by twisting the yarn on changing colour give a fabric of normal thickness, while stripes worked by carrying the yarn along the back of the work give a fabric of double thickness.

Diagonal stripes

An unusual and striking effect can be achieved by knitting stripes diagonally across a garment. Although diagonal stripes may appear complicated to work, the method is in fact very simple.

Cast on a number of stitches divisible by 5, plus 3.
1st row K3A, *K2B, K3A, rep from * to end.
2nd row P1B, *P3A, P2B, rep from * to last 2 sts, P2A.
3rd row K1A, *K2B, K3A, rep from * to last 2 sts, K2B.
4th row P1A, P2B, *P3A, P2B, rep from * to end.
Continue to work in this way moving the stripe one stitch to the right on K rows and one stitch to the left on P rows.

Herringbone stripes

These stripes are worked in almost the same way as given for diagonal stripes, but instead of moving continuously to the right as shown, try moving the stripes to the left after six rows, then back again to the right.

This pattern is very effective when used, for example, on a knitted skirt.

Vertical stripes

This is a typical example of the wide stripe which needs to have the yarn divided into small quantities. In fact any stripe over 4 stitches in width would need to be worked in this manner.

Take, for example, a sweater with five wide stripes of 21 stitches in each stripe across the front. The first row is worked by knitting 21 stitches with the first ball of A, then 21 stitches with the first ball of B, 21 stitches with the second ball of A, 21 stitches with the second ball of B, and 21 stitches with the third ball of A. Continue working in stocking stitch, as follows:

Next row (wrong side) P21 sts A, then carry yarn to the left at the front of the work, pick up the yarn B, and take it over A towards the right and P the next 21 sts with B, repeat in this way with each colour to the end of the row.

Next row K21 sts A, hold the yarn over to the left at the back of the work, take up the yarn B and bring it towards the right under the A thread, which is no longer in use, and K the next 21 sts with B, repeat in this way with each colour to the end of the row.

▲ *Diagonal striped pattern*

▲ *Joining in another colour on right side of vertical stripes*

▲ *Joining in another colour on wrong side of vertical stripes*

Chapter 32

Tweed effects in knitting

▲ *Two colour bobble tweed stitch*   ▼ *Three colour bobble tweed stitch*

▼ *Four colour bobble tweed stitch*

Striped designs are not the only way in which more than one colour may be introduced into knitted fabrics. There are many simple variations where different colours may be used effectively to give all-over patterned or tweed effects.

In many of these patterns the work is simplified by the need to use only one colour in each row, thus avoiding the weaving in or carrying across of colours not in use. Where only a few rows are worked in one colour the other colour, or colours, may be carried up the side of the work until required, care being taken not to pull them so tightly that the actual side length of the fabric is shortened. One pattern worked in two colours may take on a completely different appearance when worked in three or four colours, as illustrated.

Bobble tweed stitch
Worked over an even number of stitches.
1st row. Using 1st colour, K.
2nd row. Using 1st colour, K.
3rd row. Using 2nd colour, *K1 double by inserting needle into row below next st and K1, return this st to left-hand needle and K tog with next st on left-hand needle, K1, rep from * to end.
4th row. Using 2nd colour, K.
5th row. Using 1st colour, *K1, K1 double, rep from * to end.
6th row. Using 1st colour, K.
Continue repeating rows 3-6 as required, working 2 rows of each colour, or 2 rows each of 3 or more colours.

Horizontal fabric stripe
Worked over an even number of stitches.
1st row. Using 1st colour, K1, *yfwd, K2, lift yfwd over K2, rep from * to last st, K1.
2nd row. Using 1st colour, P.
3rd row. Using 2nd colour, work as given for 1st row.
4th row. Using 2nd colour, P.
Continue repeating rows 1-4 as required, working 2 rows of each colour, or 2 rows each of 3 or more colours.

Tweed stitch
Worked over a number of stitches divisible by 4, plus 3. Example 27 stitches.
1st row. (RS) Using 1st colour, K3, *sl 1 P-wise keeping yarn on WS, K3, rep from * to end.
2nd row. Using 1st colour, K3, *sl 1 P-wise keeping yarn on WS, K3, rep from * to end.
3rd row. Using 2nd colour, K1, *sl 1 P-wise keeping yarn on WS, K3, rep from * to last 2 sts, sl 1 P-wise, K1.
4th row. Using 2nd colour, K1, *sl 1 P-wise keeping yarn on WS, K3, rep from * to last 2 sts, sl 1 P-wise, K1.
Continue repeating rows 1-4 as required.

Striped star stitch
Worked over a number of stitches divisible by 4, plus 3. Example 27 stitches.
1st row. Using 1st colour, P.
2nd row. Using 1st colour, *insert needle into next 3 sts as if to K3 tog and K1, K1 tbl, K1 all into these sts—called 1 star—K1, rep from * ending with 1 star.
3rd row. Using 2nd colour, P.
4th row. Using 2nd colour, K2, * 1 star, K1, rep from * ending K1.
Continue repeating rows 1-4 as required.

▲ *Two colour horizontal fabric stripe*

▲ *Striped star stitch*

▲ *Three colour horizontal fabric stripe*　　　▼ *Tweed stitch*

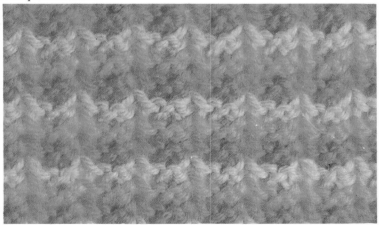

▲ *Striped fabric rib*　　　▼ *Striped vertical rib*

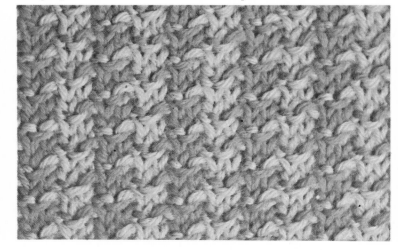

Striped fabric rib

Worked over a number of stitches divisible by 3. Example 27 stitches.

1st row. Using 1st colour, *K1, yfwd, K2 tog, repeat from * to end.

2nd row. Using 1st colour, *K1, yfwd, K2 tog, repeat from * to end.

Continue repeating rows 1 and 2 as required, working 2 rows of each colour and repeating colour sequence. Try four or six colours to give a multi-tweed effect.

Striped vertical rib

Worked over a number of stitches divisible by 4, plus 2. Example 26 stitches.

1st row. Using 1st colour, K1, *yfwd, sl 2 carrying yarn across front of work, ybk, K2, rep from * to last st, K1.

2nd row. Using 1st colour, K.

3rd row. Using 2nd colour, K1, *K2, yfwd, sl 2 carrying yarn across front of work, ybk, rep from * last st, K1.

4th row. Using 2nd colour, K.

Continue repeating rows 1-4 as required.

Chapter 33

Jacquard knitting and border patterns

Knitting Know-how

Jacquard knitting is the name given to patterned fabrics where more than one colour is used and where the pattern is knitted in at the same time as the background. It applies to the type of pattern which can be shown on a chart, in much the same way as cross stitch in embroidery is indicated, but does not include all over, multicoloured patterns formed with different stitches. The usual feature is a bold repeating design in large blocks of colour with the yarn being twisted at the back of the work to carry it along, giving a thick, woven fabric, particularly if worked in double knitting yarn. Because of this jacquard designs are often used for outdoor wear. Made in a thinner yarn, they look particularly well on skirts with one of the shades picked out for a plain matching sweater. A single jacquard motif makes a decorative patch pocket.

Two types of jacquard

There are two basic methods of knitting jacquard patterns. One is used where small motifs are being worked close together, such as on a border, or as an all-over surface design. The other is used where larger motifs are being worked and the spaces between each motif are larger in proportion.

Small motifs

When the pattern is composed of small repeats with only a few stitches in any one colour, the yarns not in use are carried across the back of the fabric until they are used again. If there are more than three stitches in a group, twist the thread not in use with the one being used, in order to avoid loose loops on the wrong side of the garment. It is essential not to drag the yarn from one group of stitches to the next, or the right side of the work will become puckered and uneven, spoiling the finished appearance.

If the garment is worked in bands of jacquard, separated by areas of stocking stitch worked in one colour only, it is advisable to use one size larger needle for the patterned bands than for the plain stocking stitch to avoid a noticeable difference in tension.

Large motifs and patterns

In any design, large diamonds and checks present a problem of their own. If they are worked in the same way as a small motif they use a great deal of unnecessary yarn, causing bulk in the fabric, and considerable care is required to keep the right side of the fabric smooth.

For this type of pattern it is best to use one ball of yarn for each area, twisting it with the next colour when moving onto the next area, as described in vertical stripes in Chapter 31. If working a design of your own decide which method you will use before beginning, based on the thickness of fabric required and the distance between the blocks of colour. In the case of published designs, the most appropriate method will almost certainly be given in the working instructions.

Working from a chart

It does not take long to learn to work from a chart and, indeed, it is often easier to read at a glance than trying to find your exact position in a maze of written instructions. Unless only two colours are used and it is obvious from the illustration which is the pattern and which is the background, you will usually find a key to the chart presented with it, describing which symbol stands for which colour.

In the charts for the 1st and 2nd border patterns a blank square denotes the background colour A, which is worked with cream; contrast colour B is pink and is indicated with a slanting line and contrast colour C, which is orange, is indicated by a dot.

The most important point in reading from a chart is to remember whether you are working in rows or in rounds. Working in rows of stocking stitch the first row on the chart, which is usually shown at the lower edge, will be the right side or knitted row and will be read along the chart from right to left. The second row will be purled and is read from left to right because you have turned the work but cannot turn the chart. If you are working in rounds then each round will begin on the chart at the right side and will, of course, be a knitted round and will be repeated to the end of the round.

To be certain that you understand these methods, try to work the border using the first chart. If you are in any doubt you can check from the following row by row instructions repeating from A to B. The border is worked over a number of stitches divisible by 21 and over 15 rows of stocking stitch, beginning and ending with a knitted row. Work 2 rows stocking stitch in A before beginning the pattern.

1st patt row. *K1 A, 3C, 8A, 3B, 6A, rep from * to end.
2nd patt row. *P5 A, 5B, 6A, 5C, rep from * to end.
3rd patt row. *K6 C, 5A, 5B, 5A, rep from * to end.
4th patt row. *P2 A, 2B, 1A, 5B, 1A, 2B, 2A, 4C, 2A, rep from * to end.
5th patt row. *K3 A, 3C, 1A, 4B, 1A, 3B, 1A, 4B, 1A, rep from * to end.
6th patt row. *P1 A, 5B, 1A, 1C, 1A, 5B, 2A, 3C, 2A, rep from * to end.
7th patt row. *K1 A, 3C, 1A, 2B, 1A, 3B, (1A, 1B) twice, 1A, 3B, 1A, 1C, rep from * to end.
8th patt row. *P1 A, 1C, (3A, 1C) twice, 3A, 4B, 3A, 1C, rep from * to end.
9th patt row. *K1 A, 3C, 1A, 2B, 1A, 3B, (1A, 1C) twice, 1A, 3B, 1A, 1C, rep from * to end.
10th patt row. *P1 A, 5B, 1A, 1C, 1A, 5B, 2A, 3C, 2A, rep from * to end.
11th patt row. *K3 A, 3C, 1A, 4B, 1A, 3B, 1A, 4B, 1A, rep from * to end.
12th patt row. *P2 A, 2B, 1A, 5B, 1A, 2B, 2A, 4C, 2A, rep from * to end.
13th patt row. *K6 C, 5A, 5B, 5A, rep from * to end.
14th patt row. *P5 A, 5B, 6A, 5C, rep from * to end.
15th patt row. *K1 A, 3C, 8A, 3B, 6A, rep from * to end.

Beginning with a purl row work 2 rows stocking stitch with A only to complete this sample.

Now try the second jacquard border pattern, following the chart in the same way.

The third jacquard pattern, showing a carnation motif, is in two colours only. The cream background is indicated by a blank square on the chart and the pink contrast by a cross. This motif can be repeated as a border, worked for example along the hem of a cardigan, or used on its own. The arrangement of the motif depends on personal taste but the finished effect can give an original touch to even the simplest garment.

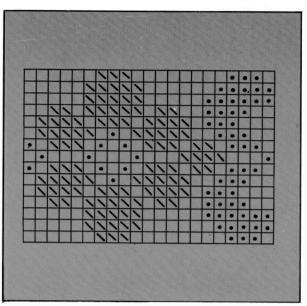

▲ *Chart for first jacquard border pattern*

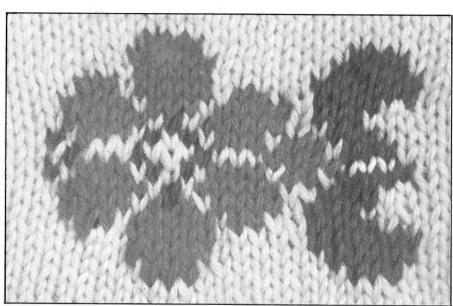

▲ *First jacquard border pattern*

▼ *Second jacquard border pattern*

▼ *Work this jacquard border pattern from the chart on the left*

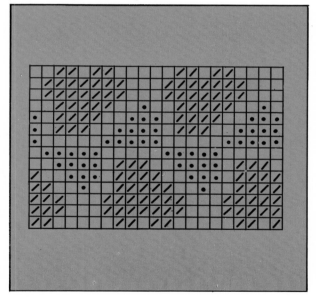

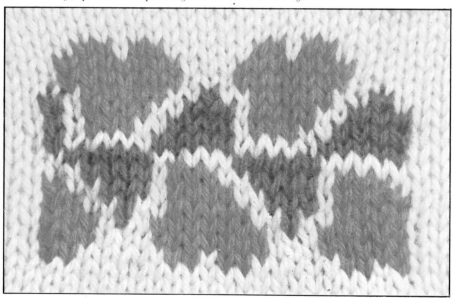

▼ *Chart for the carnation jacquard motif*

▼ *The carnation jacquard motif*

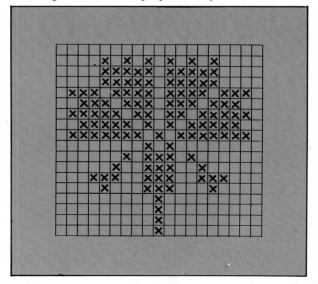

Chapter 34

Fair Isle techniques

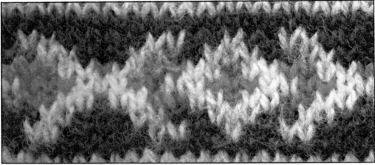

▲ *Fair Isle pattern based on a simple 'O' and 'X' design*

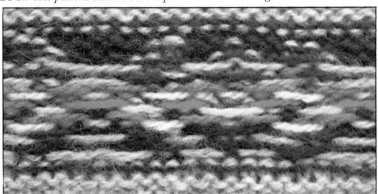

▲ *The 'O' and 'X' design, viewed from the wrong side*
▼ *Working chart for the 'O' and 'X' design*

The bands of Fair Isle pattern were based on simple 'O' and 'X' shapes, often with the Spanish cross superimposed in the centre, but were given an added subtlety by the changes of colours worked into the background in stripes, as well as the pattern itself. The softly twisted yarn was originally 'natural' in colour, which could vary from white to a dark blackish brown, whatever the colour of the sheep from which it came. These soft, natural tones gave the knitter a vast choice of shades to use in her pattern, but the many colours we know today were added much more recently, to cater for fashion demand.

The softness of the yarn is further enhanced by the seamlessness of the garment. Cardigans, sweaters and pullovers are all knitted without seams. When the armholes are reached, the stitches are left unworked, to be picked up or grafted later, so that even below the arm there is no firm seam. Shoulders, too, are grafted together, producing a softness and pliability of fabric which gives the garment an added charm and character.

Unlike most coloured or jacquard patterns, Fair Isle designs do not have the yarns twisted on the wrong side of the fabric. Each area of colour is small, and usually only two colours are used in any one row and they are carried directly from one stitch to the next to be worked in that colour.

The greatest influence and change in Fair Isle work, apart from the addition of colours which the Shetlanders are so good at blending, came about during the 1939-1945 war, when many Norwegians were stationed in Shetland. Their own coloured knitting came from similar sources to those of the Shetlanders, but the motifs used were larger and more complicated. Many Fair Isle designs now incorporate these motifs most successfully. Traditionally, the patterns are handed on from mother to daughter, but where a design is written down for others to copy the motifs are usually worked from a chart for ease of reading. Each colour is marked on the chart with its own symbol. As most of the work is made by using sets of needles to avoid seams, the right side of the work is towards the knitter who can follow the pattern visually far more quickly than attempting to read row by row instructions. Where openings are required, the work is later cut and the ends darned back in to make them secure so that the ends do not fray out.

Simple O and X design
One of the very old, often used designs, this version repeats over 14 sts.

Flower motif
This motif is worked over 30 sts.
The colours for the motif are shown on the chart colour key.
The background colours are changed as follows.
Rows 1 and 2 Fawn.
Row 3 Light green.

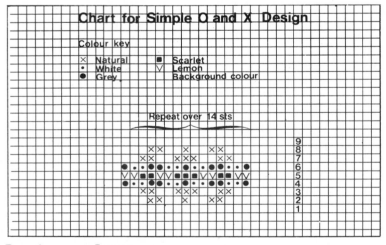

Row 4	Lemon.
Rows 5-12	White.
Rows 13-15	Stone.
Rows 16-20	Lemon.
Row 21	Light green.
Rows 22-26	Lemon.
Rows 27-29	Stone.
Rows 30-37	White.
Row 38	Lemon.
Row 39	Light green.
Rows 40 & 41	Fawn.

Star motif
This motif is worked over 36 sts. The colours used for the motif appear on the chart colour key.
The background colours are as follows:
Rows 1-10 have natural fawn background.
Rows 11-37 have white background.
Rows 38-40 have natural fawn background.

▲ *The flower motif, worked on a changing background of fawn, green, lemon, white and stone* ▼ *Working chart for the flower motif*

▲ *The star motif in tones of grey and brown on a background of* natural *fawn and off-white* ▼ *Working chart for the star motif*

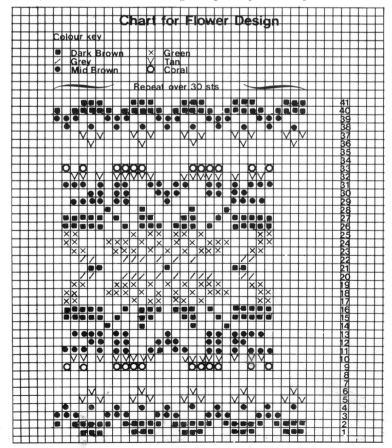

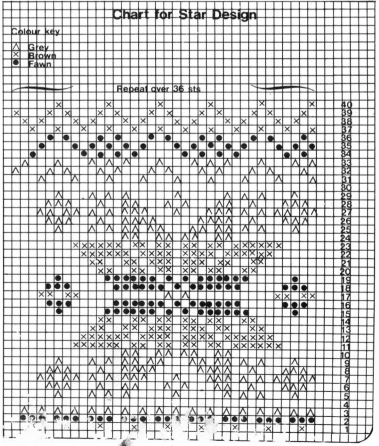

Chapter 35

Knitting with beads and sequins

The simplest method of adding beads or sequins to knitting is whilst working.

Choice of beads and sequins

Care when choosing beads and sequins for knitting will pay in the results obtained. Because large, heavy beads will drag the knitting out of shape, small beads are usually a better choice. If the beads are to be worked close together they should only cover a small area, because even with small beads a large area would soon become too heavy for the yarn.

It is always better to make sure that beads or sequins will not shed their colour, and only those guaranteed suitable for dry cleaning are advisable. All beaded and sequined garments should be dry cleaned, with the exception of those with small lightweight plastic beads, which are said to be washable.

Choice of stitch

Beads or sequins are decorative enough in themselves and should only be combined with fancy stitches if these genuinely contribute to the finished appearance.

Because of its smooth surface, stocking stitch forms the most suitable background to show the decoration to best advantage.

Threading beads or sequins onto yarn

Occasionally it is possible to buy lightweight beads or sequins with large holes, in which case there is no problem threading them onto the yarn. However, the usual bead or sequin used for knitting has a

Knitting Know-how

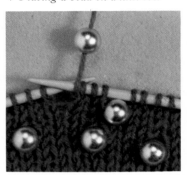
▼ *Placing a bead on a knit row*

▼ *Purling stitch after placing bead*

▼ *Placing a bead on a purl row*

▼ *Knitting stitch following bead*

relatively small hole which is not large enough to take a needle threaded with yarn.

In such a case, cut a length of sewing cotton about 8 inches long and thread both ends into the eye of the needle. Slide the needle half way along the doubled thread thus forming a loop at one end. Smooth both the ends and the loop downwards. Into the loop pass the end of the yarn for several inches and then smooth the double thickness of the yarn downwards.

Slip the beads or sequins onto the needle, over the cotton and then the yarn.

Adding beads between stitches on a purl row

Purl along the row to the bead position, take the yarn behind the needle, slip a bead along next to the needle, knit the next stitch and return the yarn ready for purling.

Continue in purl until the next bead position. Work the next bead in exactly the same way.

Adding beads between stitches on a knit row

Work to the point where the bead is to be placed. Bring the yarn forward towards you and slip a bead up close to the needle, purl the next stitch then continue knitting in the normal way until the next bead position is reached.

Adding beads (or sequins) in front of a stitch on a knit row

Knit to the required position, bring the yarn forward and slip a bead close up to the fabric, slip the next stitch from the left hand needle without knitting it and leaving the bead in front of the slipped stitch. Return the yarn to the knitting position and work to the next bead position.

Adding beads (or sequins) in front of a stitch on a purl row

Purl to the bead position. Take the yarn back to right side of work and slip bead up to the needle, slip next stitch, carry yarn across slipped stitch on

right side, bring yarn back and purl to next bead position.

Alternative method of adding sequins

The type of sequin which has a hole close to the edge must be able to hang. With either of the previous methods, the sequins would be distorted. Instead, use either of the following methods after threading the sequins onto the yarn.

Working a knit row. Knit to the point at which the sequin is to be placed, knit the next stitch through the back of the loop, pushing the sequin through the actual stitch from back to front.

Working a purl row. Work to the point at which the sequin is to be placed, push the sequin close to the needle, purl the next stitch. This stitch holds the sequin in place without having to push it through. Once the sequin is in place, continue along the row as normal on a purl row to the next sequin position.

Evening bag

Size
Top edge, approx 5in
Depth including fringe, 7in

Tension for this design
8 sts and 12 rows to 1in worked on No.10 needles

Materials shown here
Twilley's Goldfingering
1 ball
One pair No.10 needles
624 small pearl beads
One handbag frame
¼yd lining material

To work the bag
Thread beads onto ball of yarn.
Using No.10 needles, cast on 39 sts.
1st row K.
2nd and every alt row K1, P to last st, K1.
3rd row K4, *yfwd, slip bead close to work, slip next st keeping bead in front, ybk—called B1—, K5, rep from * to last 5 sts, B1, K4

▼ *Threading beads onto the yarn*

▲ *Glitter yarn enhanced by pearl beads adds glamour to an evening bag*

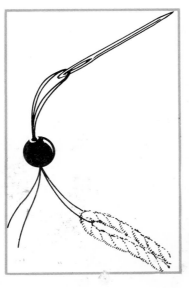

5th row K3, *B1, K1, B1, K3, rep from * to end.

7th row K2, *B1, K3, B1, K1, rep from * to last st, K1.

9th row K1, *B1, K5, rep from * to last 2 sts, B1, K1.

11th row As 7th.

13th row As 5th.

14th row As 2nd.

Rows 3-14 form the patt and are repeated throughout, the continuity of the bead lines being kept and 1 st at either end of each row being knitted and kept free of beads.

Inc one st at each end of next 6 rows. Place marker thread at each end of last row.

Work 8 rows without shaping.

Dec 1 st at each end of next and every 4th row until 41 sts remain, every alt row until 33 sts remain, then every row until 21 sts remain.

Cast off 3sts at beg of next 4 rows. Cast off.

Fringe

With RS facing, K up 72 sts between marker threads round the lower half of the bag (ie along one side, across cast off sts and along other side).

Loop row *Insert needle into next st on left hand needle, wind yarn over needle point and round 3 fingers of left

hand 3 times then round needle point once, draw loops through and return to left hand needle, K into back of loops and st (see Knitting Know-how Chapter 21), rep from * to end of row. Cast off.

Work a second side in the same way, omitting fringe.

To make up

Cut lining slightly larger than knitted section.

Place 2 sections of knitting right sides together and join along cast off edge of fringe. Seam lining along same edges. Stitch bag to frame. Insert lining and slip stitch in place.

Chapter 36

Embroidery on knitting

Knitting provides an ideal fabric for embroidery. It can be used either as a plain background for working random patterns, or the structure of the fabric can be used for counted thread types of patterns.

In decorating knitting, single stitches can be outlined in contrast colour to build up small motifs, as in Swiss darning. Alternatively, embroidery may be used to highlight a knitted pattern, a technique found in Tyrolean designs.

Swiss darning
Knitting a motif into the actual garment inevitably slows the process of knitting, and may present difficulties if rounded shapes are required. In such a case, the quickest method is to knit the garment in stocking stitch and then to darn in the motif, by outlining the stitches of the motif-area. Thread the yarn into a blunt ended needle and pass the needle through to the right side of the work at the base of a stitch. Draw the yarn through leaving a short end at the back to darn in once the work is completed. Insert the needle behind the threads at the top of the same stitch, taking the needle through to the wrong side at the right hand side of the stitch and out to the right side of the work at the left of the stitch. Then insert the needle back into the base of the same stitch. This will now have outlined one complete stitch and the process is repeated over all the necessary stitches. Darn in both ends invisibly on the wrong side.

Counted thread embroidery
In this technique, the upright and horizontal lines of the knitted stitch replace the canvas, and the spaces in the centre of stitches or between stitches are used as holes.
This is most easily worked using a blunt ended needle so that the knitted stitches are not split.

Tyrolean knitting
In these patterns the knitted stitches are used to create a self-coloured pattern which is then highlighted by the addition of small, gay coloured flowers, usually embroidered in wool. These are traditionally simple daisy shapes, sometimes formed by straight stitches like the spokes of a wheel, but more often with lazy daisy stitch. These can be used to form leaves.

Tyrolean leaf pattern
The pattern is worked over 25 stitches and makes an attractive panel on either side of cardigan button strips. (Not illustrated.)

1st row (RS) K6, P2 tog, P4, K up thread before next st tbl—called K up 1 tbl—, K1, K up 1 tbl, P4, P2 tog, K6.
2nd row K1, P4, K6, P3, K6, P4, K1.
3rd row K6, P2 tog, P3, (K1, yfwd) twice, K1, P3, P2 tog, K6.
4th row K1, P4, K5, P5, K5, P4, K1.
5th row K1, sl next 2 sts onto cable needle and hold at back of work, K2, K2 from cable needle—called C4B—, K1, P2 tog, P2, K2, yfwd, K1, yfwd, K2, P2, P2 tog, K1, sl next 2 sts onto cable needle and hold

▲ *A simple embroidery motif to link mother and daughter's outfits*

at front of work, K2, K2 from cable needle—called C4F—, K1.
6th row K1, P4, K4, P7, K4, P4, K1.
7th row K6, P2 tog, P1, K3, yfwd, K1, yfwd, K3, P1, P2 tog, K6.
8th row K1, P4, K3, P9, K3, P4, K1.
9th row K6, P2 tog, K4, yfwd, K1, yfwd, K4, P2 tog, K6.
10th row K1, P4, K2, P11, K2, P4, K1.
11th row K1, C4B, K1, P1, K5, P into front and back of next st twice, turn, K4, turn, P4, turn, K4, turn, sl 2nd, 3rd and 4th sts over first st then sl first st onto right hand needle—called Bobble 1—, K5, P1, K1, C4F, K1.
12th row As 10th.
13th row K6, inc by purling into front and back of next st, K4, sl 1, K2 tog, psso, K4, inc

in next st, K6.
14th row As 8th.
15th row K6, inc in next st, P1, K1, Bobble 1, K1, sl 1, K2 tog, psso, K1, Bobble 1, K1, P1, inc in next st, K6.
16th row As 6th.
17th row K1, C4B, K1, inc in next st, P2, K2, sl 1, K2 tog, psso, K2, P2, inc in next st, K1, C4F, K1.
18th row As 4th.
19th row K6, inc in next st, P3, K2 tog tbl, Bobble 1, K2 tog, P3, inc in next st, K6.
20th row As 2nd.
21st row K6, inc in next st, P4, sl 1, K2 tog, psso, P4, inc in next st, K6.
22nd row K1, P4, K7, P1, K7, P4, K1.
23rd row K1, C4B, K1, P13, K1, C4F, K1.
24th row K1, P4, K15, P4, K1.
These 24 rows form patt and are repeated as required.

Stem Stitch ——— Chain Stitch ● ● ● Beads

▲ *Diagram for embroidery worked in chain and stem stitches and beads*

▲ *Embroidered mittens and alternative knitted trim on red mitten*

Decorated mittens

Size
To fit an average adult hand
Length, about 10in

Tension for this design
6 sts and 8 rows to 1in
over st st worked on No.
10 needles

Materials shown here
Patons Double Knitting
Two 50g balls
One set of 4 No.10 double
pointed needles
Embroidery threads and beads

Left mitten

Using No.10 needles, cast on
48 sts and divide on 3 needles.
Cuff round *K1 tbl, P1, rep
from * to end.

Rep this round until cuff
measures 3in.
Change to st st.
1st round K22, lift thread
before next st and K into back
of it to M1 (this becomes
centre st of thumb gusset), K26.
2nd round K.
3rd round K22, M1, K1,
M1, K26.
4th round As 2nd.
5th round K22, M1, K3,
M1, K26.
6th round As 2nd.
Continue in this way until
there are 19 sts on thumb
gusset. 67 sts.

Divide for thumb
1st round K22, sl next 19
sts onto thread and leave for
thumb, K26.
Continue in rounds on 48 sts
until work measures 9in from
cast on edge or required
length to top shaping.

Shape top
1st round *K2, K2 tog, K17,
sl 1, K1, psso, K1, rep from *
once more.
2nd round *K2, K2 tog,
K15, sl 1, K1, psso, K1, rep
from * once more.
Continue dec in this way on
every round until 4 sts rem.
Break yarn and draw through
rem sts and fasten off.

Thumb
Divide 19 sts from holder onto
3 needles. K 1 round.
2nd round K1, *K2 tog, K7,
rep from * once more. 17 sts.
Work for 2in without shaping.

Shape thumb top
1st round *K2, K2 tog, rep
from * to last st, K1.
2nd round *K1, K2 tog, rep
from * to last st, K1.
3rd round K *K2 tog, rep
from * to end. Break yarn and

draw through rem sts. Fasten
off.

Right mitten

Work as for Left mitten, reversing position of thumb by working gusset after 26 sts instead
of 22 sts.

To complete

Press mittens under a damp
cloth with a warm iron,
omitting ribbing.
Embroider back as in diagram.

Alternative trim
Using No.10 needles, cast on
120 sts.
K 1 row. P 1 row. Cast off.
Allow strip to curl so that
cast on and off edges touch.
Slip stitch together if preferred
to give a firm finish. Curl
strip round to form design.

Chapter 37

How to create your own designs

This chapter tells you in simple terms how to be your own designer. Once you have mastered one of the two possible techniques, you will be able to have patterns which are exactly what you want in style and fit. Don't be too ambitious to start with—progress gradually to more complicated ideas.

1. Graph paper planning method

The graph paper planning method, most widely used by professional designers, involves planning on graph paper every stitch to be knitted—casting on and off, increasing, decreasing, and openings—and shows in diagram form what the written instructions say in words. It is not worked to scale: one small square represents one stitch and each line of squares represents one row.

2. Paper pattern method

The paper pattern method involves making a paper shape from a garment which already exists in your wardrobe. You may prefer this method if you like to follow an existing outline.

For both methods the first stages are the same. The yarn, stitch and tension must all be decided on before you can begin.

Don't over-complicate what you are trying to do

Choosing the yarn (both methods)

Decide on a simple shape for a first attempt and then consider which yarn will be most suitable for the stitch you want to use. It may sound obvious, but don't choose a double knitting yarn with an irregular surface, such as bouclé or mohair, if you have already made up your mind to use a lace stitch. Alternatively, don't pick a dainty two-ply yarn if you want to make a husky sports sweater! Once you have decided on the style, stitch and yarn, stick with it! At this stage it's so easy to be side-tracked with visions of all the gorgeous garments that you can add to your wardrobe, but be content to work on one idea at a time. Don't try to combine too many ideas in one garment.

Don't just take any old wool and start to knit

Tension (both methods)

Make a sample square, using the stitch and the yarn you've chosen, so that you can find exactly how many stitches and rows there are to 1 inch. Make this test square at least 4 inches so that you can check the tension for 1 inch over 4 inches and so stand less chance of being half a stitch out in your calculations.
Measure the square carefully with a ruler to see exactly how many stitches and rows there are to 1 inch. Note this down, because all your future work on this design must be based on this tension.

Taking your measurements (both methods)

This is the moment to make a careful note of your own measurements, or those required for the garment.
Remember that in all garments an allowance is made for movement, which is called 'tolerance'. For a bust measurement the allowance is usually about 2 inches. A loose chunky jacket may have a 'tolerance' of 4 inches added to the actual measurements.

Finding the right number of stitches to cast on (both methods)

Let us take as an example a simple jersey in old shale stitch (see Knitting Know-how Chapter 20), which, on a sample using No.10 needles and 4-ply yarn, gives a tension of 7 sts and 9 rows to 1in.

If you are making this in the ordinary way, with Back and Front each being half of the work, then the number of stitches for the Back will be half the bust measurement plus half the tolerance allowance, plus 2 stitches to allow for seaming. So, using the tension given, for a 36in bust, the sum will look like this: 18in at 7sts per in = 126 + 7 = 133 + 2 = 135.

Now it is essential to see if the stitch you have chosen will divide evenly into this total. You may have to decide whether you prefer to work with extra stitches or fewer stitches, altering the width slightly. In this case, old shale stitch requires a multiple of 11 + 2 edge stitches. The nearest to the required total of 135 is 134, and for a light jersey, one stitch fewer would be reasonable. Having given points common to both methods, let's take the differences.

Method 1 (graph paper planning)

The graph paper method is very much like making a map of what you are going to knit. Once you have calculated the number of stitches you are going to cast on, mark one square for each stitch along the first row of small squares. It is useful to develop your own code of marks, so that by glancing at the graph paper you can tell immediately whether the stitch is to be knitted or purled, decreased or cast off. For instance, a sloping line \ can be used to indicate a knit stitch and the reverse / for a purl stitch.

By now you have decided whether to have a hem or a ribbed edge and you know the number of rows to 1 inch. So, mark each line of small squares to represent one row until you have the correct number of squares marked to give you the required length of the side-seam to the beginning of the armhole.

Continue working out each step, armhole shaping and depth, neck shaping and shoulder casting off, and mark out on the graph paper until you have completed the Back and Front.

Avoid circular yokes, seamless garments and any complicated decreasing and increasing. You will be able to work out more complicated designs when you have had experience.

Make sure each side of the garment is the same length

Method 2 (paper pattern)

Trace on to paper the exact shape of an existing garment, then simply knit each piece to the same shape. Before beginning to work, check carefully that the drawing of each piece is exact. If the shape is correct the result will be much more satisfactory. Once you have begun to work, constantly check that your knitting is the same shape as the paper pattern. This is not always easy, as the unpressed knitting is not as flat as the paper pattern, but care taken to measure accurately will save disappointment or time spent in rattling down (knitter's jargon for unravelling!) your work and re-knitting.

Don't try to combine too many ideas into the one design

Pointers towards success

1. Choose a simple design to begin with. Don't put all your ideas into one design.

2. Choose the yarn and stitch carefully, so that both are suitable for the type of garment.

3. Make a large sample square before beginning the garment, using the yarn, needles and stitch you have chosen, so that you are certain about the number of stitches and rows to 1 inch.

4. Make a list of the required measurements for the garment you are going to make.

5. Decide which method you are going to use, and chart carefully or make the paper pattern with accuracy.

6. When making two similar parts, such as sleeves or fronts, use a row counter to be certain that they are exactly the same length — measuring is not sufficient.

7. The choice of materials is part of designing, so is the actual working and so is the making up. Don't try to hurry any part or the result will suffer. The choice of trimmings such as buttons is also important. Be sure that the colour and size are correct for the type of design you want to make.

105

Collector's Piece

Painting with wool

This beautiful sleeveless jacket is—
believe it or not—hand knitted! Every
patch of colour is knitted at random
and every shape is different from the
rest. Some patches are worked in
stocking stitch, others in moss stitch,
broken rib or garter stitch and even
the yarns are mixed to include plain
and marled pure new wool with a few
patches of mohair or angora.

The designer works on the principle of
planning the outline shape of her
garments. She chooses the colours and
yarns and then decides on the general
outline of the pattern shapes—here they
are irregular and angular but they
could be curved or geometric. Then,
having cast on the number of stitches
needed for the particular garment,
the knitter works a hem in one colour
and then starts taking in say, 12 stitches
of one colour, 10 stitches of the next
colour in maybe a different wool, 15
stitches of the next and so on. The knitter
sits surrounded by separate balls of the
wools and colours selected—she doesn't
carry the strands across the inside of the
work as in Fair Isle. If you look carefully,
you will see that there are at least a
dozen different balls of wool on the go
across the back of this jerkin but no
one ball is used twice across a single row.
The knitter works out the colour and
stitch patterns as she goes along,
taking care to follow the shaping. As
one colour is finished and the next
introduced, the wool is broken off and
the secret of the astonishingly tidy
inside of the jerkin is that every tail
is darned in meticulously along the
colour join lines.

It takes considerable experience and an
eye for design to be able to emulate this
kind of instinctive design but there are
two basic rules which give you a better
chance of succeeding.

One, always use wools that knit up to
the same tension, otherwise the fabric
will pucker. But if you can't resist
including a yarn with a slightly different
tension, change on to a sock needle for
the patch (as for cabling) while working
that patch so that you achieve the same
number of stitches to the inch.

Second point—careful washing and
drying can make all the difference
between a ragbag effect and a 'one-and-
only' treasure.

Baby bootees

Take your pick of these delightful baby bootees—they are quick and fun to do and make ideal gifts.

The white moccasins, shown on the left, can be worn by both boys and girls, depending on the colour of the lace trim. The slipper socks, shown centre, are designed for a baby boy while the white lace boots, shown on the extreme right, would be pretty for a baby girl.

Size
Length of foot, 4in

Basic yarn tension
8 sts and 10 rows to 1in over st st worked on No.11 needles.

Materials shown here
Lee Target 3 ply Cherub Bri-Nylon
2 ¾oz balls main shade
Small quantity of contrast for Slipper socks
Two No.11 needles
Two buttons for Slipper socks
¾yd ribbon for Moccasins and White lace boots
2yds lace for Moccasins

Abbreviations
(y2rn, —yarn twice round needle)

Slipper socks

With white cast on 42 sts.
Next row *K1, P1, rep from * to end.
Rep last row 3 times more.
Commence lace patt.
1st row K2, *P1, K4, P1, K2, rep from * to end.
2nd row P2, *K1, P4, K1,

P2, rep from * to end.
3rd row K2, *P1, K2 tog, y2rn, K2 tog tbl, P1, K2, rep from * to end.
4th row P2, *K1, P1, K first loop and then into back of 2nd loop, P1, K1, P2, rep from * to end.
Rep 1st–4th rows 7 times more. Break yarn.
With RS facing slip first 15 sts on to holder or spare needle.
Rejoin white to next st and work instep on centre 12 sts. Work 17 rows keeping pattern correct.
Next row K1, P2 tog, K1, P1, P2 tog, P1, K1, P2 tog, K1.
Break yarn.

Work slipper
With contrast colour, K15 sts from holder, K up 15 sts along side of instep, K9 sts from centre, K up 15 sts along other side of instep, K rem 15 sts. (69 sts).
K 15 rows.

Shape sole
1st row K6, K2 tog, K19, K2 tog, K11, K2 tog, K19, K2 tog, K6.
2nd, 4th, 6th, 8th and 10th rows K.
3rd row K5, K2 tog, K19, K2 tog, K9, K2 tog, K19, K2 tog, K5.
5th row K4, K2 tog, K19, K2 tog, K7, K2 tog, K19, K2 tog, K4.
7th row K3, K2 tog, K19, K2 tog, K5, K2 tog, K19, K2 tog, K3.
9th row K2, K2 tog, K19, K2 tog, K3, K2 tog, K19, K2 tog, K2.
11th row K1, K2 tog, K19,

K2 tog, K1, K2 tog, K19,
K2 tog, K1.
12th row K2 tog, K19,
K3 tog, K19, K2 tog.
Cast off.

Strap

With contrast colour cast on
45 sts.
K 2 rows.
3rd row K2, cast off 2 sts,
K to end.
4th row K to last 2 sts, cast
on 2 sts, K2.
K 2 rows. Cast off.

To make up

Join sole and back seams.
Sew strap to centre back.
Sew button on strap end.

Moccasins

Instep
Cast on 11 sts.
1st row K.
2nd row K1, *yfwd, K2 tog,
rep from * to end.
Rep 2nd row 10 times more.
Break yarn and leave sts
on holder.
Using 2 needle method cast
on 17 sts.
Using same needle on which
there are 17 sts, K up 13 sts
along side of instep, across
centre sts K2 tog, K7,
K2 tog, K up 13 sts
along other side of
instep, turn and cast on 17
sts. (69 sts).
1st row K1, *P1, K1, rep
from * to end.
2nd row Sl 1, *K into st
below next st (called K1d),
P1, rep from * to end.
3rd row Sl 1, *P1, K1d,
rep from * to last 2 sts,
P1, K1.
Rep 2nd and 3rd rows
5 times more.

Shape sole
Complete as given for slipper
socks.
Seam sole and back.

Cuff

With RS work facing K up
35 sts around ankle.
K 3 rows.
Next row K1, *yfwd, K2

tog, rep from * to end.
K 6 rows.
Next row K2, (K up 1,
K4) 3 times, K7, (K4, K
up 1) 3 times, K2. (41 sts).
Commence lace pattern
1st row K1, *yfwd, K2 tog,
rep from * to end.
Rep 1st row 8 times more.
Cast off.

To make up

Sew frill of narrow lace
around cuff and instep.
Thread ribbon through
slotting for ties.

White lace boots

Cast on 41 sts. K 4 rows.
Commence lace pattern
1st row K1, *K1, yfwd, K2
tog, rep from * to last st,
K1.
2nd row P1, *P1, yrn, P2
tog, rep from * to last st, P1.
Rep 1st and 2nd rows 5 times
more, then 1st row once.
K1 row.

Ribbon slotting
Next row K5, *yfwd, K2
tog, K4, rep from * to end.
K1 row.
Rep 1st and 2nd patt rows
once.

Divide for instep
1st row K16, *K1, yfwd, K2
tog, rep from * twice,
K1, turn.
Work 16 rows more in patt
on centre 11 sts.
Next row P2 tog, P7, P2 tog.
Break yarn. With RS of work
facing and 15 sts on needle,
rejoin yarn at beg of instep,
K up 15 sts along side of
instep, K9 sts from centre
front, K up 15 sts along other
side of instep, K15 from
needle. K1 row across all
sts (69 sts). P1 row. K1 row.
Rep last 3 rows twice more.
K2 rows.

Shape sole
As given for slipper socks.

To make up

Sew sole and back seam
and thread ribbon through
ankle slotting.

109

Christening robe in lace stitch

This lovely christening robe, designed in a delicate looking lace stitch, separated with stocking stitch and lace ladders, has all the traditional fragility of hand made lace.

Sizes
To fit birth to 6 months
Length, 27in
Sleeve seam, 5½in

Basic yarn tension
8½ sts and 11 rows to 1in over st st worked on No. 11 needles
Tension for this design
Over patt when pressed, 2 patts to 2¾in wide. Actual tension over st st, 9 sts and 12 rows to 1in worked on No.12 needles.

Materials shown here
7 ozs Peter Pan 3 ply Baby wool
One pair of No.10 needles
One pair of No.12 needles
¾yd of narrow ribbon
17 yds narrow lace, optional
Five small buttons

Note
A longer skirt may be made by working more patts before first decrease row. One ounce of wool will work approximately 4in of lace patt. The additional trimming of lace may be omitted if a more simple garment is required.

Skirt
Using No.10 needles cast on 316 sts.

K 4 rows.
Commence patt.
1st row *K2, yfwd, K2 tog, K10, (yfwd, sl 1, K2 tog, psso, yfwd, K5) 6 times, yfwd, sl 1, K2 tog, psso, yfwd, K11, yfwd, K2 tog, K1, rep from * 3 times more.
2nd row *K2, yfwd, K2 tog, P71, K1, yfwd, K2 tog, K1, rep from * 3 times more.
3rd row As 1st.
4th row As 2nd.
5th row *K2, yfwd, K2 tog, K10, (K3, yfwd, sl 1, K1, psso, K1, K2 tog, yfwd) 6 times, K14, yfwd, K2 tog, K1, rep from * 3 times more.
6th row As 2nd.
7th row *K2, yfwd, K2 tog, K10, (yfwd, sl 1, K2 tog, psso, yfwd, K1) 12 times, yfwd, sl 1, K2 tog, psso, yfwd, K11, yfwd, K2 tog, K1, rep from * 3 times more.
8th row As 2nd.
Rep 1st-8th rows 4 times more.
Work 1st dec row.
Next row *K2, yfwd, K2 tog, K6, K2 tog, K2, (yfwd, sl 1, K2 tog, psso, yfwd, K5) 6 times, yfwd, sl 1, K2 tog, psso, yfwd, K2, K2 tog tbl, K7, yfwd, K2 tog, K1, rep from * 3 times more.
Work 2nd-8th rows once, then 1st-8th rows 4 times more, noting that there is one st less on each st st panel, (2 sts less on WS rows between lace ladders).
Continue dec one st in this way on next and following 40th row until 3 dec rows have been worked. (292 sts)
Work 31 rows then dec on next row. (284 sts)
Work 23 rows then dec on next row. (276 sts)
Work 23 rows then dec on

next row. (268 sts)
Work 14 rows ending with RS row.
Next row *K2, yfwd, K2 tog, P3 tog, (P5, P3 tog) 7 times, K1, yfwd, K2 tog, K1, rep from * to end.
Next row K2, yfwd, K2 tog, K95, yfwd, K2 tog, K3, yfwd, K2 tog, K95, yfwd, K2 tog, K1.
Next row K2, yfwd, (K2 tog) twice, *yfwd, K2 tog, rep from * 45 times more, K1, yfwd, K2 tog, K3, yfwd, (K2 tog) twice, *yfwd, K2 tog, rep from * 45 times more, K1, yfwd, K2 tog, K1.
Change to No.12 needles for yoke.
1st row Cast on 3 sts, K5 yfwd, K2 tog, K94, yfwd, K2 tog, K3, yfwd, K2 tog, K94, yfwd, K2 tog, K1.
2nd row Cast on 3 sts, K5, yfwd, K2 tog, P93, K1, yfwd, K2 tog, K3, yfwd, K2 tog, P93, K1, yfwd, K2 tog, K4.
3rd row (1st buttonhole) K5, yfwd, K2 tog, K73, (yfwd, K2 tog, K5) 3 times, yfwd, K2 tog, K3, (yfwd, K2 tog, K5) 3 times, yfwd, K2 tog, K73, yfwd, (K2 tog) twice, yfwd, K2.
4th row K5, yfwd, K2 tog, P72, (K1, yfwd, K2 tog, P4) 3 times, K1, yfwd, K2 tog, K3, yfwd, K2 tog, (P4, K1, yfwd, K2 tog) 3 times, P72, K1, yfwd, K2 tog, K4.
5th row K5, yfwd, K2 tog, K73, (yfwd, K2 tog, K5) 3 times, yfwd, K2 tog, K3, (yfwd, K2 tog, K5) 3 times, yfwd, K2 tog, K73, yfwd, K2 tog, K4.

6th row As 4th.
Rep 5th and 6th rows 5 times more.

Divide for armholes
1st row Patt 48 sts, cast off 10 sts, patt to last 58 sts, cast off 10 sts, patt to last 4 sts, K2 tog, yfwd, K2.
Work on last group of sts for Right back.
Work 1 row.
Dec one st at armhole edge of next 6 rows, then every RS row until 39 sts rem.
Work 1 row.
Work 26 rows without shaping, working buttonhole on 1st and 15th rows.

Shape shoulder
1st row Cast off 7 sts, patt to end.
2nd row Patt to end.
3rd row Cast off 6 sts, patt to last 4 sts, K2 tog, yfwd, K2.
4th row Patt to end.
5th row Cast off 6 sts, patt to end.
Cast off rem sts.
With WS of work facing rejoin yarn to centre 92 sts and work to end. Complete Front on these sts. Keeping patt correct, dec one st at each end of next 6 rows, then next 3 RS rows.
Work 13 rows without shaping.

Divide for neck
1st row Patt 29 sts, cast off 16 sts, patt 29 sts.
Work right shoulder on these sts.
**Dec at neck edge on next 7 rows, then every RS row until 19 sts rem.
Work until armhole measures

Stitch detail of the christening robe's front panel

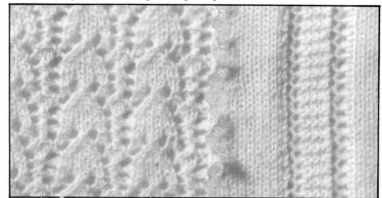

same as Right back to shoulder,
ending at armhole edge.
Cast off at beg of next and
following 2 alt rows, 7 sts
once and 6 sts twice. **
With WS of work facing,
rejoin yarn to rem sts and
work from ** to **.
With WS of work facing,
rejoin yarn to last group of
sts and complete as given
for Right back, omitting
buttonholes.

Sleeves

Using No.12 needles cast on
52 sts. K2 rows.
Continue in patt.
1st row K16, yfwd, K2 tog,
K5, yfwd, K2 tog, K3,
yfwd, K2 tog, K5, yfwd, K2
tog, K15.
2nd row P15 K1, yfwd, K2
tog, P4, K1, yfwd, K2 tog,
K3, yfwd, K2 tog, P4, K1,
yfwd, K2 tog, P15.
Keeping patt correct, inc
one st at each end of next
and every 6th row until
there are 70 sts. Continue
without shaping until work
measures 5½in, ending with
a WS row.

Shape top
Cast off 6 sts at beg of next 2
rows.
Dec one st at each end of next
and every RS row until 34
sts rem.
Dec one st at each end of
every row until 16 sts rem.
Cast off rem sts.

To make up

Press all pieces under a
damp cloth with a warm iron.
Join seam of skirt to 3in
below waistline.
Join shoulder seams.
Neckband Using No.12
needles K up 109 sts evenly
around neck edge. K3 rows.
Cast off.
Join sleeve seams. Set in
sleeves. Edge panels,
wrists, neck and lower edge
with lace if required.
Sew on buttons.
Thread ribbon through ribbon
slotting and sew ends at
sides of back opening and
centre front panel.

Shetland lace baby shawl

Because the shawl has few seams, the finished effect is fine and cobwebby.

Size
About 60in square

Tension for this design
About 4 sts and 8 rows to 1in over garter st worked on No.6 needles

---

Materials shown here
Templeton's H and O
Shetland lace 8oz
One pair No.6 needles

Outer border

Using No.6 needles cast on 8 sts.

1st row K2, (yfwd, K2 tog) 3 times.

2nd and every alt row K.

3rd row K2, yfwd, K2 tog, yfwd, K2, yfwd, K2 tog.

5th row K2, yfwd, K2 tog, yfwd, K3, yfwd, K2 tog.

7th row K2, yfwd, K2 tog, yfwd, K1, yfwd, K2 tog, K1, yfwd, K2 tog.

9th row K2, yfwd, K2 tog, yfwd, K3, (yfwd, K2 tog) twice.

11th row K1, (K2 tog, yfwd) twice, K3 tog, yfwd, K2, yfwd, K2 tog.

13th row K1, (K2 tog, yfwd) twice, K2 tog, K2, yfwd, K2 tog.

15th row K1, (K2 tog, yfwd) twice, K2 tog, K1, yfwd, K2 tog.

17th row K1, (K2 tog, yfwd) 3 times, K2 tog.

18th row K.

Rep 1st—18th rows 21 times more. Cast off.

Main border

Knit up 181 sts along straight edge of border.

1st row K.

2nd row K2, *K2 tog, yfwd, K4, rep from * to last 5 sts, K2 tog, yfwd, K3.

3rd and every alt row K.

4th row K1, *K2 tog, yfwd K1, yfwd, K2 tog, K1, rep from * to end.

6th row K2 tog, yfwd, *K3, yfwd, K3 tog, yfwd, rep from * to last 5 sts, K3, yfwd, K2 tog.

8th row K1, *yfwd, K2 tog, yfwd, K3 tog, yfwd, K1, rep from * to end.

10th row K2, *yfwd, K3 tog, yfwd, K3, rep from * to last 5 sts, yfwd, K3 tog, yfwd, K2.

12th row K1, K2 tog, yfwd, (K1, yfwd, K2 tog, yfwd, K3 tog, yfwd) twice, K7, *(yfwd, K2 tog, yfwd, K3 tog, yfwd, K1) 3 times, K6, rep from * to last 15 sts, (yfwd, K2 tog, yfwd, K3 tog, yfwd, K1) twice yfwd, K2 tog, K1.

14th row K2 tog, yfwd, (K3, yfwd, K3 tog, yfwd) twice, *K2, K2 tog, yfwd, K1, yfwd, K2 tog, K2, (yfwd, K3 tog, yfwd, K3) twice, yfwd, K3 tog, yfwd, rep from * to last 23 sts, K2, K2 tog, yfwd, K1, yfwd, K2 tog, K2, (yfwd, K3 tog, yfwd, K3) twice, yfwd, K2 tog.

16th row K1, *(yfwd, K2 tog, yfwd, K3 tog, yfwd, K1) twice, K2, K2 tog, yfwd, K3, yfwd, K2 tog, K3, rep from * to last 12 sts, (yfwd, K2 tog, yfwd, K3 tog, yfwd, K1) twice.

18th row K2, *(yfwd, K3 tog, yfwd, K3) twice, (K2 tog, yfwd) twice K1, (yfwd, K2 tog) twice, K3, rep from * to last 11 sts, yfwd, K3 tog, yfwd, K3, yfwd, K3, yfwd, K3 tog, yfwd, K2.

20th row K1, K2 tog, yfwd, K1, *yfwd, K2 tog, yfwd, K3 tog, yfwd, K4, (K2 tog, yfwd) twice, K3, (yfwd, K2 tog) twice, K4, rep from * to last 9 sts, yfwd, K2 tog, yfwd, K3 tog, yfwd, K1, yfwd, K2 tog, K1.

22nd row K2 tog, yfwd, *K3, yfwd, K3 tog, yfwd, K4, (K2 tog, yfwd) 3 times, K1, (yfwd, K2 tog) 3 times, K1, rep from * to last 11 sts, K3, yfwd, K3 tog, yfwd, K3, yfwd, K2 tog.

24th row K1, yfwd, K2 tog, yfwd, K3 tog, yfwd, K5 (K2 tog, yfwd) 3 times, *K3, (yfwd, K2 tog) 3 times, K3, K2 tog, yfwd, K4, (K2 tog, yfwd) 3 times, rep from * to last 20 sts, K3, (yfwd, K2 tog) 3 times, K5, yfwd, K2 tog, yfwd, K3 tog, yfwd, K1.

26th row K2, yfwd, K3 tog, yfwd, K5, (K2 tog, yfwd) 4 times, K1, (yfwd, K2 tog) 4 times, *K7, (K2 tog, yfwd) 4 times, K1, (yfwd, K2 tog) 4 times, rep from * to last 10 sts, K5, yfwd, K3 tog, yfwd, K2.

28th row K1, K2 tog, yfwd, K6, (K2 tog, yfwd) 4 times, K3, (yfwd, K2 tog) 4 times, *K1, K2 tog, yfwd, K2, (K2 tog, yfwd) 4 times, K3, (yfwd, K2 tog) 4 times, rep from * to last 9 sts, K6, yfwd, K2 tog, K1.

30th row K2 tog, yfwd, K6, *(K2 tog, yfwd) 5 times, K1, (yfwd, K2 tog) 5 times, K3, rep from * to last 5 sts, K3, yfwd, K2 tog.

32nd row K7, *(K2 tog, yfwd) 5 times, K3, (yfwd, K2 tog) 5 times, K1, rep from * to last 6 sts, K6.

34th row K1, K2 tog, K5, work as 30th row from * to last 5 sts, K2, K2 tog, K1. (179 sts.)

36th row K1, K2 tog, K5, *(K2 tog, yfwd) 4 times, K3, (yfwd, K2 tog) 4 times, K5, rep from * to last 3 sts, K2 tog, K1. (177 sts.)

38th row K1, K2 tog, K5, *(K2 tog, yfwd) 4 times, K1, (yfwd, K2 tog) 4 times, K1, K2 tog, yfwd, K1, yfwd, K2 tog, K1, rep from * to last 25 sts, (K2 tog, yfwd) 4 times, K1, (yfwd, K2 tog) 4 times, K5, K2 tog, K1. (175 sts.)

40th row K1, K2 tog, K5, *(K2 tog, yfwd) 3 times, K3, (yfwd, K2 tog) 3 times, K1, K2 tog, yfwd, K3, yfwd, K2 tog, K1, rep from * to last 23 sts, (K2 tog, yfwd) 3 times, K3, (yfwd, K2 tog) 3 times, K5, K2 tog, K1. (173 sts.)

42nd row K1, K2 tog, K5, *(K2 tog, yfwd) 3 times, K1, (yfwd, K2 tog) 3 times, K1, (K2 tog, yfwd) twice, K1, (yfwd, K2 tog) twice, K1, rep from * to last 21 sts, (K2 tog, yfwd) 3 times, K1, (yfwd, K2 tog) 3 times, K5, K2 tog, K1. (171 sts.)

44th row K1, K2 tog, K5, *(K2 tog, yfwd) twice, K3, (yfwd, K2 tog) twice, K1, rep from * to last 7 sts, K4, K2 tog, K1.

46th row K1, K2 tog, K5, *(K2 tog, yfwd) twice, K1, (yfwd, K2 tog) twice, K1, (K2 tog, yfwd) 3 times, K1, (yfwd, K2 tog) 3 times, K1, rep from * to last 17 sts, (K2 tog, yfwd) twice, K1, (yfwd, K2 tog) twice, K5, K2 tog, K1.

48th row K1, K2 tog, K5, *K2 tog, yfwd, K3, yfwd, K2 tog, K1, (K2 tog, yfwd) 3 times, K3, (yfwd, K2 tog) 3 times, K1, rep from * to last 15 sts, K2 tog, yfwd, K3, yfwd, K2 tog, K5, K2 tog, K1.

50th row K1, K2 tog, K5, *K2 tog, yfwd, K1, yfwd, K2 tog, K1, (K2 tog, yfwd) 4 times, K1, (yfwd, K2 tog) 4 times, K1, rep from * to last 13 sts, K2 tog, yfwd, K1, yfwd, K2 tog, K5, K2 tog, K1.

52nd row K1, K2 tog, K6, *yfwd, K2 tog, K1, (K2 tog, yfwd) 4 times, K3, (yfwd, K2 tog) 4 times, K2, rep from * to last 34 sts, yfwd, K2 tog, K1, (K2 tog, yfwd) 4 times, K3, (yfwd, K2 tog) 4 times, K1, K2 tog, yfwd, K6, K2 tog, K1.

54th row K1, K2 tog, K7, *(K2 tog, yfwd) 5 times, K1, (yfwd, K2 tog) 5 times, K3, rep from * to last 7 sts, K4, K2 tog, K1. (159 sts.)

56th row K1, K2 tog, K5,

Basic Wardrobe Knitting

*(K2 tog, yfwd) 5 times, K3, (yfwd, K2 tog) 5 times, K1, rep from * to last 7 sts, K4, K2 tog, K1.

58th row K1, K2 tog, K5, *(K2 tog, yfwd) 5 times, K1, (yfwd, K2 tog) 5 times, K3, rep from * to last 5 sts, K2, K2 tog, K1.

60th row K1, K2 tog, K5, *(K2 tog, yfwd) 4 times, K3, (yfwd, K2 tog) 4 times, K2, yfwd, K2 tog, K1, rep from * to last 27 sts, (K2 tog, yfwd) 4 times, K3, (yfwd, K2 tog) 4 times, K5, K2 tog, K1.

62nd row K1, K2 tog, K5, *(K2 tog, yfwd) 4 times, K1, (yfwd, K2 tog) 4 times, K2, yfwd, K3 tog, yfwd, K2, rep from * to last 25 sts, (K2 tog, yfwd) 4 times, K1, (yfwd, K2 tog) 4 times, K5, K2 tog, K1.

64th row K1, K2 tog, K5, *(K2 tog, yfwd) 3 times, K3, (yfwd, K2 tog) 3 times, K4, yfwd, K2 tog, K3, rep from * to last 23 sts, (K2 tog, yfwd) 3 times, K3, (yfwd, K2 tog) 3 times, K5, K2 tog, K1.

66th row K1, K2 tog, K5, *(K2 tog, yfwd) 3 times, K1, (yfwd, K2 tog) 3 times, K11, rep from * to last 21 sts, (K2 tog, yfwd) 3 times, K1, (yfwd, K2 tog) 3 times, K5, K2 tog, K1. (147 sts.)

68th row K1, K2 tog, K5, *(K2 tog, yfwd) twice, K3, (yfwd, K2 tog) twice, K6, yfwd, K2 tog, K5, rep from * to last 19 sts, (K2 tog, yfwd) twice, K3, (yfwd, K2 tog) twice, K5, K2 tog, K1.

70th row K1, K2 tog, K5, *(K2 tog, yfwd) twice, K1, (yfwd, K2 tog) twice, K5, K2 tog, yfwd, K1, yfwd, K2 tog, K5, rep from * to last 17 sts, (K2 tog, yfwd) twice, K1, (yfwd K2 tog) twice, K5, K2 tog, K1.

72nd row K1, K2 tog, K5, *K2 tog, yfwd, K3, yfwd, K2 tog, K5, rep from * to last 3 sts, K2 tog, K1.

74th row K1, K2 tog, K5, *K2 tog, yfwd, K1, yfwd, K2 tog, K4, K2 tog, yfwd, K1, yfwd, K2 tog, yfwd, K3 tog, yfwd, K1, yfwd, K2 tog, K4, rep from * to last 13 sts, K2 tog, yfwd, K1, yfwd, K2 tog, K5, K2 tog, K1.

76th row K1, K2 tog, K5, *K2 tog, yfwd, K5, K2 tog, yfwd, K3, yfwd, K3 tog, yfwd, K3, yfwd, K2 tog, K4, rep from * to last 11 sts, K2 tog, yfwd, K6, K2 tog, K1.

78th row K1, K2 tog, K9, *K2 tog, yfwd, (K1, yfwd, K2 tog, yfwd, K3 tog, yfwd) twice, K1, yfwd, K2 tog, K7, rep from * to last 5 sts, K2, K2 tog, K1.

80th row K1, K2 tog, K7, *K2 tog, yfwd, (K3, yfwd, K3 tog, yfwd) twice, K3, yfwd, K2 tog, K5, rep from * to last 5 sts, K2, K2 tog, K1.

82nd row K1, K2 tog, K4, *K2 tog, yfwd, (K1, yfwd, K2 tog, yfwd, K3 tog, yfwd) 3 times, K1, yfwd, K2 tog, K1, rep from * to last 6 sts, K3, K2 tog, K1.

84th row K1, K2 tog, K2, K2 tog, *yfwd, K3, yfwd, K3 tog, rep from * to last 10 sts, yfwd, K3, yfwd, K2 tog, K2, K2 tog, K1. (129 sts.)

86th row K1, K2 tog, K2, *yfwd, K2 tog, yfwd, K3 tog, yfwd, K1, rep from * to last 4 sts, K1, K2 tog, K1.

88th row K1, K2 tog, K2, *yfwd, K3 tog, yfwd, K3, rep from * to last 8 sts, yfwd, K3 tog, yfwd, K2, K2 tog, K1.

90th row K5, *yfwd, K2 tog, K4, rep from * to last 6 sts, yfwd, K2 tog, K4. (125 sts.)

91st row K.
Cast off loosely.

Work one more outer border and main border in the same way.
Make a third section in the same way, either casting off or leaving the sts on a holder to graft to last row of Centre. Make a fourth section but do not cast off, continuing on these 125 sts for Centre.

Centre

1st-8th rows K.
9th row K8, *yfwd, K2 tog,

K4, rep from * to last 3 sts, K3.

10th and every alt row K.

11th row K7, *yfwd, K3 tog, yfwd, K3, rep from * to last 4 sts, K4.

13th row As 9th.

15th row K.

17th row K8, yfwd, K2 tog, K to last 9 sts, yfwd, K2 tog, K7.

19th row K7, yfwd, K3 tog, yfwd, K to last 10 sts, yfwd, K3 tog, yfwd, K7.

21st row As 17th.

23rd row K.

Rep last 8 rows 27 times more, then rep 9th-14th rows once.

K8 rows more.

Cast off loosely or graft to last border section.

To make up

Slip stitch border sections to Centre sides. Slip stitch corners together.
Roll in a damp towel for 2 h____ ____ out until dry.

▲ *A perfect example of openwork stitches and fine yarn combining to make a soft and warm baby wrap*

Matinée jacket with lacy eyelets

Basic Wardrobe Knitting

Make an enchanting matinée jacket for baby. This one has an unusual two-colour band of pattern and lacy eyelets. You can either leave these open or thread with satin ribbon as an extra trimming, using the main colour or the contrast.

Sizes
To fit 18[20]in chest
Sleeve seam, 5[5¾]in
Centre back length, 9[11]in
The figures in brackets[ ] refer to the 20in size

Basic yarn tension
7 sts and 9 rows to 1 inch over st st worked on No.10 needles

Materials shown here
Peter Pan 4 ply Courtelle 3[4] oz balls in main shade, A
One oz in contrast, B
One pair No.10 needles
One large stitch holder
Four small buttons
Narrow ribbon, if required
Note K1y2rn is the abbreviation for insert needle as if to knit stitch, put yarn twice round needle, lift stitch over both loops in usual way.

Sleeves

Using No.10 needles and A, cast on 29[33]sts.
K1 row.
Next row K1, *yfwd, K2 tog, rep from * to end. K2 rows.
Next row K1[3], *inc, K2[1], rep from * to last 1[2]sts, inc [K2]. 39[47]sts.
Cont in 2-colour pattern.
1st row With A, K3, *K1y2rn, K3, rep from * to end.
2nd row With B, K3, *keeping yarn at back of work, sl 1 P dropping extra loop, K3, rep from * to end.
3rd row With B, K1, K1y2rn, K1, * yfwd, sl 1P, ybk, K1, K1y2rn, K1, rep from * to end.
4th row With A, keeping yarn at back of work, K1, sl 1P, K1, *K2, sl 1P, K1, rep from * to end.
5th row With A, K1, yfwd, sl 1P, ybk, *K1, K1y2rn, K1 yfwd, sl 1P, ybk, rep from * to last st, K1.
Rep 2nd-5th rows once more, then 2nd-4th rows once.
Continue with A only.
Next row K1, yfwd, sl 1P, ybk, K1, *K2, yfwd, sl 1P, ybk, K1, rep from * to end.
K2 rows.
Next row K1, yfwd, K1, *yfwd, K2 tog, rep from *.to last st, yfwd, K1. 41[49]sts.
K1 row.
1st patt row P1, *K1, P1, rep from * to end.
2nd patt row K.
Rep last 2 rows until sleeve measures 5[5¾]in, ending with a 2nd patt row.

Shape top
Keeping patt correct throughout, cast off 3[4]sts at beg of next 2 rows.
Dec 1 st at each end of next 4[5] RS rows. 27[31]sts.
Work 1 row.
Leave sts on holder until required.
Work the second sleeve in the same way as for the first.

Skirt

Using No. 10 needles and A, cast on 171[187]sts.
K1 row.
Next row K6, *yfwd, K2 tog, rep from * to last 5 sts, K5. K2 rows.
Next row K20, M1K, K to last 20 sts, M1K, K20. 173[189]sts.
Continue in 2-colour pattern.
1st row With A, K8, *K1y2rn, K3, rep from * to last 5 sts, K5.
2nd row K5 A, join in B, K3, *sl 1P, K3, rep from * to last 5 sts, join in length of A to work garter st border, K5 A. On patt rows when B is used, twist A and B round each other when changing colours to avoid a gap.
3rd row K5 A, with B, K1, K1y2rn, K1, *yfwd, sl 1P, ybk, K1, K1y2rn, K1, rep from * to last 5 sts, K5 A.
4th row With A, K6, sl 1P, K1, *K2, sl 1P, K1, rep from * to last 5 sts, K5.
5th row With A, K6, yfwd, sl 1P, ybk, K1, *K1y2rn, K1, yfwd, sl 1P, ybk, K1, rep from * to last 5 sts, K5.
Rep from 2nd-5th rows once more, then 2nd-4th rows once.
Next row With A, K6, yfwd, sl 1P, ybk, *K3, yfwd, sl 1P, ybk, rep from * to last 6 sts, K6.
Continue with A only.
K2 rows.
Next row K5, yfwd, K1, *yfwd, K2 tog, rep from * to last 5 sts, yfwd, K5. 175[191] sts. K1 row.
Next row K5, P1, *K1, P1, rep from * to last 5 sts, K5.
Next row K.
Rep last 2 rows until work measures 5¾[6¾] in from cast on edge.
Next row K2, yfwd, K2 tog, K1, P1, *K1, P1, rep from * to last 5 sts, K5.
Next row K.
Next row K5 patt 39[42], cast off 6[8] sts, patt 74[80], cast off 6[8]sts, patt 38[41], K5.
Work on last set of sts for Left Front.

Keeping garter st edge and patt correct, dec 1 st at armhole edge on next 4[5]RS rows.
Next row K6[8], *K2 tog, K2, rep from * to last 2 sts, K2 tog. 31[33]sts.
Leave sts on holder until required. With WS of work facing, rejoin yarn to centre group of sts for Back.
Keeping patt correct, dec 1 st at each end of next 4[5] RS rows.
Next row K2 tog[K0], *K3, K2 tog, rep from * to last 0[1]st, [K1]. 53[57]sts.
Leave rem sts on holder until required.
With WS of work facing, rejoin yarn to rem sts for Right Front. Keeping patt and garter st edge correct, dec 1 st at armhole edge on next 4[5] RS rows.
Next row K2 tog, *K2, K2 tog, rep from * to last 6[8] sts, K6[8]. 31[33]sts.

Yoke

1st row With A, K across 31[33]sts from Right Front holder, K27[31]sts from 1st sleeve, 53[57] from Back holder, 27[31] from 2nd sleeve and 31[33]sts from Left Front. 169[185] sts.
2nd row K5, yfwd, K3 tog, yfwd, *K2 tog, yfwd, rep from * to last 5 sts, K5.
3rd row K2, yfwd, K2 tog, K to end.
4th row K.
5th row K6[11], *K2 tog, K5, rep from * to last 9[13]. sts, K3 tog [K2 tog], K6[11]. 145[161]sts.
6th row K.
7th row K5, *K3, K1y2rn, rep from * to last 8 sts, K8.
Work as given for 2-colour patt at lower edge of coat, working from 2nd–5th rows once, then 2nd-4th rows once.
Next row K6[10], *yfwd, sl 1P, ybk, K3, rep from * to last 7[11]sts, yfwd, sl 1P, ybk, K6[10].
Next row K5[9], *K2 tog, K5, rep from * to last 7[12]sts, K2 tog, K5[10]. 125[140] sts.
K1 row.
Next row K2, yfwd, K2 tog, K to end.

▲ *The jacket in cream and green*

Top right: detail of the jacket

Jacket in yellow and white ►

Next row K5, K3 tog [K2 tog], *yfwd, K2 tog, rep from * to last 5 sts, K5. 123[139]sts.
K2 rows.

Next row K8 [10],K2 tog, *K6[7], K2 tog, rep from * to last 9[10]sts, K9[10]. 109[125]sts.

Next row K8, *Kly2rn, K3, rep from * to last 5 sts, K5. Work 2-colour patt as before by rep 2nd-5th rows as for Skirt, then 2nd-4th rows once.

Next row K6, *yfwd, sl 1P, ybk, K3, rep from * to last 7 sts, yfwd, sl 1P, ybk, K6.

Next row K2, yfwd, K2 tog, K1, *K1, K2 tog, rep from * to last 5[6] sts, K5[6]. 76[87] sts.
K1 row.

Next row K7[5], *yfwd, K2 tog, rep from * to last 5[6]sts, yfwd, K5[6].
K1 row. Cast off.

To make up

Join sleeve and raglan seams. Sew on buttons to correspond with buttonholes. Leave eyelets as lace pattern or thread with narrow ribbon, sewing ends to wrong side.

Chevron stripes for a little girl

Basic Wardrobe Knitting

The cleverly striped chevron patterned skirt and neat stocking stitch bodice make this delightful elfin dress ideal party wear for little girls up to four years old. The full skirt is shaped at the waist and the chevron pattern gives a scalloped edge to the hemline.

Sizes

To fit 20[22:24]in chest
Length to shoulder, 13½[15: 16½]in
Sleeve seam, 1½[2:2½]in
The figures in brackets [] refer to the 22 and 24in sizes respectively

Basic yarn tension
7 sts and 9 rows to 1in over st st worked on No.10 needles.

Materials shown here

Lister Lavenda Crisp Crepe 4 ply (1oz balls)
3[3:4] balls in main shade, A
2[2:2] balls in contrast, B
2[2:2] balls in contrast, C
1[1:1] balls in contrast, D
One pair No.10 needles
One pair No.11 needles
Three small buttons

Front

Using No.10 needles and D cast on 140[154:168] sts.
K 2 rows.
Commence patt.
1st row *K into front then into back of next st, K7[8:9], sl 1, K1, psso, K2 tog, K7[8:9], K into front then into back of next st, rep from * to end.
2nd row P.

116

Break off D.
These 2 rows form patt and are rep throughout skirt.
Continue in patt, working in stripes as follows:
14[16:18] rows C, 14[16:18] rows B, 14[16:18] rows A, 2[2:2] rows D, 8[10:12] rows C, 8 [10:12] rows B and 2[2:2] rows A.
Continue with A only.
1st and 3rd size
Next row *K2 tog, rep from * to end. 70[84] sts.
2nd size
Next row K1, *K2 tog, rep from * to last st, K1. [78] sts.
Beg with a P row work 3 rows st st.

Shape raglan
Cast off 1[2:3] sts at beg of next 2 rows.
Next row K1, sl 1, K1, psso, K to last 3 sts, K2 tog, K1.
Next row K1, P to last st, K1. **
Rep last 2 rows until 48 sts rem, ending with a WS row.

Shape neck
Next row K1, sl 1, K1, psso, K14 sts, turn.
Next row P to last st, K1.
Next row K1, sl 1, K1, psso, K to last 3 sts, K2 tog, K1.
Next row P to last st, K1.
Rep last 2 rows until all sts are worked off.
With RS of work facing, sl centre 14 sts on to a holder, rejoin A to rem sts and complete to match first side, reversing shaping.

Back

Work as given for Front to **
Rep last 2 rows until 50 sts rem, ending with a WS row.

Divide for back opening
Next row K1, sl 1, K1 psso, K29 sts, turn.
Next row K4, P to last st, K1.
Next row K1, sl 1, K1, psso, K to end.
Next row K4, P to last st, K1.
Next row (make buttonhole) K1, sl 1, K1, psso, K to last 3 sts, yfwd, K2 tog, K1.
Continue to shape raglan and work 4 sts in garter st at centre edge until 17 sts rem, working 2nd buttonhole as before on 14th row from previous buttonhole. Leave 17 sts on holder for back neck.
With RS facing, rejoin yarn to rem sts, cast on 4 sts, K to last 3 sts, K2 tog, K1.
Complete to match first side, reversing shaping, keeping 4 sts in garter st at centre edge and omitting buttonholes.

Sleeves

Using No.11 needles and A cast on 42[48:52] sts.
Work 6 rows K1, P1 rib.
Change to No.10 needles.
Beg with a K row continue in st st, inc one st at each end of 3rd and every following 4th row until there are 46[54:60] sts.
Continue without shaping until sleeve measures 1½[2:2½] in from beg, ending with a WS row.

Shape raglan
Cast off 1[2:3] sts at beg of next 2 rows.
Next row K1, sl 1, K1, psso, K to last 3 sts, K2 tog, K1.

Next row K1, P to last st, K1.
Rep last 2 rows until 6 sts rem.
Leave sts on holder.

Neckband

Join raglan seams.
Using No.11 needles and A, with RS facing, K across 17 sts on left back neck holder, K across 6 sts of left sleeve top, K up 16[18:20] sts down left front, K across 14 sts on holder at centre front, K up 16[18:20] sts up right front, K across 6 sts of right sleeve top and K across 17 sts of right back neck.
92[96:100] sts.
1st row K4, *K1, P1, rep from * to last 4 sts, K4.
Rep last row twice more.
4th row (make buttonhole) K4, *K1, P1, rep from * to last 4 sts, K1, yfwd, K2 tog, K1.
5th row As 1st.
6th row Cast off 4 sts, rib to last 4 sts, K4.
7th row Cast off 4 sts, rib to end.
Work 4 more rows in K1, P1 rib.
Cast off loosely in rib.

To make up

Press each piece on wrong side under a damp cloth with a warm iron.
Join side and sleeve seams.
Stitch underflap neatly in position at bottom of back opening.
Fold neckband in half to WS and sl st.
Sew on buttons. Press seams.

▼ *Pattern detail*　　　*Bright colours can look so pretty on little girls* ►

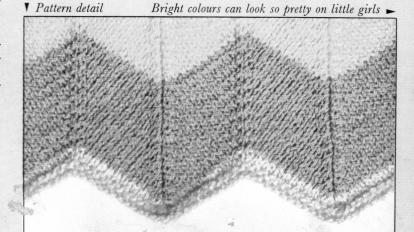

Drummer boy coat in fabric stitch

These delightful little coats are worked in a firm fabric stitch to give maximum proof against winter winds. The double breasted front fastening is worked separately and can be adapted for boy or girl. Contrast piping is made by working the invisible casting on method. Shoulder tabs and a back half belt give a military air.

Sizes
To fit a 20 [22:24] in chest
Length at centre back, 16¼ [17¾:19¼] in
Sleeve seam, 6½ [8½:10½] in
The figures in brackets [ ] refer to the 22 and 24 in sizes respectively

Basic yarn tension
Equivalent to a basic tension of 5½ sts and 7 rows to 1 inch measured over stocking stitch worked on No.8 needles.
Tension for this design
7½ sts and 13 rows on No.9 needles.

Materials shown here
Listers Lavenda Double Crepe 10 [12:14] oz in main shade, A
3oz in contrast, B
Two No.11 needles
Two No.9 needles
Two stitch holders
Ten medium buttons
Two small buttons
Small quantity of Double Knitting wool in any colour for casting on. This is removed afterwards.

Note
If the coat is being ... for a girl complete the Left Front first and mark the button positions on this front. The buttonholes are then worked on the right side. If making the coat for a boy, complete the Right Front first and work the buttonholes on the Left Front.

Back

Using No.11 needles and a length of odd wool, cast on 61 [67:73] sts. (This thread is removed later.)
** **Next row** With B, K1, * ywfd, K1, rep from * to end. 121 [133:145] sts.
Next row K1, * yfwd, sl1, ybk, K1, rep from * to end.
Next row Yfwd, sl1, ybk, * K1, yfwd, sl1, ybk, rep from * to end.
Rep last 2 rows once more. Break B and remove thread used for casting on.**
Using A and No.9 needles begin pattern.
1st row Sl1, K to end.
2nd row Sl1, K to end.
3rd row P1, * ybk, sl1, yfwd, P1, rep from * to end.
4th row K1, * yfwd, sl1, ybk, K1, rep from * to end.
These 4 rows form the pattern and are rep throughout.
Work 16 rows more.
1st dec row K29 [32:35], sl1, K1, psso, K2 tog, K55 [61:67], sl1, K1, psso, K2 tog, K29 [32:35].
Keeping pattern correct, work 15 rows more.
2nd dec row K28 [31:34], sl1, K1, psso, K2 tog, K53 [59:65], sl1, K1, psso, K2 tog, K28 [31:34].
Work 15 rows more.
Continue dec 4 sts in this way on next and every 16th row

until 89 [97:105] sts rem.
Work until 11 [12¼:13½] in, ending with a WS row.

Shape armholes
Cast off 4 [5:6] sts at beg of next 2 rows.
Dec one st at each end of next 6 rows, then next 0 [1:2] RS rows.
Work 46 [47:47] rows more.

Shape shoulders
Cast off 5 sts 0 [2:4] times and 4 sts 10 [8:6] times.
Cast off rem sts.

Left front

Using No.11 needles and a length of odd wool, cast on 37 [41:45] sts.
Work from ** to ** as for Back.
Next row With A, knit to last 22 [24:26] sts and leave these sts on holder for Front panel. Change to No.9 needles.
Continue in pattern as given for Back beginning with 2nd patt row. Work 19 rows.
1st dec row K29 [32:35], sl1, K1, psso, K2 tog, K18 [21:24].
Work 15 rows more.
2nd dec row K28 [31:34], sl1, K1, psso, K2 tog, K17 [20:23].
Work 15 rows more.
Continue dec 2 sts on next and every 16th row until 35 [39:43] sts rem.
Work until same length as Back to armhole, ending at side edge.

Shape armhole
1st row Cast off 4 [5:6] sts, patt to end.
Work one row.
Dec at armhole edge on next 6 rows then next 0 [1:2] RS rows.
Work 29 rows more without shaping.

Shape neck
Dec one st at centre front on next and every alt row until 20 [21:22] sts rem.
Work until same length as Back to shoulder, ending at the armhole edge.

Shape shoulder
Cast off 5 sts at beg of next 0 [1:2] alt rows and 4 sts at beg of next 5 [4:3] alt rows.

Right front

Cast on and work from ** to ** as for Left Front.
Next row With B and still using No.11 needles, K22 [24:26].
Slip these sts on to holder until required.
Continue in pattern with A and No.9 needles.
Work 20 rows.
1st dec row K18 [21:24], sl1, K1, psso, K2 tog, K29 [32:35].
Work 15 rows more.
2nd dec row K17 [20:23], sl1, K1, psso, K2 tog, K28 [31:34].
Work 15 rows more.
Continue as for Left Front, reversing all shapings.

Button strip

Slip 22 [24:26] sts from holder on to No.11 needles.
With B and RS work facing, K across sts from holder.
Continue in garter st (every row K) until strip is long enough to reach beg of neck shaping, when slightly stretched.
Cast off.
Mark positions for four groups of buttons.
Work strip on other side in same way working buttonholes as markers are reached as follows:
Right side facing, K3, cast off 3, K to last 6 sts, cast off 3, K2.
Next row K3, cast on 3, K to last 3 sts, cast on 3, K3.

Sleeves

Using No.11 needles and a length of odd wool cast on 25 [27:29] sts.
Work as for Back from ** to ** 49 [53:57] sts.
Continue on No.9 needles with A in 4 row patt as for Back.
Work 4 [4:12] rows.
Keeping pattern correct inc one st at each end of next and every 8th [8th:12th] row until there are 69 [73:77] sts.
Work until sleeve measures 6½ [8½:10½] in or required length.

Shape top
Cast off 4 [5:6] sts at beg of

next 2 rows.
Dec one st at each end of every RS row until 33 sts rem.
Dec one st at each end of next 7 rows.
Cast off.

Neckband

Join shoulder seams and sl st button and buttonhole strips to their respective sides.
Beginning 1 inch before seam of Front strip to Front with A, and using No. 9 needles, K up 7 sts from Right Front strip, K up 13 [14:15] sts up Right Front neck to shoulder, K up 21 [23:25] sts from Back, K up 13 [14:15] sts down Left Front neck and K up 7 sts from Left Front strip, finishing about 1 inch beyond Front strip seam to main section.
K one row.
Beginning with a 3rd patt row, work 6 rows in 4 row patt as for Back. Break A.
Change to No.11 needles and B.
1st row K1, * yfwd, sl1, ybk, K1, rep from * to end.
2nd row Yfwd, sl1, ybk, * K1, yfwd, sl1, ybk, rep from * to end.
Rep 1st and 2nd rows once.
Break B leaving a length of wool for working the invisible casting off.
Cast off using a wool needle as shown in Chapter 6.

Belt

With No.11 needles and B cast on 11 sts.
K 42 [48:54] rows. Cast off.

Shoulder tabs

With No.11 needles and B cast on 9 sts.
K 20 [22:24] rows.

Shape point
1st row K1, sl1, K1, psso, K to last 3 sts, K2 tog, K1,
K one row.
Rep last 2 rows once.
5th row K1, sl1, K2 tog, psso, K1.
6th row Sl1, K2 tog, psso, pull yarn through and finish off.
Work another tab in the same way.

▲ *Back view of the coats*

To make up

Press very lightly under a damp cloth with a warm iron.
Join side and sleeve seams.
Set in sleeves.
Fold edge of neckband sideways and sl st to cast off edge of Front strips.
Sew belt to centre back and sew a button at either end.
Stitch cast on edge of tabs close to sleeve seam at shoulder.
Sew point in place towards neckband and trim with a small button.
Sew buttons to correspond with buttonholes.
Press seams lightly.

Little drummer boy ►

▼ *Detail of invisible casting on*

Pinafore with jacquard pockets

The jacquard pockets of this pretty pinny are worked using separate balls of colour for each area to avoid weaving the yarn across the back of the work (see Knitting Know-how Chapter 33).

Sizes

To fit a 24[26:28:30]in chest
Length at centre back, 21[22:24:26]in, adjustable

Basic yarn tension
7 sts and 9 rows to 1in over st st worked on No.10 needles

Materials shown here

Sirdar 4 ply Fontein Crepe 8[9:11:12]oz main shade, A
Small quantities of contrasting colours for pockets
One pair No.10 needles
One pair No.12 needles
Set of four No.12 needles pointed at both ends
Stitch holder

Back

Using No.10 needles and A cast on 141[148:155:162] sts. Work 12 rows K1, P1 rib.
Beg with a K row continue in st st. Work 14 rows.
Next row K2 tog, K30 [32:34:36] sts, K2 tog tbl, K1, K2 tog, K67[70:73:76] sts, K2 tog tbl, K1, K2 tog, K to last 2 sts, K2 tog.
Beg with a P row work 13 rows without shaping.
Next row K2 tog, K28[30:32:34] sts, K2 tog tbl, K1, K2 tog, K65[68:71:74] sts, K2 tog tbl, K1, K2 tog, K to last 2 sts, K2 tog.

Beg with a P row work 13 rows without shaping.
Continue dec 6 sts in this way on next and every 14th row 6 times more.
Continue without shaping until work measures 15[16:17:18]in or required length to underarm, ending with a WS row.

Shape armholes

Cast off 4 sts at beg of next 2 rows, then dec one st at each end of every row until 63[68:73:78] sts rem.
Continue without shaping until armholes measure 6[6:7:7]in from beg, ending with a WS row.

Shape shoulders

Cast off 5 sts at beg of next 4 rows and 4[5:6:7] sts at beg of next 2 rows.
Cast off rem sts.

Front

Work as given for Back until work measures ½in less than Back to underarm, ending with a WS row.

Shape neck

Next row K38[41:44:47] sts, turn.
Leave rem sts on holder.
Dec one st at neck edge on every row 9[10:11:12] times in all, *at the same time* when work measures same as Back to underarm, shape armhole, ending with a WS row.

Shape armhole

Cast off 4 sts at beg of next row and dec one st at armhole edge on every row 11[12:13:14] times in all.

Continue without shaping until armhole measures same as Back to shoulder, ending at armhole edge.

Shape shoulder

Cast off at beg of next and following alt rows 5 sts twice and 4[5:6:7] sts once.
With RS work facing leave first 17[18:19:20] sts on holder for centre neck, rejoin yarn to rem sts and complete to match first side, reversing shaping.

To make up

Press under a damp cloth with a warm iron. Join shoulder seams.
Armbands. Using No.12 needles and A, with RS facing, K up 113[113:121:121] sts evenly around armhole. Work 8[8:10:10] rows K1, P1 rib, dec one st at each end of every 4th row. Cast off in rib.
Join side seams.
Neckband. Using set of four No.12 needles and A, with RS facing, K up 176[178:192:194] sts evenly around neck, including sts on holder. Work 8[8:10:10] rounds K1, P1 rib. Cast off in rib. Press seams.
Striped pockets. (make 2) Using No.10 needles and A cast on 30 sts.
Beg with a K row work in st st and stripes of 1 row B, 1 row A and 1 row C. Work 34 rows. Break off B and C and continue with A only. K 1 row. Work 5 rows K1, P1 rib. Cast off in rib.
Christmas tree pocket. (make 2) Using No.10 needles and A cast on 30 sts. Beg with a K row work in st st. Work 34 rows as given on chart using colours as given. Using A only work 6 rows K 1, P1 rib. Cast off in rib.
Boat and flower pocket. (make 2). As for Christmas tree pocket, following chart.
Windmill pocket. (make 2) Work as for Christmas tree pocket, following chart. Turn in narrow hem round edge of pockets and stitch to pinafore. Press pockets.

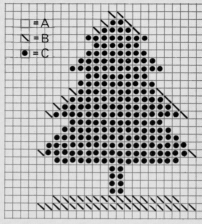

□ = A
◨ = B
● = C

▲ *Christmas tree* ▼ *flower charts*

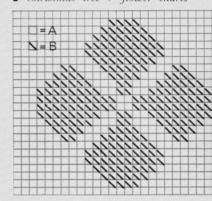

□ = A
◨ = B

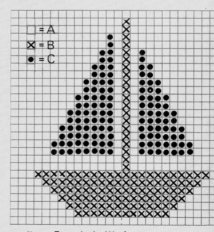

□ = A
✕ = B
● = C

▲ *Boat* ▼ *windmill charts*

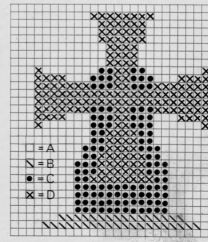

□ = A
◨ = B
● = C
✕ = D

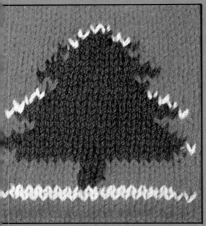

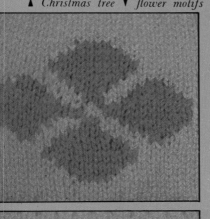

▲ *Christmas tree* ▼ *flower motifs*

▲ *Boat* ▼ *windmill motifs*

Fair Isle snow~suits

Keep out the cold with these cosy snow-suits for boys or girls. The zipped jacket has Fair Isle edges to match the hat and mitts in the next Basic Wardrobe chapter.

Sizes

To fit 24 [26:28:30] in chest
Jacket. Length to shoulder, 14½ [16:18:19½] in
Sleeve-seam, 10 [11:12½:13½] in
Trousers. To fit 25 [27:29:31] in hips
Front-seam, 9 [9:9½:9½] in
Leg-seam, 13½ [16½:19½:22½] in
The figures in brackets [ ] refer to the 26, 28 and 30in sizes respectively.

Basic yarn tension
5½ sts and 7½ rows to 1in over st st worked on No.8 needles.

Materials shown here:
Patons Double Knitting wool
Jacket. 5[5:6:7] 50g balls main shade A. Length of each contrasts B, C and D. 14 [16:18:20] in open-ended zip
Trousers. 5[5:6:7] balls main shade A, Length of elastic for waist and feet
One pair No.8 needles
One pair No.10 needles

Jacket

Back

Using No.10 needles and shade A, cast on 68[72:80:84] sts.
1st row K3, *P2, K2, rep from * to last st, K1.

122

2nd row K1, *P2, K2, rep from * to last 3 sts, P2, K1.
Rep 1st and 2nd rows 6 [7:6:8] times more, then 1st row once.
Next row Rib 12 [7:13:9] sts, (inc in next st, rib 20 [13:25:15] sts) 2 [4:2:4] times, inc in next st, rib to end.
71 [77:83:89] sts.
Change to No.8 needles.
Beg with a K row, continue in st st until work measures 9½ [10½:12:13] in from beg, ending with a P row.

Shape armholes

Cast off 3 sts at beg of next 2 rows.
Dec one st at each end of next and every alt row until 51 [55:59:63] sts rem.
Continue without shaping until work measures 14½ [16:18:19½] in from beg, ending with a P row.

Shape shoulders

Cast off 5 [5:6:6] sts at beg of next 4 rows, then 5 [6:5:6] sts at beg of next 2 rows.
Leave rem 21 [23:25:27] sts on holder.

Right front

Using No. 10 needles and shade A, cast on 32 [36:36:40] sts.
Work 15 [18:15:19] rows rib as given for Back.
24, 28 and 30in sizes only
Next row (Rib 10 [6:9] sts, inc in next st) 1 [3:2] times, rib to end. 33 [36:39:42] sts.
Change to No.8 needles.
Next row Cast off 12 sts, K to end. 21 [24:27:30] sts.
Beg with a P row, continue in st st until work measures same as Back to underarm, ending at side edge.

Shape armhole

Cast off 3 sts at beg of next row. Dec one st at armhole edge on next and every alt row until 11 [13:15:17] sts rem.
Continue without shaping until work measures same as Back to shoulder, ending at armhole edge.

Shape shoulder

24 and 26in sizes only
Cast off 5 [6] sts at beg of next row. Work 1 row. Cast off.

28 and 30in sizes only
Cast off 5 [5] sts at beg of next row and 5 [6] sts at beg of following alt row. Work 1 row. Cast off.

Left front

Using No.10 needles and shade A cast on 32 [36:36:40] sts.
Work 15 [18:15:19] rows rib as given for Back.
24, 28 and 30 in sizes only
Next row Rib 21 [15:20] sts, (inc in next st, rib 10 [6:9] sts) 1 [3:2] times. 33 [36:39:42] sts.
Change to No.8 needles and K to last 12 sts, cast off 12 sts. Break off yarn and rejoin to rem sts. Complete as given for Right front, reversing shapings.

Fair Isle bands

Using No.10 needles and shade A, with RS of Right front facing, K up 89 [97:113:121] sts along front edge.
Next row P.
Change to No.8 needles.
Working rows 1–12 from chart, keeping odd rows in K and even rows in P and working the odd st as indicated at end of K rows and beg of P rows, work 3 [3:1:1] rows from chart.

Shape neck

Cast off 8 [8:11:11] sts at beg of next row. Dec 1 st at neck edge on every alt row until 78 [86:98:106] sts rem, ending with a WS row.
Work last 2 rows from chart.
Break off contrasts B, C and D.
Change to No.10 needles.
K 1 row.
Work 2 rows of P1, K1 rib.

Cast off firmly in rib.
Using No.10 needles and shade A, with RS of Left front facing, K up 89 [97:113:121] sts along front edge.
Next row P.
Change to No.8 needles and work rows 1–12 from chart, shaping neck as follows:
Work 4 [4:2:2] rows from chart.
Cast off 8 [8:11:11] sts at beg of next row. Dec 1 st at neck edge on next and every alt row until 78 [86:98:106] sts rem.
Work last 2 rows from chart.
Break off contrasts B, C and D.
Change to No.10 needles.
K 1 row.
Work 2 rows of K1, P1 rib.
Cast off firmly in rib.

Sleeves

Using No.10 needles and shade A, cast on 32 [36:36:40] sts.
Work 15 [17:15:19] rows rib as given for Back.
Next row Work in rib, inc 4 [2:4:2] sts evenly across row. 36 [38:40:42] sts.
Change to No.8 needles.
Beg with a K row, continue in st st, inc one st at each end of 3rd [3rd:5th:3rd] and every following 7th row until there are 52 [56:60:64] sts.
Continue without shaping until work measures 10 [11:12½:13½] in, ending with a P row.

Shape top

Cast off 3 sts at beg of next 2 rows.
Dec one st at each end of next and every alt row until 32 [34:36:38] sts rem.
Cast off 3 sts at beg of next 6 [6:8:8] rows.
Cast off rem sts.

Neck border

Join shoulder seams.
Using No.10 needles and shade A, with RS facing, K up 23 [24:26:27] sts up right side of neck, K across sts on holder for Back inc 5 [5:7:7] sts evenly and K up 23 [24:26:27] sts down left side of neck.

72 [76:84:88] sts.
Beg with a 2nd row work
2½ [3½:4½:5½] in rib as given
for Back.
Cast off in rib.

Trousers (Right leg)

Using No.10 needles and
shade A, cast on 44 [48:52:56]
sts.
Work 10 rows rib as given for
Jacket back, inc 4 sts evenly
on last row. 48 [52:56:60] sts.
Change to No.8 needles.
1st row K.
2nd row P11 [12:13:14] sts,
sl 1P, P24 [26:28:30] sts,
sl 1P, P11 [12:13:14] sts.
Keeping sl st correct work
2 rows more.
Next row Inc in first st,
K22 [24:26:28], M1K, K2,
M1K, K to last st, inc in last st.
Work 8 [9:11:12] rows.
Next row Inc in first st,
work 24 [26:28:30], M1K,
work 2, M1K, work to last st,
inc in last st.
Continue inc in this way on
every following 9th [10th:
12th:13th] row until there are
84 [92:96:104] sts.
Continue without shaping
until work measures 12¾
[16:18¾:22] in from beg,
ending with a P row.
Inc one st at each end of next
and following 2 [1:2:1] rows.
90 [96:102:108] sts. Work 1
row.

Cosy set for winter days ▶

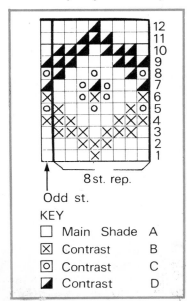

Fair Isle chart

Shape front and back edges
Cast off 2 sts at beg of next
2 rows.
Dec one st at each end of 3rd
and every following 4th row
until 68 [74:78:82] sts rem. **
Continue without shaping
until work measures 8 [8:8½:
8½] in from cast-off sts, ending
with a K row.

Shape back
1st row P48 [48:60:60] sts,
turn.
2nd and every alt row K.
3rd row P40 [40:50:50] sts,
turn.
5th row P32 [32:40:40] sts,
turn.
Continue in this way until
row P8 [8:10:10], turn,

has been worked.
Next row K.
Next row P across all sts.
Change to No.10 needles.
Work one row of K1, P1 rib.
Cast off in rib.

Left leg

Work as for Right leg to **.
Continue without shaping until
work measures 8 [8:8½:8½] in
from cast-off sts; ending with a
P row.

Shape back
1st row K48 [48:60:60] sts,
turn.
2nd and every alt row P.
Complete as given for Right
leg, reversing back shaping.

To make up

Press each piece under a damp
cloth using a warm iron.

Jacket
Stitch ends of front borders to
cast-off edge of ribbing. Join
side and sleeve seams and
set in sleeves. Fold neckband
in half to WS and sl st in place.
Sew in zip. Press seams.

Trousers
Fold legs at sl st and press
creases. Join front, back and
leg seams. Make casing stitch
at waist, insert elastic and join
ends. Stitch elastic at each side
of leg at ankles to go under
foot. Press seams.

Caps and mittens for snow~suits

These warm and cosy hat and mittens will ward off winter winds. They can be made as separates or to team with the matching jacket and trouser snow suits featured in the last Basic Wardrobe chapter. The hat can be worn as a pull-on version or made to include snug earflaps, tying under the chin. Both mitts and hat are trimmed with Fair Isle and made in strong, clear colours.

Sizes
Hat. Width all round lower edge, 18 [20] in
Mitts. Width all round above thumb, 6 [7] in
The figures in brackets [ ] refer to the larger size

Basic yarn tension
$5\frac{1}{2}$ sts and $7\frac{1}{2}$ rows to 1in over st st worked on No.8 needles
---

Materials shown here:
Patons Double Knitting wool
Hat. 2[2] 50g balls main shade A, 1[1] ball each of contrasts B, C and D
Mitts. 2[2] balls main shade A
Oddments of contrasts B, C and D
One pair No.8 needles
One pair No.10 needles

Hat

Using No.10 needles and A, cast on 128 [144] sts.
Work 4 rows K1, P1 rib, inc 1 st at end of last row.
Change to No.8 needles.
Work rows 1–12 from chart.

Break off contrast yarns B, C and D.
Change to No.10 needles.
K 1 row, dec 1 st at beg of row. Work 3in K1, P1 rib, ending with RS facing, to reverse work.
Next row P6 [2], *P2 tog, P4, rep from * to last 8 [4] sts, P2 tog, P6 [2]. 108 [120] sts.
Change to No.8 needles.
Beg with a K row, work $1\frac{1}{2}$ [2] in st st, ending with a P row.

Shape top
1st row (K7 [8] sts, K2 tog) 12 times.
2nd and every alt row P.
3rd row (K6 [7] sts, K2 tog) 12 times.
5th row (K5 [6] sts, K2 tog) 12 times.
7th row (K4 [5] sts, K2 tog) 12 times.
9th row (K3 [4] sts, K2 tog) 12 times.
11th row (K2 [3] sts, K2 tog) 12 times.
13th row (K1 [2] sts, K2 tog) 12 times.

2nd size only
15th row (K1, K2 tog) 12 times.

Both sizes
Next row (K2 tog) 12 times. 12 sts.
Break yarn, thread through rem sts, draw up and fasten off securely.

Ear flaps
Using No.10 needles and A, cast on 21 sts.
1st row K2, *P1, K1, rep from * to last st, K1.
2nd row *K1, P1, rep from

* to last st, K1.
Rep 1st and 2nd rows 8 times more.
Next row K1, K2 tog tbl, rib to last 3 sts, K2 tog, K1.
Next row K1, P2 tog, rib to last 3 sts, P2 tog tbl, K1.
Rep last 2 rows until 7 sts rem.
Continue without shaping on these sts for 7in. Cast off.

To make up

Press Fair Isle border under a damp cloth with a warm iron.
Join seam. Turn border to right side $\frac{1}{2}$in above ribbing.
Using contrast yarns, make a large pompon (see Crochet Know-how page 196) and stitch to centre of crown.
Attach ear flaps.
Press seams.

Mitts

Right hand
Using No.10 needles and A, cast on 40 [48] sts.
Work 4 rows K1, P1 rib, inc 1 st at end of last row.
Change to No.8 needles.
Work rows 1–12 from chart.
Break off contrast yarns.
Change to No.10 needles.
K 1 row, dec 1 st at beg of row.
Work 3in K1, P1 rib, ending with RS facing, to reverse work.
Next row P4 [3], *P2 tog, P3, rep from * to last 6 [5] sts, P2 tog, P4 [3]. 33 [39] sts.
Change to No.8 needles.
Beg with a K row, work 2 [4] rows st st.**

Shape thumb
1st row K18 [21], K up 1, K1, K up 1, K14 [17].
Work 3 rows.
Next row K18 [21], K up 1, K3, K up 1, K14 [17].
Work 3 rows.
Continue inc in this way until there are 41 [47] sts.
Work 1 row.
Next row K27 [30] sts, turn.
Next row P9, cast on 2 sts, turn.
Work 10 [12] rows on these 11 sts.

Shape top
1st row K2 tog tbl, K2, sl 1, K2 tog, psso, K2, K2 tog.
2nd row P.
3rd row K2 tog tbl, sl 1, K2 tog, psso, K2 tog.
Break yarn and thread through rem sts, draw up and fasten off.
With RS work facing, K up 2 sts from 2 cast-on sts at base of thumb, K14 [17].
Next row P across all 34 [40] sts. Beg with a K row, continue in st st until work measures $4\frac{1}{2}$ [5] in from end of ribbing.

Shape top
1st row K2, (K2 tog, K10 [13], K2 tog tbl, K2) twice.
2nd and every alt row P.
3rd row K2, (K2 tog, K8 [11], K2 tog tbl, K2) twice.
5th row K2, (K2 tog, K6 [9], K2 tog tbl, K2) twice.
7th row K2, (K2 tog, K4 [7], K2 tog tbl, K2) twice.
Break yarn and thread through rem sts, draw up and fasten off.

Left hand
Work as for right hand to **.

Shape thumb
Next row K14 [17], K up 1, K1, K up 1, K18 [21].
Work 3 rows.
Next row K14 [17], K up 1, K3, K up 1, K18 [21].
Work 3 rows.
Continue inc in this way until there are 41 [47] sts.
Work 1 row.
Next row K23 [26] sts, turn.
Next row Cast on 2 sts, P9, turn. Complete thumb as for Right hand.
With RS facing, K up 2 sts from 2 cast-on sts at base of thumb, K18 [21].
Next row P across all 34 [40] sts. Complete as for Right hand.

To make up

Press as given for Hat.
Join thumb and side-seam.
Fold border to right side $\frac{1}{2}$in above ribbing.
Press seams.

Fair Isle trimmed hat and mittens to team with snow suits ►

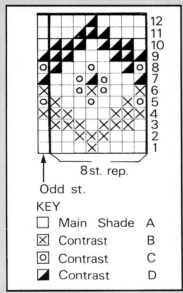

8 st. rep.

↑
Odd st.

KEY

☐	Main Shade	A
☒	Contrast	B
⊙	Contrast	C
◪	Contrast	D

Fair Isle chart ▲ *and detail* ▼

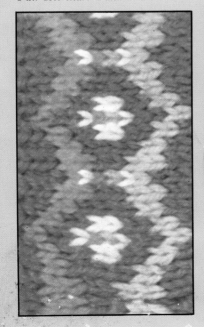

Striped sweater with raglan sleeves

Striped sweaters for a boy or a girl are child's play to knit in simple stocking stitch, and the round neckline and the easy fitting raglan sleeves make them ideal garments for indoor and outdoor play. Although stripes in contrasting colours or closely toning colours have a sporty look, the pattern can be worked in a single colour to make a simple classic sweater. The instructions cover a wide size range.

Sizes

To fit 24[26:28:30:32] inch chest
Side seam, 7½[9:10:11:12½]in
Sleeve seam, 9[10½:12¼:13½:15] in
The figures in brackets [ ] refer to the 26, 28, 30 and 32in sizes respectively.

Basic yarn tension

6 sts and 8 rows to 1in over st. st. worked on No.8 needles

Materials

Madame Pingouin (50g balls)
3[4:4:4:4] balls in main shade A
3[3:3:3:4] balls in contrast colour B, or 5[6:7:7:8] balls for a plain jersey.
One pair No.10 needles
One pair No.8 needles
One large Aero stitch holder

Back

Using No.10 needles and A, cast on 80[86:92:98:104]sts.
Work 14[16:18:18:18] rows K1, P1 rib.

Change to No.8 needles and st st.
Beg with a K row, work in stripes as follows:
1st-6th rows With A.
7th-10th rows With B.
11th-12th rows With A.
13th-14th rows With B.
15th-16th rows With A.
17th-18th rows With B.
19th-20th rows with A.
21st-24th rows With B.
These 24 rows form the patt and are rep throughout.
Work 24[34:40:48:60] more rows of patt, ending with a 24th [10th:16th:24th:12th] patt row.

Work raglan shaping

Cast off 1[1:2:2:3] sts at beg of next 2 rows.
3rd row K2, sl 1P, K1, psso, K to last 4 sts, K2 tog, K2.
4th row P.
Keeping striped patt correct, rep last 2 rows until 30[32:34:36:38]sts rem, ending with a P row.
Leave rem sts on holder.

Front

Work as for Back until 42[44:46:48:50] sts rem on raglan shaping, ending with a P row.

Shape neck

1st row K2, K2 tog tbl, K10, turn. Work right shoulder on these sts.
** Keeping raglan shaping correct as before, dec one st at neck edge on next 6 rows. Continue raglan shaping until 3 sts rem. End with WS row.**
Next row K1, K2 tog.
Last row P2 tog. Draw yarn through and fasten off.

With RS facing, slip centre 14[16:18:20:22]sts on to holder. Rejoin yarn to rem sts and work to end of row.
Work from ** to ** as for right shoulder.
Next row K2 tog, K1.
Last row P2 tog. Draw yarn through and fasten off.

Sleeves

Using No.10 needles and A, cast on 38 [40:42:44:46] sts.
Work 14[18:18:20:20] rows K1, P1 rib, inc one st at each end of last row.
Change to No.8 needles and st st. Continue working in striped patt as for Back, beg with 15th[15th:7th:7th:7th] patt row and inc one st at each end of 3rd and every 6th[6th:8th:8th:8th] row until there are 56[60:64:68:72]sts.
Work without shaping until next 24th[10th.16th:24th:12th] patt row has been completed.

Shape raglan

Cast off 1[1:2:2:3] sts at beg of next 2 rows.
3rd row K2, sl 1P, K1, psso, K to last 4 sts, K2 tog, K2.
4th row P.
Rep last 2 rows until 8 sts rem, ending with a P row.
Leave rem sts on holder.

Neckband

Using No.10 needles and A and with RS facing, K across 30[32:34:36:38]sts from Back neck, K across 8 sts from left sleeve top, K up 12 sts down neck, K across 14[16:18:20:22] sts from centre front, K up 12 sts up neck and K across 8 sts from right sleeve top. 84[88:92:96:100]sts.
Work 16[16:18:18:18] rows K1, P1 rib.
Cast off in rib.

To make up

DO NOT PRESS
Join raglan, side and sleeve seams. Fold neckband in half to WS and slip st.

Warm enough to wear outdoors ▶

Sweaters and caps in Aran

Basic Wardrobe Knitting

Warm and practical, this teenage outfit is suitable for both boys and girls. The simple design is ideal for a first attempt at Aran.

Sizes

To fit 30[32:34:36]in chest
Length to shoulder, 18[20¼:21:21¾]in
Sleeve seam, 14½[15:15½:16]in
The figures in brackets [ ] refer to the 32, 34 and 36in sizes respectively

> **Basic yarn tension**
> 4½ sts and 7 rows to 1in over st st worked on No.7 needles

Materials shown here

Robin Aran Knitting
Sweater with round neck.
10[10:11:12] 50g balls
Sweater with polo neck.
11[11:12:13] balls
Cap
2[2:2:2] 50g balls
One pair No.7 needles
One pair No.9 needles
One pair No.10 needles
One cable needle
One stitch holder

Sweater back

Using No.10 needles cast on 81[89:93:101] sts.
1st row K1 tbl, *P1, K1 tbl, rep from * to end.
2nd row P1, *K1 tbl, P1, rep from * to end.
Rep these 2 rows until twisted rib measures 2[2:2½:2½]in, ending with a 1st row.
Next row Rib 7[11:11:15], K up 1, rib 9, P up 1, rib 7,
P up 1, rib 10, K up 1, rib 8[8:10:10], P up 1, rib 8 [8:10:10], K up 1, rib 9, P up 1, rib 7, P up 1, rib 9, K up 1, rib 7[11:11:15].
90[98:102:110] sts.
Change to No.7 needles. Commence patt.
1st patt row K2, (P2, K2) 1[2:2:3] times, P2, sl next 2 sts on to cable needle and hold at back of work, K next st, K2 from cable needle, K1, sl next st on to cable needle and hold at front of work, K next 2 sts, K1 from cable needle—called C7—P2, Tw2F, P5, Tw2B, P2, C7, P2, (Tw2F, Tw2B) 4[4:5:5] times, P2, C7, P2, Tw2F, P5, Tw2B, P2, C7, P2, K2, (P2, K2) 1[2:2:3] times.
2nd patt row (K2, P2) 1[2:2:3] times, K4, P7, K2, P9, K2, P7, K2, P16[16:20:20], K2, P7, K2, P9, K2, P7, K4, (P2, K2) 1[2:2:3] times.
3rd patt row K2, (P2, K2) 1[2:2:3] times, P2, K7, P2, Tw2F, K5, Tw2B, P2, K7, P2, (Tw2B, Tw2F) 4[4:5:5] times, P2, K7, P2, Tw2F, K5, Tw2B, P2, K7, P2, K2, (P2, K2) 1[2:2:3] times.
4th patt row As 2nd patt row. These 4 rows form patt and are rep throughout the Back and Front.
Continue in patt until work measures 12[14:14½:15]in from beg, or required length to underarm, ending with a WS row.

Shape armholes

Cast off 5[6:6:7] sts at beg of next 2 rows.
Dec one st at each end of every RS row until 76[78:80:82] sts rem.
Continue without shaping until armholes measure 6[6¼:6½:6¾]in, ending with a WS row.

Shape shoulders

Cast off at beg of next and every row 5 sts 6[4:4:2] times and 6 sts 2[4:4:6] times.
Cast off rem sts.

Sweater front

Work as given for Back until armholes measure 4¼[4½:4½:4¾]in, ending with a RS row.

Shape neck

1st row Patt 30[31:31:32] sts, cast off centre 16[16:18:18] sts, patt 29[30:30:31] sts.
Complete left shoulder first.
** Dec one st at neck edge on next 7 rows then one st on every RS row until 21 [22:22:23] sts rem.
Continue without shaping until armhole measures same as Back to shoulder, ending at armhole edge.

Shape shoulder

Cast off at beg of next and following alt rows 5 sts 3[2:2:1] times and 6 sts 1[2:2:3] times. **
With RS of work facing rejoin yarn to rem shoulder sts and work right shoulder as for left shoulder from ** to **.

Sleeves

Using No.10 needles cast on 43[43:47:47] sts.
Work 2[2:2½:2½]in twisted rib as given for Back.
Change to No.7 needles and patt.
1st patt row K2[2:0:0], *(P2, K2) 1[1:2:2] times, P2, C7, P2, Tw2F, P5, Tw2B, P2, C7, P2, (K2, P2) 1[1:2:2] times, K2[2:0:0].
2nd patt row K2[2:0:0], (P2, K2) 1[1:2:2] times, K2, P7, K2, P9, K2, P7, K2, (K2, P2) 1[1:2:2] times, K2[2:0:0].
3rd patt row K2[2:0:0], (P2, K2) 1[1:2:2] times, P2,
K7, P2, Tw2F, K5, Tw2B, P2, K7, P2, (K2, P2) 1[1:2:2] times, K2[2:0:0].
4th patt row As 2nd.
Continue in patt, inc one st at each end of next and every following 8th row, working extra sts into double moss st side panels as they are made, until there are 59[63:65:69] sts.
Continue without shaping until sleeve measures 14½[15:15½:16]in from beg, or required length to underarm ending with a WS row.

Shape top

Cast off 5[6:6:7] sts at beg of next 2 rows.
Dec one st at each end of next 6 rows, then each end of every RS row until 27 sts rem.
Cast off 3 sts at beg of next 4 rows. Cast off rem 15 sts.

Neckband or polo collar

Join right shoulder seam.
Using No.10 needles and with RS of work facing, K up 20 [20:22:22] sts down left front neck, K up 16[16:18:18] sts from centre front, K up 20 [20:22:22] sts from right front neck and K up 34 [34:36:36] sts from centre back.
Work in twisted rib as given for Back, working 2in for neckband and 6in for polo collar. Cast off in rib.

To make up

Join left shoulder and neckband or collar. Turn neckband in half to WS and sl st.

Seam sleeves and set into armholes. Join side seams. Press lightly under a damp cloth with a warm iron if required, omitting ribbing.

Cap

Using No.9 needles cast on 97 sts.
Work 5 rows twisted rib as given for Sweater back.
6th row Rib 3, *K up 1, rib 2, K up 1, rib 7, K up 1,

128

rib 2, K up 1, rib 5, rep
from * to last 14 sts, K up 1,
rib 2, K up 1, rib 7, K up 1,
rib 2, K up 1, rib 3.
Change to No.7 needles.
1st row *P3, Tw2B, P2,
C7, P2, Tw2F, P2, rep from
* to last st, P1.
2nd row *P5, K2, P7, K2,
P4, rep from * to last st, P1.
3rd row *K3, Tw2B, P2, K7,
P2, Tw2F, K2, rep from *
to last st, K1.
4th row As 2nd.
Rep 1st, 2nd and 3rd rows
once more.
8th row *P3, P up 1, P2,
K2, P7, K2, P2, P up 1,
P2, rep from * to last st, P1.
9th row *P4, Tw2B, P2,
C7, P2, Tw2F, P3, rep from
* to last st, P1.
Continue in patt, noting that
there will now be 2 extra
sts on ladder panels.
Work 10 rows in patt for
Him and 14 rows in patt
for Her.

Shape top
1st dec row *P2, P2 tog tbl,
P2, K2, P7, K2, P2, P2 tog,
P1, rep from * to last st, P1.
Work 5 rows without shaping
noting that there will be 2 sts
less on each ladder panel.
2nd dec row *P1, P2 tog
tbl, P2, K2, P7, K2, P2,
P2 tog, rep from * to last
st, P1.
Work 3 rows without shaping.
3rd dec row P2 tog, *P2,
K2, P7, K2, P2, P3 tog,
rep from * to last 17 sts,
P2, K2, P7, K2, P2, P2 tog.
Work 3 rows without shaping.
4th dec row P2 tog, *P1,
K2, P7, K2, P1, P3 tog, rep
from * to last 15 sts, P1, K2,
P7, K2, P1, P2 tog.
5th dec row K2 tog, *P2,
K7, P2, sl 1, K2 tog, psso,
rep from * to last 13 sts,
P2, K7, P2, K2 tog.
Next row *P1, K2, P7, K2,
rep from * to last st, P1.
6th dec row P2 tog, *P1,
C7, P1, P3 tog, rep from * to
last 11 sts, P1, K7, P1, P2 tog.
Next row *K2, P7, K1,
rep from * to last st, K1.
7th dec row P2 tog, *K7,
P3 tog, rep from * to last
9 sts, K7, P2 tog.

▲ *The Aran sweaters with round or polo neckline and teamed with matching Aran knit cap*

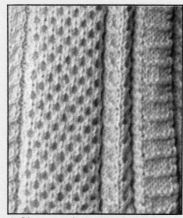

▲ *Close-up of the stitch detail*

Next row *K1, P7, rep from
* to last st, K1.
Next row *P1, C7, rep from
* to last st, P1.
8th dec row *K1, P1,
P2 tog, P1, P2 tog tbl, P1, rep
from * to last st, K1.
9th dec row *P1, K1, sl 1,
K2 tog, psso, K1, rep from
* to last st, P1.

10th dec row *K1, P3 tog,
rep from * to last st, K1.
11th dec row *P1, sl 1,
K2 tog, psso, rep from * to
last st, P1.
Break off yarn, thread
through rem sts and draw
up. Fasten off.

Brim

Using No.9 needles cast on
3 sts.
1st row K1, K1 putting yarn
twice round needle—called
K1y2rn—K1.
2nd row P1, sl 1 dropping
extra yarn, P1.
3rd row K1, K up 1,
K1y2rn, K up 1, K1.
4th row P2, sl 1 dropping
extra yarn, P2.
5th row K1, K up 1, K1,
K1y2rn, K1, K up 1, K1.
6th row P3, sl 1 dropping
extra yarn, P3.
Continue inc 2 sts in this way

on every K row until there
are 19 sts.
Keeping centre st correct
work 3 rows.
Next row K1, K up 1, K8,
K1y2rn, K8, K up 1, K1.
Keeping centre st correct
work 15 rows without shaping.
Keeping centre st correct dec
one st at each end of next
row. Work 3 rows.
Dec one st at each end of
next and every K row until
3 sts rem. Cast off.

To make up

Press pieces lightly under a
damp cloth with a warm
iron, omitting ribbing.
Seam cap from centre top
to edge.
Fold brim in half lengthwise
along sl st foldline. Sew one
long edge to centre of cap.
Sl st other long edge beneath
first.

Aran poncho and matching beret

A jaunty teenage Aran poncho and cap, designed to help you to practise Aran stitches without having to cope with complicated shaping at the same time. The poncho is made in two simple, separate strips and has a neatly fitting ribbed neckband.

Size
Each piece of the poncho measures 31in by 16½in, after pressing
Beret. To fit 20½ to 21½in circumference measured around the head

---
Tension for this design
9½ sts and 12 rows to 2in over st st worked on No.6 needles

Materials shown here
Mahony's Blarney Bainin
12 50g balls
One pair No.6 needles
One pair No.9 needles
One cable needle
One No.3·50 (ISR) crochet hook

Poncho

Using No.6 needles cast on 145 sts.
P 1 row.
Commence patt.
1st row K2, *K1 tbl, P3, K1 tbl, P2, K1 tbl, P3, K1 tbl, P11, K1 tbl, P3, K1 tbl, P2, K1 tbl, P3, K1 tbl, *, p7, sl next 2 sts onto cable needle and hold at front of work, K2, K2 from cable needle—called C4F—,P7, **, rep from * to ** once more, then from * to * once more, K2.

2nd row K2, *P1 tbl, K3, P1 tbl, K2, P1 tbl, K3, P1 tbl, K1, (K1, P1, K1 all into next st—called 3 in 1—, P3 tog) twice, 3 in 1, K1, P1 tbl, K3, P1 tbl, K2, P1 tbl, K3, P1 tbl, *, K7, P4, K7, **, rep from * to ** once more, then from * to * once more, K2. (151 sts).
3rd row K2, *K1 tbl, P3, K1 tbl, P2, K1 tbl, P3, K1 tbl, P13, K1 tbl, P3, K1 tbl, P2, K1 tbl, P3, K1 tbl, *, P6, sl next st onto cable needle and hold at back of work, K2, P1 from cable needle—called C3B—, sl next 2 sts onto cable needle and hold at front of work, P1, K2 from cable needle—called C3F—, P6, **, rep from * to ** once more, then from * to * once more, K2.
4th row K2, *P1 tbl, K3, P1 tbl, K2, P1 tbl, K3, P1 tbl, K1, (P3 tog, 3 in 1) twice, P3 tog, K1, P1 tbl, K3, P1 tbl, K2, P1 tbl, K3, P1 tbl, *, K6, P2, K2, P2, K6, **, rep from * to ** once more, then from * to * once more, K2. (145 sts).
5th row K2, *K1 tbl, P3, K1 tbl, P2, K1 tbl, P3, K1 tbl, P11, K1 tbl, P3, K1 tbl, P2, K1 tbl, P3, K1 tbl, *, P5, C3B, P2, C3F, P5, **, rep from * to ** once more, then from * to * once more, K2.
6th row K2, *P1 tbl, K3, P1 tbl, K2, P1 tbl, K3, P1 tbl, K1, (3 in 1, P3 tog) twice, 3 in 1, K1, P1 tbl, K3, P1 tbl, K2, P1 tbl, K3, P1 tbl, *, K5, P2, K4, P2, K5, **, rep from * to ** once more, then from * to * once more, K2. (151 sts).

7th row K2, *K1 tbl, P3, sl next st onto cable needle and hold at front, P1, K1 tbl from cable needle—called C2F—, sl next st onto cable needle and hold at back, K1 tbl, P1 from cable needle—called C2B—,P3, K1 tbl, P13, K1 tbl, P3, C2F, C2B, P3, K1 tbl, *, P4, C3B, P4, C3F, P4, **, rep from * to ** once more, then from * to * once more, K2.
8th row K2, *P1 tbl, K4, (P1 tbl) twice, K4, P1 tbl, K1, (P3 tog, 3 in 1) twice, P3 tog, K1, P1 tbl, K4, (P1 tbl) twice, K4, P1 tbl, *, K4, P2, K6, P2, K4, **, rep from * to ** once more, then from * to * once more, K2. (145 sts).
9th row K2, *K1 tbl, P4, sl next st onto cable needle and hold at front, K1 tbl, K1 tbl from cable needle—called C2F tbl—, P4, K1 tbl, P11, K1 tbl, P4, C2Ftbl, P4, K1 tbl, *, P3, C3B, P6, C3F, P3, **, rep from * to ** once more, then from * to * once more, K2.
10th row K2, *P1 tbl, K4, (P1 tbl) twice, K4, P1 tbl, K1, (3 in 1, P3 tog) twice, 3 in 1, K1, P1 tbl, K4, (P1 tbl) twice, K4, P1 tbl, *, K3, P2, K8, P2, K3, **, rep from * to ** once more, then from * to * once more, K2. (151 sts).
11th row K2, *K1 tbl, P3, C2B, C2F, P3, K1 tbl, P13, K1 tbl, P3, C2B, C2F, P3, K1 tbl, *, P2, C3B, P8, C3F, P2, **, rep from * to ** once more, then from * to * once more, K2.
12th row K2, *P1 tbl, K3, P1 tbl, K2, P1 tbl, K3, P1 tbl, K1, (P3 tog, 3 in 1) twice, P3 tog, K1, P1 tbl, K3, P1 tbl, K2, P1 tbl, K3, P1 tbl, *, K2, P2, K10, P2, K2, **, rep from * to ** once more, then from * to * once more, K2. (145 sts).
These 12 rows form patt and are rep throughout.
Keeping 2 sts in g st at each end, rep patt rows 5 times more.

Shape shoulder
Next row Patt 78 sts, *K1 tbl, P2 tog, P1, K1 tbl, P2, K1 tbl, P1, P2 tog, K1 tbl, *, P2 tog, P5, C4F, P5, P2 tog,

rep from * to * once more, patt next 11 sts, rep from * to * once more, K2. (137 sts).
Continue in patt for 23 more rows, noting that there will now be one st less at each side of last 3 chain cable and V panels.
Next row Cast off 78 sts, K to end. (59 sts).
Change to No.9 needles.

Neck border
1st row *K1, P1, rep from * to last st, K1.
2nd row P1, sl 1, K1, psso, *K1, P1, rep from * to last 4 sts, K1, K2 tog, P1.
3rd row K1, P1, *P1, K1, rep from * to last 3 sts, P2, K1.
4th row P1, sl 1, K1, psso, *P1, K1, rep from * to last 4 sts, P1, K2 tog, P1.
Rep last 4 rows once more, then 1st and 2nd rows once more.
Cast off in rib.
Work another piece in same way.

To make up

Press pieces under a damp cloth with a warm iron.
Join side edge of first piece to cast off edge of 2nd piece, and side edge of 2nd piece to cast off edge of first piece, including neck border edges.
Fringe. Cut a piece of stiff cardboard 1¾in wide and 5in long. Hold upright in left hand and knot yarn round near top. Using No.3·50 (ISR) hook, put hook under loop and draw yarn through then under yarn and draw loop through again, *wind yarn round card from front to back, hook under loop at front then under yarn at back, draw through loop then draw through 2 loops on hook, rep from * for required length, slipping loops off card as it becomes full. When fringe fits all round poncho, break yarn but do not fasten off last st and leave a few yards of yarn for adjustment. Rejoin yarn at other end and work 1dc into each st of fringe, adjusting length if necessary. Top st round edges of poncho.

Beret

Using No.9 needles cast on 91 sts.

Work 9 rows K1, P1 rib.

Next row P45 sts, P2 tog, P44 sts. (90 sts).

Change to No.6 needles.

1st row (RS) P.

2nd row K1, *3 in 1, P3 tog, rep from * to last st, K1.

3rd row P.

4th row K1, *P3 tog, 3 in 1, rep from * to last st, K1.

5th row As 1st.

6th row As 2nd.

7th row *P3, K1 tbl, P2, K1 tbl, P3, rep from * to end.

8th row *K3, P1 tbl, K2, P1 tbl, K3, rep from * to end.

Rep 7th and 8th rows twice more.

13th row *P3, C2F, C2B, P3, rep from * to end.

14th row *K4, (P1 tbl) twice, K4, rep from * to end.

15th row *P4, C2Ftbl, P4, rep from * to end.

16th row As 14th.

17th row *P3, C2B, C2F, P3, rep from * to end.

18th row As 8th.

Rep rows 7-18 once more.

Shape top

1st dec row P1, P2 tog, *K1 tbl, P2, K1 tbl, P2 tog, P2, P2 tog, rep from * to last 7 sts, K1 tbl, P2, K1 tbl, P2 tog, P1 (72 sts).

Work 3 rows rib tbl as now set, without shaping.

2nd dec row P2 tog, *rib 4, (P2 tog) twice, rep from * to last 6 sts, rib 4, P2 tog. (54 sts).

Work 3 rows rib tbl.

3rd dec row P1, *K1 tbl, P2 tog, rep from * to last 2sts, K1 tbl, P1. (37 sts).

Work 2 rows rib tbl.

4th dec row P1, *P2 tog, rep from * to end. (19 sts). Thread yarn through rem sts, draw up and fasten off.

To make up

Press lightly under a damp cloth with a warm iron. Join seam. Make a tassel or pompon and sew to top.

◄ *Poncho featuring a simple Aran cable pattern*

Frog-fastened coat and hat

Basic Wardrobe Knitting

This gently shaped knitted coat with matching pull-on hat will please any fashion-conscious teenage girl. The smart frog fastenings can be made in either matching or contrasting yarn or purchased ready made.

Sizes

To fit 34[36:38]in bust
Length at centre back, 35[36:37]in, adjustable
Sleeve seam, 17in, adjustable
Hat. To fit average head
The figures in brackets [] refer to the 36 and 38in sizes respectively
NB. If a coat longer than the length given for each size is required, allow an extra ball of yarn for each 1½ in in depth. If the hat is made separately allow 3 balls of yarn

---

Basic yarn tension
4½ sts and 6½ rows to 1in worked over st st on No.6 needles

Materials shown here

Wendy Diabolo Double-double Knit
22[23:24]50g balls
One pair No.5 needles
One pair No.6 needles
Four buttons
One No.3·50 (ISR) crochet hook

Coat back

Using No.6 needles, cast on 99[103:107] sts.
1st row *K1, P1, rep from * to last st, K1.
Rep 1st row 9 times more for moss st hem.

Change to No.5 needles.
Next row K15[17:19] sts, *K2 tog, K14, rep from * 4 times more, K to end. 94[98:102] sts.
Beg with a P row, work 37[41:45] rows st st.
Adjust length here.

Shape darts
1st dec row K20, sl 1, K1, psso, K to last 22 sts, K2 tog, K20.
Beg with a P row, work 7 rows st st.
Rep last 8 rows 7 times more. 78[82:86] sts.
Continue without shaping until work measures 26[26½:27] in from beg, or required length to underarm ending with a P row.

Shape armholes
Cast off 5 sts at beg of next 2 rows.
Dec one st at each end of next and following 3 alt rows. 60[64:68] sts.
Continue without shaping until armholes measure 7¼[7¾:8¼]in from beg, ending with a P row.

Shape shoulders
Cast off at beg of next and foll rows 6 sts twice, 6[7:7] sts twice and 6[7:8] sts twice.
Cast off rem 24[24:26] sts.

Coat left front

Using No.6 needles, cast on 51[53:57] sts.
Work 10 rows moss st as given for Back.
Change to No.5 needles.
Next row K15[18:21] sts, K2 tog, K14[25:14], K2 tog/K10[K0:K2 tog, K10], turn and leave rem 8 sts on holder for border. 41[44:47] sts.
Beg with a P row, work 37[41:45] rows st st, or same number as for Back.

Shape dart
1st dec row K20, sl 1, K1, psso, K to end.
Beg with a P row, work 7 rows st st.
Rep last 8 rows 7 times more. 33[36:39] sts.
Continue without shaping until work measures same as Back to underarm ending with a P row.

Shape armhole
Cast off 5 sts at beg of next row.
Work 1 row.
Dec one st at beg of next and following 3 alt rows. 24[27:30] sts.
Beg with a P row, work 20[22:24] rows st st, ending at neck edge.

Shape neck
1st row Cast off 3[4:4] sts, P to end.

2nd row K.
3rd row P2 tog, P to end.
Rep last 2 rows 2[2:4] times more. 18[20:21] sts.
Work 2[4:2] rows st st, ending at armhole edge.

Shape shoulder
Cast off at beg of next and following alt rows 6 sts once, 6[7:7] sts once and 6[7:8] sts once.

Coat right front

Using No.6 needles, cast on 51[53:57] sts.
Work 10 rows moss st as given for Back.
Next row Moss st 8 and leave these sts on holder for border, change to No.5 needles, K10, K2 tog, K14/K2 tog[K0:K14, K2 tog], K to end. 41[44:47] sts.
Beg with a P row, work 37[41:45] rows st st, or same number as for Back.

Shape dart
1st dec row K until 22 sts rem, K2 tog, K to end.
Beg with a P row, work 7 rows st st.
Rep last 8 rows 7 times more. 33[36:39] sts.
Complete as given for Left front, reversing all shapings.

Sleeves

Using No.6 needles, cast on 43[45:47] sts.
Work 10 rows moss st as given for Back.
Change to No.5 needles.
Beg with a K row, continue in st st, inc one st at each end of 21st and every following 10th row until there are 55[57:59] sts.
Continue without shaping until work measures 17in from beg, or required length to underarm. End with a P row.

Shape top
Cast off 5 sts at beg of next 2 rows.
Dec one st at each end of next and every alt row until 23 sts rem.
Cast off 3 sts at beg of next 4 rows.
Cast off rem 11 sts.

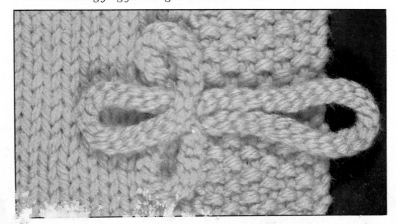

▼ *Detail showing frog fastening and the border stitch*

To make up

Press each piece under a damp cloth using a warm iron. Join shoulder, side and sleeve seams. Press seams.

Left front border

Slip border sts from holder on to No.6 needles and with RS facing, rejoin yarn and work in moss st until border is long enough to fit to neck when slightly stretched. Replace 8 border sts on holder and join border to Front.

Right front border

Work as given for Left front border but rejoin yarn to back of work.
Join border to Front.

Neckband

Using No.6 needles and with RS facing, moss st across Right front border sts, K up 16[18:20] sts to shoulder, K up 23[23:25] sts across Back neck, K up 16[18:20] sts down Left front and moss st across Left front border sts. 71[75:81] sts.
Work 9 rows moss st. Cast off in moss st.
Press borders lightly on WS. Set in sleeves.

Frog fastenings

Using No.3·50 hook make a tight chain of 14in. Miss first ch from hook and work 1ss into each ch to end. Pull out last st and leave end for sewing on. Fold into 3 loops at one end and sew to coat at neck, then sew remainder of cord in a long loop to edge of coat.
Work 4 frogs in this way down Left front and 4 more to correspond on Right front allowing long loop to protrude slightly beyond the edge of the border.
Sew on 4 buttons to Left front at end of long loop to match loops on Right front.

Hat

Crown

Using No.6 needles, cast on 83 sts, and work 30 rows moss st as given for Coat back.

Shape top

1st dec row Moss st 7, P3 tog, (moss st 11, P3 tog) 5 times, moss st 3. 71 sts.
Moss st 3 rows.
2nd dec row Moss st 11, *P3 tog, moss st 9, rep from * to end. 61 sts. Moss st 3 rows.
3rd dec row Moss st 3, P3 tog, (moss st 9, P3 tog) 4 times, moss st 7. 51 sts.
Moss st 3 rows.
4th dec row Moss st 3, *P3 tog, moss st 3, rep from * to end. 35 sts.
Moss st 1 row.
5th dec row K1, P3 tog, * moss st 3, P3 tog, rep from * to last st, K1. 23 sts.
Moss st 1 row.
6th dec row *K1, P3 tog, rep from * to last 3 sts, K1, P2 tog. 12 sts.
Next row K1, *K2 tog, rep from * to last st, K1.
Break yarn and draw through all sts, fasten off securely and sew up back seam.

Brim

Using No.6 needles, cast on 13 sts and work in moss st for 25½in. Cast off in moss st.

To make up

Join cast on edge to cast off edge. Place this seam to back seam of crown and pin evenly in position, stretching crown slightly to fit brim. Oversew to crown so that brim rolls up when finished.

133

Zip-fronted jacket

A zipped-up casual designed to fit teen to adult sizes.

Sizes

To fit 32[34:36:38:40:42]in bust or chest
Length from shoulder, 22[22:23½:23½:25:25]in, adjustable
Sleeve seam, 17[17½:17½:18:18:18]in, adjustable
The figures in brackets [] refer to the 34, 36, 38, 40 and 42in sizes respectively

> **Tension for this design**
> 12 sts and 15 rows to 2in over patt worked on No.8 needles

Materials

Patons Four Seasons (1oz balls)
14[15:17:17:18:18] balls
One pair No.9 Aero needles
One pair No.8 Aero needles
One 20[20:22:22:24:24]in Lightning open ended zip

Back

Using No.9 needles cast on 99 [105:111:117:123:129] sts.
1st row Sl 1, *K1, P1, rep from * to last 2 sts, K2.
2nd row Sl 1, *P1, K1, rep from * to end.
Rep these 2 rows 5 times more.
Change to No.8 needles.
Commence patt.
1st row Sl 1, K0[1:0:1:0:1], *P2, K2, rep from * to last 2[3:2:3:2:3] sts, P1[2:1:2:1:2], K1.
2nd row Sl 1, P0[1:0:1:0:1], *K2, P2, rep from * to last 2[3:2:3:2:3] sts, K2[3:2:3:2:3].

134

These 2 rows form patt and are rep throughout.
Continue in patt until work measures 14½[14½:15:15: 15½:15½]in from beg, or required length to underarm, ending with a WS row.

Shape raglan

Cast off 4 sts at beg of next 2 rows.
Keeping patt correct, dec one st at each end of every row until 61[55:69:63:77:71] sts rem, then every following alt row until 27[27:29:29: 31:31] sts rem.
Cast off.

Right front

Using No.9 needles cast on 49[51:55:57:61:63] sts.
Work 12 rows rib as given for Back, inc one st at beg of last row for the 34 and 42in sizes

Stitch detail showing zip

only. 49[52:55:57:61:64] sts.
Change to No. 8 needles.
Commence patt.
Sizes 32 and 40in only.
1st row Sl 1, *K2, P2, rep from * to last 4 sts, K2, P1, K1.
2nd row As 1st.
Sizes 34 and 42in only.
1st row Sl 1, *P2, K2, rep from * to last 3 sts, P2, K1.
2nd row Sl 1, P1, *K2, P2, rep from * to last 2 sts, K2.
Sizes 36 and 38in only.
Work 2 rows patt as given for 1st size Back.
All sizes.
Continue in patt until work measures same as Back to raglan shaping, ending with a RS row.

Shape raglan

Cast off 4 sts at beg of next row.
Keeping patt correct, dec one st at raglan edge on every row until 30[27:34:30:38:35] sts rem, then on every following alt row until work measures 19[19:21:21:23:23]in from beg, ending with a WS row.

Shape neck

Next row Cast off 5[5:6:5: 7:7] sts, patt to last 2 sts, K2 tog.
Continue dec at raglan edge as before, *at the same time* dec one st at neck edge on next 6 rows.
Continue shaping raglan edge only until 2 sts rem. Fasten off.

Left front

Using No.9 needles cast on 49[51:55:57:61:63] sts.
Work 12 rows rib as given for Back, inc one st at end of last row for the 34 and 42in sizes only. 49[52:55:57:61:64] sts.
Change to No.8 needles.
Commence patt.
Sizes 32 and 40in only.
1st row Sl 1, P1, *K2, P2, rep from * to last 3 sts, K3.
2nd row As 1st.
Sizes 34 and 42in only.
1st row Sl 1, *P2, K2, rep from * to last 3 sts, P2, K1.
2nd row Sl 1, K1, *P2, K2, rep from * to last 2 sts, K2.
Sizes 36 and 38in only.
Work 2 patt rows as given for 1st size Back.

All sizes.
Keeping patt correct and reversing all shaping, complete to match Right front.

Sleeves

Using No.9 needles cast on 43[45:47:49:51:53] sts.
Work 13 rows in rib as given for Back.
Next row Rib 4[1:2:3:4:1], *inc in next st, rib 4[5:5:5:5:6], rep from * to last 4[2:3:4:5:3] sts, inc in next st, rib to end. 51[53:55:57:59:61] sts.
Change to No.8 needles and patt as given for Back, inc one st at each end of 3rd and every following 7th row until there are 83[85:87:89:91:93] sts, working extra sts into patt.
Continue without shaping until sleeve measures 17[17½:17½:18:18:18]in from beg, or required length to underarm. End with a WS row.

Shape raglan

Cast off 4 sts at beg of next 2 rows.
Keeping patt correct, dec one st at each end of every row until 53[51:65:63:77:75] sts rem, then every following alt row until 15 sts rem. Cast off.

Neckband

Join raglan seams.
Using No.9 needles and with RS work facing K up 17[17:18:18:19:19] sts from right front neck edge, 15 sts from sleeve, 27[27:29: 29:31:31] sts from back neck, 15 sts from sleeve and 17[17: 18:18:19:19] sts from left front neck edge.
91[91:95:95:99:99] sts.
Beg with the 2nd row, work 2in rib as given for 1st size Back. Cast off loosely in rib.

To make up

Press lightly with a cool iron under a dry cloth on the WS.
Join side and sleeve seams.
Fold neckband in half and sl st to WS. Sew in zip.
Press seams.

His and hers zippy jackets ▶

Raglan cardigans

These useful matching cardigans are made in a wide size range for you and your daughter. The pattern panels on the front and raglan sleeves are optional and the design may be worked entirely in reversed stocking stitch. Both of these cardigans button to the neck for extra warmth and comfort.

Sizes

To fit 28[30:32:34:36:38] in bust or chest
Length at centre back, 19½[20½:22:23:23½:24]in
Sleeve seam, 13[14:16:17:18:18]in
The figures in brackets [ ] refer to the 30, 32, 34, 36 and 38in sizes respectively.

> **Basic yarn tension**
> 6 sts and 8 rows to 1in over st st worked on No.8 needles.

Materials

Madame Pingouin
5[6:7:8:9:9]50g balls
One pair No.8 needles
One pair No.10 needles
Cable needle
Seven buttons

Note

To work Cardigan entirely in reversed st st, follow instructions for sts and shaping as for patt Cardigan, omitting panel patt on Fronts and Sleeves.

Back

Using No.10 needles cast on 86[92:98:104:110:116] sts.

Work 1[1:1½:1½:1½:1½]in K1, P1 rib.
Change to No.8 needles
Beg with a P row continue in reversed stocking stitch until work measures 12[12½:13½:14:14:14] in from beg, ending with a K row.

Shape armholes

Cast off 2 sts at beg of next 2 rows.
Dec one st at each end of next and every alt row until 24[26:28:30:32:34] sts rem.
Work 1 row.
Cast off.

Left front

Using No.10 needles cast on 43[46:49:52:55:58] sts.
Work 1[1:1½:1½:1½:1½] in K1, P1 rib.
Change to No.8 needles.

Commence patt

1st row P25[27:29:32:34:36] sts, K1, P1, K1, P10, K1, P1, K1, P to end.
2nd row K2[3:4:4:5:6] sts, yfwd, sl 1, ybk, K1, yfwd, sl 1, ybk, K10, yfwd, sl 1, ybk, K1, yfwd, sl 1, ybk, K to end.
3rd row P25[27:29:32:34:36] sts, K1, P1, sl next st on cable needle and hold at front of work, P next st then K st on cable needle—called C2L—P8, sl next st on cable needle and hold at back of work, K next st then P st on cable needle—called C2R—P1, K1, P to end.
4th row K2[3:4:4:5:6] sts, yfwd, sl 1, ybk, K2, yfwd, sl 1, ybk, K8, yfwd, sl 1, ybk, K2, yfwd, sl 1, ybk, K to end.

5th row P25[27:29:32:34:36] sts, K1, P2, C2L, P6, C2R, P2, K1, P to end.
6th row K2[3:4:4:5:6] sts, sl 1 as before, K3, sl 1, K6, sl 1, K3, sl 1, K to end.
7th row P25 [27:29:32:-34:36] sts, K1, P3, C2L, P4, C2R, P3, K1, P to end.
8th row K2[3:4:4:5:6] sts, sl 1, (K4, sl 1) 3 times, K to end.
9th row P25[27:29:32:34:36] sts, K1, P4, C2L, P2, C2R, P4, K1, P to end.
10th row K2[3:4:4:4:5:6] sts, sl 1, K5, sl 1, K2, sl 1, K5, sl 1, K to end.
11th row P25[27:29:32:34:36] sts, K1, P5, C2L, C2R, P5, K1, P to end.
12th row K2[3:4:4:5:6] sts, sl 1, K6, sl 2, K6, sl 1, K to end.
13th row P25[27:29:32:34:36] sts, K1, P6, sl next st on to cable needle and hold at front of work, K next st then K st on cable needle, P6, K1, P to end.
14th row K2[3:4:4:5:6] sts, sl 1, K14, sl 1, K to end.
15th row P25[27:29:32:34:36] sts, K1, P6, make a bobble on next 2 sts by K then P then K into each st, turn.
Beg with a P row work 4 rows st st on these 6 sts.
Now with left-hand needle pass 2nd st over 1st st, 3rd st over 1st st, then sl 1st st back on to left-hand needle. Sl 5th st over 4th st and 6th st over 4th st. Replace 1st st on right-hand needle, P6, K1, P to end.
16th row K2[3:4:4:5:6] sts, sl 1, K14, sl 1, K to end.
These 16 rows form panel patt and are rep throughout.
Continue in patt until work measures same as Back to underarm, ending with a WS row.

Shape armhole

Cast off 2 sts at beg of next row, patt to end.
Work 1 row.
Dec one st at beg of next and every alt row until work measures 17[17½:19:19½:20:20½]in from beg, ending at centre front edge.

Shape neck

Cast off 6 sts at beg of next row and dec one st at neck edge on the next 5[6:7:8:9:10] rows, *at the same time* continue to dec at armhole edge as before until 2 sts rem. K2 tog. Fasten off.

Right front

Work as given for Left front, reversing all shaping and noting that 1st patt row will read as follows:
1st row P2[3:4:4:5:6] sts, K1, P1, K1, P10, K1, P1, K1, P to end.

Sleeves

Using No.10 needles cast on 42[44:46:48:50:52] sts.
Work 2[2:2½:2½:2½:2½]in K1, P1 rib.
Change to No.8 needles.

Commence patt

1st row P13[14:15:16:17:18] sts, K1, P1, K1, P10, K1, P1, K1, P to end.
2nd row K13[14:15:16:17:18] sts, sl 1, K1, sl 1, K10, sl 1, K1, sl 1, K to end.
These 2 rows set patt. Continue in patt as given for Left front, keeping centre 16 sts correct and inc one st at each end of 5th and every following 6th row until there are 66[70:74:80:84:88] sts.
Continue without shaping until sleeve measures 13 [14:16:17:18:18]in from beg, ending with a WS row.

Shape top

Cast off 2 sts at beg of next 2 rows.
Dec one st at each end of next and every alt row until 4[4:4:6:6:6] sts rem. Work 1 row. Cast off.

Borders

Using No.10 needles cast on 10 sts.
Work in K1, P1 rib.
Work ¾[1¼:1¼:½:1¼:½]in.
Next row (buttonhole row) Rib 3, cast off 3 sts, rib to end.
Next row Rib 3, cast on 3 sts, rib to end.
Make 5 more buttonholes in

this way at intervals of 2¾[2¾:3:3¼:3¼:3½]in measured from the centre of the previous buttonhole. Continue until border measures 17[17½:19:19½:20:20½] in from beg. Cast off in rib.

Work other border in same way, omitting buttonholes.

To make up

DO NOT PRESS
Join raglan, side and sleeve seams using back st and over-

sewing welts and cuffs. Oversew borders to centre front edges.

Neckband

Using No 10 needles and with RS of work facing K up 87

[93:97:107:115:119] sts evenly around neck. Work 7[7:8:8:8:8] rows K1, P1 rib making buttonhole as before on 4th and 5th rows.
Cast off in rib.
Sew on buttons.

The classic camel polo neck

Here is a ribbed sweater to make for your brother, your son or yourself.

Sizes

To fit a 32 [34:36:38] in bust or chest.
Length at centre back 23½ [23¾:24:24¼] in
Sleeve seam 17½in
The figures in brackets [ ] refer to the 34, 36 and 38in sizes respectively

Materials

Jaeger Spiral-spun Double Knitting Wool 12[13:13:14] 50g balls
Two No.9 needles
Two No.11 needles
2 stitch holders

Abbreviations

Look back to Knitting Know-How Chapter 1 to refresh your memory.

Note

For a perfect finish use the invisible casting off to complete the collar. See Knitting Know-how Chapter 6.

Back

Using No.11 needles cast on 96 [102:108:114] sts.
1st row K2, P4 [P1:P4:K3, P4], * K4, P4, rep from * to last 2 [5:0:3] sts, K2 [K4, P1: 0:K3].
2nd row P2, K4 [K1: K4: P3, K4], * P4, K4, rep from * to last 2 [5:0:3] sts, P2 [P4, K1:0:P3].
These 2 rows form the rib and are rep throughout back.
Work 22 rows more.
Change to No.9 needles and continue in rib.
Work 98 rows, or required length to armholes.

Shape armholes

Cast off 1[2:3:4] sts at beg of next 2 rows.
Dec one st at each end of next and every RS row until 82 [82:86:86] sts rem.
Work 41 [39:41:39] rows without shaping.

Shape shoulders

1st row K2, sl1, K1, psso, rib to last 4 sts, K2 tog, K2
2nd row P2, P2 tog, rib to last 4 sts, P2 tog tbl, P2.
Rep last 2 rows 8 [8:9:9] times, then 1st row once.
Leave rem 44 sts on holder.

Front

Using No.11 needles cast on 110 [116:122:128] sts.
1st row K1 [K4:P3, K4: K2], * P4, K4, rep from * to last 5 [0:3:6] sts, P4, K1 [0:P3:P4, K2].
2nd row P1 [P4:K3, P4: P2], *K4, P4, rep from * to last 5 [0:3:6] sts, K4, P1 [0:K3: K4, P2].

Work 22 rows more in rib.
Change to No.9 needles and continue in rib.
Work 98 rows or until same length as Back.

Shape armholes

Cast off 4 [5:6:7] sts at beg of next 2 rows.
Dec one st at each end of next 6 [8:8:10] rows.
Work 44 [44:46:46] rows without shaping.

Shape shoulders

Cast off 19 [19:21:21] sts at beg of next 2 rows.
Leave rem 52 sts on holder for neck.

Sleeves

Using No.11 needles cast on 54 [56:58:60] sts.
1st row P1 [2:3:4], K4, *P4, K4, rep from * to last 1 [2:3:4] sts, P1 [2:3:4].
2nd row K1 [2:3:4], P4, *K4, P4, rep from * to last 1 [2:3:4] sts, K1 [2:3:4].
Continue in rib for 22 rows more.
Change to No.9 needles and continue in rib working extra sts into rib as they are made. Work 2 rows.
Inc 1st at each end of next and every 8th row until there are 80 [84:88:92] sts.
Work until sleeve measures 17½in or required length ending with a WS row.

Shape top

1st row K2, sl1, K1, psso, rib to last 4 sts, K2 tog, K2.
2nd row P2, P2 tog, rib to last 4 sts, P2 tog tbl, P2.
Rep last 2 rows twice.
7th row as 1st.
8th row P3, rib to last 3 sts, P3.
Rep 7th and 8th rows until 32 sts rem.
Repeat 1st and 2nd rows 3 times.
Cast off.

Collar

Join left shoulder seam.
Using No.9 needles rib across sts from Back and Front holders (96 sts). Work 43 rows in K4, P4 rib.
Cast off.

To make up

Join collar and right shoulder seam.
Join side and sleeve seams.
Set in sleeves.
Press lightly using a damp cloth with a cool iron.

These jerseys have been specially designed to look good on a girl or a boy and the elasticity of the rib allows for contours! The continental shaping which has been used is of particular interest and is actually simpler to do, with better results, than the standard English type of shaping. It gives a close-fitting look, letting the clear lines of the rib reach over the shoulder from the front to the sloping back seam. The shoulder seam itself is set behind the shoulder.

Sweaters for boys or girls ►
Stitch detail of rib ▼

Tailored waistcoat

The softest random-dyed yarn makes this clever-shaped waistcoat the ideal wear for either the town or country. It is so versatile that you can wear it with trousers or any length of skirt and of course it can be made up just as successfully in plain colours. The snug, neat edging shows to full effect the special 'invisible' casting on method, see Knitting Know-how Chapter 3, and even experienced knitters will be fascinated by this clever technique.

Sizes
To fit 32 [34:36] in bust
Length at centre back, 21½ [22: 22½] in
The figures in brackets [ ] refer to the 34 and 36in sizes respectively.

Tension
Equivalent to a basic tension of 6 stitches and 8 rows to one in worked over stocking stitch on No.9 needles.

Materials
Jaeger Shadow-spun
11 [12:13] ½oz balls
One pair No.8 needles
One pair No.9 needles
One No.9 circular needle
Five small buttons

Back

Using No.9 needles and an odd length of yarn, cast on 49 [51:55] sts by the one needle method.
Next row With correct yarn, K1, *yfwd, K1, rep from * to end. 97 [101:109] sts.
Next row K1, *yfwd, sl 1, ybk, K1, rep from * to end.
Next row Yfwd, sl 1, *ybk, K1, yfwd, sl 1, rep from * to end.
Rep last 2 rows once more.
Next row K1, *P1, K1, rep from * to end.
Next row P1, *K1, P1, rep from * to end.
Rep last 2 rows 3 times more.
Change to No.8 needles and st st. Beg with a K row continue in st st, dec one st at each end of 7th and every following alt row until 81 [85: 93] sts rem, ending with a P row.
Continue in st st, inc one st at each end of 7th and every following 10th row until there are 93 [99: 105] sts, ending with a P row.
Continue without shaping until work measures 13in from beg, ending with a P row.
Shape armholes
Cast off 5 [6:7] sts at beg of next 2 rows.
Dec one st at each end of next and every alt row until 69 [73: 77] sts rem.
Continue without shaping until armholes measure 7½ [7¾: 8] in from beg, ending with a P row.
Shape shoulders
Cast off 8 sts at beg of next 2 rows and 8 [9: 10] sts at beg of following 2 rows.
Cast off rem 37 [39: 41] sts.

Left front

Using No.8 needles and correct yarn, cast on 29 [31: 33] sts.
Work in st st throughout.
K 1 row.
Cast on 3 sts at beg of next and following 2 alt rows.
Dec one st at beg of next and every alt row at side edge 8 times in all, *at the same time* inc one st at front edge on every row 10 [10: 12] times in all, ending with a P row and keeping front edge straight after last inc.
Continue in st st, inc one st at side edge on 7th and every following 10th row until there are 46 [49: 52] sts.
Continue without shaping until work measures same as Back to underarm, less ribbing, ending at armhole edge.
Shape armhole and front edge
Cast off 5 [6: 7] sts at beg of next row.
Work 1 row.
Dec one st at armhole edge on next and every alt row 7 times in all, *at the same time* dec one st at front edge on next and every following 3rd row until 16 [17: 18] sts rem.
Continue without shaping until armhole measures same as Back to shoulder, ending at armhole edge.
Shape shoulder
Cast off at beg of next and following alt row 8 sts once and 8 [9: 10] sts once.

Right front

Cast on as for Left front.
Beg with a P row continue in st st and complete as given for Left front, reversing all shaping.

Front border

Join shoulder seams.
Mark position for 5 buttons on Left front, first to come 1in above last bottom curve shaping and 5th to come 4 rows below first front edge shaping. Using No.9 needles and invisible casting on method as given for Back, cast on 217 [221: 225] sts. Change to No.9 circular needle and correct yarn, turning at the end of each row and working back. Continue as given for Back on 433 [441 :449] sts, working 8 rows in K1, P1 rib when invisible edge has been completed and making buttonholes as markers are reached on 4th and 5th ribbing rows, as follows:
Next row Rib 74 [78: 82] sts, *cast off 3 sts, rib 10, rep from *4 times more, rib to end.
Next row Rib to end, casting on 3 sts above those cast off in previous row.
Cast off in rib.

Armbands

Using No.9 needles and invisible cast on method as given for Back, cast on 63 [67: 71] sts. Complete as given for Front border, omitting buttonholes and working 4 rows K1, P1 rib.

To make up

Press each piece under a damp cloth with a cool iron omitting ribbing on Back hem and borders. Remove cast on thread. With RS facing, beg at Right front side seam and pin cast off edge of Front border round Right front edge, round neck and down Left front, making sure buttonholes come on Right front. Sew on border. Sew on armbands in same way. Join side seams including ribbing. Press seams very lightly. Sew on buttons.

Soft, subtly shaded waistcoats with neat 'invisible' cast on edge ▼
▼Details of 'invisible' edging

140

Fabric stitch sleeveless pullover

A knitted overblouse like this is a garment dear to the heart of the fashion-conscious Frenchwoman because of its many uses. Wear it with a tailored blouse and pleated skirt, or team it with trousers and chunky sweater. The interesting fabric stitch of this design gives a firm texture without being too bulky, and the deep armholes make it ideal for wearing over set-in or raglan sleeved sweaters. We suggest you make it in Madame Pingouin, which is warm but light and comes in many colours.

Sizes

To fit 34[36:38:40]in bust
Length at centre back, 26 [26½:27:27½]in
The figures in brackets [ ] refer to the 36, 38 and 40in sizes respectively

Basic yarn tension
6 sts and 8 rows to 1in
over st st worked
on No.8 needles.

Materials

Madame Pingouin
6[7:8:8]50g balls
One pair No.8 needles
One pair No.10 needles
Set of 4 No.10 needles
pointed at both ends

Back

Using No.8 needles cast on 110 [118:126:134] sts.
1st row K2, *P2, K2, rep from * to end.
2nd row P2, *K2, P2, rep

from * to end.
3rd row As 1st.
4th row As 2nd.
5th row Place the right-hand needle behind the next st, K the following st then K the first st and sl both sts off left-hand needle tog—called cross 2 —*P2, cross 2, rep from * to end.
6th row As 1st.
7th row As 2nd.
8th row As 1st.
9th row As 2nd.
10th row As 1st.
11th row P2, *cross 2, P2, rep from * to end.
12th row As 2nd.
These 12 rows form patt and are rep throughout.
Keeping patt correct, dec one st at each end of next and every following 10th row 6 times in all, then inc one st at each end of every following 12th row 4 times.
Continue without shaping until work measures 16[16:16½:16½]in from beg, ending with a WS row.

Shape armholes

Dec one st at each end of next and every following 4th row 17 [18:19:20] times in all.
Continue without shaping until armholes measure 10 [10½:10½:11]in from beg, ending with a WS row.

Shape neck and shoulders

Next row Cast off 5 sts, patt 8[10:12:14] sts, cast off 44[46:48:50] sts, patt to end.
Complete left shoulder first. Cast off at beg of next and following alt rows 5 sts twice and 4 [6:8:10] sts once. With WS of work facing, rejoin

yarn to rem sts and complete to match first side.

Front

Work as given for Back until Front measures same to underarm.

Shape armholes

Next row Dec one st at each end of this row.
Work 3 rows without shaping.
Rep last 4 rows once more.

Shape neck

Next row Dec one st, patt 34[37:40:43] sts, cast off 30 [32:34:36] sts, patt to last 2 sts, dec one st.
Complete right shoulder first. Dec one st at neck edge on next 7 rows, *at the same time* dec one st at armhole edge on every 4th row 14 [15:16:17] times more.
Continue without shaping until armhole measures same as Back to shoulder ending at armhole edge.

Shape shoulder

Cast off at beg of next and following alt row 5 sts twice and 4 [6:8:10] sts once.
With WS of work facing rejoin yarn to rem sts and complete to match first side.

To make up

Do not press.
Join shoulder-seams.
Armbands Using No.10 needles and with RS of work facing, K up 118 [126:126:134] sts evenly around armhole.
Work in K2, P2 rib.
Work 1 row.
Work 5 more rows, dec one st at each end of every row.
Cast off in rib.
Join side-seams.
Neckband Using set of 4 No.10 needles and with RS of work facing, K up 196 [204:208:216] sts evenly round neck.
Work in rounds of K2, P2 rib. Work 11 rounds.
Next round *K2, P2 tog, rep from * to end.
Cast off in rib.

Tabard in double knitting

The knights of old wore a tabard for extra warmth without bulk, and for a decorative colourful effect. Whether you wear them over casual clothes or with a dressier outfit, tabards are still the ideal garment to wear for an extra layer of warmth with maximum freedom of movement. This one opens down the front.

Sizes

To fit 34[36:38:40]in bust
Length at centre back, 31[32:33:34]in
The figures in brackets [ ] refer to the 36, 38, 40in sizes respectively

Basic yarn tension

6 sts and 8 rows to 1in over st st worked on No.8 needles

Materials

Madame Pingouin 8[9:10:11]50g balls
One pair No.8 needles
4 clasps

Back

Using No.8 needles, cast on 90[96:102:108] sts.
Beg with a K row work in st st.
Work 1 row.
Inc one st at each end of every row until there are 100[106:112:118] sts.
Commence patt.
1st-6th rows K.
7th row K.
8th row P.
Rep last 2 rows twice more.
These 12 rows form patt and are rep throughout.

Basic Wardrobe Knitting

Continue in patt until work measures 24[25:25½:26½]in from beg, ending with a WS row.

Shape armholes

Cast off 6 sts at beg of next 2 rows.
Dec one st at each end of every row until 80[84:88:92] sts rem.
Continue without shaping until armholes measure 7[7:7½:7½]in ending with a WS row.

Shape shoulders

Cast off 9 sts at beg of next 4 rows.
Cast off 8[9:10:11]sts at beg of next 2 rows.

Cast off rem sts.

Left front

Using No.8 needles cast on 40[43:46:49] sts.
Beg with a K row work in st st.
Work 1 row.
Inc one st at each end of every row until there are 50[53:56:59] sts.
Continue in patt as for Back until work measures same as Back to armhole, ending with a WS row.

Shape armhole

Cast off 6 sts at beg of next row.
Dec one st at armhole edge on every row 4[5:6:7] times.
Continue without shaping until armhole measures 5in from beg, ending at centre front edge.

Shape neck

Cast off 7 sts at beg of next row.
Dec one st at neck edge on every row 7[8:9:10] times.
Continue without shaping until armhole measures same as Back to shoulder, ending at armhole edge.

Shape Shoulder

Cast off 9 sts at beg of next and following alt row.
Cast off rem 8[9:10:11] sts.

Right front

Work as for Left front, with a RS row before armhole shaping.

To make up

DO NOT PRESS
Join shoulder seams using back st.

Armbands

K up 95[95:101:101] sts evenly around armhole with RS facing. Beg with a P row work 5 rows st st, inc one st at each end of every row. Cast off loosely.
Join side seams using back st and leaving 9in free at bottom of seams to form side vents.

Vents

K up 54 sts evenly along one side of vent, with RS facing. Beg with a P row work 5 rows st st, dec one st at bottom edge of vent and inc one st at other end of row. Cast off loosely.
Rep for 3 other vent edges.

Front facings

K up 173[179:182:188] sts along edge of Right front, with RS facing. Beg with a P row work 5 rows st st, dec one st at bottom edge on every row. Cast off loosely.
Work left front in same way.
Fold all st st edges to WS of Tabard and slip st in place, joining mitred corners.

Collar

K up 70[74:84:88]sts evenly round neck, with RS facing and beg 3 sts in from centre front edges. Beg with a K row work 5 rows g st, 4 rows st st, 6 rows g st and 12 rows st st.
Cast off loosely.
Fold collar in half to WS and slip st in place, sewing down side edges.
Sew on clasps.

▼ *The tabard with an unusual metal clasp fastening*

Tabard with link button fastening ▶

144

Sleeveless summer top

Basic Wardrobe Knitting

A skinny topper to wear with summer suits, romantic skirts and all kinds of pants.

Sizes
To fit 32[34:36:38]in bust
Length to back neck,
16¾[17:17¼:17½]in
The figures in brackets [ ] refer to the 34, 36 and 38in sizes respectively.

Basic yarn tension
7½ sts and 9 rows to
1 in over st st worked
on No.11 needles.

Materials shown here
Pingouin Age D'or
4[4:5:5]50g balls
One pair No.10 needles
One pair No.11 needles
One pair No.12 needles
One No. 2·50 (ISR) crochet hook

Back

Using No.12 needles cast on 125[131:137:143]sts.
Beg with a K row work 4 rows st st.
1st patt row Using No.10 needles K.
2nd patt row (wrong side) Using No.10 needles, K1, *K3 tog, before slipping sts off left-hand needle K into first st again then K 2nd and 3rd sts tog, slip all 3 sts off left-hand needle—called K3 into 3—rep from * to last st, K1.
3rd patt row As 1st patt row.
4th patt row As 2nd patt row.
5th-14th patt rows Using No.11 needles and beg with a K row work in st st.
146

Rep 1st–14th rows 6 times more, then 1st–10th rows once.

Shape armholes
1st row Using No.11 needles, cast off 6[6:6:9]sts, K to end.
2nd row Using No.11 needles, cast off 6[6:6:9]sts, P to end.
3rd row Using No.11 needles, cast off 3 sts, K to end.
4th row Using No.11 needles, cast off 3 sts, P to end.
5th row Using No.10 needles, cast off 3 sts, K to end.
6th row Using No.10 needles, cast off 3 sts, (1 st on right-hand needle), *K3 into 3, rep from * to last st, K1.
101[107:113:113] sts.
Rep 1st and 2nd patt rows throughout remainder of Back.
Work without shaping until armholes measure 5¾[6:6¼:6½] in, ending with 2nd patt row.

Shape neck
1st row Keeping patt correct, work 34[37:37:37]sts, cast off centre 33[33:39:39]sts, patt to end.
Complete this shoulder first.
Work 1 row.
** Cast off 3 sts at neck edge on next and following 2 alt rows.

Shape shoulder
Cast off at beg of next and following 2 alt rows 7 sts once, 9 sts once and 9[12:12:12] sts. **
With WS of work facing, rejoin yarn to rem sts for other shoulder and work 2 rows.
Complete as for first shoulder from ** to **

Front

Work as given for Back.

To make up

DO NOT PRESS.
Join shoulder and side seams using a back st seam.
Turn first 5 st st rows at lower edge to WS and slip st in place.
Neck edging Using No.2·50 (ISR) crochet hook and RS of work facing, work picot edging evenly round neck edge, *1dc, 1dc into next st, 3ch, 1dc into same place as last dc, rep from * to end. Work edging round armholes in same way.

Alternative knitted picot edging
Neck edge Join left shoulder seam.
Using No.10 needles and RS of work facing K up 13 sts down right side of Back neck, K up 33 [33:39:39]sts from centre back cast off edge, K up 13 sts up left side of Back and 13 sts down left side of Front, K up 33[33:39:39]sts from centre Front cast off edge and K up 13 sts up right side of Front. 118 [118:130:130]sts.
Work picot edge.
K into front and back of first st, turn, K2, turn, cast off 6 sts, slip st on right-hand needle back on left hand needle and rep from * until all sts have been worked off.

Armhole edging Join right shoulder seam.
Using No.10 needles and with RS of work facing, K up 92[96:100:104]sts and work as for neck edging.

Pretty, yet quick and easy to knit ▶
Stitch detail of the bodice stitch ▼

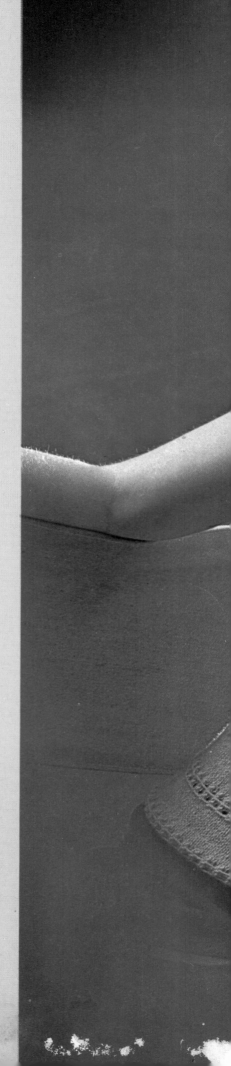

Diamond patterned jersey

This charming classic jersey is superbly simple and made in a soft light yarn for feminine flattery.

Sizes

To fit 34[36:38]in bust
Length to shoulder, 24[24½: 25]in
Sleeve seam, 17[17½:18]in
The figures in brackets [ ] refer to the 36 and 38in sizes respectively.

> **Basic yarn tension**
> 7 sts and 9 rows to 1in over st st worked on No.10 needles.

Materials shown here

Pingouin Age d'or
6[7:7]50g balls
One pair No.10 needles
One pair No.12 needles
Set of four No.12 needles pointed at both ends
Stitch holder

Front

Using No.12 needles cast on 125[131:137]sts.
Work in K1, P1 rib for 1in.
Change to No.10 needles.
Commence wide rib panels.
Next row K8[11:14], P1, *K17, P1, rep from * to last 8[11:14]sts, K to end.
Next row P8[11:14], K1, *P17, K1, rep from * to last 8[11:14]sts, P to end.
Rep last 2 rows 3 times more.

Commence diamond patt

1st row K8[11:14], P1, *K8, yfwd, K2 tog tbl, K7, P1, rep from * to last 8 [11:14] sts, K to end.

Detail of the diamond pattern

2nd and alt rows P8[11:14], K1, *P17, K1, rep from * to last 8[11:14]sts, P to end.
3rd row K8[11:14], P1, *K6, K2 tog, yfwd, K1, yfwd, K2 tog tbl, K6, P1, rep from * to last 8[11:14]sts, K to end.
5th row K8[11:14], P1, *K5, K2 tog, yfwd, K3, yfwd, K2 tog tbl, K5, P1, rep from * to last 8[11:14]sts, K to end.
7th row K8[11:14], P1, *K4, K2 tog, yfwd, K5, yfwd, K2 tog tbl, K4, P1, rep from * to last 8[11:14]sts, K to end.
9th row K8[11:14], P1, *K3, K2 tog, yfwd, K7, yfwd, K2 tog tbl, K3, P1, rep from * to last 8[11:14]sts, K to end.
11th row K8[11:14], P1, *K2, K2 tog, yfwd, K9, yfwd, K2 tog tbl, K2, P1, rep from * to last 8[11:14]sts, K to end.
13th row K8[11:14], P1, *K1, K2 tog, yfwd, K11, yfwd, K2 tog tbl, K1, P1, rep from * to last 8[11:14] sts, K to end.
15th row K8[11:14], P1, *K3, yfwd, K2 tog tbl, K7, K2 tog, yfwd, K3, P1, rep from * to last 8[11:14]sts, K to end.
17th row K8[11:14], P1, *K4, yfwd, K2 tog tbl, K5, K2 tog, yfwd, K4, P1, rep from * to last 8[11:14]sts, K to end.

19th row K8[11:14], P1, *K5, yfwd, K2 tog tbl, K3, K2 tog, yfwd, K5, P1, rep from * to last 8[11:14] sts, K to end.
21st row K8[11:14], P1, *K6, yfwd, K2 tog tbl, K1, K2 tog, yfwd, K6, P1, rep from * to last 8[11:14]sts, K to end.
23rd row K8[11:14], P1, *K7, yfwd, sl 1, K2 tog, psso, yfwd, K7, P1, rep from * to last 8[11:14]sts, K to end.
25th row K8[11:14], P1, *K8, yfwd, K2 tog tbl, K7, P1, rep from * to last 8[11:14]sts, K to end.
26th row As 2nd.
27th row K8[11:14], P1, *K17, P1, rep from * to last 8[11:14]sts, K to end.
28th row As 2nd.
Rep 27th and 28th rows 10 times more.
These 48 rows form patt.
Rep 1st–48th rows once more, then 1st–20th rows once.

Shape armholes

Keeping patt correct, cast off 3 sts at beg of next 2 rows.
Next row K1, K3 tog, patt to last 4 sts, K3 tog tbl, K1.
Work 3 rows patt without dec.
Rep last 4 rows 13[14:14] times more.

Shape neck

Next row K1, K3 tog, patt 14[14:16]sts, cast off 27 [29:31]sts, patt to last 4 sts, K3 tog tbl, K1.
Complete right shoulder first.
Dec one st at neck edge on next 6 rows, *at the same time* continue to dec on raglan edge every 4th row 4[4:5] times more. K last 2 sts tog. Fasten off.
With WS of work facing, rejoin yarn to rem sts and and complete to match first shoulder.

Back

Using No.12 needles cast on 125[131:137]sts.
Work in K1, P1 rib for 1in.
Change to No.10 needles.
Beg with a K row work in st st until Back measures same as Front to armholes, ending with a P row.

Shape armholes

Cast off 3 sts at beg of next 2 rows.
Next row K1, K3 tog, K to last 4 sts, K3 tog tbl, K1.
Work 3 rows without dec.
Rep last 4 rows 19[20:21] times more.
Leave rem sts on holder.

Right sleeve

Using No.12 needles cast on 58[60:62]sts.
Work in K1, P1 rib for 2in.
Change to No.10 needles.
Beg with a K row work in st st, inc one st at each end of 7th and every following 6th row until there are 96[100: 104]sts.
Work without shaping until sleeve measures 17[17½:18]in from beg, ending with a P row.

Shape top

Cast off 3 sts at beg of next 2 rows.
Next row K1, K3 tog, K to last 4 sts, K3 tog tbl, K1.
Work 3 rows without dec.
Rep last 4 rows 18[19:20] times more.**
Next row Cast off 6 sts, K to last 4 sts, K3 tog tbl, K1.
Work 1 row. Cast off rem sts.

Left sleeve

Work as given for Right sleeve to **.
Next row K1, K3 tog, K to end.
Next row Cast off 6 sts, P to end.
Work 1 row.
Cast off rem sts.

To make up

DO NOT PRESS
Join raglan edges of sleeves to raglan edges of Back and Front.
Neckband Using set of 4 No. 12 needles and with RS facing, K up 124[128:138]sts evenly round neck, including sts from holder.
Work in rounds of K1, P1 rib for 2in.
Cast off loosely in rib.
Join side and sleeve seams.
Fold neckband in half to WS and sl st down.

Aran style sweater

Although this smart looking sweater has an Aran look, there are no travelling stitches requiring the use of a cable needle. The zigzag lines are achieved by increasing and decreasing at either side of each pattern.

Size

To fit 38in bust
Length at centre back, 22in
Sleeve seam, about 17½in

> **Tension for this design**
> 6 sts and 8 rows to 1in over st st worked on No.9 needles

Materials

Madame Pingouin
10 50g balls
One pair No.11 needles
One pair No.9 needles

Back

Using No.11 needles, cast on 122 sts.
1st row P2, *K2, P2, rep from * to end.
2nd row K2, *P2, K2, rep from * to end.
Rep first and 2nd rows until work measures 2½in.
Change to No.9 needles and patt.
1st row K1, *P1, K2, P18, K2, P1, rep from * to last st, K1.
2nd row K1, *K1, P2, K18, P2, K1, rep from * to last st, K1.
3rd row K1, lift thread before next st and make one st by knitting into it—called K up 1—, *P1, K2, P8, P2 tog, P8, K2, P1, K up 1,

rep from * to last st, K1. 123 sts.
4th row K1, *K2, P2, K17, P2, K1, rep from * to last 2 sts, K2.
5th row K1, *P2, K up 1, K2, P2 tog, P13, P2 tog, K2, K up 1, P1, rep from * to last 2 sts, P1, K1.
6th row K1, *K3, P2, K15, P2, K2, rep from * to last 2 sts, K2.
7th row K1, *P3, K up 1, K2, P2 tog, P5, K into front and back and front and back of next st—called M4—, P5, P2 tog, K2, K up 1, P2, rep from * to last 2 sts, P1, K1.
8th row K1, *K4, P2, K6, P4, K6, P2, K3, rep from * to last 2 sts, K2.
9th row K1, *P4, K up 1, K2, P2 tog, P4, K4, P4, P2 tog, K2, K up 1, P3, rep from * to last 2 sts, P1, K1.
10th row K1, *K5, P2, K5, P4, K5, P2, K4, rep from * to last 2 sts, K2.
11th row K1, *P5, K up 1,

▼ *Close-up detail of pattern*

K2, P2 tog, P3, sl 2, K2 tog, p2sso, P3, P2 tog, K2, K up 1, P4, rep from * to last 2 sts, P1, K1.
12th row K1, *K6, P2, K9, P2, K5, rep from * to last 2 sts, K2.
13th row K1, P1, *P5, K up 1, K2, P2 tog, P5, P2 tog, K2, K up 1, P5, M4, rep from * ending last rep P6, K1.
14th row K2, *K6, P2, K7, P2, K6, P4, rep from * ending last rep K8.
15th row K1, P1, *P6, K up 1, K2, P2 tog, P3, P2 tog, K2, K up 1, P6, K4, rep from * ending last rep P7, K1.
16th row K2, *K7, P2, K5, P2, K7, P4, rep from * ending last rep K9.
17th row K1, P1, *P7, K up 1, K2, P2 tog, P1, P2 tog K2, K up 1, P7, sl 2, K2 tog, p2sso, rep from * ending last rep P8, K1.
18th row K1, *K9, P2, K3, P2, K8, rep from * to last 2 sts, K2.
19th row K1, *P9, K up 1, K2, P3 tog, K2, K up 1, P8, rep from * to last 2 sts, P1, K1.
20th row K1, *K10, P2, K1, P2, K9, rep from * to last 2 sts, K2.
21st row K1, *P4, M4, P5, K2, P1, K2, P5, M4, P3, rep from * to last 2 sts, P1, K1.
22nd row K1, *K4, P4, K5, P2, K1, P2, K5, P4, K3, rep from * to last 2 sts, K2.
23rd row K1, *P4, K4, P5, K2, P1, K2, P5, K4, P3, rep from * to last 2 sts, P1, K1.
24th row K1, *K4, P4, K5, P2, K1, P2, K5, P4, K3, rep from * to last 2 sts, K2.
25th row K1, *P4, sl 2, K2 tog, p2sso, P3, P2 tog, K2, K up 1, P1, K up 1, K2, P2 tog, P3, sl 2, K2 tog, p2sso, P3, rep from * to last 2 sts, P1, K1.
26th row K1, *K9, P2, K3, P2, K8, rep from * to last 2 sts, K2.
27th row K1, *P7, P2 tog, K2, K up 1, P3, K up 1, K2, P2 tog, P6, rep from * to last 2 sts, P1, K1.
28th row K1, *K8, P2, K5, P2, K7, rep from * to last 2 sts, K2.

29th row K1, P1, *P5, P2 tog, K2, K up 1, P5, K up 1, K2, P2 tog, P5, M4, rep from * ending last rep P6, K1.
30th row K2, *K6, P2, K7, P2, K6, P4, rep from * ending last rep K8.
31st row K1, P1, *P4, P2 tog, K2, K up 1, P7, K up 1, K2, P2 tog, P4, K4, rep from * ending last rep P5, K1.
32nd row K2, *K5, P2, K9, P2, K5, P4, rep from * ending last rep K7.
33rd row K1, P1, *P3, P2 tog, K2, K up 1, P9, K up 1, K2, P2 tog, P3, sl 2, K2 tog, p2sso, rep from * ending last rep P4, K1.
34th row K1, *K5, P2, K11, P2, K4, rep from * to last 2 sts, K2.
35th row K1, *P3, P2 tog, K2, K up 1, P5, M4, P5, K up 1, K2, P2 tog, P2, rep from * to last 2 sts, P1, K1.
36th row K1, *K4, P2, K6, P4, K6, P2, K3, rep from * to last 2 sts, K2.
37th row K1, *P2, P2 tog, K2, K up 1, P6, K4, P6, K up 1, K2, P2 tog, P1, rep from * to last 2 sts, P1, K1.
38th row K1, *K3, P2, K7, P4, K7, P2, K2, rep from * to last 2 sts, K2.
39th row K1, *P1, P2 tog, K2, K up 1, P7, sl 2, K2 tog, p2sso, P7, K up 1, K2, P2 tog, rep from * to last 2 sts, P1, K1.
40th row K1, *K2, P2, K17, P2, K1, rep from * to last 2 sts, K2.
41st row K1, P2 tog, *K2, K up 1, P17, K up 1, K2, P3 tog, rep from * ending last rep P2 tog, K1.
42nd row K1, *K1, P2, K19, P2, rep from * to last 2 sts, K2.
43rd row K1, *P1, K2, P5, M4, P7, M4, P5, K2, rep * to last 2 sts, P1, K1.
44th row K1, *K1, P2, K5, P4, K7, P4, K5, P2, rep from * to last 2 sts, K2.
45th row K1, *P1, K2, P5, K4, P7, K4, P5, K2, rep from * to last 2 sts, P1, K1.
46th row K1, *K1, P2, K5, P4, K7, P4, K5, P2, rep from * to last 2 sts, K2.
47th row K1, *P1, K up 1,

150

K2, P2 tog, P3, sl 2, K2 tog, p2sso, p7, sl 2, K2 tog, p2sso, P3, P2 tog, K2, K up 1, rep from * to last 2 sts, P1, K1.

48th row As 4th.
The patt is formed by rep rows 5—48 throughout. Work without shaping until work measures about 15½in, ending with a WS patt row.

Shape armholes
Cast off 3 sts at beg of next 2 rows.
Cast off 2 sts at beg of next 2 rows.
Cast off one st at each end of next and every alt row 7 times in all.
Work without shaping until armholes measure about 6½in, ending with a 42nd patt row.

Shape shoulders
Cast off at beg of next and every row 6 sts 8 times and 5 sts twice. Leave rem sts on holder.

Front

Work as for Back until armholes measure about 4½in, ending with a 26th patt row.

Shape neck
1st row Patt 41, turn.
Complete first shoulder on these sts.
**Cast off at neck edge on next and every alt row 3 sts once, 2 sts once and one st 7 times.
Work until armhole measures same as Back to shoulder, ending at armhole edge.

Shape shoulder
Cast off at beg of next and every alt row 6 sts 4 times and 5 sts once.**
With right side of work facing, slip centre 17 sts onto holder.
Rejoin yarn to rem sts and patt to end of row. Work 1 row.
Work second shoulder in same way from ** to **

Sleeves

Using No.11 needles, cast on 50 sts.

▲ *Aran style sweater showing overall zigzag pattern*

Work in rib as on Back until work measures 2½ in.
Change to No.9 needles and patt as on Back.
Continue working in patt as set inc one st at each end of 9th and every following 8th row until there are 75 sts.
Work until sleeve measures about 17½in ending with a WS row

Shape top
Cast off 3 sts at beg of next 2 rows.

Cast off 2 sts at beg of next 10 rows.
Cast off one st at beg of next 28 rows.
Cast off 2 sts at beg of next 6 rows.
Cast off rem sts.

Collar

DO NOT PRESS.
Join left shoulder seam.
Using No.11 needles and with right side facing. K up 120 sts evenly round neck edge.

1st row P1, K2, *P2, K2, rep from * to last st, P1.
2nd row K1, P2, *K2, P2, rep from * to last st, K1.
Rep first and 2nd rows until collar measures 5½in or required depth. Cast off.

To make up

DO NOT PRESS.
Join right shoulder seam and collar.
Join side and sleeve seams.
Set in sleeves.

Short or long coat and trousers

This smart mix and match outfit can be made with either a long or a short coat. The raised basket stitch has a rich tweed effect.

Size

To fit 32[34:36:38]in bust
34[36:38:40]in hips
Long coat. Length to shoulder 43[43½:44:44½]in, adjustable
Short coat. Length to shoulder, 31[31½:32:32½]in, adjustable
Sleeve seam, 17½in adjustable
Trousers. Inside leg, 28[28½: 29:29½]in, adjustable
The figures in brackets [ ] refer to the 34, 36 and 38in sizes respectively

Materials shown here

Sirdar Double Crepe (50g balls)
Long coat. 26[27:28:28] balls
Short coat. 22[23:24:24] balls
Trousers. 13[13:14:14] balls
One pair No.9 needles
One pair No.11 needles
Long coat. 10 buttons
Short coat. 8 buttons
One press stud
Waist length elastic
One No.3·50 (ISR) Aero crochet hook

Coat back

Using No.11 needles, cast on 177[182:187:192] sts for long coat or 157[162:167:172] sts

for short coat.
Beg with a K row, work 1½in st st ending with a K row.
Next row P2, *P twice into next st, P4, rep from * to end. 212[218:224:230] sts for long coat, 188[194:200: 206] sts for short coat.
Change to No.9 needles.
Commence raised basket st patt.
1st row K1, *with yarn at back of work sl 3P, yfwd, P3, rep from * to last st, K1.
2nd row K1, *K3, yfwd, sl 3P, ybk, rep from * to last st, K1.
3rd row As 1st.
4th row As 2nd.
5th row K1, *M1K, K3 tog,, M1K, K3, rep from * to last st, K1.
6th row P.
7th row K1, *P3, ybk, sl 3P, yfwd, rep from * to last st, K1 omitting yfwd before knitting last st.
8th row K1, *yfwd, sl 3P, ybk, K3, rep from * to last st, K1.
9th row As 7th.
10th row As 8th.
11th row K1, *K3, M1K, K3 tog, M1K, rep from * to last st, K1.
12th row P.
These 12 rows form patt and are rep throughout.
Rep 12 patt rows once more.**
Continue in patt, dec one st at each end of next and every following 12th row until 152[158:164:170] sts rem. 30 dec long coat, 18 dec short coat.
Continue without shaping until work measures 36½in from hemline for long coat or 24½in from hemline for short coat, or required length to

underarm allowing for 1½in hem and ending with a WS row.

Shape armholes

Cast off 9 sts at beg of next 2 rows.
Dec one st at each end of next and following 5[8:8:11] alt rows. 122[122:128:128] sts.
Continue without shaping until armholes measure 6½[7:7½:8]in, ending with a WS row.

Shape shoulders

Cast off at beg of next and every row 9 sts 6 times and 10 sts twice. Cast off rem 48[48:54:54] sts.

Coat left front

Using No.11 needles, cast on 92[97:102:107] sts for long coat or 82[87:92:97] sts for short coat and work as given for Back to **. 110[116:122: 128] sts for long coat and 98[104:110:116] sts for short coat.
Continue in patt, dec one st at beg of next and every following 12th row until 80[86:92:98] sts rem.
Continue without shaping until work measures same as Back to underarm, ending with a WS row.

Shape armhole

Cast off 9[9:15:15] sts at beg of next row. Work 1 row.
Dec one st at beg of next and following 5[8:8:11] alt rows. 65[68:68:71] sts.
Continue without shaping until armhole measures 4½[5:5½:6]in from beg, ending with a RS row.

Shape neck

Cast off at beg of next and following 2 alt rows 12[15:15: 18] sts once and 3 sts twice.
Dec one st at neck edge on every alt row until 38 sts rem.
Continue without shaping until armhole measures same as Back to shoulder, ending with a WS row.

Shape shoulder

Cast off 9 sts at beg of next

and following 2 alt rows.
Work 1 row.
Cast off rem 11 sts.
Mark position for buttons on Left front, first to come ½in below neck edge, last to come 6in above hemline for long coat or 4in above hemline for short coat, with 8 more evenly spaced between for long coat or 6 more for short coat.

Coat right front

Work as given for Left front, reversing all shaping and making buttonholes as markers are reached as follows:
Next row (RS) Patt 4 sts, cast off 3 sts, patt to end.
Next row Patt to end, casting on 3 sts above those cast off.

Sleeves

Using No.11 needles, cast on 57[57:62:62] sts.
Beg with a K row, work 1in in st st, ending with a K row.
Next row P2, *P twice into next st, P4, rep from * to end. 68[68:74:74] sts.
Change to No.9 needles.
Continue in patt as given for Back, inc one st at each end of 7th and every following 8th row until there are 92[92: 98:98] sts, then at each end of every 6th row until there are 116[116:122:122] sts.
Continue without shaping until sleeve measures 17½in from hemline, or required length to underarm allowing 1in for hem and ending with a WS row.

Shape top

Cast off 9[9:12:12] sts at beg of next 2 rows.
Dec one st at each end of next and following 11[14:14: 17] alt rows. 74[68:68:62] sts.
Cast off 2 sts at beg of next 12 rows, 3 sts at beg of next 6[4:4:2] rows and 4 sts at beg of next 4 rows. Cast off rem 16 sts.

To make up

Press pieces under a damp cloth with a warm iron.
Join shoulder seams.

Front and neck edge
Using No.3·50 hook and RS
facing, work 1 row dc up
Right front, round neck and
down Left front, turn and
work second row dc. Fasten off.
Join side and sleeve seams.
Set in sleeves. Turn hems to
WS and slip stitch in place.
Press seams. Sew on buttons.

Trouser left leg

Using No.11 needles, cast on
137[142:147:152] sts.
Beg with a K row, work 1½in
st st, ending with a K row.
Next row P2, *P twice into
next st, P4, rep from * to
end, 164[170:176:182] sts.
Change to No.9 needles and
work 72 rows in raised basket
st patt as given for Coat.
Next row K1, *P1, P2 tog,
K1, K2 tog, rep from * to
last st, K1. 110[114:118:122]
sts.
Next row K1, *P2, K2, rep
from * to last st, K1.
Continue in plain basket st
patt.
1st row K1, *P2, K2, rep
from * to last st, K1.
2nd row K1, *K2, P2, rep
from * to last st, K1.
3rd and 4th rows As 2nd.
5th and 6th rows As 1st.
These 6 rows form patt.
Continue in patt, dec one st at
each end of 5th and every
following 8th row until 90[96:
102:108] sts rem.
Continue without shaping
until work measures 19[19½:
20:20½]in from beg, or adjust
leg length here allowing 1½in
for hem and ending with a
WS row.
Inc one st at each end of next
and every following 8th row
until there are 102[108:114:
120] sts, then each end of
every 6th row until there are
114[120:126:132] sts, ending
with an inc row.
Inc one st at each end of next
5 rows, ending with a WS row.
124[130:136:142] sts.
Dec one st at each end of
next and following 6 alt rows,
then each end of every 4th
row until 76[82:88:94] sts
rem. Work 1[3:5:7] rows after
last dec, ending with a WS
row.**

Shape back
Next row Patt 41[45:49:53]
sts, turn and patt to end.
Next row Patt 37[41:45:49]
sts, turn and patt to end.
Continue to work 4 sts less on
every alt row until row reads
patt 17, turn and patt to end.
Change to No.11 needles.
Beg with a K row continue in
st st for 1in, ending with a
P row.
Cast off.

Trouser right leg

Work as given for Left leg to
**. Work 1 more row.

Shape back
Work as given for Left leg
until row reads patt 17, turn
and patt to end.
Change to No.11 needles.
Beg with a P row, continue in
st st for 1in, ending with a P
row. Cast off.

To make up

Press as given for Coat.
Join Back and Front seams.
Join leg seams. Turn hems at
lower edge and waist to WS
and slip stitch in place. Press
seams. Thread elastic through
hem at waist and secure.

▲ The trouser suit ▼ Stitch detail

Trouser suit with two-tone jacket

Basic
Wardrobe
Knitting

Sizes
To fit 32[34:36:38]in bust
34[36:38:40]in hip
Jacket. Length at centre
back, 27[27½:28:28½]in
Sleeve seam, 21[21:21½:21½]in
Trousers. Inside leg seam,
29[30:30½:31½]in
The figures in brackets []
refer to the 34, 36 and 38in
sizes respectively

Tension for this design
7 sts and 8 rows to 1in
over st st worked on No.10
needles
8 sts and 8 rows to
1in over patt worked on
No.10 needles

Materials shown here
Patons Limelight Courtelle,
knits as 4 ply
Jacket. 6[7:8:9] 25g balls
in dark shade, A
11[12:13:15] 25g balls in
light shade, B
7 buttons
Trousers. 17[18:19:20]
25g balls in dark shade, A
One pair No.12 needles
One pair No.10 needles
One pair No.9 needles
Waist length of elastic

Trousers left leg

**Using No.12 needles and
A, cast on 160[166:174:180]
sts and work 7 rows st st beg
with a K row.
Next row K to form ridge
for hemline.
Change to No.10 needles and
continue in st st beg with a
K row, until work measures
10[11:11½:12½]in from
hemline, ending with a P row.
154

Shape leg
Next row K39[40:42:44],
K2 tog tbl, K78[82:86:88],
K2 tog, K39[40:42:44]. 158
[164:172:178] sts.
Work without shaping until
leg measures 14[15:15½:16½]
in from hemline, ending with
a P row.
Next row K39[40:42:44],
K2 tog tbl, K76[80:84:86],
K2 tog, K39[40:42:44]. 156
[162:170:176] sts.
Work without shaping until
leg measures 18[19:19½:20½]in
from hemline, ending with a
P row.
Next row K38[39:41:43], K2
tog tbl, K76[80:84:86], K2
tog, K38[39:41:43]. 154
[160:168:174] sts.
Work without shaping until
leg measures 22[23:23½:24½]in
from hemline, ending with a
P row.
Next row K38[39:41:43], K2
tog tbl, K74[78:82:84], K2
tog, K38[39:41:43]. 152
[158:166:172] sts.
Work without shaping until
leg measures 26[27:27½:28½]in
from hemline, ending with a
P row.
Next row K37[38:40:42], K2
tog tbl, K74[78:82:84], K2
tog, K37[38:40:42]. 150
[156:164:170] sts.
Work without shaping until
leg measures 29[30:30½:31½]
in from hemline, ending with
a P row.
Mark centre of last row with
coloured thread.

Shape front and back seams
Cast off 4 sts at beg of next
2 rows, then dec 1 st at each
end of next 3 rows. 136[142:
150:156] sts. Work 1 row.
Dec 1 st at each end of next

---

and every alt row until 128
[134:142:148] st rem.
Work 7[9:9:11] rows without
shaping.
Next row K2 tog, K60[63:
67:70], K2 tog tbl, K2 tog,
K to last 2 sts, K2 tog.
124[130:138:144] sts.
Work 7 rows.
Next row K2 tog, K58 [61:
65:68], K2 tog tbl, K2 tog,
K to last 2 sts, K2 tog,
120[126:134:140] sts.
Work 5 rows.
Next row K2 tog, K56[59:
63:66], K2 tog tbl, K2 tog,
K to last 2 sts, K2 tog.
116[122:130:136] sts.
Work 5 rows.
Continue dec in this way on
next and every following 6th
row until 88[94:102:108] sts
rem.
Continue without shaping
until work measures 9[9½:9½:
10]in from coloured marker
ending with a P row.**

Shape back
***1st row** K44[47:51:54],
turn.
2nd and every alt row P.
3rd row K33[35:38:40], turn.
5th row K22[23:25:26], turn.
7th row K11[11:12:12], turn.
9th row K across all sts
picking up loop at point
where work was turned and
knitting it tog with next st to
avoid hole.
Change to No.12 needles and
work in K1, P1 rib for 1in.
Cast off evenly in rib.

Right leg

Work as for left leg from **
to **.
Next row K.
Work as for left leg from ***
to end, reading P for K and K
for P.

To make up

With WS facing, block each
piece by pinning out round
edges and omitting ribbing,
press lightly using a cool iron
and a dry cloth.
Using a flat seam for ribbing
and a fine back-stitch seam
for remainder, join front,
back and leg seams.
Fold hems at hemline to

---

wrong side and slip stitch hem
in place. Work casing stitching
inside waistband and thread
with elastic. Press seams.

Jacket back

NB When working in stripe
patt carry yarn not in use
loosely up side of work.
Using No.12 needles and A,
cast on 129[137:145:153] sts.
Work 5 rows garter st.
Change to No.9 needles, join
in B and work in patt as
follows:
1st row (RS) Using B,
*K1, yfwd, K2, sl 1, K2 tog,
psso, K2, yfwd, rep from * to
last st, K1.
2nd row Using B, P.
Rep last 2 rows twice more.
7th row Using A, as 1st.
8th row Using A, as 2nd.
These 8 rows form patt.**
Continue in patt until Back
measures 10in, ending with
RS row.
Change to No.10 needles and
continue in patt until back
measures 20in, ending with
RS facing.

Shape armholes
Keeping patt correct, cast off
3 sts at beg of next 2 rows,
then dec 1 st at each end of
every row until 109[117:125:
133] sts rem.
Work 1 row.
Dec 1 st at each end of next
and every alt row until
97[101:105:109] sts rem.
Work without shaping until
Back measures 27[27½:28:28½]
in, ending with a WS row.

Shape shoulders
Cast off 9[9:9:10] sts at beg of
next 4 rows, then 8[9:10:9]
sts at beg of following 2 rows.
Cast off rem 45[47:49:51] sts.

Left front

Using No.12 needles and A,
cast on 65[69:73:77] sts. K 5
rows.
Change to No.9 needles, join
in B and patt as follows:
1st and 3rd sizes only.
Work as for Back from ** to
**.
2nd and 4th sizes only.
1st row (RS) Using B, *K1,

yfwd, K2, sl 1, K2 tog, psso, K2, yfwd, rep from * to last 5 sts, K1, yfwd, K2, K2 tog tbl.
2nd row Using B, P.
Rep last 2 rows twice more.
7th row Using A, as 1st.
8th row Using A, as 2nd.
These 8 rows form the patt.
***All sizes** Continue in patt until Front measures 10in, ending with RS facing. Change to No.10 needles and continue in patt until Front measures 20in, ending with same patt row as Back, ending with WS row.

Shape armhole and front edge
Next row Keeping patt correct, cast off 3 sts, patt to last 2[3:2:3] sts, K2[3:2:3] tog. 61[64:69:72] sts.
Next row P.
Dec 1 st at armhole edge on every row *at the same time* dec 1 st at neck edge on next and every alt row until 50[54:58:62] sts rem.
Work 1 row.
Dec 1 st at each end of next and every alt row until 38 sts rem.
Keeping armhole edge straight, continue dec 1 st at neck edge on every alt row as before until 26[27:28:29] sts rem.
Work without shaping until Front measures same as Back to shoulder, ending with RS facing.

Shape shoulder
Cast off 9[9:9:10] sts at beg of next and following alt rows.
Work 1 row.
Cast off rem 8[9:10:9] sts.

Right front

Using No.12 needles and A, cast on 65[69:73:77] sts. K 5 rows.

Change to No.9 needles. Join in B and work in patt as follows:
1st and 3rd sizes only.
Work as for Back from ** to **.

2nd and 4th sizes only.
1st row (RS) Using B, K2 tog, K2, yfwd, *K1, yfwd, K2, sl 1, K2 tog, psso, K2, yfwd, rep from * to last st, K1.
2nd row Using B, P.
Rep last 2 rows twice more.
7th row Using B, as 1st.
8th row Using B, as 2nd.
These 8 rows form patt.
Work as for Left front from *** to end, reversing shaping.

Sleeves

Using No.12 needles and A, cast on 50[52:54:56] sts and work in K1, P1 rib for 3½in.
Next row (Rib 1, K up yarn before next st—called M1—,) 2[5:2:5] times, *inc in next st, M1, rep from * to last 2[5:2:5] sts, (rib 1, M1) 1[4:1:4] times, rib 1. 145[145:157:

157] sts.
Change to No.10 needles.
Join in B and patt as follows:
1st row (RS) Using B, *K1, yfwd, K4, sl 1, K2 tog, psso, K4, yfwd, rep from * to last st, K1.
2nd row Using B, P.
Rep last 2 rows twice more.
7th row Using A, as 1st.
8th row Using A, as 2nd.
These 8 rows form patt.
Continue in patt until sleeve measures 12½in, ending with a WS row.

Shape sleeve
Next row *K1, yfwd, K3, sl 2, K3 tog, p2sso, K3, yfwd, rep from * to last st, K1. 121[121:131:131] sts.
Next row P.
Next row *K1, yfwd, K3, sl 1, K2 tog, psso, K3, yfwd, rep from * to last st, K1.
Keeping patt correct, rep last 2 rows until sleeve seam measures 3½in, ending with WS facing.
Next row *K1, yfwd, K2,

sl 2, K3 tog, p2sso, K2, yfwd, rep from * to last st, K1. 97[97:105:105] sts.
Next row P.
Next row *K1, yfwd, K2, sl 1, k2 tog, psso, K2, yfwd, rep from * to last st, K1.
Keeping patt correct, rep last 2 rows until sleeve seam measures about 21[21:21½:21½]in, ending with same patt row as Back before armhole shaping.

Shape top
Cast off 3 sts at beg of next 2 rows.
Dec 1 st at each end of next and every alt row until 73[65:73:65] sts rem.
Work 1 row.
Dec 1 st at each end of every row until 29 sts rem.
Cast off.

To make up

Omitting garter st, block and press as for Trousers. Join shoulder, side and sleeve seams.
Set in sleeves.

Left front border
Using No.12 needles and A, cast on 11 sts.
1st row (RS) K2, (P1, K1) 4 times, K1.
2nd row (K1, P1) 5 times, K1.
Rep last 2 rows until border fits Left front and round to centre of Back when slightly stretched.
Cast off in rib.

Right front border
Work as for Left border with addition of 7 buttonholes, first to come ½in above lower edge, 7th at start of neck shaping and remainder evenly spaced between.
First mark positions of buttons on Left front then work buttonholes as markers are reached.
Buttonhole row. (RS) Rib 4, cast off 3, rib to end.
On next row cast on 3 sts above those cast off.
Join borders at centre back and stitch in position.
Press seams.
Sew on buttons.

Smart outfits for larger sizes

Five smart outfits from one pattern, specially designed for larger sizes from forty inch to forty eight inch bust. Almost an entire wardrobe, this wonderful pattern will make a sleeveless dress and jacket, a jersey and skirt, a short sleeved dress, a long sleeved dress and a sleeveless jacket.

Sizes

To fit 40[42:44:46:48]in bust
Dress. 42[44:46:48:50]in hips
Length to shoulder, 43[44:45: 46:47]in, or as required
Jacket. Length to shoulder, 25[26:27:28:29]in
Sleeve seam, 17in or as required
The figures in brackets [] refer to the 42, 44, 46 and 48in bust sizes respectively

Tension for this design
Dress. 7 sts and 9 rows to 1in over st st worked on No.10 needles
Jacket. 6½ sts and 9 rows to 1in over st st worked on No.10 needles

Materials shown here
Dress. Sirdar Fontein Crepe 4 ply
19[21:23:25:27]oz balls
One pair No.10 needles
12in zip fastener
Jacket. Sirdar Double Crepe
14[14:15:16:17] 50g balls
One pair No.10 needles
11 buttons

Dress Back

Cast on 175[183:191:199:207] sts.

1st row K1, *P1, K1, rep from * to end.
Rep 1st row until work measures 3in ending with a WS row.
Continue in st st beg with a K row.
Work 4in (for longer or shorter dress work more or less rows at this point).
1st dec row K40[42:44:46: 48], sl 1, K1, psso, K until 42[44:46:48:50] sts rem, K2 tog, K to end.
Work 7 rows st st beg with a P row.
Rep last 8 rows 19 times. more. 135[143:151:159:167] sts.
Work 39[41:43:45:47] rows without shaping.

Shape for bust
1st row K40[42:44:46:48], K up 1 tbl, K until 40[42:44: 46:48] sts rem, K up 1 tbl, K to end.
Work 7 rows st st beg with a P row.
Rep last 8 rows 5 times more. 147[155:163:171:179] sts.
Continue on these sts until work measures 35[35½:36: 36½:37]in, or required length ending with a P row.

Shape armholes
Cast off 12[13:14:14:14] sts at beg of next 2 rows.
Dec one st at beg of every row until 99[105:111:117:123] sts rem.
Work without shaping until armholes measures 8[8½:9:9½: 10]in, ending with a K row.

Shape neck
1st row P33[35:37:39:41], cast off 33[35:37:39:41], P to end.

Work on these sts for right shoulder.

Shape shoulder
1st row Cast off 7[7:8:9:9] sts, K to last 2 sts, K2 tog.
2nd row P2 tog, P to end.
Rep last 2 rows once more.
5th row Cast off 7[8:8:8:9] sts. K to last 2 sts, K2 tog.
6th row P.
Cast off rem 7[8:8:8:9] sts.
With RS facing rejoin yarn to rem sts and K to end.

Shape second shoulder
Work to correspond with first shoulder.

Dress Front

Work as given for Back until armhole shaping is complete and armholes measure 5½[6:6½:7:7½]in, ending with a K row.

Shape neck
1st row P38[40:42:44:46] sts, cast off 23[25:27:29:31] sts, P to end.
Work on last set of sts only for left shoulder, dec one st at neck edge on next and every alt row until 28[30:32: 34:36] sts rem. Work 1 row. (When working second side work 2 rows instead of 1.)

Shape shoulder
Cast off 7[7:8:9:9] sts at beg of next and following alt row, then cast off 7[8:8:8:9] sts at beg of next 2 alt rows.
With RS of work facing rejoin yarn to rem sts and work second side to correspond.

To make up

Press pieces lightly on wrong side using a damp cloth and a warm iron. Join left shoulder seam.

Neckband
With RS facing, K up 121 [125:129:133:137] sts round neck edge.
Work in moss st for 11[11:11: 12:12] rows. Cast off in moss st.
Join right shoulder seam.
Press shoulder seams.

Armbands
With RS facing, K up 133 [141:149:157:163] sts round armhole. Work in moss st for 11[11:11:12:12] rows.
Cast off in moss st.
Join right side seam and left side leaving 12in open for zip fastener about 3in below armhole. Sew in zip.
Press seams on wrong side.

Jacket Back

Cast on 127[133:139:145:151] sts.

1st row K1, *P1, K1, rep from * to end.
Rep first row 11 times more for moss st border.
Continue in st st beg with a K row.
Work until 16½[17:17½:18: 18½]in from cast on edge, ending with a P row.

Shape armholes
Cast off 8 sts at beg of next 2 rows.
Dec one st at beg of every row until 95[101:107:113:119] sts rem.
Work without shaping until armholes measure 8½[9:9½:10: 10½]in, ending with a P row.

Shape shoulders
Cast off 8[8:9:9:10] sts at beg of next 4 rows.
Cast off 7[8:8:9:9] sts at beg next 4 rows.
Cast off rem 35[37:39:41:43] sts.

Jacket left front

Cast on 81[85:89:93:97] sts.
Work in moss st as for Back for 12 rows.
Next row K to last 9 sts, moss st 9.
Next row Moss st 9, P to end.
Rep last 2 rows until work measures same length as Back to armhole, ending at side edge.

Shape armhole and border
1st row Cast off 8 sts, K to last 9 sts, moss st 9.
2nd row Moss st 9, P to end.
3rd row Sl 1, K1, psso, K to last 11 sts, K2 tog, lift thread before next st and K into back of it—called K up 1

tbl—, moss st to end.

4th row Moss st 10, P to end.

5th row Sl 1, K1, psso, K to last 10 sts, moss st 10.

6th row As 4th.

7th row Sl 1, K1, psso, K to last 12 sts, K2 tog, K up 1 tbl, moss st to end.

8th row Moss st 11, P to end.

Continue in this way for 10 more rows working the K2 tog, K up 1 tbl on 11th and 15th rows and dec at armhole edge on K rows. 65[69:73:77: 81] sts.

Work bust shaping

1st row K24[26:28:30:32], K2 tog, K24[26:28:30:32], K2 tog, K up 1 tbl, moss st to end.

2nd row Moss st 14, P to end.

3rd row K to last 14 sts, moss st to end.

4th row As 2nd.

5th row K to last 16 sts, K2 tog, K up 1 tbl, moss st to end.

6th row Moss st 15, P to end.

7th row K to last 15 sts, moss st to end.

8th row As 6th.

9th row K23[25:27:29:31], K2 tog, K to last 17 sts, K2 tog, K up 1 tbl, moss st to end.

10th row Moss st 16, P to end.

Continue to work bust dec every 8th row from last dec *at same time* working the K2 tog, K up 1 tbl before the moss st border every 4th row as before until there are 23 moss sts, ending at centre Front edge.

Shape rever

1st row Cast off 14[15:16:17: 18] sts, work to end.

2nd row K to moss st border, moss st to end.

NB The moss st border sts are now kept straight but work the K2 tog (omitting the K up 1 tbl) every 4th row as before, also working the bust dec every 8th row as before *at the same time* dec one st at neck edge every WS row until 7[8:8:8:9] bust dec have been worked and 33[32:34:36:38] sts rem. End at armhole edge.

Dress with contrast jacket ▶

▲ *Sleeveless and slimming for larger sizes*

▲ *Adaptation for a sleeveless jersey and skirt*

For 42, 44, 46 and 48in sizes only Continue on these sts until armhole measures same as Back to shoulder, ending at armhole edge.

Shape shoulder
1st row Cast off 8[8:9:9:10] sts, K to end.
2nd row For 40in size only Dec one st.
For all sizes P to end.
Rep last 2 rows once more.
5th row Cast off 7[8:8:9:9] sts, K to end.
6th row As 2nd.
Cast off rem sts.

Jacket right front

Cast on 81[85:89:93:97] sts.
Work 12 rows moss st as for Back.
Next row Moss st 9, K to end.
Next row P to last 9 sts, moss st to end.
Rep last 2 rows 11[13:15:17:

19] times more.
1st buttonhole row Moss st 3, cast off 3 sts, moss st 3, K to end.
2nd buttonhole row P to last 6 sts, moss st 3, cast on 3 sts, moss st 3.
Continue in patt making 4 more buttonholes with 24 rows between each of the buttonholes.
Next row Moss st 9, K to end.

Shape armholes
1st row Cast off 8 sts, P to last 9 sts, moss st to end.
2nd row Moss st 9, K up 1 tbl, sl 1, K1, psso, K to end.
3rd row P2 tog, P to last 10 sts, moss st 10.
4th row Moss st 10, K to end.
5th row As 3rd.
6th row Moss st 10, K up 1 tbl, sl 1, K1, psso, K to end.
Continue as set until 61[65:69:73:77] sts rem, ending at Front edge.

Work bust shaping
1st row Moss st 14, K up 1 tbl, l sl, K1, psso, K24[26:28:30:32], sl 1, K1, psso, K to end.
Continue working to correspond with Left front, working bust dec every 8th row and inc number of moss st border for rever every 4th row until 23[23:23:24:24] sts are in moss st, then shape rever and continue to match other side.

Sleeves

Cast of 65[67:69:71:73] sts.
Work in moss st for 12 rows as for Back.
Continue in st st beg with a K row. Work 4in.
Inc one st at each end of next and every 10th[10th:8th:8th:8th] row until there are 85[89:93:97:101] sts.
Work without shaping until sleeve measures 17in or

required length ending with a P row.

Shape top
Cast off 8 sts at beg of next 2 rows.
Dec one st at beg of every row until 39 sts rem.
Dec one st at each end of every row until 27 sts rem.
Cast off.

Collar

Cast on 21[25:29:33:37] sts.
Work one row moss st as given for Back.
Continue in moss st casting on 6 sts at beg of next 10 rows 81[85:89:93:97] sts.
Work 26[28:30:32:34] rows in moss st. Cast off loosely.

Cuffs

Cast on 75[77:79:81:83] sts.
Work in moss st as for Back for 6 rows.

158

▲ *Adaptation to make a short sleeved dress*

▲ *Adaptation to make a long sleeved dress and sleeveless jacket*

7th row Moss st 5, K to last 5 sts, moss st to end.

8th row Moss st 5, P to last 5 sts, moss st to end.

Rep last 2 rows once more.

11th row Moss st 5, cast off 3, K to last 5 sts, moss st to end.

12th row Moss st 5, P to last 5 sts, cast on 3 sts, moss st 5.

Rep 7th and 8th rows 8 times more, then rep 11th and 12th rows once.

Work 7th and 8th rows twice more.

Work 6 rows moss st. Cast off in moss st.

2nd cuff

Work as for first cuff to end of 10th row.

11th row Moss st 5, K to last 8 sts, cast off 3 sts, moss st 5.

12th row Moss st 5, cast on 3 sts, P to last 5 sts, moss st 5.

Rep 7th and 8th rows 8 times more, then 11th and 12th rows once.

Rep 7th and 8th rows twice more.

Work 6 rows moss st. Cast off in moss st.

Pockets

Cast on 39 sts.

Work 10 rows moss st as given for Back.

11th row Moss st 7, K to last 7 sts, moss st to end.

12th row Moss st 7, P to last 7 sts, moss st to end.

Rep last 2 rows 16 times more.

Work 4 rows moss st.

49th row Moss st 18, cast off 3 sts, moss st to end.

50th row Moss st 18, cast on 3 sts, moss st to end.

Work 4 rows in moss st. Cast off in moss st.

To make up

Press pieces on wrong side under a damp cloth with a warm iron.

Join shoulder seams, side seams and sleeve seams. Press seams.

Set in sleeves. Sew collar to neck edge placing centre of cast on sts to centre back of neck with ends in centre of revers. Sew one cuff to each sleeve with buttonhole on outer edge. Sew pocket to each front above border. Sew on buttons to correspond with buttonholes.

Mixing and matching the patterns

By using the basic patterns it is possible to adapt the garments to simple alternatives.

Dress with long sleeves

Work the dress as given, omitting armbands.

Using No.10 needles and Fontein Crepe 4 ply, work sleeves as given for the jacket, omitting cuffs.

Dress with short sleeves

Using No.10 needles and Fontein Crepe 4 ply, cast on 77[81:85:89:93] sts. Work 12 rows moss st.

Continue in st st beg with a K row, inc one st at each end of next and every 8th row until there are 85[89:93:97:101] sts.

Work without shaping until sleeve measures 5in or required length.

Complete as given for jacket sleeve.

Waistcoat

Work back, fronts and collar as given for jacket, omitting sleeves, buttonholes and pockets.

Work the armbands by first joining the shoulder seams.

Using No.10 needles and with RS facing, K up 123[127:131:135] sts.

Work 6 rows moss st. Cast off. Sear sides.

Beaded angora evening top

Basic Wardrobe Knitting

Soft angora yarn, a simple lace pattern and the sparkle of beads add up to an elegant and extremely glamorous evening top.

Size
To fit 32[34:36:38]in bust
Length to shoulder, 20¼ [20½:20¾:21]in
The figures in brackets [ ] refer to the 34, 36 and 38in sizes respectively

```
Tension for this design
6 sts and 8 rows to 1in
over patt worked on No.9
needles
```

Materials shown here
Patons Fuzzy Wuzzy 8[9:10:11] ½oz balls
One pair No.9 needles
One pair No.10 needles
One pair No.11 needles
Approx. 1050 beads
NB. Thread 350 beads onto each of 3 balls of yarn

Back

Using No.10 needles, cast on 103[109:115:121] sts.
Beg with a K row, work 5 rows st st.
Picot hemline (WS) K1, *yfwd, K2 tog, rep from * to end.
Change to No.9 needles and beaded yarn.
1st row K2, *yfwd, sl 1, push bead up to stitch so that it sits in front of slipped stitch, ybk—called B1 —, K1, rep from * to last st, K1.
2nd row P.
3rd row K1, *B1, K1, rep from * to end.

4th row P.
Rep 1st to 4th rows once.
Break off bead yarn and continue in patt.
1st patt row K1, *yfwd, K2 tog tbl, K1, K2 tog, yfwd, K1, rep from * to end.
2nd patt row P.
3rd patt row K1, *yfwd, K1, sl 1, K2 tog, psso, K1, yfwd, K1, rep from * to end.
4th patt row P.
5th patt row K1, *K2 tog, yfwd, K1, yfwd, K2 tog tbl, K1, rep from * to end.
6th patt row P.
7th patt row K2 tog, *(K1, yfwd) twice, K1, sl 1, K2 tog, psso, rep from * to last 5 sts, (K1, yfwd) twice, K1, K2 tog tbl.
8th patt row P.
These 8 rows form the patt and are rep throughout.
Work 8 rows more.

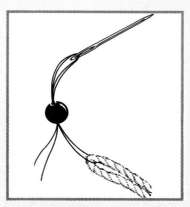

▲ *Threading bead onto the yarn*

Change to No.10 needles.
Work 16 rows.
Change to No.11 needles.
Work 8 rows.
Change to No.10 needles.
Work 16 rows.
Change to No.9 needles.
Continue in patt until work

measures 13¾in ending with 8th patt row.

Shape armholes
Cast off 6[7:8:9] sts at beg of next 2 rows.
Cast off 2 sts at beg of next 4 rows.
Dec one st at each end of next and every alt row until 73[75:77:79] sts rem.
Bead rem of Back by adding beads on every 1st and 5th patt rows between K2 tog tbl and K2 tog by slipping the stitch between and placing a bead in front of ss.
Continue until armholes measure 6½[6¾:7:7¼] in ending with a WS row.

Shape neck
1st row Patt 22[23:24:25], cast off 29 sts, patt to end.
Complete left shoulder on these sts.
2nd row P.
3rd row Cast off 3 sts, patt to end.
4th row Cast off 5[6:7:8] sts, P to end.
5th row Cast off 3 sts, patt to end.
6th row Cast off 5 sts, P to end.
7th row Cast off 2 sts, patt to end.
8th row Cast off rem 4 sts.
With WS of work facing, rejoin yarn to rem sts.
1st row Cast off 3 sts, P to end.
2nd row Cast off 5[6:7:8] sts, patt to end.
3rd row Cast off 3 sts, P to end.
4th row Cast off 5 sts, patt to end.
5th row Cast off 2 sts, P to end.
6th row Cast off rem 4 sts.

Front

Work as given for Back until armholes measure 2¾[3:3¼:3½]in ending with a WS row.

Shape neck
1st row Patt 26[27:28:29], cast off 21 sts, patt to end.
Complete right front on these sts.
2nd row P.

3rd row Cast off 3 sts, patt to end.
4th row P.
5th row Cast off 3 sts, patt to end.
6th row P.
7th row Cast off 2 sts, patt to end.
8th row P.
Dec one st at beg of next and every alt row until 14[15:16:17] sts rem.
Work until armhole measures same as Back to shoulder ending at armhole edge.

Shape shoulder
Cast off at beg of next and alt rows, 5[6:7:8] sts once, 5 sts once and 4 sts once.
With WS facing, rejoin yarn to rem sts and work left front to correspond.

Neckband

Join left shoulder seam.
Using No.10 needles and with RS of work facing and beaded yarn, K up 49 sts across Back, K up 30 sts down left front neck, 21 sts from centre front and 30 sts up right front.
**P 1 row.
2nd row K1, *B1, K1, rep from * to last st, K1.
3rd row P.
4th row K2, *B1, K1, rep from * to end.
Picot row K1, *yfwd, K2 tog, rep from * to last st, K1.
Change to No.11 needles.
Beg with a K row, work 4 rows st st. Cast off loosely.**

Armbands

Join right shoulder seam and neckband.
Using No.10 needles and beaded yarn, K up 86[90:92:96] sts evenly round armhole.
Work as for Neckband from ** to **.
Work another band in the same way.

To make up

Press lightly under a dry cloth if required.
Join side seams.
Fold hemlines to wrong side along picot rows and slip stitch in place.

Lacy dress in circular knitting

This charming scoop-necked knee-length dress, knitted in lacy stitch, is worked circularly so that there are no side seams to make up and so the skirt hangs particularly well. The sleeves are raglan-shaped, with an easy fit, and are finished with a neat ribbed cuff to match the neckline edge.

Sizes

To fit 34[36:38:40]in bust
Length from shoulder to lower edge, 45[46¾:48½:50¼]in, adjustable
Sleeve seam, 12½[12½:13½:13½]in

The figures in brackets [] refer to the 36, 38 and 40in sizes respectively

---

Basic yarn tension
7½ sts and 9½ rows to 1in over st st worked on No.10 needles

Materials shown here

Sirdar Fontein Crepe 4 ply 20[22:24:27]1oz balls
One Aero Twin-Pin No.11, 16in long
One Aero Twin-Pin No.11, 36in long
One Aero Twin-Pin No.12, 16in long
One large stitch holder

Dress

Begin at lower edge of skirt, using No.11 Aero Twin-Pin cast on 396[432:468:504]sts. Work to and fro.

1st row *K1, P1, rep from * to end.
2nd row *P1, K1, rep from * to end.
Rep these 2 rows 5 times more. Join work into a circle and continue in rounds. Place marker thread at beginning of round.

1st round *K4, yfwd, K4, sl 1, K2 tog, psso, K4, yfwd, K3, rep from * to end of round.
2nd and every alt round K.
3rd round *K5, yfwd, K3, sl 1, K2 tog, psso, K3, yfwd, K4, rep from * to end of round.
5th round *K6, yfwd, K2, sl 1, K2 tog, psso, K2, yfwd, K5, rep from * to end of round.
7th round *K7, yfwd, K1, sl 1, K2 tog, psso, K1, yfwd, K6, rep from * to end of round.
9th round *K4, (yfwd, sl 1, K2 tog, psso, yfwd, K1) 3 times, K2, rep from * to end of round.
10th round K.
These 10 rounds form patt. Rep 1st—10th rounds 7[8:9:10] times more. If the length is to be altered work more or less patterns at this point, allowing 1in for each patt. Work the 1st patt round once.
1st dec round *K2 tog, K16, rep from * to end of round. 374[408:442:476] sts.
Next round *K4, yfwd, K3, sl 1, K2 tog, psso, K3, yfwd, K4, rep from * to end of round.
Continue in patt as now set, noting that 1 less st is worked at the beg of each patt rep. Work until 5 more patts have been completed, then work 1st patt round omitting last K st of round.
2nd dec round *K2 tog, K15,

rep from * to end of round. 352[384:416:448] sts.
Next round *K4, yfwd, K3, sl 1, K2 tog, psso, K3, yfwd, K3, rep from * to end of round. Continue in patt as set, working 1 st less at beg and end of each patt rep until 3 more patts have been completed. Work 1st patt round once.
3rd dec round *K2 tog, K14, rep from * to end. 330[360:390:420] sts.
Next round *K3, yfwd, K3, sl 1, K2 tog, psso, K3, yfwd, K3, rep from * to end of round. Continue in patt as set, working 2 sts less at beg and 1 st less at end of each patt rep until 3 complete patts have been worked. Work 1st patt round once, omitting last K st.
4th dec round *K2 tog, K13, rep from * to end. 308[336:364:392] sts.
Next round *K3, yfwd, K3, sl 1, K2 tog, psso, K3, yfwd, K2, rep from * to end of round. Continue in patt as set, working 2 sts less at each end of every patt rep until 3 more patts have been completed. Work 1st patt round once.
5th dec round *K2 tog, K12, rep from * to end. 286[312:338:364] sts.
Next round *K2, yfwd, K3, sl 1, K2 tog, psso, K3, yfwd, K2, rep from * to end. Continue in patt as set, working 3 sts less at beg and 2 sts less at end of each patt rep until 3 more patts have been completed. Work 1st patt round once, omitting last K st and ending with yfwd.
6th dec round *K2 tog, K11, rep from * to end of round. 264[288:312:336] sts.
Next round *K2, yfwd, K3, sl 1, K2 tog, psso, K3, yfwd, K1, rep from * to end of round. Continue in patt as set, working 3 sts less at each end of every patt rep until work measures 30[31:32:33] in, or required length to waist.
Continue in different patt which is used throughout bodice and sleeves.

1st round *K1, yfwd, K4, sl 1, K2 tog, psso, K4, yfwd, rep from * to end of round.
2nd and every alt round K.
3rd round K2, *yfwd, K3, sl 1, K2 tog, psso, K3, yfwd, K3, rep from * to end of round ending with K1 instead of K3.
5th round K2 tog, *yfwd, K1, yfwd, K2, sl 1, K2 tog, psso, K2, yfwd, K1, yfwd, sl 1, K2 tog, psso, rep from * to last 10 sts, yfwd, K1, yfwd, K2, sl 1, K2 tog, psso, K2, yfwd, K2 tog, yfwd.
7th round *Yfwd, sl 1, K1, psso, K2, yfwd, K1, sl 1, K2 tog, psso, K1, yfwd, K3, rep from * to end of round.
9th round K1, *yfwd, sl 1, K2 tog, psso, yfwd, K1, rep from * to end of round, omitting last K st.
10th round K.
These 10 rounds form the bodice patt.
Rep 1st—10th rounds once more.
Inc round Inc for the sides as follows: *inc in first st, work in patt until 11[12:13:14] patts have been worked, inc in last st*, rep from * to * thus increasing 2 sts at each side.
Marker threads placed at each inc will make counting easy.
Work 9 rounds patt, knitting the extra inc sts.
Rep last 10 rounds 3 times more. 8 sts have now been increased at each side. Mark beg of round in centre of 8 st panel 4 sts in.
Work without shaping until work measures 39[40¼:41½:42¾]in, ending after a K round.

Shape front raglan armholes

1st row Cast off 4 sts, work in patt until 11[12:13:14] patts have been worked, K4, turn and work to and fro on these sts only.
2nd row Cast off 4 sts, P to end.
3rd row K2, sl 1, K1, psso, work to last 4 sts, K2 tog, K2.
4th row P.
Rep last 2 rows 3[5:7:9] times more.

Shape front neck

1st row K2, sl 1, K1, psso, patt 40[43:46:49] sts, turn and work on these sts only.

2nd row P.

3rd row K2, sl 1, K1, psso, patt to last 2 sts, K2 tog.

4th row P.

Rep last 2 rows 3[4:5:6] times more.

**Continue to dec at armhole edge on next and every RS row *at the same time* dec one st at neck edge on every 4th row until 21[16:23:18] sts rem. Continue to dec at armhole edge as before but keep neck edge straight until 3 sts rem, P3. Cast off.

With RS facing, sl first 36 [38:40:42] sts on stitch holder, rejoin yarn to rem sts.

1st row Patt to last 4 sts, K2 tog, K2.

2nd row P.

3rd row Dec one st, patt to last 4 sts, K2 tog, K2.

4th row Rep last 2 rows 3[4:5:6] times more.

Complete as for first side, working from ** to end.

Shape back raglan armholes

With RS facing, rejoin yarn to rem sts, cast off 4 sts at beg of next 2 rows.

3rd row K2, sl 1, K1, psso, patt to last 4 sts, K2 tog K2.

4th row P.

Rep last 2 rows 6[8:10:12] times more.

Shape back neck

1st row K2, sl 1, K1, psso, patt 34[37:40:43], turn and work on these sts only.

2nd row P.

3rd row K2, sl 1, K1, psso, patt to last 2 sts, K2 tog.

4th row P.

Rep last 2 rows 0[1:2:4] times more. Complete from ** of first side of front neck to end.

With RS of work facing, sl first 42[44:46:48] sts onto a st holder, rejoin yarn to rem sts and work to correspond with other side.

Sleeves

Using No.12 Twin-Pin, cast on 74[74:86:86] sts. Work to and fro throughout sleeve.

Work 16 rows K1, P1 rib.
Change to No.11 (16in) Twin-Pin and work in patt as given for bodice adding 1 K st at each end to allow for seaming.

1st row K1, *K1, yfwd, K4, sl 1, K2 tog, psso, K4, yfwd, rep from * to last st, K1.

2nd row P.

Continue in patt as set until 10th row has been completed then inc one st at each end of next and every 6th row until there are 98[102:106:110] sts, working the inc sts into patt as they are made.

Work without further shaping until sleeve measures 12½[12½: 13½:13½]in, ending with a P row.

Shape top

Cast off 4 sts at beg of next 2 rows.

3rd row K2, sl 1, K1, psso, patt to last 4 sts, K2 tog, K2.

4th row P.

Rep last 2 rows until 18 sts rem. Leave sts on st holder for neck ribbing.

To make up

Press each piece lightly on WS under a damp cloth and using a warm iron. Join sleeve seams.

Sew sleeve into armhole.

Slip the 42[44:46:48] sts from back st holder onto No.12 Twin-Pin, slip sts from one sleeve top onto Twin-Pin, slip 36[38:40:42] sts from front and sts from second sleeve top all onto same needle.

Join yarn to end of 18 sts of right sleeve and knit up 34 sts to st holder, rib 42[44:46: 48] sts from holder, then K up 34 sts to left sleeve, rib 18 sts sleeve and K up 66 sts to stitch holder, rib 36[38:40:42] sts from holder, K up 66 sts to right sleeve and rib 18 sts from sleeve. 314[318:322: 326] sts.

Work in rounds of K1, P1 rib for 12 rounds. Cast off in rib.

Above left: a charmingly elegant dress knitted in a fine lace pattern and tied at the waist with a silky tasselled cord

Below left: a close-up detail of the lace pattern

Bridal coat in lace stitch

This superb design represents all that is best in hand knitting. Shown here as an exquisite bridal coat, the same pattern would make an evening coat if it were knitted in a bright coloured yarn. Alternatively, by carrying the buttonloop fastening down to the hem, .the coat would make an elegant coat-dress for evening occasions. The hood is optional and can be left off, leaving a mandarin collar.

Size
To fit a 34-36in bust
36-38in hips
Length from centre back, 58in
Sleeve seam, 18in

Basic yarn tension
7 sts and 9 rows to 1in over st st worked on No.10 needles

Tension for this design
7½ sts and 9 rows to 1in over patt worked on No.10 needles

Materials shown here
Jaeger Dappelwul 4 ply
Coat. 28 1 oz balls
Hood. 3 1 oz balls
One pair No.10 needles
One No.3·00 (ISR) crochet hook
70 pearls, optional

Back

Using No.10 needles cast on 250 sts.
1st row K1, P8, *K6, yfwd, sl 1, K2 tog, psso, yfwd, K6, P16, rep from * ending P8, K1 instead of P16.
2nd and every alt row K9, *P15, K16, rep from * ending K9 instead of K16.
3rd row As 1st.

5th row As 1st.
7th row As 1st.
9th row K1, P8, *K1, yfwd, K1, yfwd, sl 1, K1, psso, K2, sl 1, K2 tog, psso, K2, K2 tog, yfwd, K1, yfwd, K1, P16, rep from * ending P8, K1, instead of P16.
11th row K1, P8, *K2, yfwd, K1, yfwd, sl 1, K1, psso, K1, sl 1, K2 tog, psso, K1, K2 tog, yfwd, K1, yfwd, K2, P16, rep from * ending P8, K1, instead of P16.
13th row K1, P8, *K3, yfwd, K1, yfwd, sl 1, K1, psso, sl 1, K2 tog, psso, K2 tog, yfwd, K1, yfwd, K3, P16, rep from * ending P8, K1, instead of P16.
15th row K1, P8, *K4, yfwd, sl 1, K1, psso, yfwd, sl 1, K2 tog, psso, yfwd, K2 tog, yfwd, K4, P16, rep from * ending P8, K1, instead of P16.
16th row As 2nd.
These 16 rows form the patt and are rep throughout.
Continue in patt until work measures 8in from beg, ending with a RS row.
1st dec row K7, K2 tog, *P15, sl 1, K1, psso, K12, K2 tog, rep from * ending sl 1, K1, psso, K7.
Continue in patt with 1 st less in the P panels at each side and 2 sts less in the rem P panels, until work measures 14in from beg, ending with a RS row.
2nd dec row K6, K2 tog, *P15, sl 1, K1, psso, K10, K2 tog, rep from * ending sl 1, K1, psso, K6.
Continue in patt until work measures 20in from beg, ending with a RS row.
3rd dec row K5, K2 tog, *P15, sl 1, K1, psso, K8, K2 tog, rep from * ending sl 1, K1, psso, K5.
Continue in patt until work measures 26in from beg, ending with a RS row.
4th dec row K4, K2 tog, *P15, sl 1, K1, psso, K6, K2 tog, rep from * ending sl 1, K1, psso, K4.
Continue in patt until work measures 32in from beg, ending with a RS row.
5th dec row K3, K2 tog,

*P15, sl 1, K1, psso, K4, K2 tog, rep from * ending sl 1, K1, psso, K3.
Continue in patt until work measures 38in from beg, ending with a RS row.
6th dec row K2, K2 tog, *P15, sl 1, K1, psso, K2, K2 tog, rep from * ending sl 1, K1, psso, K2.
Continue in patt until work measures 44in from beg, ending with a RS row.
7th dec row K1, K2 tog, *P15, sl 1, K1, psso, K2 tog, rep from * ending sl 1, K1, psso, K1. 138 sts.
Continue in patt with 2 sts in each P panel.
Work 34 rows.

Shape armholes
Cast off at beg of next and following rows 8 sts twice and 2 sts 4 times.
Dec one st at beg of every row until 104 sts rem.
Continue without shaping until armholes measure 6¾in from beg, ending with a WS row.

Shape shoulders
Cast off at beg of next and following rows 6 sts twice, 5 sts twice and 6 sts twice.

Shape back neck
Next row Cast off 5 sts, patt 14 sts, cast off 32 sts, patt to end.
Complete this side first.
1st row Cast off 5 sts, patt to last 2 sts, dec one st.
2nd row Dec one st, patt to end.
3rd row Cast off 6 sts, patt to last 2 sts, dec one st.
Work 1 row.
Cast off 5 rem sts.
Rejoin yarn to rem sts at neck edge.
1st row Dec one st, patt to end.
2nd row Cast off 6 sts, patt to last 2 sts, dec one st.
3rd row Dec one st, patt to end.
Cast off 5 rem sts.

Left front

Using No.10 needles cast on 119 sts.
1st row K1, P8, *K6, yfwd,

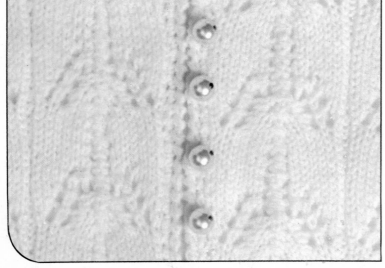

Close up of stitch detail

Lovely for autumn or spring brides ►

sl 1, K2 tog, psso, yfwd, K6, P16, rep from * ending P1, K1, instead of P16.

2nd and every alt row K2, *P15, K16, rep from * ending K9 instead of K16. Continue in patt as set until work measures 8in from beg, ending with a RS row.

1st dec row K2, *P15, sl 1, K1, psso, K12, K2 tog, rep from * ending sl 1, K1, psso, K7. Continue in patt until work measures 14in from beg, ending with a RS row.

2nd dec row K2, *P15, sl 1, K1, psso, K10, K2 tog, rep from * ending sl 1, K1, psso, K6. Continue in patt until work measures 20in from beg, ending with a RS row.

3rd dec row K2, *P15, sl 1, K1, psso, K8, K2 tog, rep from * ending sl 1, K1, psso, K5. Continue in patt until work measures 26in from beg, ending with a RS row.

4th dec row K2, *P15, sl 1, K1, psso, K6, K2 tog, rep from * ending sl 1, K1, psso, K4. Continue in patt until work measures 32in from beg, ending with a RS row.

5th dec row K2, *P15, sl 1, K1, psso, K4, K2 tog, rep from * ending sl 1, K1, psso, K3. Continue in patt until work measures 38in from beg, ending with a RS row.

6th dec row K2, *P15, sl 1, K1, psso, K2, K2 tog, rep from * ending sl 1, K1, psso, K2. Continue in patt until work measures 44in from beg, ending with a RS row.

7th dec row K2, *P15, sl 1, K1, psso, K2 tog, rep from * ending sl 1, K1, psso, K1. 70 sts. Continue in patt with 2 sts in each P panel. Work 34 rows.

Shape armhole
Cast off at beg of next and alt rows 8 sts once and 2 sts twice.
Dec one st at armhole edge on every alt row until 53 sts rem.
Continue without shaping until armhole measures 5½in from beg, ending at centre front edge.

166

Shape neck
Next row Cast off 11 sts, patt to end.
Keeping armhole edge straight, dec one st at neck edge on every row 4 times, then one st on alt rows twice, ending at armhole edge.

Shape shoulder
1st row Cast off 6 sts, patt to end.
2nd row Dec one st, patt to end.
3rd row Cast off 5 sts, patt to end.
4th row As 2nd.
5th row As 1st.
6th row As 2nd.
Keeping neck edge straight, cast off at beg of next and alt rows 5 sts once, 6 sts once and 5 sts once.

Right front

Using No.10 needles cast on 119 sts.
1st row K1, P1, *K6, yfwd, sl 1, K2 tog, psso, yfwd, K6, P16, rep from * ending P8, K1, instead of P16.
2nd and every alt row K9, *P15, K16, rep from * ending K2 instead of K16. Continue in patt as set until work measures 8in from beg, ending with a RS row.
1st dec row K7, K2 tog, *P15, sl 1, K1, psso, K12, K2 tog, rep from * ending K2.
Complete to match Left front, reversing shaping and working 1 more row before commencing armhole shaping.

Sleeves

Using No.10 needles cast on 56 sts.
1st row K3, *P2, K4, rep from * ending K3 instead of K4.
2nd row P3, *K2, P4, rep from * ending P3, instead of P4.
These 2 rows form the patt. Continue in patt inc one st at each end of 19th and every following 10th row until there are 74 sts.
Continue without shaping until sleeve measures 12½in from beg, ending with a RS row.

Next row K2, *P1, (inc one st by picking up loop between needles and P tbl, P2) 4 times, inc one st as before, P1, K2, rep from * to end. 104 sts.
Next row P2, *K6, yfwd, sl 1, K2 tog, psso, yfwd, K6, P2, rep from * to end.
Continue in patt as given for top of Back.
Work 49 more rows.

Shape top
Cast off 8 sts at beg of next 2 rows, then dec one st at beg of every row until 44 sts rem.
Cast off at beg of next and following rows 2 sts 4 times and 3 sts twice.
Cast off rem 30 sts.

Hood

Front panel
Using No.10 needles cast on 206 sts.
1st row P2, *K6, yfwd, sl 1, K2 tog, psso, yfwd, K6, P2, rep from * to end.
Continue in patt as for top of Back until work measures 7in from beg.
Cast off.

Back panel
Using No.10 needles cast on 70 sts.
Work 9in patt as given for front panel.
Cast off.

To make up

Press each piece under a damp cloth with a warm iron. Join shoulder seams.
Sew sleeves into armholes, easing fullness on each side of shoulder seam.
Join side and sleeve seams.
Join cast off and side edges of back hood panel to cast off edge of front hood panel.
Press all seams.
Hood border Thread 12 pearls onto a ball of yarn. Join in yarn and work a row of dc along face edge of hood, working one dc into each st. End with 1ch but do not turn work.
Work a row of dc back along row just worked—called crab

st—, bringing a pearl to back of work at the point of each lace panel and working the st in the usual way. Cut yarn and fasten off.
Tack hood to neck edge of coat, beg 1¼in from centre front edges of coat and easing in the fullness evenly.
Collar Join yarn to right side of neck at centre front edge. Work a row of firm dc right round neck edge, working through edges of both hood and coat. Turn with 1ch. Work 10 more rows of dc, turning with 1ch at end of every row except last row. End last row with 1ch but do not turn work.
Work a row of crab st as given for hood border.
Cut yarn and fasten off.
Front edges Join yarn to left centre front edge at top of collar and work a row of dc down left centre front edge, along cast on edges of left front, back and right front and up right centre front edge to top of collar, working into each alt row along centre front edges and into each st along cast on edges.
Cut yarn but do not turn. Thread 35 pearls on to ball of yarn.
Rejoin yarn at neck and work a row of crab st down right centre front edge, working the first 12 pearls into the first and then every 5th st and the remainder into every 9th st. Continue to work in crab st along lower edges of right front, back and left front.
Cut yarn and thread rem 23 pearls on to ball of yarn. Rejoin yarn and continue in crab st, working pearls up left front edge to match the lower 23 pearls on right front.
Continue up left front edge, working buttonloops to match 12 rem pearls on right front by working 2ch and missing one st.
Cut yarn and fasten off.
Press borders lightly.
If required, omit pearl trimming and sew on 12 small buttons, making buttonloops as given.

Slipper socks knitted in rounds

Here is an original and useful way of practising knitting and shaping in rounds. With instructions for two different sizes, to fit a small or large foot, these slipper socks are warm, comfortable and colourful.

Sizes

Striped slipper socks. To fit size 5 or 6 slipper soles
Length from top to base of heel, 22in
Bobble trimmed slipper socks. To fit size 3 or 4 slipper soles
Length from top to base of heel, excluding cuff, 15in

Basic yarn tension
$5\frac{1}{2}$ sts and $7\frac{1}{2}$ rows to 1in over st st worked on No.8 needles; 6 sts and 8 rows to 1in over st st worked on No.10 needles

---

Materials shown here

Patons Double Knitting
Striped slipper socks. 1 50g ball each of red, green, blue, orange and yellow
Slipper soles 5 or 6
Bobble trimmed slipper socks. 5 50g balls
Slipper soles size 3 or 4
One set of 4 No.10 needles pointed at both ends
Reel of shirring elastic

Striped slipper sock

Using set of 4 No.10 needles and blue cast on 77 sts, 28 on 1st needle, 21 on second needle and 28 on third needle.
1st round *P1, K5, P1, rep from * to end of round.
168

▲ *Detail of striped version*

Rep this round 7 times more.
Next round Using green, K to end.
Using green, rep 1st round 7 times more.
Next round Using red, K to end.
Using red, rep 1st round 7 times more.
Next round Using orange, K to end.
Using orange, rep 1st round 7 times more.
Next round Using yellow, K to end.
Using yellow, rep 1st round 7 times more.
These 40 rounds form striped patt, noting that 1st round with new colour is always K to end.
Continue in patt until work measures $5\frac{1}{2}$in from beg.
Next round *P1, K2, K2 tog, K1, P1, rep from * to end. 66 sts.
Continue in striped sequence, working rib as now set until work measures $13\frac{1}{2}$in from beg.

Shape leg

Next round Work 1, sl 1, K1, psso, work to last 3 sts, K2 tog, work 1.
Work 4 rounds without shaping.
Rep last 5 rounds 5 times more. 54 sts.
Continue in patt until work measures $20\frac{1}{2}$in from beg.

Divide for heel

Work across 13 sts, sl last 13 sts of round on to other end of same needle, making 26 sts for heel, divide rem sts onto 2 needles and leave for instep.
Keeping striped sequence correct work heel in rows.
1st row Sl 1, P to end.
2nd row Sl 1, K to end.
Rep these 2 rows 6 times more. Cast off.
Sl all instep sts on to 1 needle.
With RS of work facing and keeping striped sequence correct, K up 10 sts from side of heel, rib across instep sts, K up 10 sts from other side of heel. 48 sts.
Work in rows for remainder of sock.

Shape instep

1st row P7, P2 tog tbl, P1, rib 28 sts, P1, P2 tog, P to end.
2nd row K9, rib 28 sts, K9.
3rd row P6, P2 tog tbl, P1, rib 28 sts, P1, P2 tog, P to end.
4th row K8, rib 28 sts, K8.
Continue to dec in this way on every alt row until 34 sts rem, ending with a RS row.
Next row P2 tog tbl, P1, rib 28 sts, P1, P2 tog.
Next row K2, rib 28 sts, K2.
Next row P2, rib 28 sts, P2.
Keeping striped sequence correct, rep last 2 rows until work measures 7in from where sts were picked up at heel, ending with a WS row.

Shape toe

1st row K1, sl 1, K1, psso, rib to last 3 sts, K2 tog, K1.
2nd row P2, rib to last 2 sts, P2.
Rep last 2 rows until 14 sts rem, ending with a WS row.
Cast off.

To make up

Press lightly under a damp cloth with a warm iron. Sew sock to slipper sole, using zigzag stitch. Thread 4 rows shirring elastic inside top edge of each leg, on WS of work, using a blunt ended wool needle and running stitches.

Bobble trimmed slipper sock

▲ *Detail of bobble version*

Using set of 4 No.10 needles cast on 64 sts, 22 on 1st needle, 20 on 2nd needle and 22 on 3rd needle.
1st round *P1, K3, rep from * to end of round.
2nd round As 1st.
3rd round *P1, K1, make bobble by K1, P1, K1, P1, K1 all into next st, turn and K5, turn and P5, turn and K5, turn and P5 tog—called MB—, K1, rep from * to end of round.
4th to 8th rounds As 1st.
Rep last 6 rounds 3 times more then 3rd round once, then 1st round twice.
Next round P to end to mark fold line of cuff.
Work $1\frac{1}{2}$in K1, P1 rib.
Turn work inside out to reverse fabric.
Work in rib as given for 1st round until work measures $3\frac{1}{2}$in from fold line.
Next round (P1, K3) 4 times, (P1, K1, MB, K1) twice, (P1, K3) 4 times, (P1, K1, MB, K1) twice,

(P1, K3) 4 times.
Last round sets position of
bobble panels and these are
worked on every 6th round
as given for cuff.

Shape leg
Next round P1, sl 1, K1,
psso, patt to last 2 sts, K2 tog.
Work 4 rounds without
shaping.
Rep last 5 rounds 5 times
more. 52 sts.
Continue in patt until work
measures 13in from fold line.

Divide for heel
Sl last 11 sts on to spare
needle, work across first
12 sts of round on to same
needle, making 23 sts for
heel, divide rem sts on to 2
needles and leave for instep.
Keeping rib correct, work
across heel sts on rows for
2in. Cast off.
With RS of work facing K up
12 sts along side of heel,
patt across 29 sts for instep
and K up 12 sts along other
side of heel. 53 sts.
Keeping bobble panel correct
work instep in rows.
1st row P12 sts, patt 29, P12.
2nd row K2, sl 1, K1, psso,
K8, patt 29, K8, K2 tog, K2.
3rd row P11 sts, patt 29, P11.
4th row K2, sl 1, K1, psso,
K7, patt 29, K7, K2 tog, K2.
Continue in this way dec 2 sts
on every alt row until 35
sts rem ending with a WS row.
Next row K1, sl 1, K1, psso,
patt 29, K2 tog, K1.
Next row P2 sts, patt 29, P2.
Next row Sl 1, k1, psso, patt
29, K2 tog. 31 sts.
Continue in patt without
shaping until work measures
4½in from where sts were
picked up at heel.
Work in rib and bobble patt
as given for cuff, ie, bobble
on every rib, shaping toe by
dec one st at each end of next
and every following 3rd
row until 15 sts rem. Cast off.

To make up

As given for striped slipper
sock. Turn cuff to RS at fold
line.

The two slipper sock versions ▶

Jacquard pattern housecoats

Basic Wardrobe Knitting

In two lengths, this pretty lounger is worked in a jacquard pattern and trimmed with long knitted loops.

Sizes
To fit 32[34:36:38]in bust
Long version. Length from top of shoulder 48[49:50:51]in excluding loop edging
Short version. Length from top of shoulder 32[33:34:35]in excluding loop edging
Sleeve seam, 12[13:13:13½]in excluding loop edging
The figures in brackets [] refer to the 34, 36 and 38in sizes respectively

> **Tension for this design**
> 11½ sts and 12 rows to 2in over patt worked on No.7 needles

Materials shown here
Patons Camelot (50g balls)
Long version. 17[18:19:20] balls of main shade, A
8[9:10:11] balls of contrast, B
Short version. 11[12:13:14] balls of main shade. A
5[6:7:8] balls of contrast, B
One pair No.7 needles
One pair No.10 needles
15 buttons for Long version and 11 buttons for Short version

Long version

Left front

Using No.10 needles and A, cast on 73[73:79:79] sts.
Work 5 rows g st.
** Change to No.7 needles.
Commence loop patt.

1st row (RS) P.
2nd row K1, *K next st winding yarn 4 times over needle and round 1st, 2nd and 3rd fingers of left hand, then over needle again, draw 5 loops through then place loops back on left hand needle and K tog with st tbl—called ML—, K1, rep from * to end.
3rd row P.
4th row K.
These 4 rows form loop patt. Rep them twice more, then 1st and 2nd rows once. **
Join in B.
Commence patt.
1st row K1A [K1A:K0:K0], *K3B, 1A, rep from * to last 0[0:3:3] sts, K0[K0:K3B:K3B].
2nd row P1A[P1A:P0:P0], *P1A, 1B, 2A, rep from * to last 0[0:3:3] sts, P0[P0:P1A, 1B, 1A:P1A, 1B, 1A].
These 2 rows form patt and

▼ *Detail of two-colour effect*

are rep throughout.
Continue in patt until work measures 8in from top of loop edging, ending with a WS row.
Dec one st at beg of next and every following 6th row until 47[50:53:56] sts rem.
Continue without shaping until work measures 40[41:41½:42]in from top of loop edging, ending with a WS row. ***

Shape front edge
Dec one st at end of next and every alt row until 43[46:49:52] sts rem, ending with a WS row.

Shape armhole and front edge
Next row Cast off 4sts, patt to last 2sts, K2 tog.
Next row Patt to end.
Dec one st at armhole edge on every row, *at the same time* dec one st at front edge on every following 4th row until 28[31:34:35] sts rem.
Continue dec one st at front edge on every following 4th row as before, *at the same time* dec one st at armhole edge on next and every alt row until 24[25:27:29] sts rem.
Keeping armhole edge straight, continue dec one st at front edge on every following 3rd row until 18[19:20:21] sts rem.
Continue without shaping until armhole measures 7[7:7½:8]in from beg, ending with a WS row.

Shape shoulder
Cast off at beg of next and following 2 alt rows 6[7:6:7] sts once and 6[6:7:7] sts twice.

Right front

Work as given for Left front, reversing all shaping.

Back

Using No.10 needles and A, cast on 145[145:155:155] sts.
Work 5 rows g st.
Work as given for Left front from ** to **.
Join in B and work in patt as given for Left front until

Back measures 8in from top of loop edging, ending with a WS row.
Dec one st at each end of next and every following 6th row until 95[101:107:113] sts rem.
Continue without shaping until Back measures same as Front to underarm, ending with a WS row. ****

Shape armholes
Cast off 4 sts at beg of next 2 rows.
Dec one st at each end of every row until 71[77:83:85] sts rem, then one st at each end of next and every alt row until 65[69:73:77] sts rem.
Continue without shaping until Back measures same as Front to shoulder, ending with a WS row.

Shape shoulders
Cast off at beg of next and every row 6[7:6:7] sts twice and 6[6:7:7] sts 4 times.
Cast off rem 29[31:33:35] sts.

Sleeves

Using No.10 needles and A, cast on 93[93:95:95] sts.
Work 5 rows g st.
Change to No.7 needles and work 6 rows in loop patt as given for Left front.
Join in B and continue in patt as given for Left front, dec one st at each end of 5th and every following 4th row until 71[73:75:77] sts rem.
Continue without shaping until sleeve measures 12[13:13:13½]in from top of loop edging, ending with a WS row.

Shape top
Cast off 4 sts at beg of next 2 rows.
Dec one st at each end of next and every alt row until 33[37:33:31] sts rem, then one st at each end of every row until 23 sts rem. Cast off.

To make up

Press pieces lightly on WS under a dry cloth with a cool iron, omitting g st and loop edges. Join shoulder, side and sleeve seams. Set in sleeves.

Left front edge. Using No.10 needles and A, cast on 10 sts. Work in g st until edge fits from hem to beg of neck shaping when slightly stretched. Sew in position. Commence loop patt.
***** **1st, 2nd and 3rd rows** K.
4th row (K1, ML) 4 times, K2.
5th and 6th rows K. *****
Rep these 6 rows until edge fits along Left front neck to centre Back neck. Cast off.
Right front edge. Using No.10 needles and A, cast on 10 sts.
Work in loop patt as given for Left front edge from ***** to *****, noting that 4th row will read: K2, (ML K1) 4 times.
Mark positions for 15 buttons on Left front edge, first to come 14[14½:15:15½]in from lower edge and 15th to come 1in below beg of neck shaping, with 13 evenly spaced between.
Continue in loop patt until edge fits up Right front, along Right front neck to centre Back neck, making buttonholes when markers are reached as follows:
Buttonhole row (RS facing) K6, cast off 2 sts, K to end.
Next row K to end, casting on 2 sts above those cast off. Cast off.
Using flat st join centre back seam of Front edges. Sew edges in position. Press seams. Sew on buttons.

Short version

Left front

Using No.10 needles and A, cast on 61[61:67:67] sts.
Work 5 rows g st.
Work as given for Left front of long version from ** to **.
Join in B and work in patt as given for Left front of long version until work measures 8in from top of loop edge, ending with a WS row.
Dec one st at beg of next and every following 6th row until 47[50:53:56] sts rem.
Continue without shaping until Front measures 24[25:25½:26]in from top of loop

▲ *The contrast loop edging on both versions (short on left, long, right) is made of colour-mix yarn*

edging, ending with a WS row.
Complete as given for Left front of long version from ***.

Right front

Work as given for Left front, reversing all shaping.

Back

Using No.10 needles and A, cast on 121[121:131:131] sts.
Work 5 rows g st.

Work as given for Left front from ** to **.
Join in B and work in patt until Back measures 8in from top of loop edging, ending with a WS row.
Dec one st at each end of next and every following 6th row until 95[101:107:113] sts rem.
Continue without shaping until Back measures same as Front to underarm, ending with a WS row.
Complete as given for Back of long version from ****.

Sleeves

Work as given for long version.

To make up

As given for long version.
Left front edge. Work as given for long version.
Right front edge. Work as given for long version, making 11 buttonholes, the first to come 4[4:4½:4½]in from lower edge and the 11th 1in below beg of neck shaping.

Lacy bed jacket

One of the prettiest of lacy bed jackets, this design has flattering sleeves with a cape effect and has no seams to sew at all.

Size

To fit 34[36:38:40]in bust
Length at centre back, 17½[17¾:18:18¼]in
The figures in brackets [ ] refer to the 36, 38 and 40in sizes respectively

Tension for this design
8 sts and 10 rows to 1in over st st worked on No.11 Twin-Pin 8 sts and 10 rows to 1in over patt worked on No.8 needles

Materials shown here

Templeton's H and O Shetland lace
5[6:6:7] 1oz balls
One No.12 Aero Twin-Pin
One No.11 Aero Twin-Pin
One pair No.8 needles
7 small buttons
1yd 1in wide ribbon
3yds narrow ribbon
4yds narrow lace

Cape sleeves

Using No.11 Twin-Pin, cast on 199[215:231:247] sts.
Work in rows.
K 2 rows.
3rd row (ribbon slotting row) K1, *y2rn, K2 tog, rep from * to end.
4th and 5th rows K.
Change to No.8 needles and patt.
1st row (WS) K1, P to last st, K1.

2nd row K2, *insert needle into next 3 sts as if to P3 tog but work P1, K1, P1, K next st, rep from * to last st, K1.
These 2 rows form patt.
Rep 1st and 2nd rows until work measures 6in from cast on edge ending with a 2nd row.
Next row K3 tog, *P2 tog, rep from * to last 2 sts, K2 tog.
Change to No.11 Twin-Pin and work in rows.
K 2 rows.
Next row (ribbon slotting row) K1, *y2rn, K2 tog, rep from * to end.
K 2 rows.
Change to No.8 needles.
Rep 1st and 2nd rows for patt until work measures 10in from cast on edge, ending with a 2nd row.

▲ *Detail of lace and ribbon insert*

Last row K1, *P2 tog, rep from * to last 2 sts, K2 tog.
Leave sts on holder.
Work 2nd cape sleeve in same way.

Main section

Using No.12 Twin-Pin cast on 280[296:312:328] sts. Work in rows of K1, P1 rib for 2¼in.
Change to No.11 Twin-Pin and work in rows of st st, beg with a K row.
Continue in st st until work measures 12¼in from cast on edge, ending with a P row.

Divide for armholes

1st row K61[64:67:70], cast off 16[18:20:22], K126[132:138:144], cast off 16[18:20:22], K61[64:67:70].
Complete left front on last group of sts.
Next row P to last 2 sts, K2.
Next row K2, sl 1, K1, psso, K to end.
Next row P to last 2 sts, K2.
Rep last 2 rows 4[5:6:7] times more.

Shape neck

1st row K2, sl 1, K1, psso, K34, K2 tog, turn, leave rem 16[18:20:22] sts on holder.
**2nd row P to last 2 sts, K2.
3rd row K2, sl 1, K1, psso, K to last 2 sts, K2 tog.
4th row P to last 2 sts, K2.
Rep last 2 rows until 4 sts rem.
Last row K4 tog. Finish off.**
With WS facing, rejoin yarn to centre group of sts for Back.
1st row K2, P to last 2 sts, K2.
2nd row K2, sl 1, K1, psso, K to last 4 sts, K2 tog, K2.
3rd row K2, P to last 2 sts, K2.
Rep 2nd and 3rd rows 4[5:6:7] times more.

Shape back

1st row K2, sl 1, K1, psso, K34, K2 tog, turn.
Complete right back on these sts, working from ** to ** as for left front.
With RS of Back facing, slip next 36[40:44:48] sts onto holder and rejoin yarn to next st.
***1st row K2 tog, K to last 4 sts, K2 tog, K2.
2nd row K2, P to end.
Rep 1st and 2nd rows until 4 sts rem.

Last row K4 tog. Finish off.***
With WS facing, rejoin yarn to rem sts for right front.
1st row K2, P to end.
2nd row K to last 4 sts, K2 tog, K2.
Rep last 2 rows 4[5:6:7] times more.

Shape neck

1st row K2, P28, turn.
Complete as for left Back from *** to ***.

Yoke

Using No.11 Twin-Pin, K16[18:20:22] sts from Front, K up 30 sts up side of raglan, K50[54:58:62] sts from top of first cape sleeve, K up 29 sts down side of raglan, K46[50:54:58] sts from centre Back, K up 29 sts from side of raglan, K50[54:58:62] sts from second cape sleeve, K up 30 sts down side of raglan and K16[18:20:22] sts from Front. 286[302:318:334] sts. Continue in st st beg with a P row. Work 5 rows.
1st dec row K7, *K2 tog tbl, K16[18:20:22], K2 tog, K16, rep from * to last 27[29:31:33] sts, K2 tog tbl, K16[18:20:22], K2 tog, K7.
Work 3 rows.
2nd dec row K7, *K2 tog tbl, K14[16:18:20], K2 tog, K16, rep from * to last 25[27:29:31] sts, K2 tog tbl, K14[16:18:20], K2 tog, K7.
Work 3 rows.
3rd dec row K7, *K2 tog tbl, K12[14:16:18], K2 tog, K16, rep from * to last 23[25:27:29] sts, K2 tog tbl, K12[14:16:18], K2 tog, K7.
Work 3 rows.
4th dec row K7, *K2 tog tbl, K10[12:14:16], K2 tog, K16, rep from * to last 21[23:25:27] sts, K2 tog tbl, K10[12:14:16], K2 tog, K7.
Work 1 row.
5th dec row K7, *K2 tog tbl, K8[10:12:14], K2 tog, K16, rep from * to last 19[21:23:25] sts, K2 tog tbl, K8[10:12:14], K2 tog, K7.

Work 1 row.
6th dec row K7, *K2 tog tbl, K6[8:10:12], K2 tog, K16, rep from * to last 17 [19:21:23] sts, K2 tog tbl, K6[8:10:12], K2 tog, K7.
Work 1 row.
7th dec row K7, *K2 tog tbl, K4[6:8:10], K2 tog, K16, rep from * to last 15[17:19: 21] sts, K2 tog tbl, K4[6:8: 10], K2 tog, K7.
Work 1 row.
8th dec row K7, *K2 tog tbl, K2[4:6:8], K2 tog, K16, rep from * to last 13[15:17:

19] sts, K2 tog tbl, K2[4:6:8], K2 tog, K7.
Work 3 rows.
9th dec row K7, *K2 tog tbl, K0[2:4:6], K2 tog, K16, rep from * to last 11[13:15: 17] sts, K2 tog tbl, K0[2:4:6], K2 tog, K7.
Work 3 rows.
Next row K1, *K2 tog, K1, rep from * to end.
Work 5 rows.
Change to No.12 Twin-Pin and work in rows of K1, P1 rib for 1in.
Cast off.

Front edgings

Button strip
Using No.12 Twin-Pin and with RS of left Front facing, K up 190[192:196:198] sts from beg of st st to neck edge. Work 6 rows K1, P1 rib. Cast off in rib.
Mark position for 7 buttons on strip.

Buttonhole strip
Work as for button strip, working buttonholes as markers are reached on 3rd

row by casting off 3 sts and on 4th row casting on 3 sts above those cast off on previous row.

To make up

Press lightly.
Fold hem in half to wrong side and slip stitch in place.
Thread with 1in wide ribbon.
Thread narrow ribbon through sleeve slottings and sew ends. Sew lace below ribbon slottings and round yoke.

173

Matching Fair Isle sweaters

Sizes

Ladies'. To fit 36[38:40]in bust

Length at centre back, 21[22:23]in, adjustable

Sleeve seam, 18[19:20]in, adjustable

Men's. To fit 38[40:42]in chest

Length at centre back, 23½[24½:25½]in, adjustable

Sleeve seam, 17½[17½:18]in, adjustable

The figures in brackets [] refer to the Ladies' 38 and 40in sizes and the Men's 40 and 42in sizes respectively

Tension for these designs

6 sts and 8 rows to 1in over st st worked on No.9 needles

6½ sts and 8½ rows to 1in over st st worked on No.10 needles

Materials shown here

Templeton's H and O Shetland Fleece

Ladies'. 10[11:12] 1oz balls main shade, A, coral

1oz ball each of 5 shades, B, C, D, E and F, white, grey, sable, natural and dusk brown

One pair No.12 needles

One pair No.10 needles

One Aero Twin-Pin No.10

4 small buttons

One large st holder

One No. 2·50 (ISR) crochet hook

Men's. 11[12:12] 1oz balls main shade, A, natural

2 1oz balls 1st contrast, B, white

1oz ball each of 4 shades, C, D, E and F, gold, dusk brown, sable and camel

One pair No.9 needles
One pair No.11 needles
One set of 4 No.11 double point needles

Circular yoked sweater

Front

Using No.12 needles and A, cast on 113[117:121] sts. Work 4in K1, P1 rib.

Change to No.10 needles

Work in st st, beg with a K row and inc one st at each end of 7th and every following 8th row until there are 121[127:133] sts.

Continue without shaping until work measures 14[14½:15]in or length required, ending with a P row.

Shape armholes

Cast off 6 sts at beg of next 2 rows.

Dec one st at each end of next and every alt row until 103 sts rem. P 1 row.

Shape for yoke

1st row K2 tog, K33, K2 tog, leave rem 66 sts on holder. Continue on 35 sts for left side.

Dec one st at each end of every K row until 3 sts rem.

Last row K2 tog, K1. Cast off.

With RS facing, slip first 29 sts onto holder for yoke and rejoin yarn to rem 37 sts. Complete as for other side.

Back

Using No.12 needles, cast on 112[116:120] sts and work as for Front, noting that there is one st less. When shaping for yoke, leave only 28 sts instead of 29 sts on holder.

Sleeves

Using No.12 needles, cast on 60[62:64] sts.

Work 4in K1, P1 rib.

Change to No.10 needles.

Continue in st st beg with a K row, inc one st at each end of 5th and every following 6th row until there are 84[90:96] sts.

Work until sleeve measures 18[19:20]in or required length (allowing 2in for turn back cuff), ending with a P row.

Shape top

Cast off 6[6:8] sts at beg of next 2 rows.

Dec one st at each end of every K row until 36 sts rem. Leave sts on holder for yoke.

Yoke

Sew up raglan seams.

With RS facing, slip first 14 sts of Back onto holder.

Beg from centre Back with A and with first double pointed needle and K up rem 14 sts of Back, K up 31[34:37] sts from raglan side, K36 sts from sleeve holder, using 2nd needle, K up 31[34:37] sts from next raglan side, K29 sts from Front holder, K up 31[34:37] sts from next raglan side, using 3rd needle K36 sts from 2nd sleeve, K up 31[34:37] sts from last raglan side and 14 sts from centre Back. 253[265:277] sts.

Using A, P 1 row. Join in F.

Next row *K3A, 1F, rep from *, ending 1A.

Next row *P1F, 1A, rep from * ending 1F.

Next row K1A, *1F, 3A, rep from * to end of row. Break off F.

Using A, P 1 row. Break off A.

Using B, K 1 row. P 1 row.

Continue working from chart.

1st size Omit first and last 6 sts of chart 1. Work rem 19 sts of chart 1, K40 sts of both charts 2 and 1 five times, then the 15 sts of chart 2 once, ending round with first 19 sts of chart 1.

Continue with rem 24 rows of charts, beg K rows from 7th st and P rows from 19th st at front edge of garment. Dec on chart on 9th and alt rows is worked by K2 tog tbl.

*After completing 25 chart

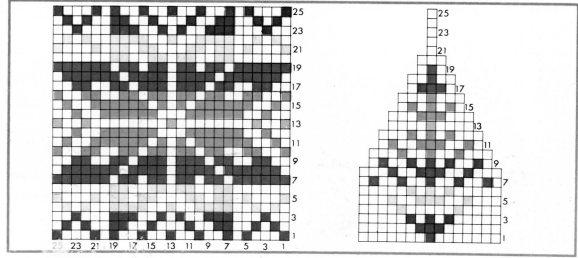

▼ *Star and tapered star motifs for yoke. Tapered stars alternate with stars*

174

rows using B, P 1 row.

Next row .*K1, K2 tog, rep from * to end of row. Break off B.

Using A, P 1 row.

Next row *K3A, 1F, rep from * to end.

Next row *P1F, 1A, rep from * to end.

Next row K1A, *1F, 3A, rep from * to end. Break off F.

Using A, P 1 row.

Next row *K2, K2 tog, rep from * to end of row. P 1 row. Change to No.12 needles. Work 1in K1, P1 rib. Cast off loosely in rib.*

2nd size Work from chart, K from 1st row of chart 1 followed by 1st row of chart 2 across 11 sts, ending with 25 sts from chart 1, noting that dec on 9th and every alt row is made by K2 tog tbl. Complete from * to * as for 1st size.

3rd size Work as for 2nd size, working every row with 6 sts in B before and after sts from charts.

All sizes Sew up Back opening leaving 4½in open. Crochet 1 row dc round both opening edges. Work 2nd row dc on RS making 4 loops for buttonholes.

Banded sweater

Back

Using No.11 needles, cast on 115[121:127] sts. Work 1½in K1, P1 rib.

Change to No.9 needles. Work in st st beg with a K row until work measures 11[11½:11½]in, ending with a P row.

Continue in st st, working 39 rows from chart. If required, continue in st st until work measures 15½[16:16]in or required length, ending with a P row.

Shape armholes

Cast off 6 sts at beg of next 2 rows.

**Next row K1, K2 tog, K to last 3 sts, sl 1, K1, psso, K1.

Next row P.**

Rep last 2 rows until 37[39: 41] sts rem, ending with a P row. Leave sts on holder.

▼ *Bottom half of banded sweater motif. Work rows 19 to 1 for top half. The whole of the star motif is worked over 39 rows*

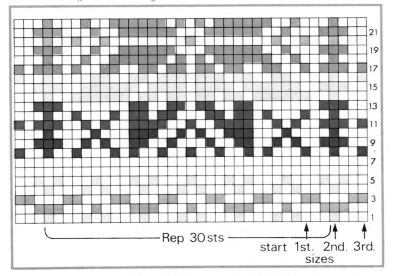

Rep 30 sts — start 1st. 2nd. 3rd. sizes

Front

Work as given for Back until 57[59:61] sts rem, ending with a P row.

Shape neck

1st row K1, K2 tog, K17, turn and leave rem sts on holder.

2nd row P to end.

3rd row K1, K2 tog, K to last 3 sts, sl 1, K1, psso, K1.

Rep 2nd and 3rd rows 6 times more, then 2nd row once.

Next row K1, K3 tog, K1.

Next row P3.

Next row K1, K2 tog.

Next row P2 tog and fasten off.

With RS facing, slip first 17 [19:21] sts onto holder. Rejoin yarn to rem sts, K to last 3 sts, sl 1, K1, psso, K1. Complete to correspond with other side.

Sleeves

Using No.11 needles, cast on 47[49:51] sts and work 3in K1, P1 rib.

Change to No.9 needles. Continue in st st beg with a K row, inc one st at each end of 5th and every following 6th row until there are 85[89:93] sts. Work until sleeve measures 19[19:19½]in or required length, ending with a P row. Place marker thread at each end of last row. Work 8 rows more.

Shape top

Rep from ** to ** as for Back until 47 sts rem, ending with a P row.

Next row K1, (K2 tog, K18, sl 1, K1, psso, K1) twice. Continue to dec in centre of every 6th row 4 times more, *at same time* dec at each end of every K row until 9 sts rem, ending with a P row. Leave sts on holder.

Neckband

Join raglan seams, sewing last 8 rows of sleeve top above marker threads to cast off sts at armhole.

Using No.11 needles and with RS facing, K across sts of right Sleeve, Back neck and left Sleeve, knitting 2 tog across each raglan seam, K up 14 sts down Front neck, K Front sts and K up 14 sts up other side of neck. 98[102:106] sts.

Work 2½in in K1, P1 rib. Cast off loosely in rib.

To make up

Yoked sweater

Pin out and press with a warm iron over a damp cloth, omitting ribbing. Sew up side and sleeve seams. Sew on buttons to correspond with loops.

Banded sweater

Press work with a warm iron over a damp cloth. Join side and sleeve seams. Fold neckband in half to wrong side and slip stitch in place. Press seams.

Man's fabric stitch waistcoat

Men's waistcoats are having a big revival for casual as well as formal wear.

Sizes

To fit 38[40:42:44]in chest
Length at centre back, 20½ [21½:22:23] in.
The figures in brackets [ ] refer to the 40, 42 and 44in sizes respectively.

Basic yarn tension

6 sts and 8 rows to 1in over st st worked on No.8 needles.

Materials

Madame Pingouin
6[6:7:7] 50g balls
One pair No.8 needles
One pair No.10 needles
Five buttons
Stitch holder

Back

Using No.8 needles cast on 119[125:131:137] sts.
1st row K1, *P1, K1, rep from * to end.
2nd row P1, *K1, P1, rep from * to end.
Continue in K1, P1 rib until work measures 11 [11½:12: 12½] in from beg.

Shape armholes

Cast off 6 sts at beg of next 2 rows.
Dec one st at each end of every row until 81[85:89:93] sts rem.
Continue without shaping until armholes measure 5½[6:6:6½] in from beg.
Inc one st at each end of next and every following 10th row

until there are 87[91:95:99] sts.
Continue without shaping until armholes measure 9½[10:10:10½] in from beg.

Shape shoulders and neck

Next row Cast off 7 sts, rib 28[29:30:31], cast off 17 [19:21:23] sts, rib to end.
Complete left shoulder first.
Cast off at armhole edge at the beg of next and following alt rows 7 sts twice and 5[6:7:8] sts once, *at the same time* cast off 3 sts at neck edge on following 3 alt rows.
With WS of work facing rejoin yarn to rem sts and complete to match first side.

Left front

Using No.8 needles cast on 3 sts.

Commence patt and shaping

1st row P1, K1, P1.
2nd row Inc in first st (centre edge), K to last st, inc in last st (outside edge).
3rd row K twice into first st, P1, K1, P1, K twice into last st.
4th row K twice into first st, K to last st, K twice into last st.
Keeping patt correct, inc one st at each end of every row 3[5:7:9] times more.
Continue to inc one st at centre edge on every row 12 times more, *at the same time* cast on at outside edge 9 sts 4 times. 63[67:71:75] sts.
Dec one st at outside edge on every 8th row 4 times, then inc one st at this edge on every 6th row 6 times,

at the same time, when inc at centre front edge are completed, work straight for ¼[½:¾:1]in, ending at centre front edge and working a buttonhole on next 2 rows as follows
Next row Patt 2 sts, cast off 2 sts, patt to end.
Next row Patt to last 2 sts, cast on 2 sts, patt 2 sts.
Work 4 more buttonholes in this way at intervals of 2½ [2½:2½:2¾]in measured from centre of previous buttonhole.
Work until outside edge measures 10½[11:11½:12]in from beg, ending at side edge.

Shape armhole and front

Next row Cast off 6 sts, patt to last 2 sts, work 2 tog.
Dec one st at neck edge on every following 3rd row 21[22:23:24] times more, *at the same time* dec one st at armhole edge on every row 14(16:18:20) times continuing until armhole measures 5½ (6:6:6½) in from beg, then continue armhole shaping by inc one st at beg of next and every following 10th row 3 times in all. Continue until armhole measures same as Back to shoulder, ending at armhole edge.

Shape shoulder

Cast off at beg of next and every alt row 7 sts 3 times and 5[6:7:8] sts once.

Right front

Work as given for Left front, reversing all shaping and omitting buttonholes.

To make up

DO NOT PRESS.
Join shoulder seams using back st.
Armbands Using No.10 needles and with RS facing, K up 102 [108:108:114] sts evenly round armhole. K 2 rows. Cast off.
Right front edge Using No.10 needles beg at side edge and K up 43 [45:47:49] sts to centre point. K 2 rows, inc one st at centre point on each row. Cast off.
Using No.10 needles, beg at centre point and K up 25[27:29:31] along shaped edge, 65[68:71:74] along centre front straight edge, 64[67:67:70] along shaped edge of neck and 19[20:21:22] sts to centre back neck. K 2 rows, inc one st at centre point on each row. Cast off.
Left front edge Using No.10 needles beg at centre back neck and K up 19[20:21:22] sts, 64[67:67:70] along shaped edge of neck, 65 [68:71:74] along centre front straight edge and 25 [27:29:31] along shaped edge to centre point.
K 2 rows, inc one st at centre point on each row. Cast off.
Using No.10 needles, beg at centre point and K up 43 [45:47:49] sts to side edge. K 2 rows, inc one st at centre point on each row. Cast off.
Join side and armband seams. Join Right and Left front edges at centre point. Neaten buttonholes and sew on buttons.

The waistcoat front is in rice stitch, giving a fabric effect ▼

Aran cardigan

The charm of Aran is that it suits both men and women. This authentic pattern is for a 36 to 44in chest.

Sizes

To fit a 36[38:40:42:44]in bust or chest
Length at centre back, 24[24½:25:25½:26]in, adjustable
Sleeve seam, 17[17½:18:18½:19]in, adjustable
The figures in brackets [ ] refer to the 38, 40, 42 and 44in sizes respectively

---

Basic yarn tension
4¾ sts and 6¼ rows to 1in over st st worked on No.7 needles.

Tension for this design
5 sts and 7 rows to 1in over double moss stitch worked on No.7 needles.

Materials shown here

Marriner Regency Bainin wool 14[15:16:17:18]50 g balls
One pair No.7 needles
One pair No.10 needles
One cable needle
Two stitch holders
Five buttons

Back

Using No.10 needles cast on 94[98:102:106:110]sts.
1st row *K1 tbl, P1, rep from * to end.
Rep 1st row 7 times more.
Next row K to end, inc 16 sts evenly across row. 110[114:118:122:126]sts.
Change to No.7 needles.

178

1st row (wrong side) (K1, P1) 3[4:5:6:7] times, *K2, P6, K7, P4, K6, P6, K2*, P32 sts, rep from * to * once, (K1, P1) 3[4:5:6:7] times.
2nd row (K1, P1) 3[4:5:6:7] times, *P2, sl next 2 sts on to cable needle and hold at back of work, K2, K2 from cable needle—called C4B—K2, P6, K2, sl next 2 sts on to cable needle and hold at front of work, P1, K2 from cable needle—called K2F—P6, C4B, K2, P2*, (C4B, sl next 2 sts on to cable needle and hold at front of work, K2, K2 from cable needle—called C4F) 4 times, rep from * to * once, (K1, P1) 3[4:5:6:7] times.
3rd row (P1, K1) 3[4:5:6:7] times, *K2, P6, K6, P2, K1, P2, K6, P6, K2*, P32 sts, rep from * to * once, (P1, K1) 3[4:5:6:7] times.
4th row (P1, K1) 3[4:5:6:7] times, *P2, K6, P5, sl next st on to cable needle and hold at back of work, K2, P1 from cable needle—called P1B—K1, K2F, P5, K6, P2*, K32 sts, rep from * to * once, (P1, K1) 3[4:5:6:7] times.
5th row (K1, P1) 3[4:5:6:7] times, *K2, P6, K5, P2, K1, P1, K1, P2, K5, P6, K2*, P32 sts, rep from * to * once, (K1, P1) 3[4:5:6:7] times.
6th row (K1, P1) 3[4:5:6:7] times, *P2, K2, C4F, P4, P1B, K1, P1, K1, K2F, P4, K2, C4F, P2*, (C4F, C4B) 4 times, rep from * to * once, (K1, P1) 3 [4:5:6:7] times.
7th row (P1, K1) 3 [4:5:6:7] times, *K2, P6, K4, P2, (K1, P1) twice, K1, P2, K4, P6,

K2*, P32 sts, rep from * to * once, (P1, K1) 3 [4:5:6:7] times.
8th row (P1, K1) 3[4:5:6:7] times, *P2, K6, P3, P1B, (K1, P1) twice, K1, K2F, P3, K6, P2*, K32 sts, rep from * to * once, (P1, K1) 3[4:5:6:7] times.
9th row (K1, P1) 3[4:5:6:7] times, *K2, P6, K3, P2, (K1, P1) 3 times, K1, P2, K3, P6, K2*, P32 sts, rep from * to * once, (K1, P1) 3[4:5:6:7] times.
10th row (K1, P1) 3[4:5:6:7] times, *P2, C4B, K2, P2, P1B, (K1, P1) 3 times, K1, K2F, P2, C4B, K2, P2*, (C4B, C4F) 4 times, rep from * to * once, (K1, P1) 3[4:5:6:7] times.
11th row (P1, K1) 3[4:5:6:7] times, *K2, P6, K2, P2, (K1, P1) 4 times, K1, P2, K2, P6, K2*, P32 sts, rep from * to * once, (P1, K1) 3[4:5:6:7] times.
12th row (P1, K1) 3[4:5:6:7] times, *P2, K6, P1, P1B, (K1, P1) 4 times, K1, K2F, P1, K6, P2*, K32 sts, rep from * to * once, (P1, K1) 3[4:5:6:7] times.
13th row (K1, P1) 3[4:5:6:7] times, *K2, P6, K1, P2, (K1, P1) 5 times, K1, P2, K1, P6, K2*, P32 sts, rep from * to * once, (K1, P1) 3[4:5:6:7] times.
14th row (K1, P1) 3[4:5:6:7] times, *P2, K2, C4F, P1, K2F, (P1, K1) 4 times, P1, P1B, P1, K2, C4F, P2*, (C4F, C4B) 4 times, rep from * to * once, (K1, P1) 3[4:5:6:7] times.
15th row (P1, K1) 3[4:5:6:7] times, *K2, P6, K2, P2, (K1, P1) 4 times, K1, P2, K2, P6, K2*, P32 sts, rep from * to * once, (P1, K1) 3[4:5:6:7] times.
16th row (P1, K1) 3[4:5:6:7] times, *P2, K6, P2, K2F, (P1, K1) 3 times, P1, P1B, P2, K6, P2*, K32 sts, rep from * to * once, (P1, K1) 3[4:5:6:7] times.
17th row As 9th.
18th row (K1, P1) 3[4:5:6:7] times, *P2, C4B, K2, P3, K2F, (P1, K1) twice, P1, P1B, P3, C4B, K2, P2*, (C4B, C4F) 4 times, rep

from * to * once, (K1, P1) 3[4:5:6:7] times.
19th row As 7th.
20th row (P1, K1) 3[4:5:6:7] times, *P2, K6, P4, K2F, P1, K1, P1, P1B, P4, K6, P2*, K32 sts, rep from * to * once, (P1, K1) 3[4:5:6:7] times.
21st row As 5th.
22nd row (K1, P1) 3[4:5:6:7] times, *P2, K2, C4F, P5, K2F, P1, P1B, P5, K2, C4F, P2*, (C4F, C4B) 4 times, rep from * to * once, (K1, P1) 3[4:5:6:7] times.
23rd row As 3rd.
24th row (P1, K1) 3[4:5:6:7] times, *P2, K6, P6, sl next 3 sts on to cable needle and hold at front of work, K2, K2, P1 from cable needle, P6, K6, P2*, K32 sts, rep from * to * once, (P1, K1) 3[4:5:6:7] times.
These 24 rows form patt and are rep throughout Back. Continue in patt until work measures 15[15½:16:16½:17]in or required length to underarm, ending with a WS row.

Shape armholes

Cast off 8 sts at beg of next 2 rows.
1st raglan row K1, sl 1, K1, psso, patt to last 3 sts, K2 tog, K1.
2nd raglan row K1, P1, patt to last 2 sts, P1, K1.
Rep these 2 rows until 32 [34:36:38:40]sts rem.
Cast off.

Left front

Using No.10 needles cast on 29 sts and work 24 rows K1, P1 rib for pocket lining. Leave sts on holder.
Using No.10 needles cast on 48[50:52:54:56]sts.
Work 8 rows twisted rib as given for Back.
Next row K to end, inc 8 sts evenly across row. 56 [58:60:62:64]sts.
Change to No.7 needles.
Commence patt.
1st row (wrong side) K1, P16, K2, P6, K7, P4, K6, P6, K2, (K1, P1) 3[4:5:6:7] times.
2nd row (K1, P1) 3[4:5:6:7] times, P2, C4B, K2, P6, K2,

K2F, P6, C4B, K2, P2, (C4B, C4F) twice, K1. Continue in patt as set until 24 rows have been worked, K front edge st on every row.
Next row K1, P16, K2, sl next 29 sts on to stitch holder, work in patt across 29 pocket lining sts, K2, (K1, P1) 3[4:5:6:7] times.
Continue until work measures same as Back to armhole, ending at armhole edge.

▲ *Stitch details of Aran patterns*

Shape armhole and neck
Next row Cast off 8 sts, patt to last 2 sts, dec one. Work 1 row.
Next row K1, Sl 1, K1, psso patt to end.
Next row Dec one, patt to last 3 sts, P1, K1.
Continue in this way dec one st at armhole edge on every alt row and one st at neck edge on every 3rd row 16[17:18:19:20] times in all, until all sts are worked off. Pull yarn through, finish off.

Right front

Work as given for Left front, reading patt row in reverse and reversing all shapings.

Sleeves

Using No.10 needles cast on 46[48:50:52:54]sts.
Work 3in twisted rib as given for Back.
Next row K to end, inc 14 sts evenly across row. 60 [62:64:66:68]sts.
Change to No.7 needles.
1st row K1[K2:P1,K2:K1, P1,K2:P1,K1,P1,K2], P6,

K2, P16, K2, P6,K2,P16,K2, P6, K1[K2:K2,P1:K2,P1, K1:K2,P1,K1,P1].
2nd row P1[P2: K1, P2: P1,K1,P2:K1,P1,K1,P2], C4B,K2,P2,(C4B,C4F) twice, P2, C4B, K2, P2, (C4B, C4F) twice, P2, C4B, K2, P1[P2:P2,K1:P2,K1,P1:P2, K1,P1,K1].
Continue in patt as set, working 2 honeycomb panels and 3 plaited cables and inc one st at each end of next and every 6th row until there are 80[84:88:92:96]sts. Work inc in double moss st.
Continue without shaping until sleeve measures 17 [17½:18:18½:19]in, or required length ending with a WS row.

Shape top
Cast off 8 sts at beg of next 2 rows.
Work 1st and 2nd raglan rows as given for Back until 2[4:6:8:10]sts rem. Cast off.

Buttonhole band

Using No.10 needles cast on 10 sts. Work in twisted rib as given for Back.
Work 3 rows.
Next row Rib 4 sts, cast off 2 sts, rib 4 sts.
Next row Rib 4 sts, cast on 2 sts, rib 4 sts.
Continue in rib working 4 more buttonholes in this way at 3[3¼:3½:3¾:4]in intervals, until band measures 56[58: 60:62:64]in when slightly stretched. Cast off.

To make up

Using No.10 needles and with RS pocket top facing, work 7 rows twisted rib as given for Back. Cast off. Complete other pocket top in same way. Set in sleeves. Join side and sleeve seams. Sew round pocket linings and sides of pocket tops. Sew on button-hole band, with buttonholes on Left front for a man's garment and Right front for a woman's. Sew on buttons to correspond. Press very lightly under a damp cloth with a warm iron.

Seamless jersey in fisherman's knitting

Basic Wardrobe Knitting

Your first project in fisherman's knitting is a seamless sweater for an outdoor man. The firmness of the fabric, which results from the traditional stitch, makes this an ideal garment to wear in cold or windy weather.

Size
To fit 38[40:42:44]in chest
Length at centre Back, 23[23:23½:23½]in
Sleeve seam, 18in, adjustable
The figures in brackets [] refer to the 40, 42 and 44in sizes respectively

> **Tension for this design**
> 7 sts and 9 rows to 1in over st st worked on No.10 Twin-Pin

Materials shown here
Templeton's Double Knitting 22[23:24:25] 1oz balls
One No.12 16in or 24in Aero Twin-Pin
One No.10 16in or 24in Aero Twin-Pin
One set of 4 No.12 double pointed needles
One set of 4 No.10 double pointed needles

NB This jersey is entirely seamless and requires no making up after knitting. Yarn should be joined at mock seams by leaving ends to darn into work on completion.

Jersey

Using No.12 Twin-Pin, cast on 264[276:288:300] sts.
1st row *P1, K2, P1, rep from * to end. Join into a

180

circle and place marker thread before first st to mark beginning of round.
Next round *P1, K2, P1, rep from * to end of round. Rep last round until work measures 3in.
Change to No.10 Twin-Pin.
Next round *P into front and back of next st to make one st, K130[136:142:148], P1, rep from * once.
Continue in st st with mock seam sts.
1st round *K1, P1, K130 [136:142:148], P1, rep from * once more.
2nd round *P2, K130[136:142:148], P1, rep from * once more.
Rep 1st and 2nd rounds until work measures 12in from cast on edge ending with a 1st round.
Begin yoke pattern and underarm gusset.
1st round *K into front and back and front of first st, P132[138:144:150], rep from * once more.
2nd round *K3, P132[138:144:150], rep from * once more.
3rd round *K3, P1, K130 [136:142:148], P1, rep from * once more.
Rep 3rd round once more.
Rep 2nd round twice more.
7th round *Inc once in each of next 2 sts, K1, P1, K130 [136:142:148], P1, rep from * once more.
8th round *K5, P1, K130 [136:142:148], P1, rep from * once more.
9th round *K5, P132[138:144:150], rep from * once more.
Rep 9th round once more.
Rep 8th round once more.

12th round *K5, P1, (K2, P2) 32[34:35:37] times, K2 [0:2:0], P1, rep from * once more.
13th round *Inc, K2, inc, K1, P1, K130[136:142:148], P1, rep from * once more.
14th round *K7, P1, (P2, K2) 32[34:35:37] times, P2 [0:2:0], P1, rep from * once more.
15th round *K7, P1, K130 [136:142:148], P1, rep from * once more.
Continue in this way, working centre 130[136:142:148] sts in 4 row patt, keeping seam sts correct and inc one st at each side of each gusset on every 6th row until 14 rows more have been worked. There should now be 11 sts between seam sts on gusset.
Break yarn at end of last round.

Divide for armholes
Slip gusset sts and seam sts (13 sts at each side) onto holder or thread until required. Work Front on centre 130[136:142:148] sts working in rows.
**1st row P.
2nd row K.
3rd row K.
4th row P.
Rep 1st—4th rows once more then 1st and 2nd rows once.

Work centre patt panel
1st patt row K.
2nd patt row P.
3rd patt row K2[5:8:11], *K10, P1, K10, rep from * to last 2[5:8:11] sts, K to end.
4th patt row K1, P1[4:7:10], * P9, K3, P9, rep from * to last 2[5:8:11] sts, P to last st, K1.
5th patt row K2[5:8:11], *K8, (P1, K1) twice, P1, K8, rep from * to last 2[5:8:11] sts, K to end.
6th patt row K1, P1[4:7:10], * P7, (K1, P2) 3 times, P5, rep from * to last 2[5:8:11] sts, P to last st, K1.
7th patt row K2[5:8:11], *K6, P1, K2, P3, K2, P1, K6, rep from * to last 2[5:8:11] sts, K to end.
8th patt row K1, P1[4:7:10], * P5, K1, P2, (K1, P1) 3 times, P1, K1, P5, rep from *

9th patt row K2[5:8:11], *K4, (P1, K2) twice, P1, (K2, P1) twice, K4, rep from * to last 2[5:8:11] sts, K to end.
10th patt row K1, P1[4:7:10], *P3, (K1, P2) twice, K3, (P2, K1) twice, P3, rep from * to last 2[5:8:11] sts, P to last st, K1.
11th patt row K2[5:8:11], *K5, P1, K2, (P1, K1) 3 times, K1, P1, K5, rep from * to last 2[5:8:11] sts, K to end.
12th patt row K1, P1[4:7:10], *P4, (K1, P2) twice, (K1, P2) 3 times, P2, rep from * to last 2[5:8:11] sts, P to last st, K1.
13th patt row K2[5:8:11], *K6, P1, K2, P3, K2, P1, K6, rep from * to last 2[5:8:11] sts, K to end.
14th patt row K1, P1[4:7:10], *P5, K1, P2, (K1, P1) 3 times, P1, K1, P5, rep from * to last 2[5:8:11] sts, P to last st, K1.
15th patt row K2[5:8:11], *K7, (P1, K2) 3 times, K5, rep from * to last 2[5:8:11] sts, K to end.
16th patt row K1, P1[4:7:10], *P6, K1, P2, K3, P2, K1, P6, rep from * to last 2[5:8:11] sts, P to last st, K1.
17th patt row K2[5:8:11], *K8, (P1, K1) 3 times, K7, rep from * to last 2[5:8:11] sts, K to end.
18th patt row K1, P1[4:7:10], *P7, (K1, P2) 3 times, P5, rep from * to last 2[5:8:11] sts, P to last st, K1.
19th patt row K2[5:8:11], *K9, P3, K9, rep from * to last 2[5:8:11] sts, K to end.
20th patt row K1, P1[4:7:10], *P8, (K1, P1) 3 times, P7, rep from * to last 2[5:8:11] sts, P to last st, K1.
21st patt row K2[5:8:11], *K10, P1, K10, rep from * to last 2[5:8:11] sts, K to end.
22nd patt row K1, P1[4:7:10], *P9, K3, P9, rep from * to last 2[5:8:11] sts, P to last st, K1.
23rd patt row As 21st.
24th patt row K1, P1[4:7:10], *P10, K1, P10, rep from * to last 2[5:8:11] sts, P to last st, K1.

▲ A modern interpretation of the traditional fisherman's gansey

25th patt row K.
26th patt row P.
P 1 row. K 2 rows. P 1 row.
Rep last 4 rows once more.
P 1 row. K 2 rows.
Next row P2[0:2:0], *K2,
P2, rep from * to end.
K 1 row.

Next row K2[0:2:0], *P2,
K2, rep from * to end.
Rep last 4 rows until 14 rows
more have been worked.
P 1 row. K 1 row.

For 42 and 44in sizes only
K 1 row. P 2 rows. K 1 row.**

For all sizes divide for shoulders

1st row K48[50:52:54], then
complete this shoulder on
these sts.
***2nd row** P2 tog, P to end.
3rd row P to last 2 sts, P2
tog.
4th row K2 tog, K to end.
5th row K to last 2 sts, K2
tog.
6th row P2 tog, P to end.
7th row P to last 2 sts, P2
tog.
8th row K2 tog, K to end.
9th row K to last 2 sts, K2
tog.
P 2 rows.
K 1 row.
Leave sts on holder.***
With RS facing, slip centre
34[36:38:40] sts onto holder
and leave for neckband.
Rejoin yarn to rem sts and K
to end. Complete other
shoulder to correspond,
working from *** to ***,
reversing shaping

Back

With RS facing, rejoin yarn
to rem 130[136:142:148] sts
and work from ** to ** as
for Front.

Work shoulders

K 1 row. P 2 rows. K 1 row.
Rep last 4 rows twice more.
Cast off right shoulder as
follows:
Hold Back and Front together
with WS touching.
Cast off both shoulders
together on RS by *K first
st from Back and Front tog,
K next 2 sts tog, lift first st
over 2nd, rep from * until all
shoulder stitches are cast off.
Slip centre 50[52:54:56] sts
onto holder for neckband and
cast off 2nd shoulder in same
way.

Neckband

Using No.10 Twin-Pin, K sts
from Back holder, K up 14 sts
down right side of neck, K
across sts from Front holder
and K up 14 sts up left side of
neck.
1st round *P1, K2, P1, rep
from * to end.
Rep 1st round for 1in.
If preferred, neckband may be
made longer and folded in

half to WS and slip stitched in
place.

Sleeves

Using set of 4 No.10 needles,
with RS facing, work gusset
sts on first needle, P1, K11,
P1, K up 110[110:118:118]
sts evenly around armhole,
dividing the stitches over 3
needles. Work in rounds.
1st round P1, K11, P1, K2,
*P2, K2, rep from * to end.
2nd round P1, K2 tog tbl,
K7, K2 tog, P1, K to end.
3rd round P1, K9, P3, *K2,
P2, rep from * to end.
4th round P1, K9, P1, K to
end.
Rep last 4 rounds until 12
more rounds have been
worked dec one st each side of
gussets every 6th round.
Next round P1, K5, P to end.
Rep last round once more.
Next round P1, K5, P1, K to
end.
Next round P1, K2 tog tbl,
K1, K2 tog, P1, K to end.
Next 2 rounds P1, K3, P to
end.
Next 2 rounds P1, K3, P1,
K to end.
Next round P1, K3, P to end.
Next round P1, K3 tog,
P to end.
Next round P3, K to end.
Next round P1, K1, P1, K
to end.
Next round P3, K2 tog tbl,
K to last 2 sts, K2 tog.
Next round P1, K1, P1, K
to end.
Next round P3, K to end.
Next round P1, K1, P1, K
to end.
Rep last 4 rounds until
57[61:61:65] sts rem.
Work until sleeve measures
15in or 3in less than required
length, dec one st at beg of
last round.
Change to No.12 needles.
1st round *P1, K2, P1, rep
from * to end.
Rep 1st round until cuff
measures 3in. Cast off in rib.

To complete

Press lightly on wrong side
under a damp cloth using a
warm iron. Darn in ends
including joining first row ends
to complete lower edge
circle. Do not press heavily.

Chapter 1

Introduction to crochet

Crochet is a boon for the busy woman who can only spare ten minutes at a time. Once the three basic movements have been mastered, there are dozens of patterns, like the Old America squares on the opposite page (see Chapter 4 for how to make the squares). They can be carried around in a handbag, worked individually, and then sewn up into anything from a bedspread to a waistcoat. Yet though crochet is simple, it provides marvellously crisp textures and colour effects.

If you knit, you will notice that anything you crochet uses more yarn than something which is knitted. But because the crochet rows are deeper you will finish the work much faster, whether it's a man's tie or an evening dress.

The tools of the trade

Until July 1969 there were two ranges of crochet hooks available in Britain—a wool and a cotton range.

Since July 1969 the International Standard range came into being which consists of one range for thick and fine work alike. All hook sizes given in future pages refer to the International Standard range and will be followed with the initials (ISR). The chart below shows clearly what number this would have been prior to the change-over.

ISR hooks	old Wool sizes	ISR hooks	old Cotton sizes
7.00	2	2.00	1½
6.00	4	1.75	2½
5.50	5	1.50	3½
5.00	6	1.25	4½
4.50	7	1.00	5½
4.00	8	0.75	6½
3.50	9	0.60	7
3.00	10		
2.50	12		
2.00	14		

The following tools will also be helpful:
- [ ] Rustless steel pins
- [ ] Scissors
- [ ] Sewing needles—some with blunt points for certain finishing processes
- [ ] A washable bag in which to keep work clean
- [ ] Iron and ironing board with felt pad or blanket
- [ ] Rigid inch rule
- [ ] Cloths suitable for pressing

Take care with yarn

All types of yarns are suitable for crochet—whether thick or thin, natural or man-made fibres—not only the fine cottons or linens used for the more traditional types of fine crochet.

If you are not absolutely certain that you have come to grips with tension, then it is wisest to buy the brand of yarn specified in the instructions. A different brand may make it difficult for you to obtain the correct measurements. But as in knitting, if you can obtain the numbers of stitches and rows given in the instructions, then you can use any other yarn that gives the same number of stitches and rows to the inch. (See Yarn Chart, pages 10/11). Always buy sufficient quantity to complete the garment so that all the yarn comes from the same dye lot. Another dye lot may vary very slightly and cause unwanted stripes. When working with balls of crochet cotton, always use the end from the centre of the ball as it runs more smoothly when being worked.

Take care with tension

Tension is one of the most important factors towards successful work. If you do not get the number of stitches and rows to one inch that are stated in the instructions your garment cannot have the correct measurements when completed.

Beginners should practise trying to obtain the correct tension, but if it proves impossible to obtain at the same time as holding hook and yarn comfortably, then different hook sizes should be tried.

Before beginning a garment, work a four inch square. If you find you have fewer stitches to the inch than given, then use a hook one size smaller: if on measuring you find you have too many stitches to the inch, then you must use a hook which is one size larger.

Abbreviations

Below you find a list of the most commonly used abbreviations. More complicated abbreviations will be given and explained as they occur.

alt	=alternate(ly)	inc	=increase
beg	=beginning	oz	=ounce
ch	=chain	patt	=pattern
cl	=cluster	rep	=repeat
cm	=centimetre	RS	=right side
dc	=double crochet	ss	=slip stitch
dec	=decrease	sp	=space
dtr	=double treble	st(s)	=stitches
gr(s)	=group(s)	tr	=treble
g	=gramme	tr tr	=triple treble
htr	=half treble	WS	=wrong side
in	=inch(es)	yrh	=yarn round hook

N.B. It should be noted that yrh is the first movement in crochet and forms an important part of every stitch.

An asterisk * indicates repeats. Follow the instructions after the * once, and then repeat from the * as many times as specified.

Repeat instructions in brackets as many times as specified.

For example: (5ch, dc into next dc) 5 times, means to make all that is in brackets 5 times in all.

How to start

The beginning of crochet is to make a slip loop in the yarn and place it on the hook.

1. To make a slip loop. Wrap yarn around first and second fingers of left hand. Insert hook under front loop and draw the back loop through to form a new loop, slipping it off fingers and transferring it to the hook. Pull the loop tight.

2. Holding yarn and hook. Before making a chain, which is the next step, it is necessary to know how to hold the hook and the yarn correctly.

The hook is held in your right hand in the same way as you hold a pen or pencil. This means you hold it between thumb and first finger, letting the hook rest against the second finger, which controls it in moving through the stitches.

The left hand is used to hold the work as it is made, and to control the yarn from the ball. Control the yarn by passing it over the first and second fingers of the left hand, then under the third finger and round the little finger—loosely letting the yarn flow.

3. Chain. Hold the stitch you have made between thumb and first finger of left hand.

Pass hook from left to right under the yarn over your left hand fingers, and round the hook. This is called 'yarn round hook' (yrh) and is a most important part of all stitches. Draw yarn through loop on hook. This makes 1 chain (ch).

4. Repeat this action until you have as many chain stitches as you need, taking care to move your left hand thumb and finger up the chain to hold the stitch you have just made.

Practise making chains until you can hold hook and yarn comfortably.

To fasten off. Cut yarn about six inches from work. Thread loose end through the one remaining loop on the hook and pull it tightly.

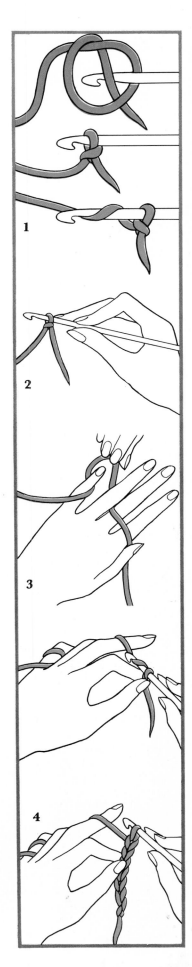

183

Chapter 2

Doubles, trebles and slip stitch

Crochet is based on a few very simple stitches from which all patterns are made. To begin, make a chain and then work back along that chain with your chosen stitch. The top edge of this row forms a new chain base for the next row. At this stage always remember to pick up the top two loops of the chain formed by the previous row, unless the design instructions state otherwise. This gives a flat surface and a firm fabric. (Sometimes there will be instructions for working into back or front loop to give a ridged effect.)

Double crochet (dc)

Make the required length of chain, plus two turning chain stitches (usually just called chain).

1st row. Miss the first two chain.* Insert hook in next chain, yarn round hook, draw through loop (2 loops on hook), yarn round hook, and draw through both loops (1 loop on hook). This makes one double crochet. Repeat from * to end of chain. Turn.

2nd row. 2 chain, miss first double crochet.* Insert hook through next double crochet (picking up both loops), yarn round hook, draw loop through (2 loops on hook), yarn round hook, draw loop through both loops on hook (1 loop on hook), repeat from * in every double crochet, working last double crochet into turning chain on previous row. Turn.

Repeat 2nd row until the work measures the required length. Fasten off.

Do check the number of stitches at the end of each row, to make sure you have worked the full number of stitches.

Treble stitch (tr)

Make the required length of chain plus 3 turning chain.

1st row. Miss first 3 chain, * yarn round hook, insert hook into next chain, yarn round hook, draw through one loop (3 loops on hook), yarn round hook, and draw through 2 loops (2 loops on hook), yarn round hook, and draw through remaining 2 loops on hook (1 loop on hook). This forms 1 treble. Repeat from * to end of chain, turn.

2nd row. 3 chain, miss the first treble * 1 treble in next treble, repeat from * to end of row, working last treble into third chain of turning chain, turn.

Repeat 2nd row until the work measures the required length. Remember to check the number of stitches you have worked at the end of each row to maintain the shape of your work.

Always take good care to draw up the first loop to its full height. Proper loop formation gives the finished stitch its full and soft appearance. If the top of the stitch is finished off too loosely a ragged effect will be produced.

Turning chains

When working rows (as opposed to rounds), it is necessary to add extra chain stitches at the beginning of each row as a 'fake' stitch to bring you up to the level of stitching for this row. These extra stitches are called turning chain and count as the first stitch of the row to be worked (unless otherwise stated). To compensate for this extra stitch, you must miss the first stitch of the row and work the first actual pattern stitch into the second stitch of the previous row. At the end of each row the last stitch is then worked into the turning chain of the previous row.

These turning chain give a neat, firm edge to your work. The following table is a guide to the number of chain to be worked to give the right depth of the stitch being replaced.

N.B. Some patterns give instructions for working the turning chain at the end of the row before turning to start the next row. You may do this if you prefer, but in this book the turning chain is given at the beginning of each row.

Double crochet	— 2 turning chain
Half treble	— 2 turning chain
Treble	— 3 turning chain
Double treble	— 4 turning chain
Triple treble	— 5 turning chain

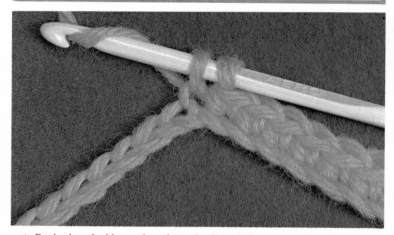

▲ *Beginning double crochet along the first chain*

▼ *Treble crochet gives a deeper row*

Variations of the treble stitch

1. Half treble (htr)
Make the required length of chain.

1st row. Miss first 2ch, * yrh, insert hook into next ch, yrh, draw through one stitch (3 loops on hook), yrh, draw through all loops on hook (1 loop on hook), (this makes 1 htr), repeat from * to end of ch. Turn.

2nd row. 2ch, * 1 htr into next htr, rep from * to last htr, 1 htr into 2nd of 2 turning ch. Turn. Rep 2nd row for length required.

2. Double treble or long treble (dtr)
To start off first work the required length of chain.

1st row. Miss first 4ch, * yarn twice round hook—called y2rh-insert hook into next ch, yrh, draw loop through ch, yrh, draw loop through first 2 loops on hook, yrh, draw loop through next two loops on hook, yrh, draw loop through last 2 loops on hook, (this makes 1 dtr), rep from * to end of ch. Turn.

2nd row. Work 4 ch. Work 1 dtr into next dtr, rep from * to end of row, working last dtr into 4th ch or turning ch. Turn. Rep 2nd row for length required.

Triple or quadruple treble
Work these stitches in the same way as double treble, passing the yarn three or four times, respectively, round the hook, instead of twice. Then work the loops off in the same way, two at a time, until one loop remains on hook.

3. Treble round treble
This stitch is frequently used in designs where a deeply ridged effect is required. Make the ridge by working round the treble in the previous row, instead of working into the chain at the top of the stitches. Shown here is a sample of treble already worked, with the hook in position to work the next stitch round the treble in the previous row. The ridge is made by the top chain on the previous row being left free on the reverse side of the work.

4. Treble between treble
To crochet with the stitches alternating more definitely, work into the space between the trebles in the previous row. The illustration shows ordinary treble with the hook in position to work the next treble into the space in the previous row.

The last two stitches show how you can change the appearance of a familiar stitch by varying the way you insert the hook.

Single crochet or slip stitch (ss)

This stitch is used chiefly for joins or in fancy patterns, and it is the shortest in height of all the crochet stitches.

Make the required length of chain.

1st row. Miss end ch, * pass hook through top loop of next ch, yrh, draw yarn through both stitches on hook, rep from * to end of ch. Turn. This makes 1 ss.

2nd row. 1 ch, * 1 ss into next ss, rep from * working last ss into turning ch of previous row.

Repeat second row for length required. Fasten off.

The yarn used on these two pages is
Patons Double Knitting

▲ *Half treble stitch*

▲ *Double treble or long treble stitch*

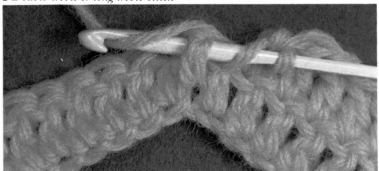

▲ *Treble round treble stitch*

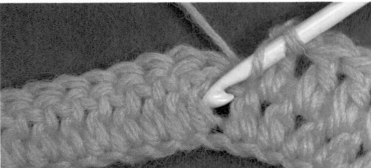

▲ *Treble between treble stitch*

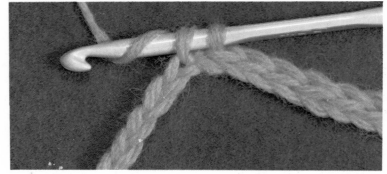

▲ *Single crochet, or slip stitch*

Chapter 3

Increasing and decreasing

Increasing and decreasing stitches play a very important part in crochet and after you have had a little practice you will find them quite simple. Once you know how to do them you are ready to tackle almost any crochet garment.

Increasing

1. The simplest way to increase is to work two stitches into one. This can be done at each end of a row, or at one end only.

2. The second method is to add as many chain as the number of stitches to be increased, plus the turning chain at the end of the row. This way, an increase at the left side of the work is made at the end of a right side row, and an increase at the right side of the work is made at the end of a wrong side row. When the work is turned, the new chain is worked the same as a commencing chain.

3. Mark the place where the increase is to be made with a length of coloured thread. If the increase is to be made to the right, work two stitches into the stitch before the marker.

4. If the increase is to be made to the left, work these stitches into the stitch after the marker.

If the increases are to be repeated in following rows, they are moved one stitch to the right, or one stitch to the left, depending on which side the increase is required.

5. To make a double increase, follow the same instructions but work three stitches instead of two into the foundation stitch.

Decorative increasing

You can make a more decorative increase this way. Mark the place where the increase is to be made on the wrong side of the work. Then, working on the wrong side, make one chain before the marker if you want the increase to be to the left, or after the marker if you want it to be to the right. On the next row (right side) work the increase stitch into the chain made on the previous row.

2. *Increasing with a chain*

3. *Increasing to the right. This is made by marking the position for increasing, and working two stitches into one to the right of the marker*

4. *Increasing to the left. This is made by marking the position for increasing, and working two stitches into one to the left of the marker*

1. *Increasing by working two stitches into one. This is the simplest method, and can be worked at either end of a row*

5. *Double increasing. This is the same method as for single increasing, but three stitches instead of two, are worked into one*

Decreasing

To decrease one stitch at the side edge, miss the first stitch at the beginning of the row and insert the hook into the second stitch. Work to the last two stitches in the normal way, miss the next stitch and insert the hook into the last stitch.

To decrease several stitches, work the row and turn, leaving the stitches to be decreased at the end of a row, unworked.

6. There is a way to avoid ugly steps in your work where several stitches have to be decreased at once. For example, if three are to be decreased, work along the row to the last three stitches, miss the next two and work one slip stitch into the last stitch: turn with one chain, miss the slip stitch, work a double crochet into the next stitch, and then continue along the row in the normal way.

Decreasing a stitch in the middle of a row

7. Work two double or treble crochet but keep the last loop of each stitch on the hook. Then draw a loop through all the loops that are remaining on the hook.

Marking position for decreases

When making decreases in the middle of a row make sure you mark the spot with a length of contrasting coloured yarn. Then work the decrease in the two stitches before the marker if it is a right decrease, or in the two stitches after it, for a left decrease.

For example, to decrease on double crochet, insert the hook into the first of these two stitches, yrh, and draw one loop through, keeping it on the hook. Insert the hook into the second stitch, yrh and draw another loop through so that there are three loops on the hook. Then, yrh, draw loop through all loops.

When decreasing or increasing on garments, use the methods that leave the neatest edges as it will be easier to make up.

6. Decreasing at the end of a row. This can be worked on either side, producing the slanting edge shown

7. Decreasing a stitch in the middle of a row. It is very important to use a marker, to keep the decreasing even

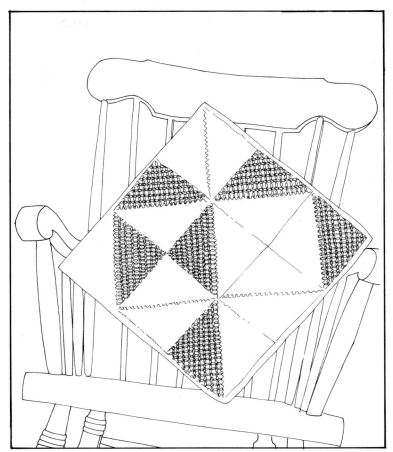

This attractive cushion cover has been made from crocheted squares each made up of two colours and then joined together. This method could be used for anything which is made with squares—a waistcoat, handbag, or an afghan coverlet would all look lovely in carefully chosen colours

Cushions made with coloured squares

The cushion is made with squares crocheted in two colours, and then sewn together to form a cover. Each square measures 5½ inches square. You can use oddments of yarn but do make sure you choose yarns of similar thickness.

To make a square

Work 3 ch.

1st row. Work 2 tr into 3rd ch from hook. Turn. Continue in rows of tr working 3 ch at beg of each row to turn, and inc 2 tr at each end of every row. Work until about 7½ inches wide.

Join contrast yarn with ss and continue, dec 2 tr at each end of every row by leaving last loop of each 3 tr to be decreased on hook, and drawing yarn through all loops. This decreases 2 tr. Work until 3 tr rem.

Last row. Work 3 tr, leaving last loop of each on hook, then draw loop through all loops on hook.

Work 8 more squares and sew together on wrong side.

To make the border

Work 2 rows of dc round edges, working 2 extra dc into corners. Work another side in the same way.

You can, if you like, instead of working two sides, just work one and back it with any strong fabric in a contrasting or blending colour. Vary the arrangement of the squares and colours too, to make your very own arrangements.

Chapter 4

Crochet in rounds

Crochet in rounds produces beautiful results from the simplest Old America squares to the finest Irish crochet.

To make a circle

Make the central circle from a short chain, looped round to form a circle and joined by 1 ss into the first ch. Into this first circle work twice the number of stitches of the original chain, and complete the round by joining to the first stitch with a ss. Shape is made in the next rounds by the position of the increased stitches.

N.B. Before making anything in crochet of any size, you must know how to join yarn securely. Join new yarn with a slip stitch, work the chain to form the first stitch and work over both the ends for a few stitches.

▼ *Joining chain to form a circle*   ▼ *The disc when almost complete*

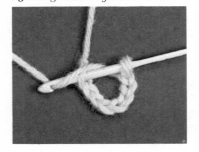 

Crocheting into spaces (sp)

When following a pattern it is often necessary to work into a space made in the previous row, instead of working into or round the stitch. The illustration shows the third round of an Old America square and illustrates how to change to a different coloured yarn with a slip stitch while working into a chain space.

'*Wrong' side of the Old America square*

Afghan squares are so bright and easy

An afghan is the name given to a knitted or crocheted rug or coverlet. These are often made in strips or sections for easy handling, then made up when all the sections are complete. The beautiful rug shown on the opposite page is made of small squares crocheted in a traditional, much-used design called the Old America Square.

It is common to use odd lengths of wool or left-over scraps of any colour for making afghans but, if you have to buy wool, the afghan can take on added sophistication by having a planned colour scheme. Choose one colour for the background or main colour, and two or more colours to tone or contrast. Arrange the finished squares at random as in the illustration, or in lines, or squares of colour for a neat, symmetrical design.

To make an Old America Square

Using 2 different colours.

Work 4ch with the contrast yarn, joining to form a circle with a ss.
1st round. 3 ch, 2tr into circle, 1 ch, * 3tr into circle, 1 ch, rep from * twice. Join into 3rd ch with ss. Break yarn.
2nd round. With main colour, join into last sp with ss, 2ch, 2tr into same sp, 1 ch, 3 tr into same sp, 1 ch * 3 tr, 1 ch, 3 tr, 1 ch into next sp, rep from * twice, join into 3rd ch with ss. Break yarn.
3rd round. With contrast yarn join into last sp with ss. Continue working groups of 3 tr with 1 ch between along sides, and 2 groups of 3 tr with 1ch between into each corner.
Work 3 more rounds in this way.
When enough squares are ready, sew together on wrong side, or crochet together, using double crochet.
Finish ends by darning into same colour yarn so that it is invisible. Either side of the crochet can be treated as the right side.

◄ *Working into a space*

The colour scheme for this richly blending afghan was taken from the colours seen in a harbour in Malta, where these pictures were taken ►

Chapter 5

Multi-coloured waistcoat in squares

You have already seen how to work squares in two colours only in Crochet Know-how Chapter 4. This waistcoat design is based on different colour permutations using four colours and a total of 62 squares, plus 2 half squares for the front shaping. You can make every square different by varying the number of colours and also their sequence used for each square. If you want to do a special colour combination, make each square the same.

For the waistcoat shown you need a total of 9 50g balls of double knitting yarn and a No.4·00 (ISR) crochet hook. But remember that if you intend to use one main colour as the last round of every square, you will need more of this colour in proportion to the three contrasting colours.
The measurements are for a 34–36in bust size, with an underarm length of 17½in. This size is based on a 3½in square, joined together in rows of ten. To vary the bust size, use a different size of hook to work a smaller or larger square. For example, to make a 30–32 in size use a hook which will work a 3in square, ten of which when joined together will give you the size you want. Add extra rows of squares to alter the length of the waistcoat to a sweeping midi worn over flowing evening trousers. Take away one or two rows and you have a snug little bolero.

Size
To fit a 34–36in bust
Length to centre back, 24½in

Crochet Know-how

Tension
Each square measures 3½ x 3½in worked on No.4·00 (ISR) crochet hook

Materials
Double knitting yarn
3 50g balls main colour, 2 balls each of 3 contrast colours
One No.4·00 (ISR) crochet hook

To make a square

Work 4ch. Join with s ss to first ch to form circle.
1st round. 3ch, 2tr into circle, 2ch, *3tr into circle, 2ch, rep from * twice.
Join with a ss to 3rd of first 3ch.
2nd round. 2ch, work 3tr, 2ch, 3tr into first 2ch space to form corner, *1ch, work 3tr, 2ch, 3tr into next 2ch space to form corner, rep from * twice. Join with a ss to 1st of first 2ch.
3rd round. 3ch, 2tr into first ch space, 1ch, *work 3tr, 2ch, 3tr into corner 2ch, 1ch, 3tr into next 1ch space, 1ch, rep from * twice, work 3tr, 2ch, 3tr into last corner space, 1ch. Join with a ss to 3rd of first 3ch.
4th round. 2ch, 3tr into next 1ch space, 1ch, *work 3tr, 2ch, 3tr into corner 2ch space, 1ch, 3tr into 1ch space, 1ch, 3tr into 1ch space, 1ch, rep from * twice, work 3tr, 2ch, 3tr into last corner 2ch space, 1ch, 2tr into next ch space. Join with a ss to 1st of first 2ch. Fasten off.

Make 61 more squares in this way, varying theme by using one colour or two, three or four colour combinations.

To make a half square

Work 32ch.
1st row. Into 3rd ch from hook work 1tr, 1tr into next ch, 1ch, miss 1ch, work 1tr into each of next 3ch, 1ch, miss 1ch, work 1tr into each of next 3ch, 1ch, miss 1ch, work 1tr into each of next 3ch leaving last loop of each tr on hook, miss 1 ch, work 1tr into each of next 3ch leaving last loop of each tr on hook, yrh and draw through all 7 loops on hook, 1ch, miss 1ch, work 1tr into each of next 3ch, 1ch, miss 1ch, work 1tr into each of next 3ch, 1ch, miss 1ch, work 1tr into each of last 3ch. Turn.
2nd row. 3ch, into 1st ch loop work 3tr, 1ch, miss 3tr, 3tr into next ch loop, 1ch, miss 3 tr, work 3tr into next ch loop leaving last loop of each tr on hook, miss corner cluster, work 3tr into next ch loop leaving last loop of each

tr on hook, yrh and draw through all 7 loops on hook, 1ch, miss 3tr, work 3tr into next ch loop, 1ch, miss 3tr, work 3tr into next ch loop, 1tr in turning ch. Turn.
3rd row. 3ch, into 1st ch loop work 3tr, 1ch, miss 3tr, 3tr into next ch loop leaving last loop of each tr on hook, miss corner cluster, work 3tr into next ch loop leaving last loop of each tr on hook, yrh and draw through all 7 loops on hook, 1ch, miss 3 tr, 3tr into next ch loop, 1tr into turning ch. Turn.
4th row. 3ch, work 3tr into first ch loop leaving last loop of each tr on hook, miss corner cluster, work 3tr into next ch loop leaving last loop of each tr on hook, yrh and draw through all 7 loops on hook, 1tr into turning ch. Fasten off.
Make one more half square in the same way varying colours if required.

To make up

Darn in all ends. Press each square under a damp cloth with a warm iron. Sew or crochet 10 squares together to form one row and join 5 rows in same way. (50 squares). To 4 centre squares of last row join 2 rows of 4 squares for centre back. (58 squares). Miss first and last square at end of last row and join 2 rows of one square to 2nd and 9th squares, leaving 3rd and 8th squares on last row to form underarm. Join half motif to 1st and 10th squares of last row to form neck shaping. Join 2nd square to first of 4 centre back squares and 9th square to 4th of 4 centre back squares to form shoulders. Press.
With RS facing beg at underarm square of lower edge and work 1 round dc up front, round neck, down front and round lower edge. Join with ss to first st. Work round armholes in same way. Press. If preferred work a picot edge (see Crochet Know-how page 200).

Chapter 6

Ideas for motifs

Motifs have endless uses, not only for cushions and covers but also for fashion ideas. A change of colours, yarn or shape of motif can completely alter the finished look.

Colours and yarns

Try out several colour ideas until you find something you particularly like. It could be a collection of gay chunky wools worked with a large hook so that the motifs grow quickly and are then joined (see Crochet Know-how Chapter 4) to form a long scarf. Or trim the lower edges and sleeves of an evening blouse with a row of motifs worked in a fine metallic yarn. Just remember, if you are using only one colour you do not need to break the yarn but simply continue the next round, omitting the slip stitch used to join in the new colour.

Instructions are given for the same colour combinations as those shown in the illustrations. Try using your own choice of colours and see the difference if you work in only one or two. Or work with the palest colour in the centre and graduate out to the darkest.

Square motif

With centre colour, work 10ch. Join into a circle with a ss.
1st round. Using same colour, work 3ch to form the first st, work 23tr into circle. Join with ss into 3rd of first ch. Break yarn.
2nd round. Using 1st contrast, join to top of last st of preceding round with a ss, work 3ch to form first st, 5ch, 1tr into same st as first st, 7ch, *miss 5 tr of preceding round, work 1tr, 5ch, 1tr all into next tr, 7ch, rep from * twice. Ss to 3rd of first 3ch.
3rd round. 3ch to form first st, work 4tr, 5ch, 5tr all into first 5ch space of preceding round, 3ch, *miss 7ch space, 5tr, 5ch, 5tr all into next 5ch space, 3ch, rep from * twice. Join with ss into 3rd of first 3ch. Break yarn, leaving end for darning.
4th round. Using second contrast, join as before, work 3ch to form first st, 1tr into each of next 4tr of preceding round, work 3tr, 5ch, 3tr all into next 5ch space, work 1tr into each of next 5tr, 7ch, *1tr into each of next 5tr, work 3tr, 5ch, 3tr all into next 5ch space, 1tr into each of next 5tr, 7ch, rep from * twice. Join with ss to 3rd of first 3ch. Break yarn and leave end for darning.
5th round. Join in third contrast as before, work 3ch to form first st, 1tr into each of next 7tr of preceding round, 9tr into next 5ch space, 1tr into each of next 8tr, 3ch, 1dc into 4th (centre) ch of 7ch, 3ch, *1tr into each of next 8tr, 9tr into next 5ch space, 1tr into each of next 8tr, 3ch, 1dc into 4th ch of 7ch, 3ch, rep from * twice. Join with ss to 3rd of first 3ch. Break yarn, leaving end for darning.
6th round. Join in fourth contrast as before, 1ch, work 1dc into each tr or dc of preceding round, working 3dc into each 3ch space. Join with ss to first ch. Break yarn and darn in end. Take care when doing this to darn into the same colour, so that the ends are invisible and the pattern not spoilt. If you have used wool or cotton, pin out the motif forming a good, regular shape and press under a damp cloth with a warm iron. Do not press too heavily so that the stitches are flattened. Do not press man-made fibres. Sew the motifs together at points where they touch each other.

Star motif with 8 points

Using centre colour, work 7ch. Join into a circle by working a ss into the first ch.
1st round. Work 2ch to form first st, work 23dc into circle. Join to 2nd of 2ch with ss. Break yarn and leave end for darning.
2nd round. Join contrast yarn with ss to top of last st worked, 4ch, 1tr into same st as first st, 1ch, *miss 2dc of preceding round, 1tr, 2ch, 1tr all into next dc, 1ch, rep from * 6 times. Join with ss into 2nd of first 4ch.
3rd round. With same colour, work 2ch, 1tr, 2ch, 2tr all into first 2ch space of preceding round, 1dc into next 1ch space, *2tr, 2ch, 2tr all into next 2ch space, 1dc into next 1ch space, rep from * 6 times. Join with ss into 2nd of first 2ch. Break yarn.
4th round. Join in first colour as before, 2ch, 2tr, 1ch, 3tr all into first 2ch space of preceding round, 1dc on each side of dc of preceding round, *3tr, 1ch, 3tr all into next 2ch space, 1dc on each side of next dc, rep from * 6 times. Join with ss to 2nd of 2ch. Break yarn, leaving an end for darning.
5th round. Join in contrast as before, 2ch, 1dc into each of next 3tr, 1dc, 3ch, 1dc all into first 1ch space, 1dc into each of next 4sts, *1dc into each of next 4sts 1dc, 3ch, 1dc all into next 1ch space, 1dc into each of next 4sts, rep from * 6 times. Join with ss to 2nd of first 2ch. Break yarn and darn in all ends. Complete as for square motif if pressing is required.

◄ *Star motif*

▲ *Square motif*

Catherine wheels

To make the large round

Work 4ch. Join into circle with ss.

1st round. Work 3ch, * (yrh, insert hook into the circle and draw a loop through) twice, yrh and draw through all loops, 1ch, rep from * 7 times more. Join with ss into 3rd ch. Cut yarn and fasten off.

2nd round. Join new colour into last ch sp with a ss, 2 ch, (1tr, 2ch) into same sp,* (2tr, 2ch) into next ch sp, rep from * six times (8 tr groups). Join with a ss into 2nd ch. Cut yarn and fasten off.

3rd round. Join new colour into last ch sp with a ss, 2ch, (1tr, 1ch, 2tr, 1ch) into same sp,* (2tr, 1ch, 2 tr, 1ch) into next ch sp, rep from * to end (16 tr groups). Join as before. Cut yarn and fasten off.

4th round. Join new colour into last sp with ss, 2ch, (2tr, 1ch) into same sp,* (3tr, 1ch) into next ch sp, rep from * to end (16 tr groups). Cut yarn and fasten off.

5th round. Change colour and rep 4th round once more.

To make the small round

Make a ch and work 1st round as above but do not break yarn.

2nd round. 2ch, (1tr, 2ch) into next sp,* (2 tr, 2ch) into each sp to end. Join with ss. Cut yarn and fasten off.

Chapter 7

Decorative trimmings

Small crochet trims are easy to handle, quickly worked, perfect for using up all those left-over odds and ends, and are a marvellous way of adding finish and individuality to clothes and accessories. Take a baby's bonnet, trim it with bunches of cord and pastel rosettes like a miniature bouquet of flowers, and fasten mittens and bootees with ties trimmed to match. Add a bold military touch to a jacket with a richly scrolled frogged fastening, and bobble buttons. Dangle groups of crochet spirals from the ends of a slender cord belt. Make them in glittering yarn to fringe an evening bag or let the whole idea go to your head with narrow cords or flower rosettes to twist into an elaborate party hairstyle.

Cords and rosettes trim a baby's outfit

Cords, rosettes and spirals

You can make a pretty bag for a little girl out of colourful felt, with a crocheted cord handle and a bunch of rosettes in one corner to give a decorative touch. Trim your key ring by adding a few spirals made in brightly coloured wool.

To make a cord
Work 7 ch, joining to form a circle with a ss. Work 2 ch, work 1 tr into each ch. Do not join with a ss but continue working round with 1 tr into each previous tr until required length is reached. Finish off. You can trim the cord with rosettes and spirals.

To make a rosette
Work 16 ch.
1st row. Into 4th ch from hook work 1 tr, 3 tr into same sp,* 5tr into next ch, rep from * to end. Finish off.
You will see the rosette forms a small curl or rose shape. The ends can be secured by a few small stitches sewn through the centre. The longer the chain, and the thicker the yarn and hook which you use, the larger the rosette will be.

To make a spiral
Work 20ch.
1st row. Work 2tr into 4th ch, * 3tr in next ch, rep * to end of ch. Cut yarn and finish off the spiral.

Bag and key with crochet trims

Buttons

Small buttons like the ones shown are not just decorative—they're practical too! They often make a smart alternative to ordinary buttons on knitted or crocheted garments.

To make a button
Work 4 ch, joining to form a circle with a ss.

1st round. 1 ch, work 7 dc into circle. Do not join with a slip stitch. Cont. in dc working * 2dc into next dc, 1dc into each of next 2dc, rep from * 8 times. Work 1dc into each of next 12dc. Dec by working as follows: * insert hook into next dc, yrh, draw through loop, (2 loops on hook) insert hook into next dc, yrh, draw through loop (3 loops on hook), yrh, draw through all loops on hook, 1dc into next dc, rep from * 5 times until opening is almost closed, stuffing with cotton wool as you work. Finish off and close any opening which is left.

You can vary the size of the button by increasing more or fewer stitches at the beginning. The number of stitches you work before decreasing will alter its depth.

Begin the button with a flat circle ▼

Continue working over the filling ▼

Buttonholes

Making buttonholes for a crocheted garment presents no problems. It is simple to work them into the main fabric as you go along, either horizontally or vertically.

Horizontal buttonholes
Work until the position for the buttonhole is reached. When this is made as part of the main fabric of, say, a cardigan, always finish at the centre front edge, before working the buttonhole row. On the next row, work a few stitches to where the buttonhole is required, work two or more chain stitches to suit the size of the button, miss the corresponding number of stitches in the row below (picture 1), then pattern to end of row. On the following row, work in pattern over the chain stitches made in the previous row to complete buttonhole (picture 2).

Vertical buttonholes
Work until the position for the buttonhole is reached. On the next row work a few stitches to where the buttonhole is required, turn and work back and then work the required number of rows over these stitches to take the size of button being used, ending at inner edge (picture 3). Work in slip stitch down inner edge of rows to the last complete row worked, work across the remaining stitches for the same number of rows, then continue across all stitches (picture 4).

1. *Horizontal buttonholing by chains*

2. *Horizontal buttonhole completed*

3. *Vertical buttonholing by rows*

4. *Vertical buttonhole completed*

Pompons
and tufts

Pompons and tufted fringes are a fascinating trim for so many things. Add a cluster of jewel-bright pompons to cushions, a nursery rug or a cot cover. Use a large, important pompon to make a 'pull' for a roller blind. A huge pompon will cheer up a plain woolly cap—and you can add a matching pompon to a scarf. All too often, instructions just say 'finish with a pompon', but give no details about making one. This chapter tells you what to do.

Small pompons or bobbles

To make these, wind lengths of yarn round two or more fingers. When you think you have wound enough yarn for the size of pompon you want, slip the strands carefully off the fingers and tie tightly round the centre. With sharp scissors, snip both looped ends of yarn and arrange them to form a ball. It may be necessary to trim untidy ends so that the finished shape is neat and round.

Make cord belts with pompons or knot cord ends and fray out as tassels

Large pompons

For large pompons, a cardboard frame is required. Decide on the diameter of the pompon you want and draw two circles of this diameter on to the cardboard. From the centre of each circle cut out a smaller circle: the larger this inner circle, the more wool you will need to complete the pompon and the heavier it will be when finished. If you haven't a compass, a cup or small bowl will be large enough to draw the outer circle and a coin or egg-cup is often a good size for the inner circle.

Place the two circles together and with one or more strands begin to wind the yarn around the frame as evenly as possible. When the centre hole is almost filled, thread the yarn into a blunt-pointed needle and continue until the hole is completely filled. To make a well-shaped, fat pompon you must continue to work until the centre circle is tightly filled.

When you have done this take a sharp pair of scissors and begin to cut the strands of yarn at the outside edge, working in line with the edge of the cardboard, placing the scissors between the cardboard circles. Once you have cut all the strands you are ready to begin the final stage.

Gently, with the tips of the scissors, begin to open the cardboard rings until they are far enough apart for you to tie a strong strand of yarn tightly round all the threads where they pass through the centre of the rings. If the pompon is to be sewn on a garment you may like to leave the ends of the tying yarn hanging so that you can use them for sewing on. Once the centre is tied, continue to remove both rings of cardboard.

Fluff the pompon into a complete ball and trim uneven ends.

For a multi-coloured pompon, work all the colours together: if you want a striped effect, work round the ring in one colour and then in another, or work in sections of one colour only if you want to make a patchwork pompon.

Tufted fringing

From the illustration, you can see how to give a baby's poncho a soft, frothy edge by adding a tufted fringe.

The number and size of the tufts on each strand can be altered as you want and also the distance between the tufts. You can make a short, thick fringe by working only a few chain stitches between each tuft, or a deeper, more delicate fringe by spacing the tufts much further apart—you simply work more chain stitches between the tufts.

Begin by preparing the tufts. Decide on the size you want and cut a piece of card this width and several inches long. Then wind the yarn round the full length of the cardboard and cut along the edges. If each tuft on the strand is to be a different width then you will require one piece of card for each width. The illustrations on the opposite page show a strand of wool made with three different sized tufts.

Now prepare the strands. Begin the first strand by making 9 chain stitches with a crochet hook. Open out the last chain stitch and place the required number of threads in the loop. When the tuft is in place, pull the open stitch tight to grip all the threads in the centre of the tuft. Continue by making 9 chain stitches before inserting the next tuft.

Complete the number of tufts required in this way and join the strand, when completed, to the edge of the work with a slip stitch. Cut the yarn and fasten off the ends. Join other strands at even intervals along the edge to be trimmed. Finally, when the fringe is completed, you can anchor each tuft even more securely by working several small stitches through the centre of tuft and chain with a fine, matching sewing thread or wool.

▲ *Winding the yarn onto the frame*

▲ *Working the chain between tufts*   ▲ *Joining a tuft to the chain*

▼ *Baby's poncho with tufted fringe and pompon tie*

▲ *Cutting yarn between circles*   ▼ *The finished pompon*

Chapter 8

Braids, borders and edgings

One of the great things about crochet is the many different types of trimming you can make with it. Braids and borders can look very attractive if you use a combination of colours, and they can be worked in a wide range of materials from fine cotton to coloured string to make cushion and curtain edges, hat bands, belts and hairbands. Crochet edgings in a single colour are also pretty and need not be limited to trimmings for household linen or crochet garments. They look just as attractive as borders for knitted garments. Try trimming a plain sweater with a crochet edging in a contrast colour, as shown in the illustration on the opposite page, to make a simple neckline look more interesting.

Braids and borders

Braid in two colours

With blue, work a chain the required length, of a number divisible by 10, plus 1.

1st row. With blue, work 1htr into 3rd ch from hook, 1htr into each ch to end. Break yarn. Turn and work other side of ch. Join blue with ss to first st of commencing ch, 2ch, 1htr into each st to end. Break yarn and finish off. Complete remaining rows on one side before turning and working the other side to correspond.

2nd row. Join cream with ss to first st, 2ch, 1dc into each of next 2htr, *miss 2htr, insert hook into space between 2 rows of htr along commencing ch immediately below 2nd missed st, yrh and draw through a long loop to reach row being worked, 1dc into first htr missed, yrh and draw through both loops on hook, 1dc into each of next 3htr, rep from * to end. Break yarn and fasten off. Do not turn work.

3rd row. Join cream with ss to 2nd of first 2ch, 2ch, *2ch, yrh, insert hook into same st as last st, yrh and draw through 2 loops, yrh and insert hook into same st, yrh and draw through all 3 loops on hook, miss 3dc, 1dc into next dc, rep from * to end. Break yarn and fasten off. Turn work.

Complete as for first side, working 2nd row with long st sloping in

opposite direction, thus — join cream with ss to 2nd of first 2ch, 2ch, 1dc into each of next 2htr, *insert hook into same space as first long st on other side, yrh and draw a long loop through, 1dc into next htr, yrh and draw through 3 loops on hook, 1dc into each of next 3htr, rep from * to end. Break yarn and fasten off. Do not turn work. Complete as for first side. Darn in all ends.

Border 1 in three colours

Work a chain the required length with blue. Turn.

1st row. With blue, 1dc into 2nd ch from hook, 1dc into next ch, *3ch, miss 2ch, 1dc into each of next 2ch, rep from * to end. Turn. Break off blue and fasten off.

2nd row. With cream, join with ss into first dc, 1ch, 1dc into next dc, *into 3ch space work 1dc, 3tr, 1dc, 1dc into each of next 2dc, rep from * to end. Turn. Break off cream and fasten off.

3rd row. With light green, join with ss to first dc, 1 dc into first dc, 2ch, join with ss into side of last dc to form picot, 1dc into next dc, *2ch, 1dc into 2nd of 3tr, 2ch, 1dc into next dc, 1 picot as before, 1dc into next dc, rep from * to end. Break off green and darn in all ends.

Border 2 in three colours

Work a chain the required length with blue. Turn.

1st row. With blue, 1dc into 2nd ch from hook, *1dc into next ch, rep from * to end. Break off blue and fasten off. Turn.

2nd row. With cream, join with ss into first dc, 1dc into same dc, *7ch, miss 3dc, into 4th dc work 1dc, 1ch, turn and work 4dc into 7ch space, 1ch, turn, work 1dc into each of 4dc just worked, 1dc into last dc worked before 7ch, rep from * to end. Break off cream and fasten off. Turn.

3rd row. With light green, join with ss into first dc, *1dc into each of first 3dc, into 4th dc work 3dc, 3dc into part of 7ch space not covered by dc, miss 1dc, rep from * to end. Break off light green and darn in all ends.

Edgings

The simplest of all edgings is formed by working two or more rows of double crochet along the garment edge.

The first row of crochet must be worked evenly on to the knitted edge for a neat and attractive crochet design. If the stitches of this first row are worked unevenly, the finished appearance will be completely spoilt.

Here we give you four more edges which can be worked just as quickly and easily. Use them as borders on the front of a plain cardigan or round the cuffs and neck of a basic sweater to give a couture finish to your favourite pattern.

Crab stitch edging

This is the simplest of all the variations of double crochet and can be worked backwards and forwards along an edge in rows, or continuously round a circular opening, such as a cuff.
1st row. Work along edge using double crochet. If working a circular edge, join with a slip stitch to the first stitch.
2nd row. If the work is circular, work back along the round already made, making one double crochet in each double crochet and working from left to right instead of the normal right to left. If you are working in rows then do not turn the work but simply make one double crochet in each double crochet already made. Fasten off.

Reversed crab stitch edging

1st row. Work along edge using double crochet. Turn.
2nd row. 2ch, miss first double crochet, *1dc into next dc, rep from * to end. Do not turn.
3rd row. Into each dc of previous row work 1dc, working from left to right. Fasten off.

Twisted stitch edging

1st row. Work along edge using double crochet. Turn.
2nd row. *Insert hook into first dc, yrh and draw a loop through loosely, turn the hook on itself in order to twist the stitches, yrh and draw through all loops, rep from * to end. Fasten off.

Cluster stitch edging

1st row. Work along edge using double crochet. Break yarn.
The 2nd row is worked in the same direction as the 1st.
2nd row. Join yarn with ss to first dc, 2ch, *1dc into next st, (yrh, insert hook into ch to right of dc just worked and draw through one loose st) 3 times into same stitch, yrh and draw through all loops, 1ch, miss 1dc, rep from * to end. Fasten off.

▲ *Crab stitch edging*
▼ *Reversed crab stitch edging*

▼ *Twisted stitch edging*

▼ *Cluster stitch edging*

Sweater showing crochet neck edging

Crochet
Know-how

More ideas for edgings

Picot edgings

Picot edgings can be made in thick wools to give a chunky edge or in cotton for a delicate cobweb effect.

Small picot edging

* Work 3ch, into the first of these 3ch work 2dc. Without turning the work rep from * until the strip is the required length. Finish off.

Lace picot

Work 2ch, * into the first of these 2ch insert the hook, yrh, and draw through one loop. There are now 2 loops on hook.
Into the loop nearest the hook point work 2ch. Slip both loops off hook and insert hook back only into the loop further to the left of work. Without turning the work, rep from * until the edging is the required length. Finish off.

Ring picot

* Work 5ch, into the first of these 5ch work 1tr. Without turning the work, rep from * until the edging is the required length. Finish off.

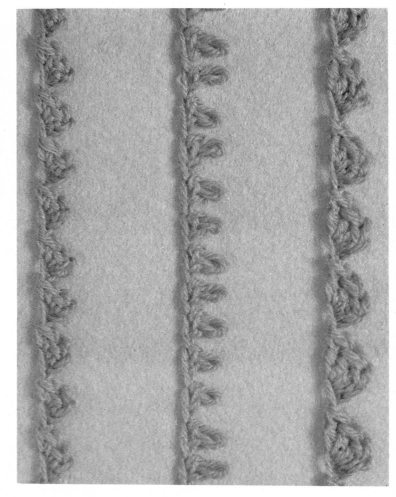

Left to right: small picot edging, lace picot, leaf picot

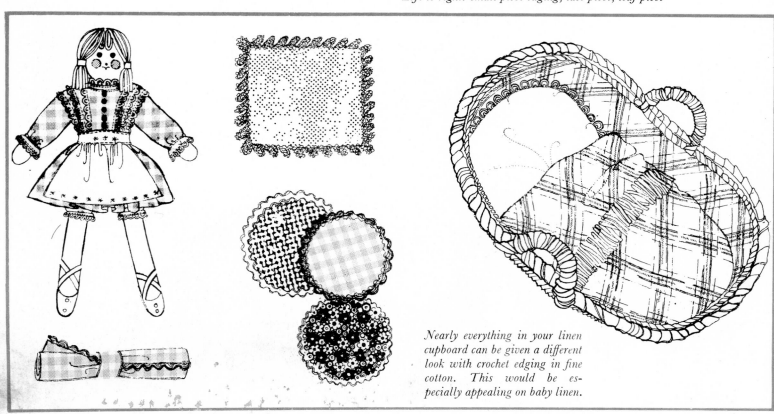

Nearly everything in your linen cupboard can be given a different look with crochet edging in fine cotton. This would be especially appealing on baby linen.

Ribbon—threaded edgings

These edgings are pretty in a variety of yarns, but, whichever yarn you choose, don't use too small a crochet hook, since the work must be open enough to allow the ribbon to slide through easily.

Clover edging

Work a number of chains divisible by 8, plus 1, for the required length.

1st row. 1dc into 2nd ch from hook, *1dc into next ch, rep from * to end. Turn.

2nd row. 2ch, miss first dc, *3ch, miss 3dc and into next dc work 1dc, 5ch to form picot, (1dtr into same dc, 1 picot of 5ch) twice and 1dc all into same dc forming clover group, 3ch, miss 3dc, 1dc into next dc, rep from * to end. Finish off.

Thread ribbon between dc of first row.

Scalloped edging

Crochet a number of chains divisible by 4, plus 2, for the required length.

1st row. 1dc into 4th ch from hook, *1ch, miss 1ch, 1dc into next ch, rep from * to end. Turn.

2nd row. 2ch, *6ch, miss 1ch and 1dc and 1ch of previous row, 1dc into next dc, rep from * to end. Turn.

3rd row. 2ch, *3dc into next 6ch loop, 3ch, 1ss into side of last dc worked to form picot, 3dc into same 6ch loop, 1dc into dc between loops, rep from * to end. Finish off. Thread ribbon in first row.

▲ *Clover edging*   ▼ *Scalloped edging*

Threaded trimmings give a charming edge to a little dress or a shawl

Mitred corners and 'V'necks

Crochet Know-how

Crochet tunic with 'V' neck

Although most crochet patterns give detailed instructions it is useful to know how shaping is worked, particularly when adapting a favourite design to crochet. Previous chapters tell you various methods of increasing and decreasing and all about tension. This chapter gives instructions for working a pointed, and a rounded mitred corner, sleeve underarm shaping and 'V' necklines.

The tunic illustrated here shows the effective use of 'V' neck shaping, which is defined by an edging in a single contrasting colour. The contrasting colour theme can be continued at the hem and round the armholes. A 'V' neck tunic is a smart and useful addition to any wardrobe as it can be worn with a variety of separates to liven up the most ordinary outfit. Team it with a skirt and polo-neck sweater or with an open-necked shirt and trousers as illustrated.

Pointed mitred corner

To make a separate band having a pointed mitred corner, first measure the length of band required and make the necessary number of chain. Mark the stitch which is to be the innermost point of the corner with coloured thread. The band is worked from the inside to the outside edge.

1st row. (right side). Work 1dc into 2nd ch from hook, then work 1dc in to each ch to the last ch before the marked corner ch, work 2ch and continue working 1dc into each ch to end. Turn.

2nd row. 2ch, work 1dc into each dc and 1dc into each of the 2ch at corner. Turn.

Continue in this way, working 2ch at corner on every RS row working 1 more dc on each RS row before making the 2ch and working 1dc into each of these 2ch on WS rows until the band is the required depth. Fasten off.

Any number of chain may precede and follow the corner stitches, depending on the angle of the corner, but always

work one more stitch before corner chain on each RS row.

Rounded mitred corner

Prepare the band as for pointed mitred corner.

1st row. (right side). Work 1dc into 2nd ch from hook, then 1dc into each ch to marked corner st, work 3dc into corner st and 1dc into each ch to end. Turn.

2nd row. 2ch, work 1dc into each dc to end. Turn. Repeat these 2 rows until band is the required depth, working 3dc into centre stitch of the 3 corner stitches on each RS row.

Sleeve underarm shaping

To give a good underarm fit, the same number of stitches should be decreased on the back and front of a garment and at the commencement of the sleeve top shaping. Work until the back and front side seams and the sleeve seam are the required length.

1st row. Ss over first 5 sts, work 1dc into each dc to last 5 sts. Turn.

2nd row. 2ch, miss 1dc, work 1dc into each dc to last 2 dc, miss 1dc, work 1dc in last dc. Turn.

Repeat the 2nd row for a depth of 1½in.

'V' neckline

The depth of the 'V' neck is entirely a matter of choice, but bear in mind that the deeper the 'V', the more gradual the shaping, and that a high 'V' must decrease more rapidly in order to complete the shaping before reaching the shoulder level. On a 34in bust size an average depth for a 'V' neck is approximately 10in from the shoulder, which means that the shaping must be commenced at least 3in before the armhole shaping. Mark the position of the centre stitch and work each side separately.

1st row. (right side). 2ch, work 1dc into each dc, miss 1dc before marked centre st, work 1dc in centre st. Turn.

2nd row. 2ch, work in dc to end. Repeat 2nd row twice more.

5th row. 2ch, work 1dc into each dc, miss last dc but one at

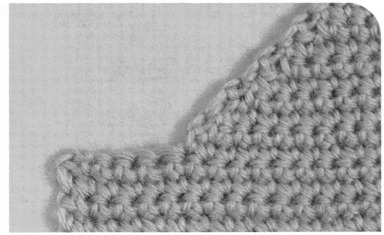

▲ *Pointed mitred corner*　　　▲ *Rounded mitred corner*　　　▲ *Sleeve underarm shaping*　　　▼ *'V' neck shaping*

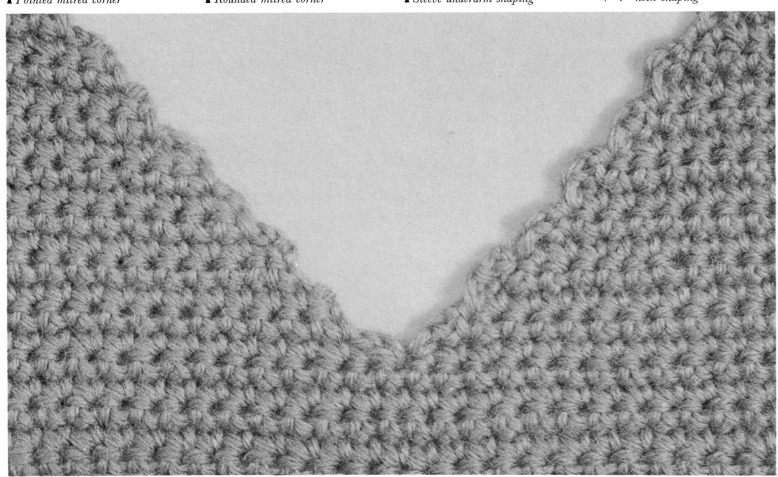

neck edge, work 1dc in last dc. Turn.

Repeat rows 2-5 until required number of stitches have been decreased at neck edge, then continue without shaping, if necessary, to a depth of 10in. With RS of work facing, rejoin yarn to centre st.

1st row. 2ch, miss 1 dc, work 1dc into each dc to end. Turn. Work 3 rows without shaping.

Repeat these 4 rows to match first side.

An alternative method of shaping may be worked as follows:

1st row. (right side). 2ch, work 1dc into each dc to last 2sts before centre st, insert hook in next dc, yrh and draw loop through, insert hook in last dc, y h and draw loop through, (3 loops on hook),

yrh and draw through all loops in hook (1 dec made), work 1dc in centre st. Turn.

Work 3 rows without shaping.

5th row. 2ch, work 1dc into each dc to last 3dc, 1dec in next 2dc, 1dc in last dc. Turn.

Repeat rows 2-5 until required number of stitches have been decreased at neck edge, then continue without shaping, if necessary to a depth of 10in.

With RS of work facing, rejoin yarn to centre st.

1st row. 2ch, insert hook in next st, yrh, draw loop through, insert hook in next st, yrh and draw loop through, yrh and draw through 3 loops on hook, work 1dc in each dc to end. Turn. Work 3 rows without shaping.

Repeat these 4 rows to match first side.

Chapter 10

Tubular crochet

The technique of tubular crochet is the same as knitting in rounds, and has the advantage of doing away with bulky seams. Almost any crochet stitch can be adapted to this method but remember that the right side of the work is always facing you. It is particularly useful for working seamless skirts, handbags, hats or layette garments.

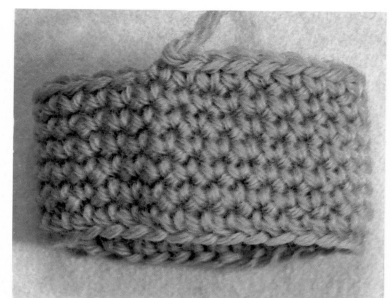

▲ *Tubular Russian stitch*   ▼ *Tubular twisted stitch*

▲ *Joining foundation chain into a ring*   ▼ *Tubular rib stitch*

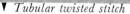

▼ *Tubular rose stitch*

Tubular crochet

Commence with the number of chains which are required to give the total circumference of the article being made. Join into a ring with a slip stitch into the first foundation chain. Continue working in rounds with the chosen stitch for the necessary depth. With the stitches illustrated here it is not necessary to join the end of each round with a slip stitch but it is advisable to mark the beginning of the first round with a coloured thread, so that you know where to finish.

Tubular rib stitch

Work each round in double crochet on a foundation chain joined into a ring but insert the hook into the back loop only of each double crochet.

Tubular Russian stitch

Work each round in double crochet on a foundation chain joined into a ring.

Tubular twisted stitch

Work a foundation chain joined into a ring. Insert hook in centre of foundation chain with the hook pointing downwards, pass the hook over the yarn on the left index finger and, to make 3rd loop on hook, yrh by working from left to right, pull yarn through chain, pass the yarn over the hook from left to right (instead of the normal way from right to left), pull yarn through 3 loops on hook. This completes one stitch. On following rounds insert hook through both loops of stitch in previous round.

Tubular rose stitch

Work each round in half trebles on a foundation chain joined into a ring.

Handbag: *join required number of ch into circle. Work patt for depth needed. Seam bottom edge, gather top edge on to frame.*
Bolster: *make ch as for handbag. Work in patt for length of bolster. Make 2 catherine wheel motifs. Pad bolster, stitch 1 motif to each end.*
Napkin ring: *make ch as for bag. Work in patt for required depth.*

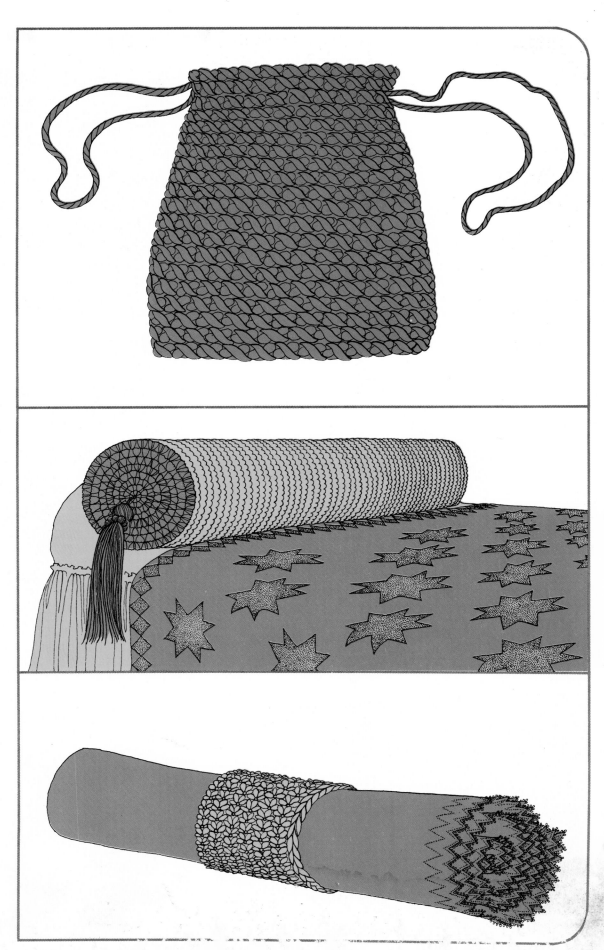

Chapter 11

Introduction to fabric stitches

These very firm, fabric-like stitches are used for garments which receive a lot of wear—suits, jackets, skirts, coats and dresses, for instance. When you are working these stitches, choose a plain double knitting quality rather than a fancy yarn, or the fabric effect tends to become lost. You will find that the close, compact nature of the stitches uses yarn rather quickly, so allow a little extra when you are working out a garment pattern.

When you have completed all the stitch samples, they could be stitched together to make a colourful cushion cover. If you keep each square 4 inches by 4 inches and allow 9 squares for the front and the back of the cushion, you will arrive at a cushion measuring 12 inches square. Three of each pattern in different, vividly contrasting colours would make a completely original and individual furnishing accessory.

Double double crochet

Make a chain of required length.

1st row. Insert hook into 3rd ch from hook, draw yarn through, yrh, draw through 1 loop, yrh, draw through 2 loops on hook to form 1 double double crochet, work 1 double double crochet in each ch to end. Turn.

This row forms pattern and is repeated throughout, inserting the hook into each st of the previous row and beg each row with 2ch as turning ch.

Up and down stitch

Make a number of chain divisible by 2, plus 1.

1st row. Into 3rd ch from hook work 1dc, *1tr into next ch, 1dc into next ch, rep from * to end. Turn.

2nd row. 2ch, *1dc into tr, 1tr into dc, rep from * to last st, 1dc in last st. Turn.

The 2nd row forms pattern and is repeated throughout.

Double up and down stitch

Make a number of chain divisible by 4, plus 1.

1st row. Into 3rd ch from hook work 1dc, 1tr into each of next 2 ch, *1dc into each of next 2 ch, 1tr into each of next 2 ch, rep from * to end. Turn.

2nd row. 2ch, 1dc into 2nd tr, *1tr into each of next 2 dc, 1dc into each of next 2 tr, rep from * to last 2 sts, 1tr into each of last 2 dc. Turn.

The 2nd row forms pattern and is repeated throughout.

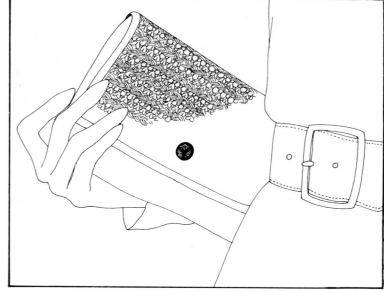

Fabric-look clutch bag in double double crochet

Raised basket weave stitch

Make a number of chain divisible by 4, plus 3.

1st row. Into 2nd ch from hook work 1dc, 1dc into ch each to end. Turn.

2nd row. 2ch, 1dc into each dc to end. Turn.

3rd row. 2ch, work 1dc into each of next 2 dc working into the back loop only of the row below, *work 1dc into next dc inserting the hook in the corresponding st on the row below the previous row and drawing up a long loop, work 1dc into each of next 3dc working into back loop only of the row below, rep from * to end. Turn.

4th row. As 2nd.

5th row. 2ch, *work 1dc into next dc inserting the hook in the corresponding st on the row below the previous row and drawing up a long loop, work 1dc into each of next 3dc working into back loop only of the row below, rep from * to last 2 sts, work 1dc in next dc inserting hook and drawing up a loop as before, 1dc in back loop only of last dc. Turn.

Rows 2–5 form pattern and are repeated throughout.

Leaf stitch

Make a number of chain divisible by 2, plus 1.

1st row. Into 3rd ch from hook work 2dc, miss 1ch, *2dc into next ch, miss 1ch, rep from * to last st, 2dc in last st. Turn.

2nd row. 2ch, *miss 1dc, work 2dc into 2nd dc of group, rep from * to end. Turn.

The 2nd row forms pattern and is repeated throughout.

Little leaf stitch

Make a number of chain divisible by 2, plus 1.

1st row. Into 3rd ch from hook work 1dc, 1ch, 1dc into same st, miss 1ch, *1dc, 1ch, 1dc into next st, miss 1ch, rep from * to last st, 1dc, 1ch, 1dc into last st. Turn.

2nd row. 2ch, *into ch between 2dc of previous row work 1dc, 1ch, 1dc, rep from * to end. Turn.

The 2nd row forms pattern and is repeated throughout.

Up and down stitch ▲
Double up and down stitch ▼

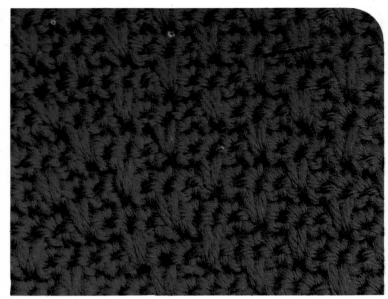

Raised basket weave stitch ▲
Leaf stitch ▼

Double double crochet ▼

Little leaf stitch ▼

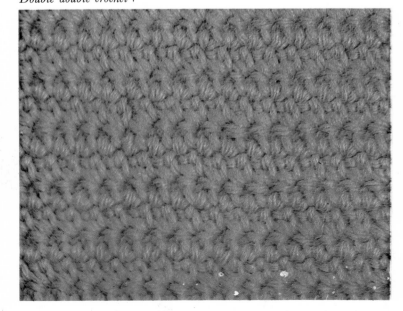

More firm fabric stitches

There are many variations of the closely-worked crochet stitches which give a fabric effect. The ones shown here produce a slightly bulkier fabric than those on the previous page as the stitches are grouped together in chunky clusters. To make the attractive peasant skirt illustrated, simply work two strips of crochet, one for the skirt back and one for the front, using any of the fabric stitches in this chapter. Work in a single bright colour or, for extra sparkle, in horizontal stripes of contrasting colours. Join the two strips down the long sides and the gather up the waist on a cord to tie in front. Work a fringe around the hem.

Cluster stitch
Make a number of chain divisible by 3.
1st row. Into 3rd ch from hook work 2tr, miss 2ch, *1dc and 2tr into next ch, miss 2ch, rep from * to last st, 1dc in last st. Turn.
2nd row. 2ch, 2tr into first dc, *1dc and 2tr into each dc of previous row, rep from * ending 1dc in turning ch. Turn.
The 2nd row forms pattern and is repeated throughout.

Claw stitch
Make a number of chain divisible by 2.
1st row. Into 4th ch from hook work 1tr, *miss 1ch, 2tr into next ch, rep from * to end.
2nd row. 3ch to form 1st st, 1tr into st between 1st and 2nd tr of previous row, * work 2tr between next 2tr of previous row, rep from * to end. Turn.

Elongated basket stitch
Make a number of chain divisible by 3, plus 1.
1st row. Into 2nd ch from hook work 1dc, 1dc in each ch to end. Turn.
2nd row. 2ch, 1dc into each dc to end. Turn.
3rd row. 3ch, 1tr into each of next 2dc, *(inserting hook in the space between one st and the next on first dc row, work 1tr drawing up a long loop) 3 times, 1tr into each of next 3dc, rep from * to end. Turn.
4th row. As 2nd.
5th row. 3ch, (inserting hook between one st and the next on row below previous row, work 1tr drawing up a long loop) twice, *1tr into each of next 3dc, (inserting hook between one st and the next on row below previous row, work 1tr drawing up a long loop) 3 times, rep from * to end. Turn.
Rows 2–5 form pattern and are repeated throughout.

Paving stone stitch
Make a number of chain divisible by 2.
1st row. Into 3rd ch from hook work 1tr, 2ch, 1dc into next ch, *miss 2ch, 2tr into next ch, 2ch, 1dc into next ch, rep from * to end. Turn.
2nd row. 2ch, *work 2tr, 2ch and 1dc into 2ch loop of previous row, rep from * to end, 1dc in turning ch. Turn.
The 2nd row forms pattern and is repeated throughout.

Straw stitch
Make a chain divisible by 10, plus 6.
1st row. Into 3rd ch from hook work 1dc, 1dc into each of next 3ch, *1tr into each of next 5ch, 1dc into each of next 5ch, rep from * to end. Turn.
2nd row. 3ch, 1tr into each of next 4dc, *1dc into each of next 5tr, 1tr into each of next 5dc, rep from * to end. Turn.
3rd row. 2ch, 1dc into each of next 4tr, *1tr into each of next 5dc, 1dc into each of next 5tr, rep from * to end. Turn.
Rows 2 and 3 form pattern and are repeated throughout.

▲ *Cluster stitch, a particularly close fabric stitch*

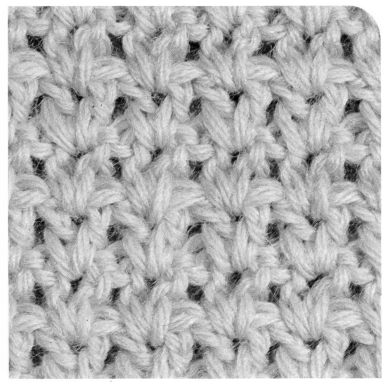

▲ *Claw stitch, a fairly firm fabric stitch suitable for lightweight jackets*

◄ *Elongated basket stitch* ▲ *Paving stone stitch* ▼ *Straw stitch*

Chapter 12

Introduction to jacquard effects

Jacquard effects can be obtained in crochet using two or more colours. As working in several colours makes a close fabric it is advisable to use a crochet hook one size larger than one would normally choose for the thickness of the yarn. Jacquard fabrics are ideal for warm outer garments.

Jacquard patterns give working instructions in two ways, either by rows or by means of a chart. Where the former method is used, the background or main colour will be given as main shade A, the second colour to be used will be given as contrast colour B, and so on. If a chart is used, the main shade is represented by a white, open square and the contrast colour by a black dot. Subsequent colours would then be represented by different symbols, such as an X or O and these would be shown in the instructions. In the jacquard patterns illustrated both methods are given so that you may become familiar with them.

Where the yarn has to be carried over 3 or more stitches in a pattern, it may be advisable in the following row to work over the yarn, when working the central stitch or stitches of a block. To do this on the right side of the work, insert the hook through the stitch to be worked and under the loop of yarn on the wrong side, then work the stitch in the usual way. When working on the wrong side, insert the hook under the loop of yarn and then into the stitch to be worked and complete the stitch in the usual way. In the following pattern instructions this will be referred to as, 'working over main or contrast thread'. This prevents over-long loops at the back of the work and makes it easier to keep an even tension.

Using contrast yarn in jacquard

When a contrast colour has to be brought in during the work, the last 2 loops of the last stitch in the main colour are drawn through with the yarn of the contrast colour, always keeping the yarn on the wrong side of the work. (See illustration).

Reverting to main colour in jacquard

When reverting to the main colour, after working a group of stitches in a contrast colour, the last 2 loops of the last stitch in the contrast colour are drawn through with the yarn of the main colour, always keeping the yarn on the wrong side of the work. (See illustration).

Two-colour square jacquard pattern

The pattern comprises multiples of 7 stitches, plus 6 and turning chain. Make 22ch, using A.

1st row. Using A, work 1tr into 4th ch from hook, 1tr in each ch to end. Turn. 20 tr.

2nd row. (right side) Join in contrast colour B, work 2ch in A and 3rd ch in B, miss 1st tr, *using B work 1tr in each of next 4 tr ending 4th tr by drawing A through last 2 loops on hook, using A work 1tr in each of next 3 tr ending 3rd tr by drawing B through

Above: working with the contrast yarn in jacquard crochet
Below: reverting to the main colour yarn

last 2 loops on hook, rep from * to last 5 sts, using B work 1tr in each of next 4tr ending 4th tr by drawing A through last 2 loops, 1tr in turning ch with A. Turn.

3rd row. (wrong side) Keeping yarn not in use on wrong side work 2ch in A, 3rd ch in B, miss 1st tr, using B work 1tr in next tr, 1tr in each of next 2tr working over main colour loop of row below, 1tr in next tr drawing A through last 2 loops, * using A work 1tr in next tr, 1tr in next tr working over contrast colour loop of row below, 1tr in next tr drawing B through last 2 loops, using B work 1tr in next tr, 1tr in each of next 2tr working over main colour loop, 1tr in next tr drawing A through last 2 loops, rep from * to last tr, 1tr in turning ch with A. Turn.

4th row. Using A work 3ch, miss 1st tr, 1tr in each tr to end, working over yarn loops on 2 central tr of each block in B and 1 central tr of each block of A, ending with 1tr in turning ch. Turn. These 4 rows form pattern and are repeated throughout. They can also be worked from the chart.

Two-colour diamond jacquard pattern.

This pattern comprises multiples of 6 stitches, plus 1 and turning chain. Make 21 ch, using A.

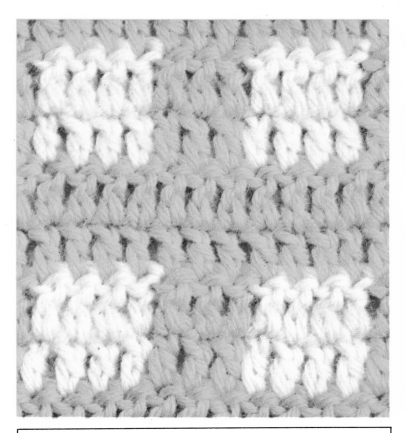

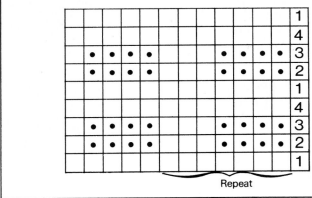

Above: two-colour square jacquard pattern
Below: chart for the two-colour square jacquard pattern

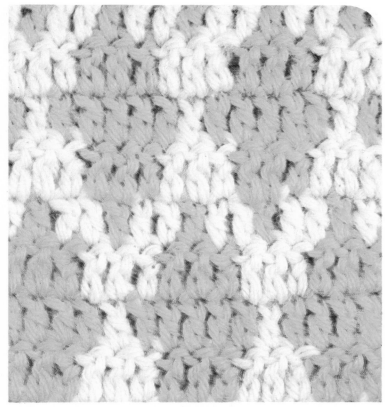

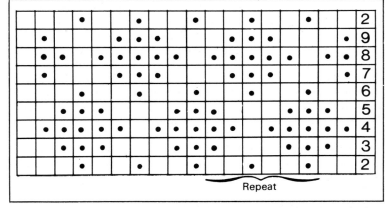

Above: two-colour diamond jacquard pattern
Below: chart for the two-colour diamond jacquard pattern

1st row. Using A, work 1tr into 4th ch from hook, 1tr into each ch to end. Turn. 19tr.

2nd row. (right side) Using A work 3ch, join in B, miss 1st tr, using A work 1tr in next 2 tr drawing B through last 2 loops of last tr, *using B work 1tr in next tr drawing A through last 2 loops, using A work 1tr in next 2tr drawing B through last 2 loops of last tr, rep from * to last 4tr, using B work 1tr in next tr drawing A through last 2 loops, using A work 1tr in last 3tr working last tr in turning ch. Turn.

3rd row. (wrong side) Keeping yarn not in use on wrong side work 3ch in A, miss 1st tr, 1tr in next tr drawing B through last 2 loops, *using B work 1tr in each of next 3tr working over yarn loop on central tr and drawing A through last 2 loops of last tr, using A work 1tr in each of next 3tr working over yarn loop on central tr and drawing B through last 2 loops of last tr, rep from * to last 5tr, using B work 1tr in each of next 3tr working over yarn loop on central tr and drawing A through last 2 loops of last tr, using A work 1tr in last 2 tr working last tr in turning ch. Turn.

Continue changing yarns in this way and working over loops on row below, keeping yarn not in use on wrong side of work.

4th row. Work 2ch in A, 3rd ch in B, miss 1st tr, *using B work 1tr in next 5tr, using A work 1tr in next tr, rep from * to end working last tr in turning ch. Turn.

5th row. As 3rd.

6th row. As 2nd.

7th row. Work 2ch in A, 3rd ch in B, miss 1st tr, using B work 1tr in next tr, *using A work 1tr in next 3tr, using B work 1tr in next 3tr, rep from * to last 5tr, using A work 1tr in next 3tr, using B work 1tr in next tr, using A work 1tr in turning ch. Turn.

8th row. Work 2ch in A, 3rd ch in B, miss 1st tr, using B work 1tr in next 2tr, * using A work 1tr in next tr, using B work 1tr in next 5tr, rep from * to last 4tr, using A work 1tr in next tr, using B work 1tr in next 2tr, using A work 1tr in turning ch. Turn.

9th row. As 7th.

Rows 2–9 form pattern and are repeated throughout. They can also be worked from the chart.

Chapter
12 continued

More jacquard patterns from charts

Whether working jacquard patterns in two colours or more, the method is the same as that given on page 210. Jacquard patterns produce a rather thick fabric and for this reason it is better to limit the colours used to three when working garments.

Base designs for jacquard crochet on geometric shapes or simple designs—cross stitch embroidery patterns can be used as a guide for motifs. Don't attempt anything too complicated because the depth of crochet stitches will not allow very fine detail.

Copy the design you have chosen on to squared graph paper calculating one stitch for each square. Show the stitches to be worked in the main colour as an empty square and the stitches to be worked in a contrast colour as a black dot in a square. If you wish to use a third colour in the design, show the stitches as a crossed square. Work the design in double crochet or treble, remembering that double crochet will give a closer overall pattern, whereas treble stitches are fairly long and will distort a rounded shape.

When changing from one colour to another, remember to draw through the last loops of the last stitch with the yarn of the next colour. Always keep the yarns not in use at the back of the work and when working over a group of stitches remember to work over the loop of yarn on the row below, to avoid overlong loops at the back of the work.

The white cottage motif shows how a simple design can be converted into a chart and worked in crochet. Designs such as this could be worked for pockets or as motifs for cushions.

You can use up oddments of yarn while practising the three jacquard patterns on these pages, trying out colour variations of the patterns. If test squares of crochet are worked to the same size they can be joined together to make a colourful rug.

▼ *Two-colour triangle jacquard pattern*

▲ *Three-colour geometric jacquard pattern showing one repeat*
▼ *Chart for three-colour geometric jacquard pattern*

▼ *Chart for two-colour triangle jacquard pattern*

▲ *Two-colour checked jacquard pattern*
▼ *Chart for two-colour checked pattern*

▲ *A simple picture worked in crochet from a chart. Using six colours, the motif produces a rather thick fabric suitable for a mat or pot holder. Chart for cottage motif* ▼

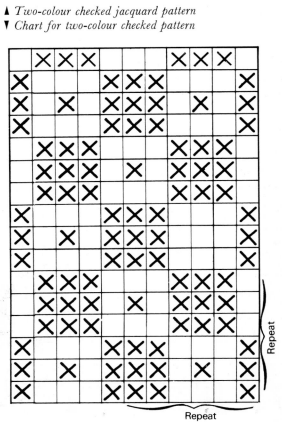

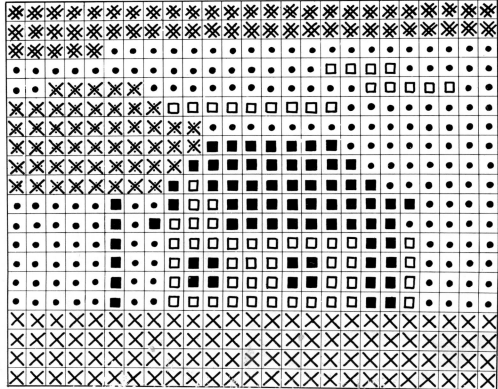

Chapter 13

Crochet plaid patterns

These patterns are amusing to work using odd scraps of different coloured yarns, and the results can be most original. Worked in thick wool they make extremely attractive rugs for either the house or the car. However, if the rug is to be used on an uncarpeted floor, it is advisable to back the work with a non-slip textured fabric such as fine foam rubber. Cotton yarn makes a most effective washable bath mat.

The plaid pattern is prepared in two separate stages. The net background is made first, on to which the vertical rows of chains are then worked to form the pattern. The colours can be as varied as you like, both on the background and the vertical chains, and a very authentic looking plaid can be produced in this way. If you want to make your own original pattern, remember to keep the background rows in each colour in their correct sequence and also the sequence of colours for the chains, or the results could look rather haphazard.

▲ *The net background formed from evenly spaced trebles*
▼ *Working vertical chains to form the plaid pattern*

Preparing the net background
Make an even number of chain.
1st row. Work 1tr into 5th ch from hook, *1ch, miss 1ch, 1tr into next ch, rep from * to end. Turn.
2nd row. 4ch, miss 1st tr and 1st space, *1tr in next tr, 1ch, miss 1 space, rep from * ending with 1tr into 3rd ch of turning ch. Turn. The 2nd row forms the pattern and is repeated for the required length, changing colours as required.

Working vertical chains to form plaid pattern
Contrast yarn is used double throughout. Make a slip loop in contrast yarn. Holding right side of net background facing you, begin at bottom right-hand corner of work and insert hook through slip loop. Keep working threads at back of work and insert hook from the front into the first space of the net background and work towards the top of the background, thus:
Draw yarn through space and through the stitch on hook.
Continue working from * to * until the top of the work is reached then work last chain stitch over top of net background and through loop on hook.
Make vertical chains in this way into all spaces across net background, changing colours as required. Particular care must be taken with the tension of the chains to avoid any distortion of the net background.

Crochet plaid pattern
This pattern requires multiples of 12ch, plus 8, to give a pattern repeat of 6 spaces, plus 4 spaces, and an additional 3 turning ch.
Make sample as follows:
Using main colour make 35ch (12 × 2, +8, +3 = 35).
1st row. Work 1tr into 5th ch from hook, *1ch, miss 1ch, 1tr into next ch, rep from * to end. Turn. 16 spaces.

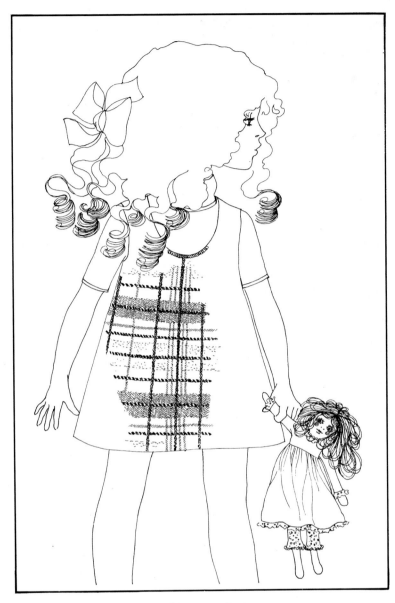

▲ *A colourful lassie in her plaid pattern dress*

▲ *The right side of the three colour crochet plaid pattern*
▼ *The wrong side of the three colour crochet plaid pattern*

▼ *An example of a crochet plaid pattern in two colours*

2nd row. 4ch, *miss 1 space, 1tr in next tr, 1ch, rep from * ending with 1tr into 3rd ch of turning ch. Turn.
Repeat 2nd row twice more.
Join in 2nd colour and repeat 2nd row.
Join in 3rd colour and repeat 2nd row.
Join in main colour and repeat 2nd row 4 times.
Join in 2nd colour and repeat 2nd row.
Join in 3rd colour and repeat 2nd row.
Join in main colour and repeat 2nd row 4 times. Fasten off. Using main colour double, make a slip loop. Insert hook into loop and then into first space at bottom right-hand corner of net background. Hold yarn at back of work and draw yarn through space and through loop on hook. Work towards the top of the background in this way in each space. Fasten off.
Repeat in next 3 spaces.
Using 2 strands of 2nd colour, work into 5th space in same way.
Using 2 strands of 3rd colour, work into 6th space in same way.
Repeat with main colour in next 4 spaces, 2nd colour in next space, 3rd colour in next space and main colour in last 4 spaces.
Fasten off.

Chapter 14

Crochet Know-how

Lacy-look stitches

This chapter shows how groups of stitches can be built up to form fancy and lacy-looking patterns. All the stitches on these pages are open stitches with the exception of lattice stitch, which forms an attractive diamond pattern on a close fabric background.

Any leftover oddments of yarn can be used to practise these stitches, using a medium size hook.

Fan stitch

Make a number of chain divisible by 8, plus 1.

1st row. Into 2nd ch from hook work 1dc, work 1dc into each ch to end. Turn.

2nd row. 2ch, 1dc into each dc to end. Turn.

3rd row. 5ch, miss 3dc, *(1tr, 3ch, 1tr) into next dc, 2ch, miss 3dc, 1tr in next dc, 2ch, miss 3dc, rep from * ending with 1tr in last st. Turn.

4th row. 2ch, *2dc in next space, 1ch, 5dc in next space between tr, 1ch, 2dc in next space, 1ch, rep from * ending with 2dc in last space, omit last ch and work 1dc in turning ch. Turn.

5th row. 2ch, 1dc in first dc, 1ch, work petals thus: *yrh, insert hook into first dc of 5dc of previous row, yrh, pull through loop, yrh, put hook into same dc, yrh, pull through loop, yrh, put hook into same dc, yrh, pull through loop, yrh, pull through all 7 loops on hook, rep from * into each of next 4dc, 1ch, miss 1ch and 2dc, work 1dc into next 1ch space, 1ch, miss 2dc and 1 ch, rep from * ending with 1dc and omitting last ch. Turn.

6th row. 5ch, *1dc in space between 2nd and 3rd petals of next petal group, 2ch, 1dc in space between 3rd and 4th petals, 2ch, (1tr, 2ch, 1tr) all into next dc between petal groups, 2ch, rep from * omitting 2ch and 1tr from last rep. Turn.

7th row. 2ch, 3dc into first space, work 2dc into every space to end, 1dc in 2nd ch of turning ch. Turn.

Rows 2–7 form pattern and are repeated throughout.

Lattice stitch

Make a number of chain divisible by 4, plus 3.

1st row. Into 2nd ch from hook work 1dc, work 1dc into each ch to end. Turn.

2nd row. 2ch, 1dc into each dc to end. Turn.

3rd row. As 2nd.

4th row. 2ch, 1dc into each of next 2dc, insert hook from front to back of work in first st of 1st row, yrh, draw up long loop, yrh and pull through first loop on hook, miss 4sts on 1st row, insert hook from front to back in next space, *yrh, draw up long loop, yrh and pull through first loop on hook, yrh and draw through all 3 loops on hook, miss 1dc behind this st, work 1dc in each of next 3dc, insert hook into same space as last loop worked, yrh, draw up loop, yrh and draw through first loop on hook, miss 4sts on 1st row, insert hook from front to back in next space, rep from *, ending with 3dc. Turn.

Rep 2nd row 3 times more.

8th row. 2ch, 1dc into next dc, insert hook into st formed where loops join in 4th row, yrh, draw up loop, yrh and draw through first loop on hook, yrh and draw through both loops, miss dc behind this st, work 1dc into each of next 3dc, *insert hook from front to back in same place as first loop, yrh, draw up loop, yrh and draw through first loop on hook, insert hook in st joining next 2 loops on 4th row, yrh, draw up loop, yrh and draw through first loop on hook, yrh, draw through all 3 loops on hook, miss 1dc behind this st, work 1dc into each of next 3dc, rep from * to end, with last loop pulling yarn through first loop on hook, insert hook in last dc on 4th row, yrh, draw through loop, yrh, draw through all 3 loops on hook, miss 1dc behind this st, work 1dc into each of next 3dc. Turn.

Rep 2nd row 3 times more.

12th row. 2ch, 1dc into next 2dc, insert hook from front to back into st formed on 8th row, yrh, draw up loop, yrh, pull through first loop on hook, *insert hook into next joining loops in 8th row, yrh, draw up loop, yrh, draw through first loop on hook, yrh, draw through all 3 loops on hook, miss 1dc behind this st, work 1dc into each of next 3dc, insert hook in same place, yrh, draw up loop, yrh and draw through first loop on hook, rep from * ending with 3dc. Turn.

Rows 5–12 form pattern and are repeated throughout.

Triangle stitch

Make a number of chain divisible by 3, plus 2.

1st row. Into 2nd ch from hook work 1dc, 1dc into each ch to end. Turn.

2nd row. 4ch, *miss 2dc, work 1tr into next dc, insert hook into 2nd missed dc behind tr just worked, work 1tr, 1ch, rep from * ending 1tr. Turn.

3rd row. 2ch, miss first tr, work 1dc into each st to end, ending 1dc into 3rd ch of turning ch. Turn.

Rows 2 and 3 form pattern and are repeated throughout.

Crazy stitch

Make a number of chain divisible by 6, plus 2.

1st row. Into 2nd ch from hook work 1dc, *2ch, miss 2ch, work 3tr into next ch, 2ch, miss 2ch, 1dc into next ch, rep from * ending with 1tr in last ch. Turn.

2nd row. *2ch, 1dc into space before 3tr group of previous row, 2ch, 3tr into 3rd tr of previous row, rep from * ending with 1tr in space between last dc and turning ch. Turn.

The 2nd row forms pattern and is repeated throughout.

Chainmail stitch

Make a number of chain divisible by 2, plus 1.

1st row. Into 2nd ch from hook work 1dc, 1dc into each ch to end. Turn.

2nd row. 3ch, miss first dc, *insert hook in next st, yrh, draw yarn through, yrh, draw through first loop on hook, yrh, draw through first loop on hook, yrh, draw through 2 loops on hook, 1ch, miss 1dc, rep from *, ending 1tr in last st. Turn.

3rd row. 2ch, work 2dc into each space of previous row to end. Turn.

Rows 2 and 3 form pattern and are repeated throughout.

Using these stitches for a stole

Any of these attractive fancy stitches can be used to make a huge stole.

Begin and end with two rows of trebles and allow for five extra stitches at each end of the rows, to give a border effect. When completed, trim the short edges with a row of scallops, by working four chain, missing one treble, then working one double crochet into the next treble.

If you wish, add a fringe to the scalloped row.

Fan stitch ▲
Chainmail stitch ▼

Lattice stitch ▲
▼ *A pretty edging for a stole crocheted in triangle stitch*

Triangle stitch ▲

Crazy stitch ▼

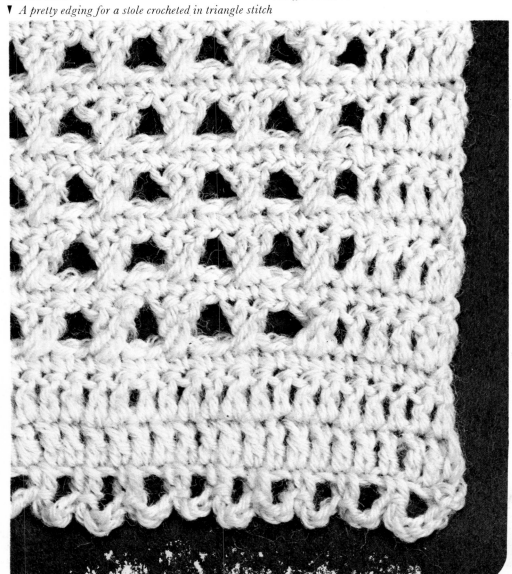

Crochet
Know-how

Arch stitches

These simple crochet stitches, based on a series of chains to form arches, comprise a very popular group of patterns. As these stitches are so open and lacy they have a great variety of uses—from chunky stoles and ponchos to gossamer baby shawls and fashion garments.

A pretty way to try out arch stitches would be to make long lacy sleeves to fit into a sleeveless dress. Choose the shape of sleeve you want and either buy or make a paper pattern. As you work the sleeve, increase and decrease to obtain the shape, keeping to the pattern outline as closely as possible. You will find a straight, long sleeve or trumpet-shaped sleeve easiest to work. The illustration shows the use of festoon stitch on a trumpet shape sleeve.

Simple arch stitch
Make a loose chain divisible by multiples of 4, plus 2.
1st row. Into 2nd ch from hook work 1dc, *5ch, miss 3 ch, 1dc into next ch, rep from * to end working 1dc in last ch. Turn.
2nd row. *5ch, 1dc in first ch loop, rep from * to end. Turn. The 2nd row forms pattern and is repeated throughout.

Fancy arch stitch
Make a loose chain divisible by multiples of 4, plus 2, noting that 1st row of chain loops should be an odd number of loops to keep pattern symmetrical.
1st row. Into 2nd ch from hook work 1dc, *5ch, miss 3 ch, 1dc into next ch, rep from * to end working 1dc in last ch. Turn.

▼ *Simple arch stitch*

▲ *Fancy arch stitch which has an asymmetrical effect*

▲ *Festoon stitch consisting of trebles and double crochet forming arches*

2nd row. *3ch, 3tr into central ch of loop, 3ch, 1dc into central ch of next loop, rep from * ending with 1dc into dc of previous row. Turn.
3rd row. 5ch, *1dc into centre tr of 3tr group, 3ch, 3tr into next dc of previous row, 3ch, rep from * ending 2ch, 1tr into top of turning ch. Turn.
4th row. *3ch, 3tr into next dc, 3ch, 1dc into centre tr of next tr group, rep from * ending with 1dc into turning ch. Turn.
Rows 3 and 4 form pattern and are repeated throughout.

Festoon stitch on arches
Make a loose chain divisible by multiples of 4, plus 2.
1st row. Into 2nd ch from hook work 1dc, 1dc into each ch to end. Turn.
2nd row. 3ch, miss first dc, *1tr into next dc, 3ch, 1tr into same dc, miss 3dc, rep from * to last 2dc, miss 1dc, 1tr into last dc. Turn.
3rd row. 1ch, 1dc into first tr, *5dc into 3ch loop, rep from * ending

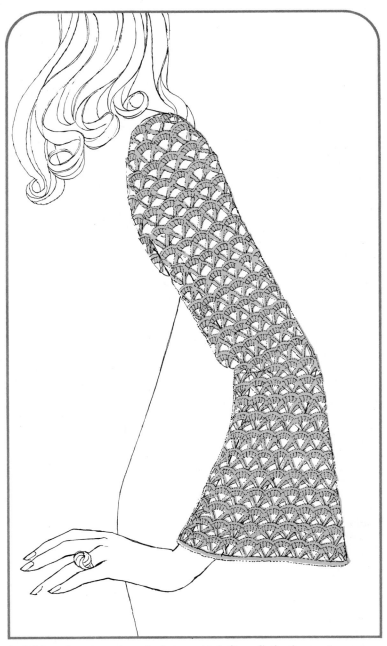

▲ *Arch stitch with picots results in a firmer look*

▲ *Arch stitch with clusters, ideal for stoles and ponchos*

with 1dc into top of turning ch. Turn.
4th row. 3ch, *1tr into centre dc of 5dc group, 3ch, 1tr into same dc, rep from * ending with 1tr into last dc. Turn.
Rows 3 and 4 form pattern and are repeated throughout.

Arch stitch with picots

Make a loose chain divisible by multiples of 4, plus 2.
1st row. Into 2nd ch from hook work 1dc, *5ch, miss 3 ch, 1dc into next ch, rep from * ending with 1dc into last ch. Turn.
2nd row. 3ch, *1dc into 5ch loop, 3ch, sl st into first ch to form picot, 1dc into same ch loop, 4ch, rep from * ending with 1tr into last dc of previous row. Turn.
3rd row. 7ch, *1dc, 1 picot, 1dc all into 4ch loop, 4ch, rep from * ending with 1tr into top of turning ch. Turn.
4th row. 3ch, *1dc, 1 picot, 1dc all into 4ch loop, 4ch, rep from * ending with 1 picot, 1dc into 7ch loop, 1tr into 4th ch of turning ch. Turn.
Rows 3 and 4 form pattern and are repeated throughout.

▲ *Make a long lacy sleeve in festoon stitch for a distinctive touch*

Arch stitch with clusters

Work a loose chain divisible by multiples of 4, plus 2.
1st row. Into 2nd ch from hook work 1dc, 1dc into each ch to end. Turn.
2nd row. 1ch, 1dc into next dc, *4ch, miss 3dc, 1dc into next dc, rep from * ending with 1dc into last dc. Turn.
3rd row. 1ch, 1dc into next dc, into first loop work 1dc, into same loop, (yrh, draw yarn very loosely through ch loop) 3 times, yrh and draw through all loops on hook, yrh and draw through single loop on hook—called 1 cluster—1dc into same loop, 4ch, *1dc, 1 cluster, 1dc all into next ch loop, 4ch, rep from * ending with 1dc into last dc. Turn.
4th row. 5ch, *into next 4ch loop work 1dc, 1 cluster, 1dc, 4ch, rep from * ending 1dc into each of last dc. Turn.
5th row. 1ch, 1dc into next dc, *into next 4ch loop work 1dc, 1 cluster, 1dc, 4ch, rep from * ending by missing 4ch of last rep, then 1dc into 2nd of first 5ch. Turn.
Rows 4 and 5 form pattern and are repeated throughout.

Chapter 15

Introduction to filet crochet

Crochet Know-how

Filet lace is one of the most interesting forms of crochet and its uses are manifold. Worked in fine cotton, it makes beautiful and long-wearing net curtains. In thicker yarn, such as vest cotton, filet crochet can make anything from a pretty bedspread to a fashionable sweater. This chapter describes how to work a net ground—a fabric of spaces joined by trebles—and includes a chart for filet crochet.

Net ground
This consists of a fabric of spaces joined by trebles made by working, *2ch, 1tr, rep from * for required length, ending with 1tr. The next and following rows are worked in the same way, working the trebles into the trebles of the previous row.

Beginning with a block
To begin the first row with a block of trebles, make 3 extra chain to stand as the first treble and make next treble in the 4th chain from hook. Complete first block of 4 trebles by working 1 treble in each of the next 2 chain.

Beginning with a space
To begin the first row with a space, make 5 extra chain of which the first 3 chain stand as the first treble. Then work 1 treble in the 8th chain from hook.

Fabric beginning with a block of trebles
If the row begins with a block over a block of trebles, without increase or decreases, turn work, make 3 chain to stand as first treble, miss first treble and work 1 treble into next 3 trebles, or required number of trebles to complete block.

▲ Net ground of trebles and spaces
▼ Fabric beginning with a block of trebles

▲ Beginning with a block of trebles
▼ Fabric of alternating trebles and spaces

▲ Beginning with a space
▼ Making net fabric beginning with a space

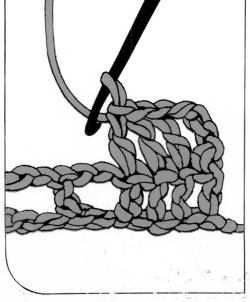

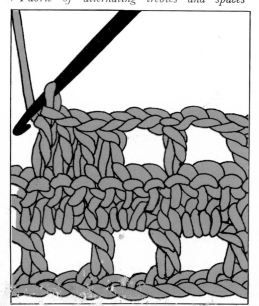

Fabric of alternating trebles and spaces

If the row begins with a block of trebles over a space, make 3 chain to stand as first treble, *work 2 treble into space of previous row, 1 treble into next treble, rep from * to end. If the row begins with a space over a block of trebles, make 5 chain, miss 3 treble and work 1 treble into last treble of block. Vary blocks of trebles and spaces as pattern requires.

Net fabric of trebles and spaces

If the row begins with a space over a space, without increases or decreases, turn work, make 5 chain and work 1 treble into 2nd treble of previous row.

Sample of filet crochet

Working methods of filet crochet are very often given by means of a chart, but unlike knitting each square on the chart does not necessarily represent just one stitch. A chart and row by row instructions are given for this sample so that you may become familiar with this method. In this case, each open square on the chart represents a 2 chain space plus a connecting treble, and each cross represents a block of 2 trebles plus a connecting treble. Begin at the bottom right-hand corner of the chart for the 1st row, turn

work and read from left to right for the 2nd row, and so on. Make 50 ch.

1st row. Work 1 tr into 8th ch from hook, (standing as first tr and first 2ch space), *2ch, miss 2 ch, 1tr in next ch, rep from * to end. Turn. (15 spaces).

2nd row. 5ch, (standing as first tr and first 2ch space), miss 2ch space, 1 tr in next tr, 2 tr in next 2ch space, 1tr in next tr, 2tr in next 2ch space, 1tr in next tr, (2 blocks), 2ch, miss 2ch space, 1tr in next tr, (1 space), (2tr in 2 ch space, 1tr in tr) twice, (2ch, miss 2ch space, 1tr in tr) 3 times, (2tr in 2ch space, 1tr in tr) twice, 2ch, miss 2ch space, (2tr in 2ch space, 1tr in tr) twice, 2ch, miss 2ch, 1tr in top of 3rd turning ch. Turn.

3rd row. 5ch, miss 1tr and 2ch, 1tr in next tr, 2 blocks over next 2 blocks working 1tr in each tr, 1 space over 1 space, 2ch, miss 2tr, 1tr in tr, (1 space over 1 block), 1tr into each of next 3tr, 2tr in 2ch space, 1tr in 1tr, (1 block over 1 space), 1 space over 1 space, 2tr in 2ch space, 1tr in 1tr, 1tr in each of next 3tr, (1 block over 1 space, 1 block over 1 block), 1 space over 1 block, 1 space over 1 space, 2 blocks over 2 blocks, 2ch, miss 2ch, 1tr into 3rd of turning ch. Turn.

Continue working in this way from the chart, noting that 14 rows form one complete pattern repeat.

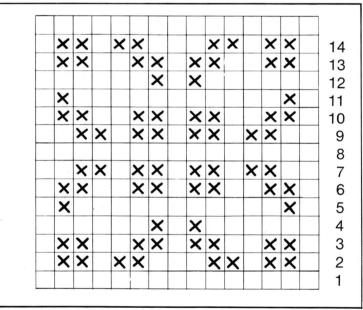

▲ *Chart for filet crochet pattern*
◀ *Part of the filet crochet pattern worked from instructions and chart*
▼ *The filet crochet pattern makes a pretty dressing table mat*

Shaping corners in filet

Shaping and making corners in filet crochet is not difficult but the continuity of the pattern must be kept correct. Here are some useful hints for increasing and decreasing on spaces and blocks and a pretty filet crochet edging to try out.

Decreasing a space at the end of a row
At the end of the row where shaping is required do not work last space but turn work, make 5 chain and work 1 treble in 2nd treble of row below (figure 1).

Decreasing a space at the beginning of a row
Work last space of previous row, turn. On next row work 1 chain, 1 slip stitch in each of the next 2 chain stitches, 1 slip stitch in next treble, 5ch, miss 2 ch, ltr in next tr, *2ch, miss 2ch, ltr in next tr, rep from * to end (figure 2).

Increasing a space at the beginning of a row
Complete the row before shaping is required, turn work. On next row make 7ch (2 for base, 3 for side and 2 for top of space), work 1tr in last tr of previous row, *2ch, miss 2ch, ltr in next tr, rep from * to end (figure 3).

Decreasing a block at the end of a row
Work in pattern to the last 4 trebles, work 1 treble, turn.
Next row. Work 3ch if next row commences with a block, 3tr and then continue in pattern. Begin with 5ch if next row commences with a space, miss 2ch or 2tr, depending on whether you are working over a space or a block, ltr in next tr, continue in pattern.

Increasing a block at the beginning of a row
Complete to the end of the row before shaping is required, turn work and make 5ch. Work 1tr into 4th ch from hook and 1tr into 5th ch from hook, then continue working in pattern to end.

Filet crochet edging
Work this edging from the chart, noting that each open square represents a space and each dot a block of trebles. Make 24ch and start 1st row 1tr into 4th ch from hook, 1tr into each of next 2ch, (2ch, miss 2ch, 1tr into next ch) 5 times, 1tr into each of next 3ch. Turn. 1 blk, 5 sps, 1 blk formed. Working next and foll alt rows from left to right on the chart (even numbered rows) and the odd numbered rows from right to left, cont in patt from chart, repeating the 8 rows from * to * as reqd, and ending with an 8th row.

Shape corner
1st row. Work as 1st patt row.
2nd row. 3ch, 1 blk, 1sp, 3 blks, 1sp, turn.
3rd row. 5ch, 1tr into next tr (makes first sp), 1sp, 2blks, 1sp, 1blk.
4th row. 3ch, 1 blk, 1sp, 1 blk, 1sp, 1 blk, turn.
5th row. Ss over blk, 3ch, 1 blk, 2sps, 1 blk.

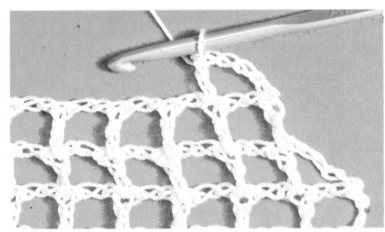

▲ **1.** *Decreasing a space at the end of a row*

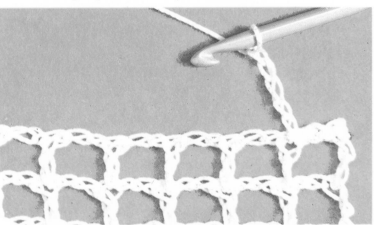

▲ **2.** *Decreasing a space at the beginning of a row*
▼ **3.** *Increasing a space at the beginning of a row*

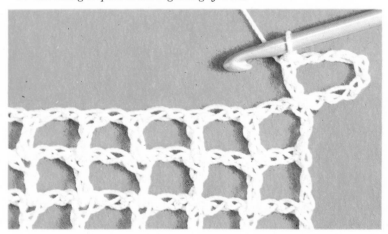

6th row. 3ch, 1 blk, 1sp, 1 blk, turn.
7th row. Ss over blk, 5ch 1tr into next tr (for 1sp), 1 blk.
8th row. 3ch, 2 blks, turn works sideways, 3ch, 3tr into side of last tr, 2ch, ss to top corner of next blk, 2ch, 1tr into top corner of next blk, turn.
9th row. 1sp, 1 blk.
10th row. 3ch, 1 blk, 1sp, 1 blk, 2ch, ss to top of corner of next blk, 2ch, 1tr into 3rd of 5ch (sp), turn.
11th row. 2 blks, 1sp, 1 blk.
12th row. 3ch, 1 blk, 1sp, 3 blks, 1sp, 2tr into next sp, ss to corner, turn.
Cont in patt from 1st patt row for the required length.

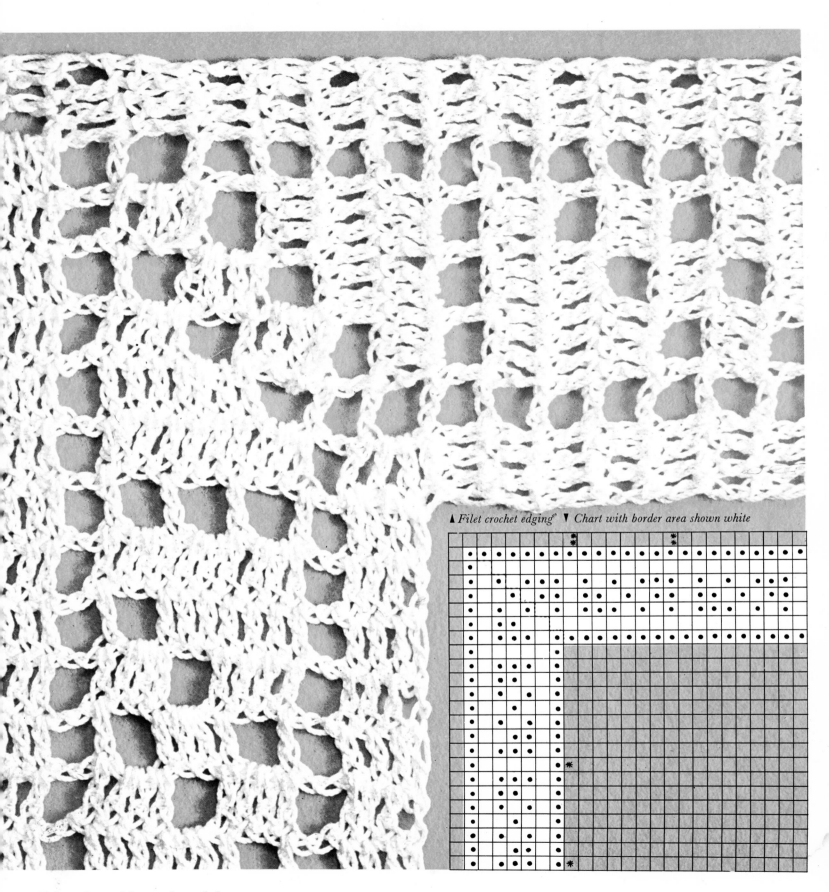

▲ *Filet crochet edging* ▼ *Chart with border area shown white*

Trimming with crochet edging

Filet crochet can be used for both edgings and for insertions on household linens. For edgings, make a narrow hem on the cloth first, machine stitching it or hemming by hand. The crochet edging is attached with either back stitch or slip stitch, working along the edge of the crochet. For insertion crochet use a decorative stitch, but make sure that the stitch does not conflict with the pattern of the crochet.

Chapter 16

Traditional Irish crochet lace

Traditional Irish crochet lace is renowned throughout the world and, as with Aran and Shetland knitting, is synonymous with all that is beautiful in handicrafts.

This chapter deals with the preparation of three net backgrounds and gives directions for working various decorative motifs.

Shown here is a delightful snood that is sure to start your fingers itching.

Irish crochet can be used to make a wide range of garments, from the finest and most intricate of wedding gowns and baby robes, to simpler things such as shawls, scarves and stoles. Irish crochet makes pretty edgings too, worked in fine crochet cotton. The basic principle in this chapter consists of a net background onto which the traditional motifs, such as shamrock, roses and leaves, are then sewn. The variations which can be achieved must be seen to be believed, and if you ever have the opportunity to see an exhibition of this breathtakingly beautiful craft a visit is well worth while—if only for the countless ideas you will glean.

The illustration below shows a delicate example of Irish crochet worked in the finest cotton. The rose motif is set off against a background of diamond picot net, forming a traditional design called Bebe crochet.

▼ *A beautiful example of Irish crochet*

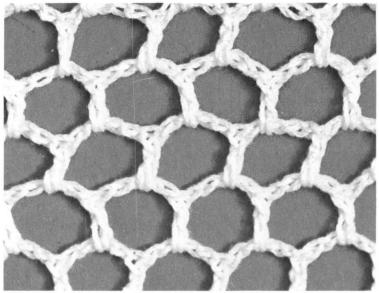

▲ *Honeycomb pattern net*

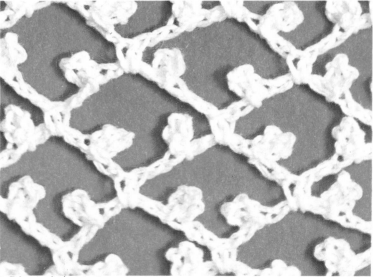

▲ *Diamond picot pattern net*
▼ *Shamrock pattern net*

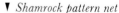

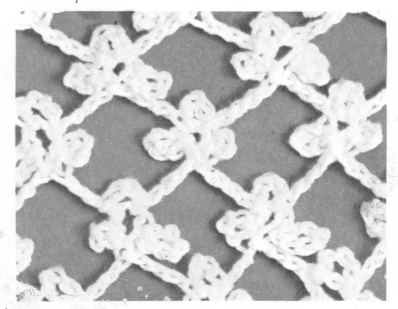

Net backgrounds

The patterns for the net backgrounds given here form the basis of many beautiful pieces of Irish crochet.

Honeycomb pattern net
Make a chain divisible by 4, plus 11.
1st row. Into 10th ch from hook work 1 tr, *4ch, miss 3ch, 1tr into next ch, rep from * to end. Turn.
2nd row. 8ch, 1tr into first 4ch loop of previous row, *4ch, 1tr into next 4ch loop, rep from * to end. Turn.
The 2nd row forms pattern and is repeated throughout.

Diamond picot pattern net
Make a chain divisible by 7, plus 2.
1st row. Into 2nd ch from hook work 1dc, *2ch, make 5ch and ss into first of these 5ch to form picot, 3ch, 1 picot, 2ch, miss 6ch, 1dc into next ch, rep from * to end. Turn.
2nd row. 2ch, 1 picot, 3ch, 1 picot, 2ch, 1dc into 3ch loop between picots of previous row, *2ch, 1 picot, 3ch, 1 picot, 2ch, 1dc into next 3ch loop, rep from * to end. Turn.
The 2nd row forms pattern and is repeated throughout.

Shamrock pattern net
Make a loose chain divisible by 5.
1st row. *Ss into 5th ch from hook to form picot, 7ch, ss into 5th ch from hook to form 2nd picot, close the shamrock by working 1ss into bottom of first picot, miss 4ch, 1dc into next ch, 8ch, rep from * ending 1dc in last ch. Turn.
2nd row. 11ch, work 1ss into 2ch space between picots of previous row, 4ch, 1ss into same 2ch space, *8ch, 1ss into 5th ch from hook, 7ch, 1ss into 5th ch from hook, 1ss into bottom of first picot, 3ch, 1ss into 2ch space of next 2 picot group, 4ch, 1ss into same 2ch space, rep from * to end. Turn.
The 2nd row forms pattern and is repeated throughout, ending with 1dc into 3rd ch of 11 turning chain.

Snood

Materials shown here
1 ball Twilley's Lysbet: One No.2·50 (ISR) crochet hook: Length round hat elastic

To work
Using No.2·50 (ISR) hook make 39 ch.
Work as given for honeycomb patt net, inc one sp at beg of each row by working 1 extra tr and 4ch into first sp until there are 14 sp. Work 6 rows without shaping, then dec one sp at beg of each row until 8 sp rem. Do not break off yarn.

To make up

Using No.2·50 (ISR) hook work edging along sides and ends, *2dc into next sp, 1dc into next sp, rep from * along all 4 sides. Join with ss to first dc. Work 2 more rounds dc. Finish off. Thread elastic through edging and secure on WS. Trim with motifs.

Glamorous snood in honeycomb net. The motifs are on page 22 ►

Collector's Piece

These delicate lace cuffs are an example of the exquisite results once achieved in Irish crochet. Worked at the end of the 19th century with the finest cotton and crochet hook, they show a variety of motifs including roses, trefoils and grapes on a net background. Crochet work of such delicacy first appeared in Ireland towards the middle of the 19th century in the work school of the Ursuline nuns in County Cork, and gradually spread to the northern counties. Country people, both men and women, flocked to learn the new skill, as they desperately needed a money-making cottage craft. Irish crochet became very popular as a fashion accessory just before the First World War, both at home and abroad. The smartest women were to be seen with crochet lace trims on their dresses, jackets, hats and parasols. Under the pressure of modern living, few people have the time, skill or patience required to produce quite such delicate works of art, but with a little perseverance beautiful examples of the craft can still be achieved.

Irish crochet motifs

Here are four pretty motifs which are used on the net backgrounds given on page 225. The rose motif was used on the Medici snood.

To give greater depth to Irish crochet lace, particularly when working in a very fine cotton, an almost three-dimensional effect is achieved by working over a separate thread of yarn. To begin work, estimate the length of separate thread you will require to complete a motif, then work a row of double crochet over this thread for the required number of stitches.

On the 2nd row, work one double crochet into each double crochet, still working over the thread, and by pulling the thread tightly the rows of double crochet can be made to lie in a curve.

To work a ring, first coil the separate thread into a loop once or twice, depending on the thickness required, then work a round of double crochet over this thread, joining with a slip stitch to complete ring. Where rings are required at varying intervals, continue working in double crochet over the separate thread until the next position is reached, then coil the thread in the same way and work another ring of double crochet.

Irish crochet rose motif

Work 8ch and close into a circle with a ss.
1st round. 1ch, into circle work 15dc, ending with ss into first ch.
2nd round. *Work 1dc and 1htr into 1st dc, work 3tr into

next dc, work 1htr and 1dc next dc, rep from * ending with a ss into 1st dc.
3rd round. Work 1dc into same place as ss, *10ch, 1dc between 2dc of previous round, rep from * ending with a ss into 1st dc.
4th round. Work 15dc into each ch loop, ending with a ss into 1st dc. Fasten off.

Irish crochet leaf and stem motif

Begin with 12dc worked along a separate thread and leaving an end long enough to form the stem later. Turn.
1st row. 1ch, work 10dc over thread and with hook inserted between one dc and the next of previous row. Turn.
2nd row. 1ch, work 5dc over thread and on dc sts of previous row, then work 9dc on thread only. Turn.
3rd row. 1ch, work 12dc over thread and on dc sts of previous row. Turn.
4th row. 1ch, work 6dc over thread and on dc sts of previous row, then work 9dc on thread only. Turn.
5th row. 1ch, work 15dc over thread and on dc of previous row. Turn.
6th row. 1ch, work 6dc over thread and on dc of previous row, then work 6dc on thread only. Turn.
7th row. 1ch, work 12dc over thread and on dc of previous row, then work 1tr into the first free st of 2nd row of 2nd petal and 1dc into 2nd free st. Turn.
8th row. 1ch, work 5dc over thread and on dc of previous row, then work 5dc on thread only. Turn.

9th row. 1ch, work 10dc over thread and on dc of previous row, 1tr into the first free st of 2nd row of 1st petal and 1dc into 2nd free st, work 4dc on thread only and attach this tail to the base of the leaves with a ss. Fasten off.
For the stem, return to the ends of yarn left at the beginning and work in dc over thread only. Fasten off.

Irish crochet branch and leaves motif

For each leaf, begin with 14dc worked over a thread. Turn. On the return row work 1ch, then, working over the thread and into the front loop only of the dc of the previous row, work 13dc and 6dc into last dc. Continue working along other side of these dc, again working over thread and picking up facing loops of the sts, work 11dc. Turn.
On the return row work 1ch, working over thread and picking up both loops of all sts work 15dc, 5dc in dc at tip of leaf and 12dc along other half of leaf. Turn.
Working back in the same way, work 1ch, 14dc, 5dc into tip of leaf and 14dc on other half of leaf. Fasten off.
Make a second leaf in the same way.
For the branch, work 13ch and join to the base of one leaf with a ss. Work back along this ch with a row of dc or tr. Attach second leaf to completed branch as illustrated.

Irish crochet three petal flower motif

Over a triple loop of separate thread work 24dc and join into a circle with a ss.
1st round. *Work 21dc over thread only, miss 7dc of circle, 1ss into next dc of circle, rep from * twice more.
2nd round. Fill inside of each petal formed by working 1tr, 1ch, into every alt dc of circle. Join with ss to petal edge. Fasten off. For the stem, work 13ch and join to the space between two petals with a ss. Work back along this ch with a row of dc or tr. Fasten off all ends.

▲ *Work double crochet over thread*
▼ *Working 2nd row over thread*

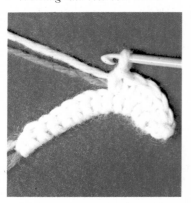

▲ *Working ring over loop of thread*
▼ *Work along thread for next ring*

Irish crochet rose motif ▲   *Leaf and stem motif* ▲

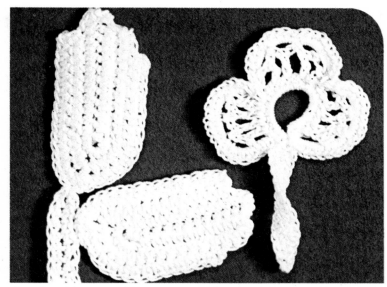

Branch and leaves motif ▲   *Three petal flower motif* ▲

Irish rose cameo

Size

Oval motif 1¾in by 1¼in worked on No.0·75 (ISR) crochet hook.

A larger round motif (5in diameter) can be worked using the materials indicated below.

Materials

Oval motif Reel of sewing cotton or machine twist No.50
One No.0·75 (ISR) crochet hook
Oval brooch frame
Silk and cardboard for backing
Large motif 1 ball Twilley's Crysette
One No.2·50 (ISR) crochet hook

Centre rose motif

Make 8ch. Join into a ring with ss into first ch.
1st round 1ch, work 12dc into ring. Join with ss.
2nd round *5ch, miss 1dc, 1dc in next dc, rep from * all round. Join with ss. (6 loops).
3rd round Into each loop work 1dc, 1htr, 5tr, 1htr, 1dc. Join with ss. (6 petals).

Background

4th round *7ch, ss into same dc as worked on 2nd round from back, rep from * to end. Join with ss. (6 loops).
5th round Into each loop work 1dc, 1htr, 7tr, 1htr, 1dc. Join with ss.
6th round *1ch, work 5ch and

join with ss to first ch to form picot, 2ch, 1 picot, 1ch, join to 2nd tr of next petal with 1dc, 1ch, 1 picot, 2ch, 1 picot, 1ch, join to 5th tr of same petal with 1dc, rep from * to end.
7th round Continue with loops of ch and picot, joining each with 1dc into centre of 2ch loop of previous round.
8th round Continue with loops of 9ch, joining each with 1dc into centre of 2ch loop of previous round, end round with 4ch joined to centre of first 9ch loop.
9th round 5dc into same loop, 10dc into each following loop 11 times, 5dc into rem half loop. Join with ss.
10th round 1ch, *1dc into each of next 4dc picking up back loop only, 5ch, miss 1dc, rep from * to end. Join with ss. Fasten off, leaving 12in end of thread for sewing motif to backing.

To make up oval motif

Wet crochet to shrink it. While still damp pin out to shape on padded surface with pin in every 5ch loop of last round. Leave until dry before removing pins. Cut silk and card to fit brooch frame, allowing ⅜th in to cover edge of card. Run tacking thread ⅛th in from edge of material, cover card and secure at back. Attach motif to backing working sts right through backing.

Cameo with fine Irish rose motif ▲

Chapter 17

Crochet Know-how

Introduction to Tunisian crochet

If you can knit but have never tried to crochet, Tunisian crochet is the answer because both techniques are combined in the working—and in the appearance of the finished fabric.

Tunisian crochet

Tunisian crochet is the complete marriage between crochet and knitting and draws on the techniques of both crafts to achieve the finished fabric. Because of the way in which it is worked, Tunisian crochet produces strong, thick fabrics which are ideal for sportswear, coats, suits and heavier garments, although lighter fabrics can also be achieved. Depending on the stitch used, the finished appearance can resemble crochet or it can look surprisingly like knitting.

Tunisian crochet hooks

The fabric is not produced with an ordinary, short crochet hook but with a special Tunisian crochet hook which looks exactly like a knitting needle with a hook at the end instead of a point. These are available in one length but, just as with crochet hooks, in a large range of sizes, the most commonly used being Nos.3·00, 3·50, 4·00, 4·50 and 5·00. As with both knitting and crochet, the size of hook required depends on your own particular tension, the thickness of the yarn being used and the firmness required for the final fabric. Experimenting with yarns and hook sizes will soon give you a very clear idea of how to achieve the desired results.

Working Tunisian crochet

Tunisian crochet takes from crochet the basic principle of beginning with a chain, see Crochet Know-how Chapter 1. But instead of completing one stitch and then passing on to the next, it becomes like knitting and one loop from each stitch is lifted onto the hook as you work along the length of starting chain, from the right towards the left.

Although one row has now been worked, it requires a second row to complete the pattern. This is worked from left to right without turning the work round and reduces the number of loops until only one remains, when you should again have reached the right hand edge of the work.

Once you have practised a little you will find the work grows quickly and is not in any way complicated.

Classic Tunisian stitch

Begin with a chain consisting of an even number of stitches.
Foundation row. Insert hook into 2nd ch from hook, put yarn round hook—called yrh—, and draw one loop through ch, *insert hook into next ch, yrh and draw through one loop, rep for * to end. The number of loops on the hook should now be the same as the number of chain worked at the beginning.

2nd row. Do not turn work, yrh and draw loop through first loop on hook, *yrh and draw through 2 loops on hook, rep from * until one loop remains. This is working from left to right hand edge.

3rd row. 1ch, *insert hook from right to left through first upright thread of previous row, yrh and draw through one loop, rep from * into every upright thread working along the row to the left. Once again, the number of loops on the hook should be the same as the number of chain worked at the beginning.

4th row. As 2nd.

The 3rd and 4th rows are repeated for the required length. Always finish with a 2nd row and for a neat finish work 1 row double crochet into the last row of upright threads.

Because of the way in which Tunisian crochet is worked, it has a tendency to twist sideways. This can be corrected when the finished work is pressed but can be lessened by not making the fabric too tight. It will be tighter if the 'yrh' is not pulled adequately through the stitch so that only a tiny loop is formed and also if the yarn is held too tightly, or if too fine a hook is used. When starting to work towards the right never pull the first stitch so tightly that you flatten or pull down the height of the row.

Treble Tunisian stitch

Worked over an even number of chain.
Foundation row. Yrh, insert hook into 3rd ch from hook, yrh and draw through ch, yrh and draw through 2 loops, *yrh, insert hook into next ch, yrh and draw through 2 loops, rep from * to end.
2nd row. As 2nd row of classic Tunisian stitch.
3rd row. 2 ch, *yrh and insert hook from right to left into upright thread of previous row, yrh and draw through one loop, yrh and draw through 2 loops, rep from * to end.
4h row. As 2nd row of classic Tunisian stitch.
The 3rd and 4th rows are repeated for the required length.

Eyelet Tunisian stitch

Worked over an even number of chain.
Foundation row. Yrh twice, insert hook into 3rd ch from hook, yrh, draw through one loop, yrh, draw through 2 loops, *miss 1ch, yrh twice, insert hook into next ch, yrh and draw through one loop, yrh and draw through 2 loops, rep from * to end.
2nd row. As 2nd row classic Tunisian stitch.
3rd row. 2ch, *yrh twice, insert hook into upright thread *and* slightly sloping upright thread to right of it made in previous row, yrh and draw through one loop, yrh and draw through 2 loops, rep from * to end.
4th row. As 2nd.
The 3rd and 4th rows are repeated for the required length.

Tunisian stocking stitch

Worked over an even number of chain.
Foundation row. As given for classic Tunisian stitch.
2nd row. As 2nd row of classic Tunisian stitch.
3rd row. 1ch, *insert hook from front to back *between* upright threads of previous row, yrh and draw through one loop, rep from * to end.
4th row. As 2nd.
The 3rd and 4th rows are repeated for the required length. It is important to draw through a loop that is fairly loose on the hook, otherwise the work will be very close and thick.

▲ *Working the first row of Tunisian crochet, from right to left*

▲ *Working the second row, from left to right, without turning the work round*

▲ *Working the third row, inserting the hook into the upright thread of previous row*

▲ *Classic Tunisian stitch*

▲ *Working treble Tunisian stitch*   ▼ *Tunisian stocking stitch*

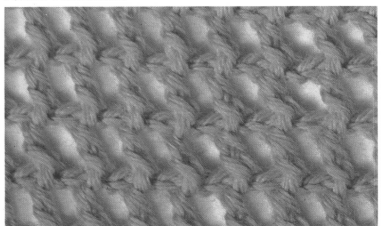

▲ *Eyelet Tunisian stitch*

▼ *Tunisian crossed stitch*

Tunisian crossed stitch

Worked over an even number of chain.
Foundation row. As given for classic Tunisian stitch.
2nd row. As 2nd row of classic Tunisian stitch.
3rd row. 1ch, *insert hook into 3rd upright thread of previous row, yrh and draw through one loop, insert hook into 2nd upright thread and draw through one loop, rep from * to end, working into 5th then 4th, 7th then 6th upright threads, etc.
4th row. As 2nd.
5th and 6th rows. As classic Tunisian stitch.
7th row. As 3rd.
8th row. As 4th.
The 5th to 8th rows are repeated for the required length.

Shaping in Tunisian crochet

▲ *Increasing one stitch at the beginning of a row*

To be able to make garments in Tunisian crochet it is necessary to understand how to increase and decrease while working the fabric. This section deals with the technique and also explains how to make buttonholes.

The method of working Tunisian crochet makes it easy to work with two yarns simultaneously, and this technique can be used with many of the stitches to achieve tweed-like textures and a thickness of fabric which is not always possible with crochet. Experiment with two different weights of yarn— a smooth with a rough for instance—for a tweedy look.

Increasing one stitch at beginning of a row

To increase one stitch at the beginning of a right side row, or the right-hand edge of the work, work 1 chain then insert the hook under the horizontal thread between the first and second upright threads, yrh and draw through one loop. Continue working into next and following upright threads in the normal way.

Increasing one stitch at end of a row

Work in the same way as given for the beginning of the row by inserting the hook under the horizontal thread between the second to last and last stitches, yrh and draw through one loop. Work the last stitch in the usual way.

Increasing two or more stitches at beginning of a row

To increase more than one stitch at the beginning of a row, work that number of chain. Into the chain work classic Tunisian stitch and continue along the row.

Increasing two or more stitches at end of a row

At the left-hand end of a right side row, put onto the hook the required number of slip stitches. Continue to work the next row in the usual way.

Decreasing one stitch at right hand edge

Insert the hook through 2 upright threads, yrh and draw through only one loop, working to the end of the row in the normal way.

Decreasing one stitch at end of a row

Work in the same way as given for the beginning of a row by inserting the hook through the last 2 upright threads together, yrh and draw through only one loop.

Working a buttonhole

Mark the position for a buttonhole with pins on the right side of the work before beginning the right side row. Work to the beginning of the marked position. Wind yarn round the hook for the number of stitches over which the hole must stretch, miss this number of stitches and continue to the end of the row. On the next row work off each loop of yarn as if it were one stitch.

▲ *Increasing one stitch at the end of a row*
▼ *Increasing two or more stitches at the beginning of a row*

▼ *Increasing two or more stitches at the end of a row*

▲ *Decreasing one stitch at the right hand edge*

▲ *Winding yarn round the hook for a buttonhole*
▼ *Working the 2nd row of the buttonhole*

Tunisian rib stitch

Worked over an even number of chain.

1st and 2nd rows. As given for classic Tunisian stitch, see Crochet Know-how page 230.

3rd row. 1ch, *insert hook into 3rd upright thread of previous row, yrh and draw through one loop, insert hook into 2nd upright thread, yrh and draw through one loop, continue from * in this way working in groups of 2 and crossing the threads by working the 5th then 4th, 7th then 6th, etc, ending with one st in last upright thread.

4th row. As classic Tunisian stitch.

Repeat 3rd and 4th rows as required. If this pattern is worked over stitches which are being decreased or increased, care must be taken to see that the crossed stitches come immediately above the crossed stitches of the previous row, or the ribbed effect will be spoilt.

Tunisian diagonal rib stitch

Worked over an even number of chain.

1st and 2nd rows. Work as given for classic Tunisian stitch.

3rd and 4th rows. Work as given for rib stitch.

5th row. 1ch, work into next upright thread, yrh and draw loop through, then work one stitch into each of next 2 stitches, working the furthest away first then returning to work the missed one, rep to end of row.

6th row. As given for 2nd row of classic Tunisian stitch.

Repeat 3rd to 6th rows as required.

Tunisian cluster stitch

This stitch can be varied to suit the purpose for which it is required. It is worked on a ground of classic Tunisian stitch, working the clusters where required by making 4 or 5 chain before continuing the next stitch. The chain or cluster formed should be left on the right side of the work. Use cluster stitch distributed evenly on the fabric as an all-over pattern, or grouped together in geometric areas.

▲ *Tunisian rib stitch*

▲ *Tunisian diagonal rib stitch*
▼ *Tunisian cluster stitch*

Chapter 18

Crochet loops for a stole

Although very effective, the technique of working crochet loops is simple and quick. The stole pattern incorporates both openwork and looped fringing rows.

The technique used for looping stitches in crochet makes it possible to create openwork rows of any depth required or, alternatively, to work rows of loops into the actual crochet to form fringing. The same fringing worked all over the fabric creates a fluffy fur-like surface.

Working openwork rows

This effect is worked by pulling a long loop the required length out of a simple double crochet all along one row and then working the tips of the loops together on the following row with double crochet.

Several rows may then be worked before another open-work row is made or, alternatively, a very lacy fabric can be achieved by working openwork rows on every alternate row.

To make a sample, work 20ch.
1st row Work 1dc into 2nd ch from hook, *1dc into next ch, rep from * to end. Turn.
2nd row 1ch, *1dc into next st, rep from * to end.
3rd row As 2nd.
4th row Insert hook into first st, yrh and draw through 1 loop on hook, yrh and draw through both loops and drawing the new loop out to the required length, *insert hook into next st, yrh, draw through 1 loop, yrh, draw through long loop pulling it up to the required length, slip hook out of loop and rep from * to end of row. It may be found that it is easier to keep the loop on the hook until several are made so that it is simple to keep them the same length.

5th row Work a number of chain the same length as the loop, insert hook into top of loop, yrh, draw through 1 loop, yrh and draw through both loops, * insert hook into next loop, yrh and draw through 1 loop, yrh and draw through both loops, rep from * along row to end.
Work several rows dc before repeating 4th row as required.

Fringing

Fringing can be worked over the fingers but is more even when the length of loops is controlled by a piece of card cut to the depth required.
Before beginning to crochet, cut a piece of card which is strong enough not to bend to the required depth and sufficiently long to hold easily. It is not necessary to have the card the full length of a row. Several loops can be worked and then the card moved along.
To make a sample, cut a piece of card 1in deep and 6in long. Work 20ch.
Work 2 rows dc. Turn.
3rd row Hold card in left hand, the base level with top of previous row. Take yarn over top of card and down behind the card. Insert the hook into the first st and draw yarn from the back through 1 loop, yrh and draw through both loops, rep from * to end of row. Turn. Withdraw the card.
4th row 1ch, 1dc into each st. Work next row as 3rd row or if a less dense fringe is required, work several rows dc before again working a loop row.
Long, dainty fringes can be worked by cutting a deep piece of card and by spacing the rows an inch or more apart. On the other hand, short, thick, fur-like fringes can be made by working over a narrow card with thick yarn and working every alternate row as fringe.

Looped stole

Size
Approx 23in wide by 76in long

Materials
Twilley's Cortina 16 25g balls

One No. 4·00 (ISR) Aero crochet hook
One piece stiff card 2in deep by 8in long

Stole
Cut the card required to control the depth of fringing before beginning to crochet. Work 96ch.
1st row Into 2nd ch from hook work 1dc, *1dc into next ch, rep from * to end. Turn.
2nd row 1ch, *1dc into next dc, rep from * to end. Turn.
3rd row As 2nd.
4th row (WS and fringe row) 1ch, *hold card behind and above work, the base level with top of last row, take yarn up and over top of card and down behind it, insert hook into next st and draw loop of yarn from behind base of card through one st, yrh and draw through both loops, rep from * to end.
5th row As 2nd.
Rep 4th and 5th rows 10 times more.
Continue in openwork patt. Work 2 rows dc as 2nd row of fringe.
3rd row Draw loop on hook out to ½in long, *insert hook into next dc, yrh and draw through one st, yrh and draw through both loops until ½in long, leave loop on crochet hook until a few sts have been worked or slip it off and continue with next st as preferred, rep from * to last st, work ss into last st, 4ch. Turn.
4th row Loop of last ch on hook, *insert hook into top of next long loop, yrh and draw through one st, yrh and draw through both loops, rep from * to end.
5th and 6th rows Work all sts in dc.
Rep 3rd, 4th, 5th and 6th rows once.
11th, 12th, 13th and 14th rows Work in dc.
Rep 3rd, 4th, 5th and 6th rows twice.
Rep last 18 rows until work measures 38in. Finish off ends. Work a second piece in the same way. Slip stitch both pieces together.

Working the loops together after an openwork row

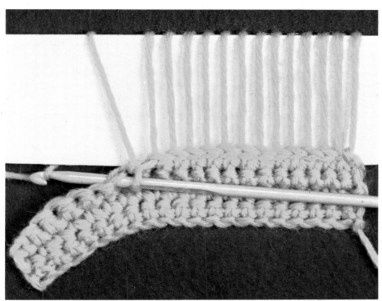

▲ *Bringing yarn from back of card through first stage of double crochet*
A fine stole worked in a combination of openwork rows and fringing ►

▲ *Yarn round hook ready for final stage of double crochet on fringe row*
▼ *The looped fringe when the card has been removed*

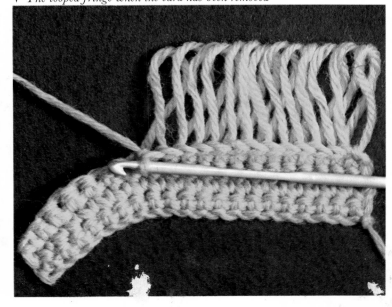

Chapter 19

Introduction to hairpin crochet

Hairpin, or fork, crochet is so called because the main tool used resembles a long hairpin or tuning fork.

Types of hairpins or forks

There are two styles available. One resembles a "square U" and is available in light alloy in 9 sizes from ½in to 3in. It is easily held in the hand and is ideal for light yarns and cottons. Because of the small size very delicate work can be produced. When the prongs become full the worked loops are slipped off the ends.

The second type is a hairpin frame which consists of two lightweight rods connected at top and bottom by plastic bars. By slotting the rods into different positions on the bars, the width between the rods can be altered. The positions do not, however, allow for very small sizes or half inch variations. This type is very suitable for the heavier yarns and more bulky work because the prongs are held in position by the bars at top and bottom thus making the frame rigid. This keeps the tension even as it stops the bars being pulled together when working. When the frame is full the bottom bar is removed, the completed loops slipped off, and the bar replaced.

Working double crochet

Make a slip knot in the yarn and take the top bar off until you have placed the slip knot on the right hand rod. Replace the bar. Draw the loop out so that the knot is exactly central

between the bars. Hold the yarn behind the left rod with the index finger and thumb of the left hand and turn the frame towards you from right to left until the right hand rod has reversed to the left side. The yarn will now pass round the other rod and should be held again by the left hand behind the left hand rod. Insert crochet hook through loop, draw a single thread through, yrh, draw through loop to complete one stitch. *Insert crochet hook through loop and draw a single thread through so that there are two loops on the crochet hook, yarn round hook and draw through both loops to complete one double crochet. Keeping loop on hook, pass the hook through to the back of the frame and turn the frame towards you from right to left as before. Repeat from *, turning the frame after each stitch. The frame is always turned the same way.

To finish off, break the yarn and draw through the last double crochet.

Double double crochet

Work as for double crochet, working two double crochet instead of one by making the first into the loop as before and the second under both threads of the loop.

Double crochet on two threads

Work as for double double crochet but make both first and second double crochet under both threads of loop.

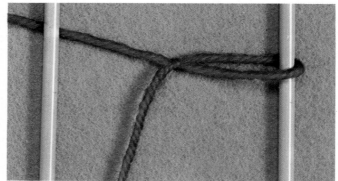

▲ *The slip knot loop on the frame*

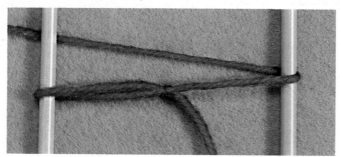

▲ *The loop after turning the frame once*

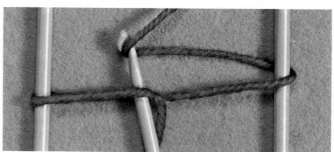

▲ *Drawing the first loop through with a crochet hook*

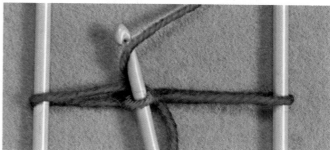

▲ *Completing the first stage of the centre stitch*

▲ *Completing the second stage of the centre stitch*

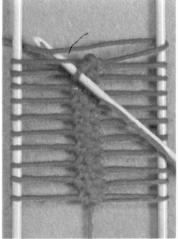

▲ *1st double double crochet stitch*

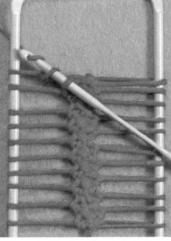

▲ *2nd double double crochet stitch*

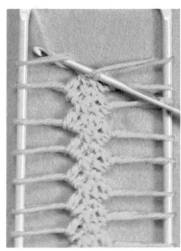

▲ *1st stitch of tr on two threads*

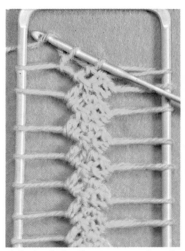

▲ *2nd stitch of tr on two threads*

▲ *1st stitch of dc on two threads*
▼ *Joining strips with crochet hook*

▲ *2nd stitch of dc on two threads*

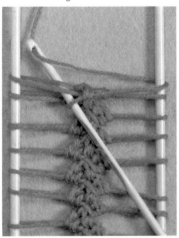

▲ *Stage 1 dc with tr on 2 threads*

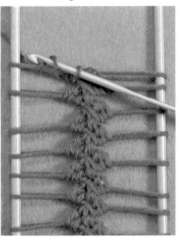

▲ *Stage 2 dc with tr on 2 threads*
▼ *Joining strips with chain stitch*

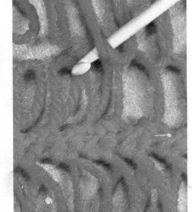

Treble crochet on two threads

Work as for double with treble crochet, making both stitches treble and working them both under two threads of the loop.

Double with treble crochet on two threads

Work as for double double crochet on two threads, making one double crochet under both threads of loop and then putting yarn round hook and working one treble under both threads of loop.

Joining strips with a crochet hook

Place the two strips together horizontally. Using the crochet hook, lift one of the loops from the first strip and one from the second. Draw the second loop through the first then pick up the second loop of the first strip. Draw this through loop on hook then pick up second loop from second strip and draw the loop through. Continue in this way along the strips until they are joined together. Make sure that the final stitch is securely sewn to prevent it unravelling.

Joining with chain stitch

Place two strips together horizontally and work from right to left. Make a slip knot and place on crochet hook. *Insert hook through first loop of first strip and first loop of second strip, yarn round hook and draw through. Repeat from * until all the loops are joined, then finish off thread by drawing it through last stitch.

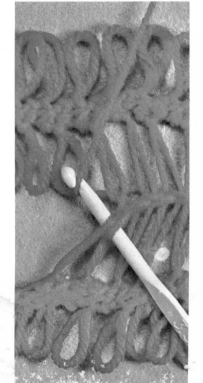

Hairpin crochet cushion

This section deals with more complex groupings.

Designs in hairpin crochet are made by joining long strips of loops together. The method used to anchor the stitches as they are made can vary, but the joining of the loop stitches is what gives each design its originality.

Fan shaped grouping

Work 3 strips of hairpin crochet using dc on 2 threads (see Crochet Know-how page 236).
Before joining the strips, work 1 row dc along each side as follows:
1st side *Work 1dc into group of 10 loops, work 1dc into each of next 10 loops, rep from * to end.
2nd side *Work 1dc into each of next 10 loops, work 1dc into group of next 10 loops, rep from * to end.
The strips will now be curved instead of straight and are ready to join together with crochet.
Join yarn to first st at right side of first strip with ss. Work 5ch, work 1dc into 2nd st of left side of 2nd strip, *3ch, 1dc into 2nd st from last st on 1st strip, 5ch, 1dc into 2nd st from last st on 2nd strip, rep from * until strips are joined together. Other strips are joined in the same way.

Peacock tail grouping

Work strips as for preceding design, working the edge grouping as follows:
1st side *(Work 1dc into group of 3 loops, 3ch) 3 times, twisting loops over so that they lie as

shown in the illustration, work 1dc into next 9 loops twisted, 3ch, rep from * to end.
Work 2nd side in same way arranging the 9-loop groups so that they come in the centre of the three 3-loop groups.
When the stitches are grouped, join the strips in the same way as for Fan grouping, or slip st edges tog.

Hairpin crochet cushion

Size
About 14in diameter

Tension for this design
Worked on a Quad frame or crochet fork measuring about 3in from outer edges

Materials shown here
Twilley's Cortina
2 25g balls colour A
1 25g ball colour B
One Quad frame or crochet fork
One No.3·00 (ISR) Aero crochet hook
One No.2·00 (ISR) Aero crochet hook
Blunt ended wool needle
Small safety pins
Cushion pad to fit

Front

1st strip for centre
Using colour A and No.2·00 crochet hook, work strip of 66 loops at either side of centre stitches worked in double double crochet (see Crochet Know-how page 236).

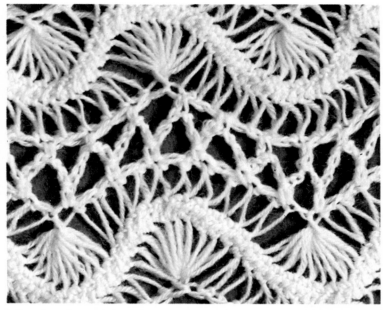

▲ *Fan shaped grouping*

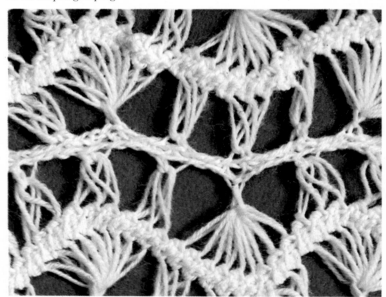

▲ *Peacock tail grouping*

Finish off ends, joining first and last centre stitches together so that strip forms a circle. Thread wool needle with short length of A and thread through the inner side loops of strip. Draw up to form centre of cushion and finish off ends securely.

2nd strip
Using B, work as for 1st strip until there are 132 loops at either side of middle stitches. Finish off. Join first and last stitches so that strip forms circle.

Join 1st and 2nd strips
Using No.2·00 crochet hook,

work the two strips together. Slip 2 loops from first strip onto hook, slip 4 loops from second strip onto hook and draw through first 2 loops. Slip next 2 loops from first strip onto hook and draw through loops already on hook, slip next 4 loops from second strip onto hook and draw through loops on hook. Continue in this way until all loops are joined. Thread a piece of yarn through last group and sew in place. Leave loops on other side of 2nd strip grouped ready for next joining row. Slip 12 loops onto a safety pin. Repeat

▲ *Cushion worked combining both methods of joining strips, with and without additional threads*

Back

Using B and No.2·00 crochet hook, work 7ch. Join into circle with ss into first ch.

1st round 7ch, (1dtr in circle, 3ch) 7 times. Join to 4th of first 7ch with ss.

2nd round Ss to centre of ch loop, 7ch, (1dtr in next ch loop, 3ch, 1dtr in same loop, 3ch) 7 times. Join to 4th ch with ss.

3rd round Ss to centre of ch loop, 7ch, (1dtr in next loop, 3ch, 1dtr in same loop, 3ch, 1dtr in next loop, 3ch) 7 times. Join to 4th ch with ss. 21 dtr.

Continue in rounds in this way, working 2dtr into a ch sp where an increase is required, spacing the number of increases evenly round the circle.

Work so that next round has 28 dtr.

5th round Has 40dtr.
6th round Has 45dtr.
7th round Has 48dtr.
8th round Has 54dtr.
9th round Has 62dtr.
10th round Has 68dtr.
11th round Has 74dtr.
12th round Has 78dtr.
13th round Has 86dtr.
14th round Has 94dtr.
15th round Has 98dtr.
16th round Has 104dtr.
17th round Has 116dtr.
Finish off.

Joining Front and Back

Place Back on top of Front, right sides out. With Back facing, insert No.2·00 crochet hook through ch loop of Back and draw through 2 loops from edge of 4th Front strip, insert hook into next ch loop of Back and draw through next 2 loops from 4th strip, drawing them through 2 loops already on hook. Continue in this way until three quarters of the way round cushion. Insert pad and continue until all the loops are joined through the Back ch loops. Fasten the last loops securely with a thread.

Make a tassel with A, about 8in long, and attach to centre.

until all loops are on pins (11 groups in all).

3rd strip

Using A, work strip as for 1st strip until there are 176 loops at either side of middle stitches. As the strip lengthens, place loops onto safety pins in groups of 16. This makes counting and joining simpler. Fasten off ends and join first and last middle stitches together, forming circle.

Join 2nd and 3rd strips

Using A and No.3·00 crochet hook, join with 1dc to middle stitches of 2nd strip between two groups of 12 loops. 1dc into all 16 loops of first group on 3rd strip removing safety pin, *11ch, 1dc into middle sts on 3rd strip before second group of 16, 1dc into next group of 12 loops on 2nd strip removing pin, 11ch, 1dc into middle sts on 2nd strip before next group, 1dc into next group of 16 loops on 3rd strip, rep from * until all loops are joined, completing circle with 1ss into first dc.

4th strip

Using B, work as for 1st strip until there are 232 loops on either side of middle sts, slipping loops off frame in groups of 8 on safety pins for next joining row. Fasten off ends, joining first and last middle sts to form circle.

Join 3rd and 4th strips

Using No.2·00 crochet hook, slip 3 loops from 3rd strip onto hook, slip 4 loops from first safety pin of 4th strip onto hook and draw through loops already on hook, slip next 3 loops from 3rd strip onto hook and draw through loops, slip next 4 loops from 4th strip onto hook and draw through loops. Continue in this way until all loops are joined, securing last group with thread.

239

Hairpin crochet bedspread

Many fascinating items can be assembled from strips of hairpin crochet. For a first large-scale project, try this bedspread. The illustration shows a similar hairpin crochet bedspread made in a thicker yarn.

Size

About 80in by 52in excluding fringe (length and width are easily adapted)

Tension for this design
Worked on a Quadframe at full width using 3 balls of yarn together throughout

---

Materials shown here

Templeton's H and O
Shetland lace
36 1oz balls
One Quadframe
One medium sized crochet hook

Strips

Using 3 strands of yarn, make a slip loop and place on right hand upright of Quadframe. Hold yarn behind left side with left hand and turn the frame towards the left (see Crochet Know-how page 236).
Insert the crochet hook into the loop in the centre of the frame and draw the thread through to form a loop on the crochet hook, insert the hook under loop in centre of frame and draw yarn through (2 loops on hook), yrh and draw through both loops, *turn frame to left after passing hook and the loop on it to the back, insert hook into loop and

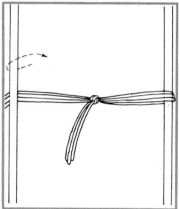

▲ *The first loop on the frame*

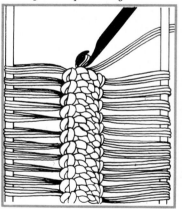

▲ *Working the centre stitch*

draw thread through, insert hook under loop and draw thread through (2 loops on hook), yrh and draw through both loops, rep from * until the frame is full, slip loops off returning the last 2 loops at each side to frame and repeating until strip measures 80in or required length. Fasten off centre thread securely and remove work from frame.
Work another 18 strips or number for width required.

Joining

Insert crochet hook into first 2 groups of three threads at bottom right hand side of first strip and draw first 2 groups of three threads from bottom of left hand side of 2nd strip through, *draw next 2 groups of three threads from first strip through loop on hook, draw next 2 groups of three threads from 2nd strip through loop on hook, rep from * until all loops are joined. Sew last loop in place.

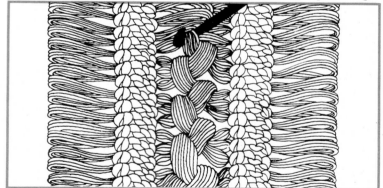

▲ *Joining the strips of hairpin crochet together*
▼ *Alternative edging for bedspread which could be used instead of the fringe*

Join other strips together in same way.

Fringe

Cut lengths of yarn 10in long. Take 6 threads, fold in half and knot into beginning of long side. Work along edge.

Alternative edging

Work 1 length of hairpin crochet as given for the bedspread until long enough to trim the edges or to reach round bedspread as required.

Inner edge

Using crochet hook, join double yarn to first loop on right hand side of strip and work *8ch, 1dc into next 3 loops, rep from * to end.

Outer edge

Using crochet hook, join double yarn to first loop on left hand side, *6ch, into 4th ch from loop work 1dc, 2ch, 1dc into next loop, rep from * to end forming a picot edge.

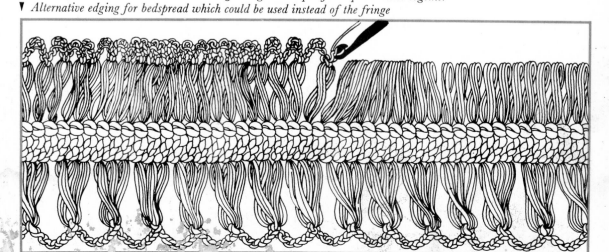

Chapter 20

Beads and sequins in crochet

▲ *Slipping bead close to fabric on a wrong side double crochet row*

▲ *Completing the double crochet stitch after placing bead on wrong side row*

This page covers crocheting beads or sequins directly into a piece of work.

Beads or sequins worked into crochet are an attractive way of giving additional interest and colour.

Choice of beads and sequins

The choice of beads will depend on the thickness of the yarn to be used. Never choose large, heavy beads for a fine yarn because they will pull it out of shape. The finer or softer the yarn, the smaller the beads need to be. If the beads are to decorate a garment, make sure that they are suitable for dry cleaning.

Because they are so light, most sequins are suitable, provided they are able to be dry cleaned.

Threading beads or sequins

Where a bead or sequin with a large hole is to be used, it is possible to thread directly onto the yarn with a needle before working.

Most beads and sequins, however, have a small hole through which the bulk of the yarn and needle eye would not pass. In this case, cut a piece of sewing cotton 8in long and thread both ends into the eye of the needle. Slide the needle half way along the doubled thread thus forming a loop at one end. Smooth both the ends and the loop downwards. Into the loop pass the end of the yarn for several inches and then smooth the double thickness of the yarn downwards.

Thread the beads or sequins onto the needle, over the cotton and then the yarn.

Double crochet

Although the beads lie on the right side of the fabric, they may be worked in on either a right side or a wrong side row. It is possible to leave several stitches between beads and several plain rows between bead rows.

Adding on a wrong side row. Begin a wrong side row in the normal way, working along to the bead position. Insert hook into next stitch, yrh and draw through loop, slip bead up close against the right side of the work, yrh taking the yarn from just beyond the bead and draw through both loops.

Adding on a right side row. Work to the first bead position. Insert the hook into the next stitch from back to front, slip bead up close to hook, yrh from beyond bead and draw the loop through to the back of the work, yrh and draw through all sts. Continue along the row.

Treble crochet

Adding on a right side row. Work to the first bead position, yrh, slip bead up close to the hook, insert hook into next st, yrh and draw through loops, yrh and draw through two loops, yrh and draw through remaining loops.

Adding on a wrong side row. The bead is added just before the last stage of the tr. Work in tr to bead position, yrh, insert hook into next st, and draw loop through, yrh and draw through two loops, slip bead up close to fabric on RS, yrh taking yarn from beyond bead and draw through remaining loops.

▲ *Putting yarn round hook from beyond bead on right side double crochet row*

Choker

Size
Depth of choker, 1in
Length of choker, 12in, adjustable

Tension for this design
Centre motif measures $1\frac{5}{8}$in

Materials shown here
Coats Mercer Cotton No.20
1 ball
One No.1·25 (ISR) crochet hook
Two hooks and eyes for fastening
28 pearl beads (if length is altered additional beads will be required)

Centre motif
Thread 8 beads onto yarn.
1st round Wind yarn 10 times round tip of finger, remove from finger and work 32dc into ring, join with ss into first dc.
2nd round 1dc into same place as ss, *5ch, miss 3dc, 1dc into next dc, rep from * omitting 1dc at end of last rep, join with ss into first dc.
3rd round 2dc into first ch loop, insert hook into same ch loop, slip bead up to hook, yrh from beyond bead and draw loop through ch letting bead come to front of work, yrh and draw through both loops—called 1 bead dc—, 3ch, 5tr into bead dc worked before 3ch, 2ch, 1 ss into same dc—called 1 shell—, 2dc into

▲ *Yarn round hook for first stage of treble on right side row*

▲ *Treble wrong side row*

▲ *Completing treble*

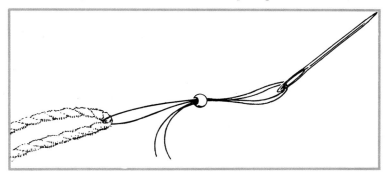

▲ *Method for threading beads or sequins onto yarn*

▲ *A pretty beaded choker which is simple to make in crochet cotton*

same ch loop, *into next ch loop work 2dc, 1 bead dc, 1 shell and 2dc, rep from * ending with ss into first dc. Fasten off.

First side of neckband
Thread 10 beads onto yarn or additional beads if length is to be altered.

1st row Commence with *3ch, 1tr into 3rd ch from hook—called 1 ring—, rep from * 19 times more or until work measures ½in more than required length from outer edge of Centre motif to centre back of neck, having an even number of rings. Do not turn.

2nd row *Into next ring work 1dc, 2ch, 1dc*, rep from * to * to within last ring, into next ring work 1dc, 2ch, 3dc into

end of ring, 2ch and 1dc into other side, working into opposite side of rings rep from * to * to within opposite side of last ring, into last ring work 1dc, 2ch and 2dc, join with ss into first dc.

3rd row Ss into first ch loop, 1dc into same ch loop, *5ch, 1dc into next ch loop, 3ch, 1dc into next ch loop, rep from * to within 3dc at end of neckband, omitting 1dc at end of last rep, miss 1dc, 1dc into next dc, **3ch, 1dc into next ch loop, rep from ** ending with 3ch, miss 1dc, 1dc into next dc, 3ch, join with ss into first dc.

4th row *Into next ch loop work 2dc, 1 bead dc, 1 shell and 2dc, 3dc into next ch loop, rep from * to within dc

at end of neckband, 3dc into next ch loop, 1ss into next dc, 3ch, 3tr into each ch loop to within last 2 loops, 2ch, 1ss into next dc, 3dc into each of next 2ch loops, join with ss into first dc. Turn.

5th row 1ch, 1dc into each of next 6dc, 3dc over next 2ch loop, 1dc into each tr, 3dc over next 3ch loop, 1dc into each of next 6dc. Turn.

6th row 1ch, 1dc into first dc, 1ch, 1ss into centre tr of any shell on centre motif, 1ch, 1ss into last dc on neckband, 1dc into each of next 7dc, 1ch, 1ss into centre tr of next shell on centre motif, 1ch, 1ss into last dc on neckband, 3dc into next dc, 1dc into each dc to within last 9dc, 3dc into next dc, 1dc into each dc to end.

Second side of neckband
Work first 5 rows as given for first side of neckband.

6th row 1dc into each of first 8dc, 3dc into next dc, 1dc into each dc to within last 9dc, 3dc into next dc, 1dc into next dc, 1ch, miss 2 shells at top of centre motif, 1ss into centre tr of next shell, 1ch, 1ss into last dc on neckband, 1dc into each of next 6dc, 1ch, 1ss into centre tr of next shell on centre motif, 1ch, 1ss into last dc on neckband, 1dc into next dc. Fasten off.

To make up
Press under a damp cloth with a hot iron on a felt or foam pad to protect beads.
Sew hooks and eyes to ends of neckband to fasten.

243

Chapter 20 continued

Beaded accessories

Unusually pretty collar and earrings with sewn-on beads.

Size
To fit average neck
Centre front depth, about 2½in

Tension for this design
7htr to 1in worked on No.2·00 crochet hook

Materials shown here
Twilley's Lysbet
One 25g ball
One No. 2·00 (ISR) crochet hook
102 beads
One button
Earring mounts

Beaded collar

Using No. 2·00 hook, work 107ch.
1st row Into 2nd ch from hook work 1htr, *1htr into next ch, rep from * to end. Turn.
2nd row 2ch, 1htr into each of next 3htr, *2htr into next htr, 1htr into each of next 4htr, rep from * to end. Turn.
3rd row *5ch, miss 3htr, 1dc into next htr, rep from * to end. Turn.
4th row Into each 5ch loop work 6dc ending with ss into last st. Break off yarn.
5th row With RS facing, rejoin yarn to centre of 3rd loop with ss, 1dc into next dc, 1htr into next dc, *miss first dc in next loop, work 1htr into each of next 5dc, rep from * to 3rd loop from end, 1htr into next dc, 1dc into next dc, ss into next dc. Break off yarn.
6th row With RS facing, rejoin the yarn with a ss to the centre of 5th loop from end, 1dc into next st, 3ch, miss 3 sts, 1dc into each of next 2

The beaded collar in champagne coloured yarn with yellow beads

Matched with earrings, a beaded crocheted collar resembles jewellery ▶

sts, 4ch, miss 3 sts, *1dc into each of next 2dc, 5ch, miss 3 sts, rep from * 17 times more, 1dc into each of next 2 sts, 4ch, miss 3 sts, 1dc into each of next 2 sts, 3ch, miss next 3 sts, 1dc into next st, ss into next st. Turn.

7th row Ss into first st, work 4dc into first loop, 5dc into 2nd loop, work 7dc into each loop until 2 loops rem, 5dc into next loop, 4dc into last loop, ss into last st. Break off yarn.

8th row With RS facing, rejoin yarn to centre of 3rd loop on preceding row with ss, 1dc into next st, 1htr into next st, *miss first st in next loop, work 1htr into each of next 6 sts, rep from * to 3rd loop from end of preceding row, 1htr into next st, 1dc into next st, ss into next st. Break off yarn.

9th row With WS facing, rejoin yarn to centre of 5th loop on preceding row, 4ch, miss 4 sts, 1dc into each of next 2 sts, 5ch, miss 4 sts, 1dc into each of next 2 sts, *6ch, miss 4 sts, 1dc into each of next 2 sts, rep from * 8 times more, 5ch, miss 4 sts, 1dc into each of next 2 sts, 4ch, miss 4 sts, ss into next st. Turn.

10th row Into first loop work 4dc, into 2nd loop work 6dc, work 7dc into every loop until 2 rem, work 6dc into next loop and 4dc into last loop, ss into last st. Break off yarn.

11th row With RS facing, rejoin yarn into centre of 3rd loop on preceding loop row with ss, 1dc into next st, 1htr into next st, *miss first dc of each loop, 1htr into each of next 6dc, rep into each loop until 3 rem, 1htr into next st, 1dc into next st, ss into next st. Break off yarn.

12th row With WS facing, rejoin yarn to centre of first loop on first row of loops with ss, 4ch, ss into base of 4ch, work 5dc into loop just formed, 1dc into 4 sts to centre of 2nd loop, 5ch, ss into base to form loop, 6dc into loop, 1dc into 4 sts to

centre of 3rd loop, 6ch, ss to form loop, 10dc into loop, *1dc into each st to centre of next loop, 6ch, ss into base to form loop, 12dc into loop, rep from * 5 times, continue in this way working 3 loops of 7ch with 14dc in loop, then loops of 8ch with 16dc in each loop until only 12 loops rem to be worked to complete collar and dec in size to correspond with other end. Finish off.

To make up

Sew beads at ends of each loop arch and at base of loops on last row.
Sew button on one end, make button loop to correspond.

Earrings

Using No.2·00 hook, begin at centre, work 5ch. Join with ss into first ch to form circle.
1st round 3ch, work 15tr

into circle. Join with ss to 3rd of first 3ch.
2nd round 1ch, *1dc into next tr, 5ch, ss into last dc, work 8dc into loop just formed, 1dc into next tr, rep from * to end. Join with ss to first ch. Finish off.

To make up

Sew a bead at base of each loop and one in centre.
Stitch securely to mounts.

245

Hooded baby jacket

Crocheted in a crisp cluster stitch to make a firm yet lightweight fabric, this hooded jacket is a perfect garment to keep baby warm and snug. Designed to be suitable for either a boy or a girl, the body of the jacket is made in one piece and then divided at armhole level. The hood is made separately and sewn on.

Sizes
To fit a 18[20]in chest
Length, 10¾[11½]in
Sleeve seam, 6½[7½]in
The figures in brackets[] refer to the 20in size only

Tension for this design
6 motifs and 12 rows to 4in over patt worked on No.4·00 (ISR) crochet hook.
One motif consists of 2 clusters worked into the same st

Materials shown here
Pingouin Age d'Or
3 50g balls
One No.4·00 (ISR) Aero crochet hook
One No.3·50 (ISR) Aero crochet hook
Three buttons

▼ *Detail showing rows of cluster stitch alternating with double crochet*

Body

Using No.4·00 (ISR) hook make 87[99]ch loosely.
1st row Yrh, insert hook into 5th ch from hook, yrh, pull loop through, (yrh, insert hook into same ch, yrh, pull loop through) twice, yrh and pull through all 7 loops on hook to form 1 cluster—called 1cl—2ch, 1cl into same st as last 1cl, 1ch, *miss 2ch, 1cl into next ch, 2ch, 1cl into same ch as last 1cl, 1ch, rep from * ending with 1tr into last ch. Turn. 28[32] motifs.
2nd row 1ch, *2dc into next 2ch sp, 1dc into next 1ch sp, rep from * to end. Turn.
3rd row 3ch, 1cl into 2nd dc, 2ch, 1cl into same dc, 1ch, *miss 2dc, 1cl into next dc, 2ch, 1cl into same dc, 1ch, rep from * ending with 1tr into last st. Turn.
4th row As 2nd.
Rows 3 and 4 form patt and are rep throughout.
Continue in patt until work measures 6[6½]in from beg.

Divide for armholes
1st row Work in patt over first 7[8] motifs only, 1tr into next st. Turn.
Complete Right front on these sts.
Continue until work measures 8¾[9½]in from beg, ending at armhole edge.

Shape neck
Continue in patt working one motif less at neck edge on next following 2 alt rows. Finish off.

Left front
Rejoin yarn to sts for Left front, working 1tr into first st, then working in patt over last 7[8] motifs only.
Complete to correspond with Right front.

Back
Rejoin yarn to centre 14[16] motifs and work in patt until Back measures same as Fronts to shoulder. Finish off.

Sleeves

Using No.4·00 (ISR) hook make 30[33]ch.
Work in patt as given for Body. 9[10] motifs.
Work 4 rows.
Continue in patt, inc 1cl at each end of next and every following 4th row until 2 motifs at each side have been inc.
Continue without shaping until sleeve measures 6½[7½]in, or required length to top of sleeve. Finish off.

Hood

Using No.4·00 (ISR) hook make 54[60]ch.
Work in patt as given for Body. 17[19] motifs.
Work 2 rows.
Keeping patt correct, inc 1cl at each end of next and following 3 alt rows until there are 21[23] motifs.
Continue without shaping until Hood measures 5¼[5½]in from beg.

Shape back
1st row Ss over first 7[8] motifs and continue on centre 7 motifs only.
Dec 1cl at each end of next and following 3 alt rows.
Continue without shaping until Hood measures 10[10¾] in from beg. Finish off.

To make up

Join shoulder and sleeve seams. Set in sleeves.
Cuffs Using No.3·50 (ISR) hook work 3 rows dc along lower edge of sleeves.
Last row Without turning work, work 1 row of crab st by working from left to right, working 1dc into each dc to end. Finish off.
Body Work as given for Cuffs from centre front neck edge around Body to other neck edge, making 3 evenly spaced buttonholes on 3rd row, on Right front for a girl and Left front for a boy, by working 4ch and missing 4sts.
Hood Seam back of Hood to side edges. Work round front edge of Hood as given for Cuffs. Sew Hood around neck edge of Body. Sew on buttons.

Blue for a boy in chunky crochet ▶

Tunic suit for a toddler

If frills and furbelows aren't the style for your baby, then why not crochet this simple, crisply styled tunic and pant suit. You could make it all in one colour, or it would look extra smart with the pants and trimming worked in a contrasting colour, say navy with white, or yellow with orange.

Sizes

To fit 18 [20, 22] inch chest. The figures in brackets [ ] refer to 20 inch and 22 inch sizes respectively.

> **Tension**
> 2½ 'V' groups and
> 3 rows to 1in.

Materials

6 [8, 9] oz Robin Casino Crepe 4 ply
1 No. 3·50 (ISR) crochet hook
4 small buttons
¾ yard elastic

Tunic front

Work 66 [70, 74] ch, loosely.
1st row 2 tr into 4th ch from hook, * miss 1 ch, 2 tr into next ch. rep from * to last ch, 1 tr into last ch. Turn.
2nd row 3 ch, * 2 tr into next tr, miss 1 tr, rep from * to last tr, 1 tr into 2nd ch of turning ch. Turn. 31 [33, 35] complete 'V' groups.
The 2nd row forms the 'V' pattern and is rep throughout.
Work 4[5, 6] rows.
Dec at each end of next row by making only 1 tr into first and last 'V' of previous row. This means that in the next row two less 'Vs' are worked

than before the dec.
Continue patt, dec in this manner at each end of every 6th [7th, 8th] row until 28 [29, 30] rows in all have been worked. 23 [25, 29] complete 'V' groups.

To shape armholes

1st row Ss over 4 sts, 3 ch, work in patt to last 4 sts. Turn
Work 9 [10, 11] rows.
19 [21, 25] complete 'V' groups.

To shape neck

Work 3 rows on 7 [8, 9] 'V' groups. Finish off.
Work other shoulder in same way.

Tunic back

Work as given for Front until armhole shaping row has been completed.
Next row Work across half the sts, turn, and complete one side on these sts, working as given for Front.
Finish off.
Rejoin yarn and work other side in same way.

Sleeves

Work 32 [34, 36] ch, loosely.
Work 3 rows in patt as given. 14 [15, 16] complete 'V' groups.
Inc at each end of next row by adding 1 tr to first and last 'V', each of which will become a 'V' in the following row, thus adding 2 'V' groups after inc.
Continue patt, inc each end of every 4th row until 18 [20, 22] rows have been worked.

Shape sleeve top

1st row Ss over 4 sts, 3 ch, patt to last 4 sts. Turn
Work 8 [9, 10] rows, dec at each end of every alternate row. Finish off.

Front trimming

Work 20 ch.
Work 7 rows dc.
Work corded edge around both long sides, and one short end, as follows—
1 row dc, working from left to right instead of the usual right to left, to give an extra twist to the stitch, and inserting hook under both horizontal threads of the edge stitches.

Pants

Work 48 [52, 56] ch loosely.
Work in patt as given for Tunic Front for 23 [24, 25] rows.
22 [24, 26] complete 'V' patterns.

To shape crutch

Next row Ss across 15 [17, 19] sts, 3 ch, work next 8 'V' groups, 1 tr. Turn.
Work 6 rows on central sts.
Next row Work to end, in place of turning ch work 15 [17, 19] ch loosely.
Break off the yarn.
At the other end of same row, join yarn and work 16 [18, 20] ch loosely. Turn.
Work across all sts in patt.
Work 23 [24, 25] rows.
Finish off.

To make up tunic

Join shoulder seams. Sew in sleeves, join the sleeve and the side seams.
Back opening. With right side of work facing, beg at base of left side of opening and work 1 row dc evenly up left side, round neck and down right side. Turn and work 2nd row. Mark position for 3 buttons on the left side.
3rd row Work to top of right side, level with first marker* miss 2 dc, 2 ch. Work in dc until next marker is reached, rep from * until

3 buttonholes have been worked, complete row. Turn.
4th row Work up right side of opening and round neck using dc. Turn.
5th row Work in corded edge st round neck to top of the opening.
Work corded edging around wrists and lower edge.
Sew tab trimming neatly to centre front.
Press very lightly with a dry cloth using a cool iron.
Sew on buttons.

To make up pants

Fold in half at crutch. Join side seams.
Work corded edging loosely round leg openings.
Thread elastic through waist edge, and sew ends together to form circle.
Press lightly.

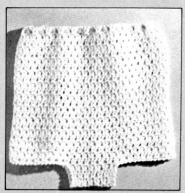

▲ *The matching pants*
Crocheted tunic for a toddler ►
▼ *Back view of tunic*

Coat and hat for a little girl

Light yet warm, this little unlined crocheted coat and matching hat makes a charming spring outfit for two-to-three year olds.
The coat skirt is worked in a fabric stitch and the sleeves in double crochet.

Sizes
To fit a 21[22:23]in chest
Length at centre back, 13¼ [14:15¼]in, adjustable
Sleeve seam, 6½[7¼:8½]in, adjustable
The figures in brackets [ ] refer to the 22 and 23in sizes respectively.

> **Tension for this design**
> 9 sts and 10 rows to 2in over dc worked on No. 4·00 (ISR) crochet hook

Materials
Madame Pingouin (50g balls)
7[7:8] balls main shade, A
1[1:2] balls contrast, B
One No.3·00 (ISR) crochet hook
One No.4·00 (ISR) crochet hook
One No.5·00 (ISR) crochet hook
Three buttons

Back yoke

Using No.4·00 (ISR) hook and A work 53[55:57]ch.
1st row Into 2nd ch from hook work 1dc, 1dc in each ch to end. Turn.
2nd row 2ch, 1dc in each dc to end. Turn. 52[54:56]dc including turning ch.
Work 2nd row 2[2:4] times more.

Shape armholes
1st row Ss over 4 sts, work 1 dc in each dc to last 4 sts. Turn.
Work 1 row. 44[46:48]dc.
3rd row Ss over 2[2:3]sts, work 1dc in each dc to last 2[2:3] sts. Turn.
Work 19[19:21] rows on rem 40[42:42]sts.

Shape shoulders
1st row Ss over 4 sts, work 1dc in each of next 11[12:12] dc. Turn.
Complete shoulder on these sts.
2nd row Ss over 2dc, 1dc in each of next 9[10:10]dc. Turn.
3rd row Ss over 3[4:4]dc, 1dc in each dc to end. Turn.
4th row 2ch, 1dc in next 5[5:5]dc. Turn.
5th row Ss over 3dc, 1dc in each dc to end. Turn.
6th row 2ch, 1dc in each of next 2dc. Pull yarn through rem loop and finish off.
Rejoin yarn to last 15[16:16] sts and work other shoulder to correspond.

Left front yoke

Using No.4·00 (ISR) hook and A work 32[33:34]ch.
1st row Into 2nd ch from hook work 1dc, 1dc in each ch to end. Turn.
2nd row 2ch, 1dc in each dc to end. Turn. 32[33:34]dc including turning ch.
Work 2nd row 2[2:4]times more.

Shape armhole
1st row Ss over 5 sts, 1dc in each dc to end. Turn.
Work 1 row.

3rd row Ss over 2[2:3]sts, 1dc in each dc to end. Turn.
Work 16[16:18]rows dc.

Shape neck
1st row Ss over 6 sts, 1dc in each dc to end. Turn.
2nd row 2ch, 1dc in each of next 16[17:17]dc. Turn.
3rd row Ss over 2 sts, 1dc in each dc. Turn.
4th row Ss over 4 sts, 1dc in each of next 9[10:10]dc. Turn.
Work 1 row.
6th row Ss over 3[4:4]sts, 1dc in each of next 3dc. Turn.
Work 1 row.
Pull yarn through rem loop and finish off.

Right front yoke

Work as given for Left front yoke, reversing shapings and working 3 buttonholes, the first on the 3rd row and the third just below centre neck edge, as follows:
2ch, 1dc in each of nest 2dc, 2ch, miss 2dc, 1dc in each dc to end. Turn.
Work 1dc into each ch on the following row so that the number of dc rem the same.

Coat skirt

Join yoke side seams and shoulder seams.
Using No.4·00 (ISR) hook and A, join with ss to centre front edge of Left front yoke.
1st row 2ch, 1dc in each dc along lower edge of Left front yoke, Back yoke and Right front yoke. 115[119:123]dc, including turning ch.
Change to No.5·00 (ISR) hook and work 1 row dc.
Continue in patt.
1st row 1ch, insert hook between next 2dc 1 row below, yrh and draw a long loop up to level of row being worked, yrh and draw through both loops on hook—called 1 long dc—*1dc in next dc, 1 long dc between 2nd and 3rd dc from previous long dc, rep from * to end, ending with 1dc in last st. Turn.
2nd row 1ch, 1dc in each dc to end. Turn.
3rd row 1ch, *1 long dc in previous patt row, 1dc in next dc, rep from * to end. Turn.
Rep 2nd and 3rd patt rows to form patt.
Continue in patt until skirt measures 6[6½:7½]in from beg, or 2in less than required length, ending with a 2nd row.
Continue in patt, working 2 rows B, and 2 rows A alternately until 3 bands of B have been worked ending with a 3rd patt row. Work 1 row ss with B to finish edge. Break yarn and draw through rem loop and finish off.

Right sleeve

Using No.4·00 (ISR) hook and A work 27[29:31]ch.
Work in dc as given for yoke inc one st at each end of 3rd and every 3rd [4th: 4th] row until there are 39[39:43]sts. Work in dc until sleeve measures 4½[5¼: 6½]in, or 2 in less than required length.

Shape top
1st row Ss over 4sts, 1dc in each dc to last 3dc. Turn.
Work 1 row. 32[32:36]dc.
3rd row Ss over 2[2:3]dc, 1dc in each dc to last 2[2:3] dc. Turn.
Work 1 row. 28[28:30]dc.
5th row Ss over 2dc, 1dc in each dc to last 2dc. Turn.
Work 1 row.
Rep last 2 rows 1[1:2] times more. Pull yarn through rem loop and finish off.

Left sleeve

Work as given for Right sleeve reversing top shaping.

Cuff

Using No.4·00 (ISR) hook and A, join with ss to first st of lower edge 2ch, work 25[25:27]dc evenly along edge.
Change to No.5·00 (ISR) hook and work 1 row dc.
Continue in 2 row patt as

given for skirt, beg with B and working until there are 3 bands of B, ending with 3rd patt row. Complete with 1 row ss using B.

Edgings

Using No.4·00 (ISR) hook and B beg at lower edge of Right front and work up 8dc along edge of border, join in A and continue up centre front edge working 38[42:50] dc to neck edge, 3dc in corner st, work 12[12:13]dc to shoulder seam, 13dc along back neck edge and 12[12:13] dc down other front neck, 3dc in corner st and 38[42: 50]dc down left front to beg of border, complete with 8dc in B. Fasten off all ends.

Collar

Using No.4·00 (ISR) hook and A with RS of work facing, work 33[33:35]dc evenly around neck beg and ending in 4th dc from centre corner dc.
Change to No.5·00 (ISR) hook and work 2 rows dc, inc 8 sts evenly on first row. Change to B and patt as given for skirt, working until 3 bands of B have been worked and ending with a 3rd patt row. Complete with 1 row ss using B. Using B work 8dc along each short edge of collar. Finish off ends.

To make up

DO NOT PRESS
Seam sleeves and sew in place. Sew on buttons to correspond with buttonholes.

Hat

Using No.3·00 (ISR) hook and A work 5ch. Join into a circle with a ss into first ch.
1st round 1ch to form 1st st, work 9dc into circle. Join with ss to 1st ch.
2nd round 2ch, 1dc in same st, *2dc in next dc, rep from * to end. Join with ss.
3rd round 1ch to form 1st st, 2dc in next dc, *1dc in next dc, 2dc in next dc, rep

from * to end. Join with ss.
4th round 1ch, 1dc in each dc. Join with ss. 30 sts.
5th round 1ch, 1dc in next dc, 2dc in next dc, *1dc in next 2 dc, 2dc in next dc, rep from * to end. Join with ss. 40 sts.
6th and 7th rounds 1ch, 1dc in each dc to end. Join with ss.
8th round 1ch, 1dc in each of next 2dc, 2dc in next dc, *1dc in next 3dc, 2dc in next dc, rep from * to end. Join with ss. 50 sts.
9th round 1ch, 1dc in each of next 3dc, 2dc in next dc, *1dc in next 4dc, 2dc in next dc, rep from * to end. Join with ss. 60 sts.
10th round 1ch, 1dc in each dc to end. Join with ss.
11th round 1ch, 1dc in each of next 4dc, 2dc in next dc, *1dc in next 5dc, 2dc in next dc, rep from * to end. Join with ss. 70 sts.
12th round 1ch, 1dc in each of next 5dc, 2dc in next dc, *1dc in next 6dc, 2dc in next dc, rep from * to end. Join with ss. 80 sts.
Work 2 rounds without shaping.
Inc 6 sts evenly in next round.
Work 1 round.
Rep last 2 rounds 1[1:2] times more. 92[92:98]sts.
Continue in rounds without shaping until work measures 6[6:6½]in from centre to edge.
Turn work and crochet brim.
Work 1 round inc 6sts evenly.
Work 3 rounds inc 10 sts evenly in each round.
Work 1 round without shaping.
Work 2 rounds dec 10 sts evenly in each round. 108 [108:114]sts. Turn work and work 1 round dc. Join with ss.
Turn work and with B work 1st patt row. Join with ss.
Turn work and with B work 1 round dc. Join with ss.
Turn work and with A work 3rd patt row. Join with ss.
Turn work and with A work 1 round ss. Join with ss.
Break yarn and finish off ends.
DO NOT PRESS.

Crocheted coat bordered in pink ►

Lacy-sleeved dress for a little girl

A pretty dress for a little girl's special occasions, worked in a soft, lightweight yarn in basic stitches.

Sizes
To fit 23[24:25]in chest
Length at centre back, 17¾[18½:19¼]in
Sleeve seam, 8¾[9¼:9¾]in
The figures in brackets [] refer to the 24 and 25in sizes respectively

---
Tension for this design
18dc and 25 rows to 4in worked on No.3·50 (ISR) crochet hook

Materials shown here
Pingouin Age d'Or
5[5:6] 50g balls
One No.3·50 (ISR) crochet hook
One small button

Front

Using No.3·50 (ISR) hook make 70[73:76]ch.
1st row Into 2nd ch from hook work 1dc, 1dc into each ch to end. Turn.
2nd row 1ch, *1dc in next dc, rep from * to end. Turn.
Continue in dc, dec one dc at each end of 9th and every following 10th row 5 times in all. 59[62:65]dc.
Continue without shaping until work measures 12½[13:13½]in from beg.

Shape armholes
1st row Ss over 3dc, work in dc to last 3dc. Turn.
2nd row Work in dc to end. Turn.

3rd row Ss over 2dc, work in dc to last 2dc. Turn.
4th row Work in dc to end. Turn.
Rep 3rd and 4th rows once more.
Next row Ss over 1dc, work in dc to last dc. Turn. 43[46:49]dc.
Continue without shaping until armholes measure 2¾[3:3¼]in from beg.

Shape neck
Next row 1ch, 1dc into each of next 15[16:17]dc. Turn.
Complete left shoulder first.
Continue in dc, dec 2dc at beg of next row and 1dc at beg of following alt row.
Continue without shaping until armhole measures 4¾[5:5¼]in from beg, ending at armhole edge.

Shape shoulder
1st row Ss over 5dc, work in dc to end. Turn.
2nd row Work in dc to end. Turn.
3rd row Ss over 4dc, work in dc to end. Finish off.
With RS of work facing, miss centre 11[12:13]dc, rejoin yarn to last 16[17:18]dc and work right shoulder to match left shoulder, reversing shaping.

Close-up of lace sleeve stitch

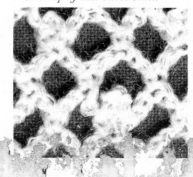

Back

Using No.3·50 (ISR) hook make 62[66:70]ch.
Work as given for Front, dec one st at each end of 11th and every following 12th row 4 times in all.
54[58:62]dc.
Continue without shaping until Back measures same as Front to underarm.

Shape armholes
1st row Ss over 2dc, work in dc to last 2dc. Turn.
2nd row Work in dc to end. Turn.
Rep 1st and 2nd rows once more.
5th row Ss over 1dc, work in dc to last dc. Turn. 44[48:52]dc.
Continue without shaping until armhole measures 1in from beg.

Divide for back opening
Next row 1ch, work 1dc into each of next 21[23:25]dc. Turn.
Complete right back first.
Continue working in dc until armhole measures same as Front to shoulder, ending at armhole edge.

Shape shoulder
1st row Ss over 5dc, work in dc to end. Turn.
2nd row Work in dc to end Turn.
3rd row Ss over 4dc, work in dc to end. Finish off.
With RS of work facing, rejoin yarn to rem sts and work left back to match right back, reversing shaping.

Sleeves

Using No.3·50 (ISR) hook make 23[25:27]ch.
1st row Into 2nd ch from hook work 1dc, 1dc into each ch to end. Turn.
2nd row 1ch, *1dc into next dc, rep from * to end. Turn.
3rd row 3ch, miss 1dc, 1dc into next dc, *2ch, miss 1dc, 1dc into next dc, rep from * to end. Turn. 11[12:13] sps.
4th row *5ch, 1dc into next 2ch sp, rep from * to end. Turn.

5th row *5ch, 1dc into 3rd ch of 5ch sp of previous row, rep from * to end. Turn.
6th row *5ch, 1dc into next sp, 3ch, 1dc into same sp as last dc—called 1 picot—5ch, 1dc into next sp, rep from * to last 1[0:1] sp, 5ch, 1 picot in last sp[0: 5ch, 1 picot in last sp]. Turn.
7th row As 5th.
8th row *5ch, 1dc into next sp, 5ch, 1 picot into next sp, rep from * to last 1[0:1] sp, 5ch, 1dc in last sp[0: 5ch, 1dc in last sp]. Turn.
Rows 5-8 form patt and are rep throughout.
Continue in patt until sleeve measures 8¾[9¼:9¾]in from beg, or required length to underarm.

Shape top
Next row Keeping patt correct, ss over 2ch to centre of first ch sp, 1dc into 3rd ch of 5ch loop, work in patt to last sp, 1dc into 3rd of last 5ch loop. Turn.
Rep the last row 8 times more. Finish off.

Sleeve frill
Using No.3·50 (ISR) hook and with RS of sleeve facing, work frill along lower edge.
1st row Rejoin yarn to first dc, *5ch, 1dc into next dc, rep from * to end. Turn.
2nd row As 5th row of sleeve patt. Finish off.

Collar

Using No.3·50 (ISR) hook make 47[49:51]ch.
1st row Into 2nd ch from hook work 1dc, 1dc into each ch to end. Turn.
Work 2 rows dc.
4th row As 3rd of sleeve patt.
5th row As 4th of sleeve patt.
6th row As 5th of sleeve patt. Finish off.

To make up

DO NOT PRESS
Join shoulder, side and sleeve seams. Sew in sleeves. Sew collar around neck edge. Work a loop buttonhole at top of back opening. Sew on button to correspond.

Fringed waistcoats

Western-style waistcoats to delight the hearts of adventurous boys and girls.

Sizes
To fit 24[26]in chest
Length at centre back, 10½ [11¾]in
The figures in brackets [] refer to the 26in size only

Tension for this design
5tr and 3 rows to 1in worked with No.3·00 (ISR) crochet hook

Materials shown here
Wendy 4 ply Courtelle Crepe 5[6]23½g balls
One No.3·00 (ISR) Aero crochet hook

Back

Using No.3·00 (ISR) hook make 64[68]ch.
1st row Into 3rd ch from hook work 1tr, work 1tr into each ch to end. Turn.
2nd row 2ch, *1tr between next 2tr of previous row, rep from * to end. Turn.
The 2nd row forms the patt and is rep throughout.
Continue in patt until work measures 4¼[5⅛]in from beg.

Shape armholes
1st row Ss over 3tr, patt to last 3tr. Turn.
2nd row Ss over 2tr, patt to last 2tr. Turn.
5 sts have now been dec at each side.
Continue dec 1tr at each end

of every row 2[3] times. Continue without shaping until work measures 9¾[10¼]in from beg.

Shape shoulders
1st row Ss over 6[7]tr, 1ch, patt to last 7[8] sts, 1dc in next st, ss in same st. Fasten off.

Left front

Using No.3·00 (ISR) hook make 33[35]ch.
1st row Into 3rd ch from hook work 1tr, work 1tr into each ch to end. Turn.
2nd row 2ch, *1tr between next 2tr of previous row, rep from * to end. Turn.
Continue in patt until work measures 3⅝[4¼]in from beg.

Shape neck
Dec 1tr at centre front edge on every row 5[3] times, 1tr on every following 2nd row 5[7] times and 1tr on every following 3rd row 2[2] times, *at the same time* shape armhole as given for Back when work measures same length as Back to underarm.
Continue without shaping until work measures same as Back to shoulder.
Finish off.

Right front

Work as given for Left front, reversing shaping.

To make up

Join side and shoulder seams. Work 2 rows dc around all edges, including armholes. Make a cord for the front lacing, using 4 strands of yarn and No.3·00 (ISR) hook, working a ch the required length.
Cut lengths of yarn 9½[12½]in long for the fringe. Fold 4 strands of yarn in half and pull centre of folded threads through ch at lower edge to form fringe. Rep into every 2nd st along lower edge of waistcoat. Trim ends of fringe if required.
Thread cord through centre front edges to for lac

All set in crochet waistcoats, fringed and laced, to round up outlaws ►
▼ *Close-up of the main pattern stitch*

Crochet head scarf

Make this delightful crochet head scarf to guard against playful summer breezes. It is worked in a simple arch stitch and buttons neatly under the chin so that it cannot slip off.

Front view and button fastening ▲

Back view showing edging ▼

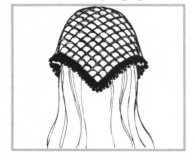

Size
To fit an average head

Materials
Madame Pingouin
1 50g ball
1 No.2·50 (ISR) Aero
crochet hook.
1 button

Headscarf

Work 6ch. Join into a loop by working 1 dc into the first ch worked. Turn and work 1st row into top of this loop.

1st row 6ch, 1dc into first of 6 ch, 5 ch, 1 dc into 3rd ch of loop. Turn.
2nd row 6 ch, 1 dc into first of 6 ch, (5ch, 1dc into 3rd ch of next loop) twice. Turn.
3rd row 6 ch, 1 dc into first of 6 ch, (5ch, 1dc into 3rd ch of next loop) 3 times. Turn. **4th, 5th, 6th, 7th and 8th rows** are worked as for 3rd row increasing number of times stitches in brackets are worked by one rep each row.
9th row 5 ch, 1 dc into 3rd ch of first 5 ch loop, (5ch, 1 dc into 3rd ch of next loop) 8 times. Turn.
10th row As 9th.
11th row 6 ch, 1 dc into first of 6 ch, (5 ch, 1 dc into 3rd ch of next loop) 9 times. Turn. Continue in this way inc one loop on each of 8 rows then working 2 rows without inc. Rep until 36 rows have been worked.

To work edging
Do not turn at end of last row
1st row Work 84 dc evenly along side to Back point (formed by first loop), 84 dc along other side to front edge, work 3 dc into each loop along this front edge. Join to first dc with ss.
2nd row Work 1 dc in each dc working 2 dc in each of 3 dc at each corner. Join to first dc with ss.
3rd row *7ch, 1 dc into next dc, rep from * to end of 2nd side only omitting the Front edge. Finish off.
Do not press.
Sew button to left hand front corner using first loop at right hand front corner as buttonhole.

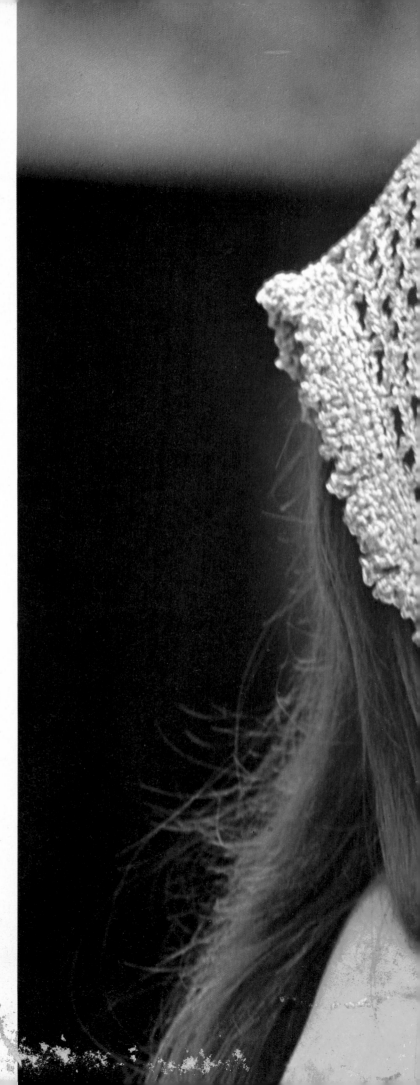

Gipsy shawl with tassel trim

These striking shawls are a simple way to practise shaping in crochet. This chapter also introduces the making of that most effective trimming, the large tassel.

Size
Approximately 36in from neck edge to bottom of centre point

Tension for this design
3 tr and 1 row to 1 in worked on No.6·00 (ISR) crochet hook, using 2 strands of yarn

---

Materials shown here
Lister Lavenda Double Knitting
One colour version. 18oz main shade, A
3 colour version. 8oz main shade, A
9oz contrast colour, B
3oz contrast colour, C
One No.6·00 (ISR) crochet hook

Shawl
Using No. 6·00 (ISR) hook and 2 strands of A, make 284ch.
Base row Work 1tr in 3rd ch from hook, 1tr in next ch, *1ch, miss 1ch, 1tr in each of next 3ch*, rep from * to * 32 times more, 1ch, miss 1ch, (1tr in each of next 3ch leaving last loop of each tr on hook, yrh and draw through 4 loops on hook, miss 1ch) twice, 1tr in each of next 3ch leaving last loop of each tr on hook, yrh and draw through 4 loops on hook, rep from * to * 34

times. Turn.
1st row 6ch, *1tr in next ch sp, 3ch*, rep from * to * 33 times, miss next 3 tr groups, rep from * to * 34 times, 1tr in turning ch. Turn.
2nd row 3ch, miss first ch sp, 3tr in next ch sp, *1ch, 3tr in next ch sp*, rep from * to * 30 times, 1ch, (3tr into next ch sp leaving last loop of each tr on hook, yrh and draw through 4 loops on hook) 3 times—called corner group —rep from * to * 32 times, 1tr into 3rd of first 6ch. Turn.
3rd row 6ch, *1tr in next ch sp, 3ch*, rep from * to * 31 times, miss corner group, rep from * to * 32 times, 1tr in turning ch. Turn.
4th row 3ch, miss first ch sp, 3tr in next ch sp, *1ch, 3tr in next ch sp*, rep from * to * 28 times, 1ch, work corner group in next 3 ch sps, rep from * to * 30 times, 1tr into 3rd of first 6ch. Turn.
5th row 6ch, *1tr in next ch sp, 3ch*, rep from * to * 29 times, miss corner group, rep from * to * 30 times, 1tr in turning ch. Turn.
Continue with A or break off 1 ball of A and join in 1 ball of B.
6th row 3ch, miss first ch sp, 3tr in next ch sp, *1ch, 3tr in next ch sp*, rep from * to * 26 times, 1ch, work corner group in next 3 ch sps, rep from * to * 28 times, 1tr into 3rd of first 6ch. Turn.
Continue in this way dec 1 tr group at each end and on centre group on every alt row until 33 patt rows ave been worked and

changing colours for 3 colour version, as follows:
At the end of 11th row break off 2nd ball of A and join in 2nd ball of B.
At the end of 18th row break off 1st ball of B and join in 1st ball of C.
At the end of 26th row break off 2nd ball of B and join in 2nd ball of C.
Complete using C only.
34th row 3ch, miss first ch sp, work corner group in next 3 ch sps, 1tr into 3rd of first 6ch. Turn.
35th row 3ch. Join with a ss to top of end of corner group. Fasten off. Darn in all ends.

Edging
Using No.6·00 (ISR) hook, 2 strands of A for 1 colour version and 2 strands of B for 3 colour version, with RS of work facing, join yarn with a ss to end of commencing ch.
Next round *1ch, into next ch sp work 1dc, 2tr, 1dc,

rep from * along all edges, missing 1 ch sp and working into next ch sp along neck edge. Join with a ss into same place as first ss. Fasten off. Darn in ends.

Tassels
Make 3 tassels in A for 1 colour version and 1 each in A, B and C for 3 colours version. Cut 40 lengths of yarn each 24in long for 1 tassel. Fold in half and tie round securely leaving 2 ends of yarn approximately 12in long. Bind off top of tassel securely. Insert hook through top fold loop of tassel and draw through 2 ends of yarn, work 6ch. Fasten off. With RS of work facing sl 6ch through centre of corner group at point and fasten off securely. Work 2 more tassels in same way.

To make up
Press lightly on WS under a damp cloth using a warm iron.

Have a fling with several tones of one colour or work in a single shade ►
Close-up of a tassel ▼ *Shawl fabric stitch detail* ▼

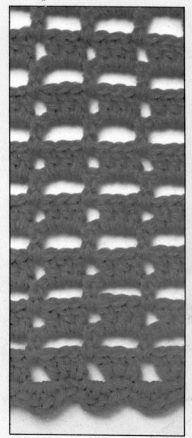

258

Diamond patterned shawl

Work this beautiful triangular shawl, with its pattern of alternating large and small diamonds, finished with a deep looped fringe.

Size
Shawl measures about 50in from centre point across centre of work to straight edge, excluding fringe

---

Tension for this design
1 large diamond measures about 3¾in across centre

Materials shown here
Pingouin Age d'Or
8 50g balls
One No.4·50 (ISR) Aero crochet hook
One No.2·00 (ISR) Aero crochet hook
One piece of card 8in long by 5½in deep

Shawl

Begin at centre back point and work towards longest edge.
Using No.4·50 hook, work 1ch.
1st row 3ch, into first ch worked (yrh, insert hook into ch, yrh and draw through loop, yrh and draw through 2 loops) 5 times, yrh and draw through all loops on hook—called 1cl—, 2ch, 1cl in same st.
2nd row 3ch, 1cl in top of edge cl of previous row, 2ch, 1cl between 2cl of previous row, 2ch, 1cl in top of edge cl.
3rd row 3ch, 1cl in edge st (the first and last clusters are always worked into the top of

260

---

cl on previous row, the other cl being worked into spaces), 5ch, 1cl before centre cl, 2ch, 1cl after centre cl, 5ch, 1 edge cl.
4th row 3ch, 1 edge cl, 5ch, 1dc in next sp, 5ch, 1cl between 2cl, 5ch, 1dc in next sp, 5ch, 1 edge cl.
5th row 3ch, 1 edge cl, 2ch, 1cl, 5ch, 1dc in next sp, 5ch, 1dc in next sp, 5ch, 1cl, 2ch, 1 edge cl.
6th row 3ch, 1 edge cl, (5ch, 1cl, 5ch, 1dc in next sp) twice 5ch, 1cl, 5ch, 1 edge cl.
7th row 3ch, 1cl, 5ch, 1dc in next sp, 5ch, 1dc in next sp, 5ch, 1cl, 2 ch, 1 cl, 5ch, 1dc, 5ch, 1dc, 5ch, 1cl.
8th row 3ch, 1cl, 2ch, 1cl, 5ch, 1dc, 5ch, 1cl, 2ch, 1cl, 2ch, 1cl, 5ch, 1dc, 5ch, 1cl, 2ch, 1cl.
9th row 3ch, 1cl, (2ch, 1cl, 5ch, 1dc, 5ch, 1dc, 5ch, 1cl) twice, 2ch, 1cl.
10th row 3ch, 1cl, (5ch, 1cl, 5ch, 1dc) 4 times, 5ch, 1cl, 5ch, 1cl.
11th row 3ch, 1cl, (5ch, 1dc, 5ch, 1dc, 5ch, 1cl, 2ch, 1cl) twice, 5ch, 1dc, 5ch, 1dc, 5ch, 1cl.
12th row 3ch, 1cl, (5ch, 1dc, 5ch, 1cl) 6 times.
13th row 3ch, 1cl, (5ch, 1dc, 5ch, 1cl, 2ch, 1cl, 5ch, 1dc) 3 times, 5ch, 1cl.
14th row 3ch, 1cl, (5ch, 1dc, 5ch, 1cl, 2ch, 1cl, 2ch, 1cl) 3 times, 5ch, 1dc, 5ch, 1cl.
15th row As 11th, rep sts in brackets 3 times.
16th row As 12th, rep sts in brackets 8 times.
17th row As 13th, rep sts in brackets 4 times.
18th row As 10th, rep sts in brackets 8 times.

Continue working in this way alternating diamonds with cl of 4 between diamonds with cl of 9.
Work until 3½ diamonds have been completed counting from point. Keeping diamond with large cluster correct, work 1 repeat replacing small clusters with large ones, then continue as before.
Work until there are 11 complete diamonds then work half diamond until there are 3cl in the diamond.
Work 1 row dc round edge, working 5dc in 5ch loops and 3dc in 2ch loops.
Next row *3ch, miss 1dc, 1dc in next dc, rep from * around all edges.
Complete by working fringe on 2 sides only, working loops round cardboard strip (see Crochet Know-how Chapter 18).

▼ *Detail of the shawl opposite*

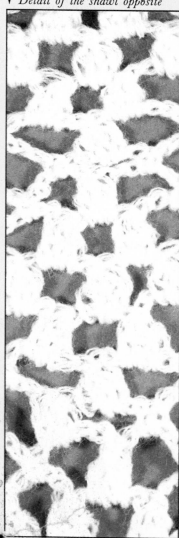

Waistcoat in Tunisian crochet

This buttoned top is an ideal first garment project for Tunisian crochet. The stitch texture combined with the rainbow yarn makes an interesting tapestry effect. The secret of success in Tunisian crochet garments is not to pull the yarn too tightly otherwise the fabric will take a bias.

Sizes

To fit 32[34:36:38]in bust
Side seam, 11½in
The figures in brackets [ ] refer to the 34, 36 and 38in sizes respectively

Tension for this design
4½ sts and 4 rows to 1in over classic Tunisian stitch worked with No. 4·50 Tunisian crochet hook

Materials shown here

Patons Double Knitting 5[6:7:8] 50g balls in random 1[1:2:2] balls in contrast
One No. 4·50 (ISR) Aero Tunisian crochet hook
One No.4·00 (ISR) Aero crochet hook, 6 buttons

Back

Using No. 4·50 Tunisian crochet hook, work 62[66:70:74]ch.
1st row (forward row working from right to left) Insert hook into 2nd ch from hook, yrh and draw through loops, *insert hook into next ch, yrh and draw through loop, rep from * to end of ch.

62[66:70:74] loops on hook. Do not turn work.
2nd row (backward row worked from left to right without turning work) Yrh and draw through one loop, *yrh and draw through 2 loops, rep from * to end of row. One loop rems on hook. These 2 rows form one complete row.
3rd row (forward row worked from right to left) *Insert hook into first vertical or upright thread on front of work from right to left, yrh and draw through loop, rep from * into each vertical thread to end of row. 62[66:70:74] loops on hook.
4th row (backward row worked from left to right) As 2nd.
The 3rd and 4th rows form the patt and are rep throughout (see Crochet Know-how Chapter 17, classic Tunisian stitch).
Inc one st at each end of next and every following 4th row until there are 76[80:84:88] sts (see Crochet Know-how page 232 for increasing).
Work until 10in or required length to underarm ending with one loop on hook at right hand edge of work.

Shape armholes

1st row (forward row) Work 1ss into next 8[9:10:11] vertical sts, patt 58[60:62:64] sts omitting last 9[10:11:12] sts.

Detail of Tunisian crochet which is worked one row forward, one back

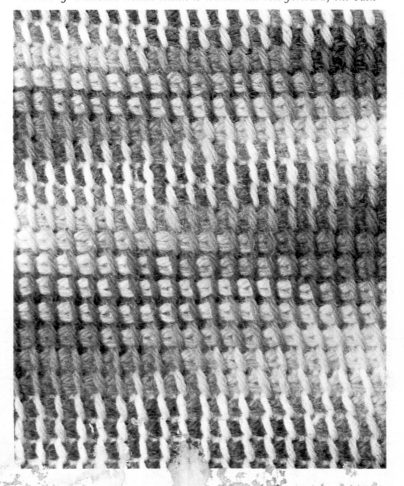

2nd row (backward row) Work to end on 58[60:62:64] sts.
Dec one st at each end of next 6 forward rows. 46[48:50:52]sts.
Work on these sts without further shaping until armholes measure 6[6¼:6½:6¾]in ending at armhole edge with one loop on hook.

Shape shoulders

1st row Work 1ss into each of first 3 vertical threads, patt to end omitting last 4 sts.
2nd row Patt back along row.
Rep last 2 rows once more. Finish off.

Left front

Using No.4·50 Tunisian crochet hook, work 31[33:35:37] sts.
Work 1st to 4th rows as given for Back.
Continue in classic Tunisian stitch inc one st at beg of next and every following 4th row until there are 38[40:42:44] sts.
Work without further shaping until same length as Back to underarm ending at side edge.

Shape armhole

1st row 1ss into next 8[9:10:11] vertical threads, patt 29[30:31:32] sts.
2nd row Patt back along row.
Dec one st at armhole edge on next 6 forward rows.
Work 4 rows (2 forward, 2 backward rows) ending at side edge with one loop on hook.

Shape neck

1st row Work 18 loops omitting last 5[6:7:8] sts.
2nd row Work back along row.
3rd row Work 15 loops omitting last 3 sts.
4th row Work back along row.
5th row Work 13 loops omitting last 2 sts.
6th row Work back along row.
Dec one st at neck edge on next 2 forward rows.
Work without further shaping until armhole measures same as Back to shoulder, ending at

side edge with one loop on hook.

Shape shoulder

1st row Work 1ss into each of first 3 vertical threads, patt to end.
2nd row Work back along row. Rep 1st and 2nd rows once more. Finish off.

Right front

Work as for Left front reversing all shaping.

To make up

Join shoulder seams.

Armhole edgings

Using No.4·00 hook, contrast wool and with RS facing, work 60[64:68:72]dc round armhole. Work 4 rows. Join side seams.

Lower edging

Using No.4·00 hook, contrast wool and with RS facing, work 120[126:132:138] sts along lower edge.
Work 6 rows dc, turning at end of each row with 1ch. Finish off.

Front edging

Using No.4·00 hook, contrast wool and with RS facing, work 50dc along Right front, 1dc into top corner, 20[21:22:23]dc up to shoulder, 24[26:28:30]dc along Back neck, 20[21:22:23]dc down other side, 1dc in corner of Left front and 50dc along lower edge.
Work 1 row dc working 3dc into corner sts.
Mark position for 6 buttonholes on Right front and work 3ch over marker missing 3ch on next row, still working 3dc into corner sts.
Work 1 row more, working 3dc into corner sts and 1dc into each ch over buttonholes. Finish off.
Press lightly under a damp cloth using a warm iron.
Sew on buttons to correspond with buttonholes.

Waist hugging top for warmth ▶

Crocheted jersey with a ribbed look

The ribbed effect of this neat jersey is achieved by working from side edge to side edge on both the body and sleeves. Collar, cuffs and welt are knitted in rib.

Sizes
To fit 34[36:38:40]in bust
Length to shoulder, including welt 22[22½:23:23½]in
Sleeve seam, 17½in including cuff.
The figures in brackets [] refer to the 36, 38 and 40in sizes respectively

---

Tension for this design
15 sts and 18 rows over patt to 4 sq in worked on No.4·50 (ISR) crochet hook

---

Materials
Madame Pingouin
11[11:12:12]50g balls
One No.4·50 (ISR) Aero crochet hook
One pair No.10 needles

Back

Beg at side edge.
Using No.4·50 (ISR) hook make 56ch.
1st row Into 2nd ch from hook work 1dc, *1dc into next ch, rep from * to end. Turn.
2nd row 2ch, *1dc into next dc working into back loop only, rep from * to end. Turn.
The 2nd row forms patt and is rep throughout.
Work 2[2:2:4] rows in patt.
Continue in patt, inc one st at end of next row.
Work 1 row.

264

Shape armhole
Next row Work 20[22:24:26] ch, work in patt along ch and across rem sts. 77[79:81:83] sts.
Continue in patt, inc one st at shoulder edge on 6th[8th: 8th:8th] row and every following 6th row, counting from armhole, until there are 80[82:84:86] sts.
Work 13[13:15:15] rows without shaping.
This completes one half Back. Work other half to correspond, dec instead of inc and ss over 20[22:24:26] sts for armhole. Finish off.

Front

Work as given for Back.

Sleeves
Beg at side edge.
Using No.4·50 (ISR) hook make 10ch.

1st row 1ss into each ch to end. Turn.
2nd row 2ch, *1dc into next st working into back loop only, rep from * to end. Turn.
3rd row 10ch, 1ss into each ch, work 1dc into back loop only of each dc. Turn.
4th row As 2nd.
Continue in patt, inc 10 sts at beg of next and every 2nd row in this way until 5 groups of 10 sts have been added to the first group of 10 sts, *at the same time* shape sleeve top by inc one st at end of 5th and beg of 6th rows, at end of 7th and beg of 8th and continuing in this way until there are 78[80:82:84] sts in all.
Work 1 row.
Next row Work 18[18:18:20] ch for saddle top of sleeve, ss along ch and work in patt along rem sts.
Work 6 rows without shaping. This completes half the sleeve. Work other half to correspond, dec instead of inc and ss over groups of 10 sts for underarm seam.

To make up

DO NOT PRESS.
Cuffs. Using No. 10 needles and with RS facing, K up 46[48:50:52] sts along lower edge of sleeve. Work 1½in K1, P1 rib. Cast off in rib.
Back welt. Using No.10 needles and with RS facing, K up 110[114:118:122] sts along lower edge of Back. Work 1½in K1, P1 rib. Cast off in rib.
Front welt. Work as given for Back welt.
Join saddle top of sleeves along shoulder edge of Left front and Back, and Right front, leaving Back seam open.
Collar. Using No.10 needles and with RS facing, K up 108 [108:116:116] sts evenly around neck.
Work 6in K1, P1 rib. Cast off in rib.
Join Right back seam and collar. Sew in sleeves to armholes.
Join side and sleeve seams.

◄ *Detail of the ribbed effect*
Jersey with a saddle top shoulder ►

Lacy jersey and pompon cap

This lacy looking crocheted jersey, worked in a simple shell panelled stitch, is matched up with a jaunty, pomponned cap worked in a cluster stitch. Although they are of dissimilar patterns, the cap and jersey, both crocheted in the same yarn, combine to make an attractive ensemble, linked by the deeper toned edging worked on the cap, on the jersey neckline and on the welt.

Sizes

To fit 34[36:38]in bust
Length at centre back, 23½in
Sleeve seam, 16in
The figures in brackets [] refer to the 36 and 38in sizes respectively

Tension for this design
7tr and 5 rows to 2½in worked on No.4·50 (ISR) crochet hook

Materials shown here

Pingouin Classic Crylor
Jersey. 5[6:6] 50g balls main shade, A, 1[1:1] ball contrast colour, B
One No.4·50 (ISR) crochet hook
Cap. 2 balls main shade, A
Small quantity contrast colour B
One No.4·50 (ISR) crochet hook
One No.5·50 (ISR) crochet hook

Jersey back

Using No.4·50 (ISR) hook and A, work 68[72:76]ch.
1st row Into 2nd ch from hook work 1 dc,*1dc in next ch, rep from * to end. Turn.
2nd row (RS) 3ch, 1tr into each of next 7[9:11] sts, *miss 3 sts, work 4tr, 1ch, 4tr all into next st to form 1 group, miss 3 sts, 1tr in each of next 8 sts, rep from * ending last rep with 8[10:12]tr. Turn.
3rd row 3ch, 1tr into each of next 7[9:11]tr, *3ch, 1dc in centre of group, 3ch, 1tr into each of next 8tr, rep from * ending last rep with 8[10:12]tr. Turn.
These 2 rows form patt and are repeated throughout.
Continue in patt until work measures 16in from beg, or required length to underarm ending with a 3rd patt row.

Shape raglan

1st row Ss over 3[4:5] sts, patt to last 3[4:5] sts. Turn.
Continue in patt, dec one tr at each end of every row until side panel trs have been worked off and group panel sts are reached. Then dec across groups by working ½ group less on WS rows, then continue to dec 1tr at each end of every row until 1[2:3]tr, 1 group, 8tr, 1 group, 1[2:3]tr rem. Finish off.

Jersey front

Work as given for back, shaping raglan in same way until 5[6:7]tr, 1 group, 8tr, 1 group, 5[6:7]tr, rem.

Shape neck

Work shoulders separately on sts outside groups on either side of central panel working 1tr less at armhole edge as before, *at the same time* dec 1tr at neck edge on every 2nd row until all sts have been worked off. Finish off.

Sleeves

Using No.4·50 (ISR) hook and A, work 32[32:34]ch.
1st row As given for back.
2nd row 3ch, 1tr into each of next 4[4:5] sts, miss 3 sts, 1 group, miss 3 sts, 1 tr into each of next 8 sts, miss 3 sts, 1 group, miss 3 sts, 1tr into each of next 5[5:6] sts. Turn.
3rd row 3ch, 1tr into each of next 4[4:5] sts, 3ch, 1dc in group, 3ch, 8tr, 3ch, 1dc in group, 3ch, 5[5:6]tr. Turn.
Continue in patt, inc one tr at each end of every 4th row until there are 13[13:14]tr at either side of groups.
Continue without shaping until sleeve measures 16in from beg, or required length to underarm ending with a 3rd patt row.

Shape raglan

1st row Ss over 3[4:5] sts, patt to last 3[4:5] sts. Turn.
2nd row Ss over 2 sts, patt to last 2 sts. Turn.
Rep 2nd row 3 times more.
Continue dec 1tr at each end of every row until 4[4:6]tr rem. Finish off.

To make up

DO NOT PRESS.
Join raglan, side and sleeve seams.
Edges Using No.4·50 (ISR) hook and B, with RS of work facing, work 2 rounds dc around sleeve edges and 4 rounds dc round neck edge. Finish off.

Cap

Using No.5·50 (ISR) hook and 3 strands of A, work 3ch. Join into a circle with ss into first ch.
1st round 2ch, work 5dc into circle. Join with ss into 2nd of first 2ch.
2nd round Yrh, insert hook into first st, yrh and pull up a long st, yrh, insert hook into same st, yrh and draw up a loop, yrh and draw through all 5 loops on hook, 1ch— this forms 1 cluster—, work 1 cluster in same st, *2 clusters in next dc, rep from * to end. Join with ss to top of first cluster.
3rd round *1 cluster in next sp between clusters of previous row, 2 clusters in next sp, rep from * to end. Join with ss to top of first cluster.
4th round *1 cluster in each of next 2 sp, 2 clusters in next sp, rep from * to end. Join with ss to top of first cluster.
5th round *1 cluster in each of next 3 sp, 2 clusters in next sp, rep from * to end. Join with ss to top of first cluster.
6th round *1 cluster in each of next 4 sp, 2 clusters in next sp, rep from * to end. Join with ss to top of first cluster.
7th round *1 cluster in each of next 5 sp, 2 clusters in next sp, rep from * to end. Join with ss to top of first cluster.
8th round *1 cluster in next sp, rep from * to end. Join with ss to top of first cluster.
Rep 8th round 3 times more.
Change to No.4·50 hook.
12th round 2ch, *1dc in next sp, rep from * to end. Join with ss to 2nd of first 2ch.
13th round 2ch, *1dc in next dc, rep from * to end. Join with ss to 2nd of first 2ch.
Break off yarn and darn in ends.

Peak

Using No.5·50 (ISR) hook and 3 strands of A, work 20 ch.
Work every row dc, dec one st at beg of every row until 12dc rem. Finish off.

To make up

Sew peak in place. Using No.4·50 (ISR) hook and 3 strands of B work 1 row dc along all edges. Trim top with large pompon, see Crochet Know-how page 196.

Peaked cap and a lacy look jersey ▶

266

High-necked jacket

This elegant, high-buttoned crocheted cardigan has been cleverly designed in a range of sizes to suit both slim and comfortable figures.

Sizes

To fit 34[36:38:40:42:44]in bust
Length at centre back, 21½[21½:22:23½:24]in
Sleeve seam, 16½[17:17:17½:17½:18]in, adjustable
The figures in brackets [ ] refer to the 36, 38, 40, 42 and 44in sizes respectively

Tension for this design
For 34, 36 and 38in sizes, 1 motif of 3tr and 1 picot measures approximately ¾in worked on No.3·50 (ISR) hook. For 40, 42 and 44in sizes, 1 motif of 3tr and 1 picot measures approximately 1in worked on No.4·00 (ISR) hook

Materials shown here
Pingouin Age d'Or 6[6:7:7:8:8] 50g balls
One No.3·50 (ISR) crochet hook for 34, 36 and 38in sizes
One No.4·00 (ISR) crochet hook for 40, 42 and 44in sizes
Seven buttons

Back

Using No.3·50[3·50:3·50: 4·00:4·00:4·00] (ISR) hook, make 87[91:95:87:91:95]ch.
1st row (WS) Into 6th ch from hook work 1dc, *3ch, 1dc into first of 3ch to form 1 picot, 1dc in next ch, 2ch, miss 2ch, 1dc in next ch,

rep from * to end of row. Turn.
2nd row 3ch, 2tr into 2ch sp of previous row, *2ch, 3tr into next 2ch sp, rep from * to end of row. Turn.
3rd row 4ch, *work 1dc, 1 picot, 1dc all into next 2ch sp, 2ch, rep from * ending with 1dc after 2nd last tr of previous row. Turn.
The 2nd and 3rd rows form patt and are rep throughout. Continue without shaping until work measures 14 [14:14:15:15:15]in from beg, ending with a 2nd row.

Shape armholes
1st row 1ss into each of next 2sts, 2dc into next sp omitting picot, patt to last sp, 2dc into sp omitting picot. Turn.
2nd row 1ss in next st, work 1dc, 1htr, 1tr all into next sp, patt to last sp, work 1tr, 1htr, 1dc into last sp. Turn.
3rd row As 1st.
4th row 1ss into next st, 3ch, 2tr into next sp, patt to last sp, 3tr in last sp. Turn.
Continue without shaping until armholes measure 7[7:7½:8:8:8½]in from beg.

Shape shoulders
Keeping patt correct work 2 patt less at each end of next and following alt row.
Work 1 row in patt.
Work 1[1:1½:1:1:1½] patt less on next row. Finish off.

Left front

Using No.3·50[3·50:3·50: 4·00:4·00:4·00] (ISR) hook make 47[51:59:47:51:59]ch.
Work as given for Back until Left front measures same as

Back to armhole, ending with a 2nd patt row.

Shape armhole
Work ½ patt less at armhole edge on next 6 rows. Continue without shaping until armhole measures 5[5:5½:6:6:6½]in from beg.

Shape neck
Keeping patt correct work 1 patt less at neck edge 2[3:3:2:3:3] times, then ½ patt less 1[1:2:1:1:2] times. Continue without shaping until armhole measures same as Back to shoulder, ending at armhole edge.

Shape shoulder
Work 2 patt less at shoulder edge of next and following alt row. Work 1 row. Work 1[1:1½:1:1:1½] patt less on next row.
Finish off.

Right front
Work as given for Left front, reversing all shaping.

Sleeves
Using No.3·50[3·50:3·50: 4·00:4·00:4·00] (ISR) hook make 35 [39:39:35:39:39]ch.
Work in patt as given for Back, inc one tr at each end of 6th and every following 2nd row, working the tr into patt as they are made, until there are 4 complete motifs extra at each end.
Continue without shaping until sleeve measures 16½ [17:17:17½:17½:18]in from beg, or required length to underarm.

Shape top
Work ½ patt less at each end of every row 13[14:14: 13:14:14] times. Finish off.

To make up

DO NOT PRESS. Leave each piece flat between damp towels until dry. Join shoulder, side and sleeve seams. Set in sleeves.
Front borders. Using No.3·50[3·50:3·50:4·00: 4·00:4·00] (ISR) hook work 1 row dc up Right front, round neck and down Left front, working 3dc in Front corner sts. Turn.
Work 3 more rows dc in same way.
5th row (buttonhole row) Mark positions for 7 buttons on Left front, first to come 8 sts from lower edge and the 7th to come in neckband with 5 more spaced evenly between. Work in dc to end, making buttonholes as markers are reached by making 3ch and missing 3dc. Work 3dc into corner sts and dec 7dc evenly around neck edge, work in dc to end. Turn.
6th row Work in dc to end, working 3dc into 3ch sp of previous row. Turn.
Work 3 more rows dc, dec 7 times evenly around neck edge on 3rd row.
Last row Work 1 row dc continuing along lower edge of Cardigan. Finish off.
Sleeve edges. Work 1 row dc along cuff edge of each sleeve. Finish off.
Sew on buttons to correspond with buttonholes.

▼ *Stitch detail   Casually elegant teamed with a skirt►*

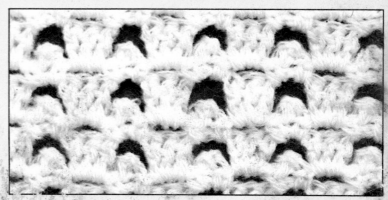

Button-through coat dress

This crocheted midi-cardigan in softest cotton can be worn as a button-through coat dress or as a tunic over trousers. Make it in sparkling white as shown here or try French navy with scarlet and grey for the contrasting midriff panel.

Sizes

To fit 32[34:36:38]in bust
34[36:38:40]in hips
Length to shoulder, 41[41½: 41½:42]in, adjustable
The figures in brackets [] refer to the 34, 36 and 38in sizes respectively

---

Tension for this design
5tr and 2½ rows to 1in worked on No.3·50 (ISR) crochet hook

Materials shown here

Twilley's Stalite Soft Knitting Cotton No.3
8[9:10:11] 50g balls main shade, A
1[1:2:2] balls contrast, B
1[1:1:1] ball each of contrasts C and D
One No.3·50 (ISR) crochet hook
One No.3·00 (ISR) crochet hook
Nine buttons

Bodice

Using No.3·50 (ISR) hook and B, make 136[146:156: 166]ch and work bodice in one piece to underarm.
Base row Into 2nd ch from hook work 1dc, 1dc into each ch to end. Turn. 135[145: 155:165]sts.

270

Commence coloured patt.
1st row Using B, 2ch, miss first dc, 1dc into each dc to end. Turn.
2nd and 3rd rows As 1st.
4th row Using D, 2ch, 1dc in first dc, *1dc in next dc, miss 1dc, 1dc in next dc, 2dc in each of next 2dc, rep from * to last 4dc, 1dc in next dc, miss 1dc, 1dc in next dc, 2dc in last dc. Turn. 162[174: 186:198]sts.
5th row Using D, 2ch, 1dc in first dc, *1dc in next dc, miss 2dc, 1dc in next dc, 2dc in each of next 2dc, rep from * to last 4dc, miss 2dc, 1dc in next dc, 2dc in last dc. Turn.
6th and 7th rows Using C, as 5th. Break off C.
8th row Using D, 2ch, miss first dc, *1tr in next dc, 1dtr into each of next 2dc, 1tr in next dc, 1dc into each of next 2dc, rep from * to last 5dc, 1tr in next dc, 1dtr into each of next 2dc, 1tr in next dc, 1dc in last dc. Turn.
9th row Using C, 2ch, miss first st, *1dc in next st, 2dc into each of next 2 sts, 1dc in next st, miss 2 sts, rep from * ending miss 1st. Turn.
10th row As 9th. Break off C.
11th and 12th rows Using D, as 9th and 10th. Break off D.
13th row Using B, 2ch, miss first dc, 1dc in next dc, *miss next st, 1dc into each of next 5 sts, rep from * to last 4 sts, miss next st, 1dc into each of last 3 sts. Turn. 135[145:155: 165]sts.
Work rows 1-12 once more.
Change to No.3·00 (ISR) hook and using E work 4 rows dc across all sts. 162[174:

186:198]sts. Break off B.
Change to No. 3·50 (ISR) hook and join in A.
1st row 3ch, miss first st, *1tr in next st, rep from * to end. Turn.
Rep this row until work measures 8½ from beg, or required length to underarm ending with a WS row.

Divide for Back and Fronts

1st row Work in tr across 35[38:40:43]sts. Turn.
Complete Right front on these sts.
Next row Ss across first st, work in tr to end. Turn.

Shape Right front neck

Next row Ss across 9[9:10: 10]sts, work in tr to last st but one. Turn.
Next row Ss across first st, work in tr to last st but one. Turn. 22[25:26:29]sts.
Rep last row until 12[13:14: 15]sts rem.
Continue without shaping until armhole measures 6½[7: 7:7½]in from beg. Finish off.
With RS of work facing, miss next 11[11:13:13]sts, rejoin yarn and work in tr across next 70[76:80:86]sts. Turn.
Complete Back on these sts.
Next row Ss across first st, work in tr to last st but one. Turn.
Rep last row until 54[58:62: 66]sts rem.
Continue without shaping until Back measures same as Right front to shoulder. Finish off.
With RS of work facing, miss next 11[11:13:13]sts, rejoin yarn to rem sts and work to end.
Complete Left front on these sts.
Next row Work in tr to last st but one. Turn.

Shape Left front neck

Next row Ss across first st, work in tr to last 9[9:10:10] sts. Turn.
Next row Ss across first st, work in tr to last st but one. Turn.
Rep last row until 12[13:14: 15]sts rem.
Complete to match Right front.

Skirt

Using No. 3·00 (ISR) hook, A and with RS of work facing, rejoin yarn with ss to first st of Left front.
1st row 3ch, 1tr into each of next 3[7:4:1]sts, (2tr into next st, 1tr into each of next 8[7:7:7]sts) 14[16:18:20] times, 2tr into next st, 1tr into each of next 4[8:5:2]sts. Turn. 150[162:174:186]sts.
2nd row 3ch, miss first st, * 1tr in next st, rep from * to end. Turn.
Change to No. 3·50 (ISR) hook. Work 3 rows tr.

Shape skirt

1st inc row 3ch, 1tr into each of next 11[12:13:14]sts, (2tr into next st, 1tr into each of next 24[26:28:30]sts) 5 times, 2tr into next st, 1tr into each of last 12[13:14:15]sts. Turn. 156[168:180:192]sts.
Work 3 rows tr.
2nd inc row 3ch, 1tr into each of next 11[12:13:14]sts, (2tr into next st, 1tr into each of next 25[27:29:31]sts) 5 times, 2tr into next st, 1tr into each of last 13[14:15:16]sts. Turn. 162[174:186:198]sts.
Work 3 rows tr.
3rd inc row 3ch, 1tr into each of next 12[13:14:15]sts, (2tr into next st, 1tr into each of next 26[28:30:32]sts) 5 times, 2tr into next st, 1tr into each of last 13[14:15:16]sts. Turn. 168[180:192:204]sts.
Work 5 rows tr.
4th inc row 3ch, 1tr into each of next 12[13:14:15]sts, (2tr into next st, 1tr into each of next 27[29:31:33]sts) 5 times, 2tr into next st, 1tr into each of last 14[15:16:17]sts. Turn. 174[186:198:210]sts.
Work 5 rows tr.
5th inc row 3ch, 1tr into each of next 13[14:15:16]sts, (2tr into next st, 1tr into each of next 28[30:32:34]sts) 5 times, 2tr into next st, 1tr into each of last 14[15:16:17]sts. Turn. 180[192:204:216]sts.
Work 7 rows tr.
6th inc row 3ch, 1tr into each of next 13[14:15:16]sts, (2tr into next st, 1tr into each of next 29[31:33:35]sts) 5 times, 2tr into next st, 1tr into each

of last 15[16:17:18]sts. Turn. 186[198:210:222]sts.

Work 7 rows tr.

7th inc row 3ch, 1tr into each of next 14[15:16:17]sts, (2tr into next st, 1tr into each of next 30[32:34:36]sts) 5 times, 2tr into next st, 1tr into each of last 15[16:17:18]sts. Turn. 192[204:216:228]sts.

Work 7 rows tr.

8th inc row 3ch, 1tr into each of next 14[15:16:17]sts, (2tr into next st, 1tr into each of next 31[33:35:37]sts) 5 times, 2tr into next st, 1tr into each of last 16[17:18:19]sts. Turn. 198[210:222:234]sts.

Work 9 rows tr.

9th inc row 3ch, 1tr into each of next 15[16:17:18]sts, (2tr into next st, 1tr into each of next 32[34:36:38]sts) 5 times, 2tr into next st, 1tr into each of last 16[17:18:19] sts. Turn. 204[216:228:240] sts.

Continue without shaping until work measures 40½[41: 41:41½]in from top of shoulder, or required length less ½in. Finish off.

To make up

Press on WS under a damp cloth using a warm iron. Join shoulder seams.

Armbands Using No. 3·00 (ISR) hook, B and with RS facing work 1 row dc round armhole. Turn. Work 2 more rows dc. Finish off.

Front borders Using No. 3·00 (ISR) hook and B, with RS facing, work in dc up Right front edge, round neck, down Left front and round lower edge, working 3dc into each corner st. Turn.

Next row (buttonhole row) Work in dc, making 9 buttonholes on Right front edge, the 1st to come just below neck shaping and rem 8, 2½in apart, by working 3ch and missing 3dc, and working 3dc into each corner st. Turn.

Next row Work in dc to end working 3dc into each 3ch buttonhole on previous row. Finish off.

Join armbands. Press borders. Sew on buttons to correspond with buttonholes.

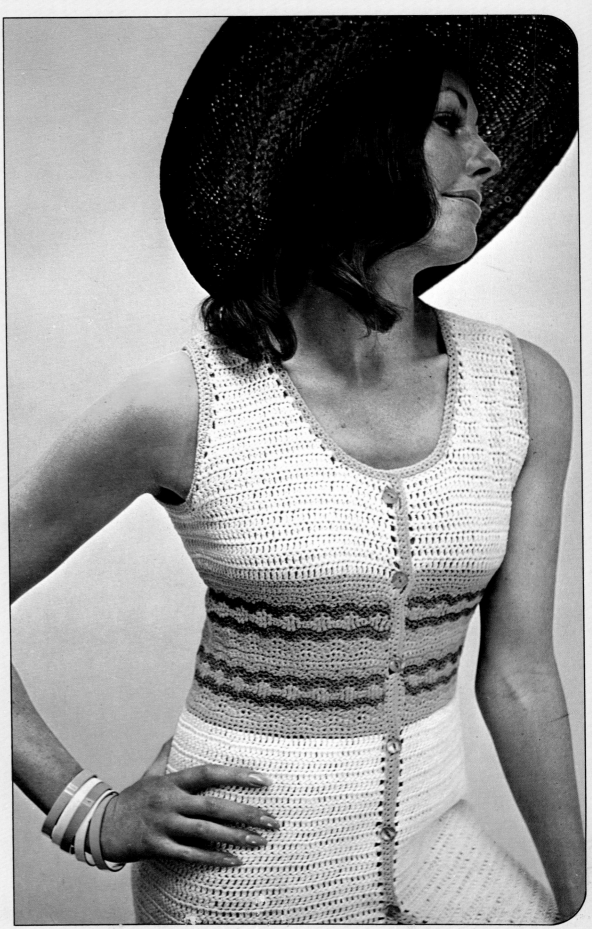

Charleston dress in crochet

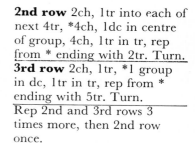

Basic Wardrobe Crochet

A young styled dress with the lively look of the 'roaring twenties'. A cleverly shaped treble panel ensures a perfect fit and the brief patterned yoke lends a demure touch. Wear it as a cool summer dress, as a dashing tunic over slim trousers, or add a glittering belt for evening glamour.

Sizes

To fit a 34[36:38]in bust
36[38:40]in hips
Length at centre back, 31¾in
The figures in brackets [ ] refer to the 36 and 38in sizes respectively

Tension for this design
One patt rep of 8tr and 1 group and 7 rows to 3in over patt worked on No.3·00 (ISR) crochet hook

Materials

Madame Pingouin
11[11:12] 50g balls
One No.3·00 (ISR) crochet hook
One button

Back

Using No.3·00 (ISR) hook make 125[129:133]ch.
1st row Into 2nd ch from hook work 1dc, *1dc into next ch, rep from * to end. Turn.
2nd row 2ch, 1tr into each of next 5[7:9] sts, *miss 3 sts of previous row, work 4tr, 1ch, 4tr all into next st to form group, miss 3 sts of previous row, 1tr into each of next 8

sts, rep from * ending last rep with 6[8:10]tr. Turn.
3rd row 2ch, 1tr into each of next 5[7:9] sts, *4ch, 1dc into ch sp in centre of tr group, 4ch, 1tr into each of next 8 sts, rep from * ending last rep with 6[8:10]tr. Turn.
4th row 2ch, 1tr into each of next 5[7:9] sts, *into dc in centre of group work 4 tr, 1ch, 4tr group, 1tr into each of next 8 sts, rep from * ending last rep with 6[8:10]tr. Turn.
Rep 3rd and 4th patt rows until work measures 4in, ending with a 4th patt row.
1st dec row 2ch, 1[2:3]tr, work next 2tr tog to dec thus: (yrh, insert hook into next st, yrh and draw loop through, yrh and draw through 2 loops) twice, yrh, draw through all 3 loops on hook, 2[3:4]tr, *4ch, 1dc in centre ch of group, 4ch, 1tr into each of next 3tr, dec by working 2tr tog as before, 1tr into each of next 3tr, rep from * ending last rep by working 2tr tog in centre of the panel.

Continue in patt noting that there will be one tr less in each panel.
Dec one tr in the centre of each panel in this way when work measures 8, 16 and 19in. There should now be 2[4:6]tr at each side and 4tr in central panels.
Work 2in without shaping. Inc one tr in centre of each panel by working 2tr into one st.
Continue without shaping until work measures 25in from beg, ending with a 3rd patt row.

Shape armholes

1st row Ss to centre of 1st group, 3ch, 3tr into same st as base of ch, work in patt to last group, 4tr in dc. Turn.
2nd row 1ch, 1tr into each of next 5tr panel, work in patt to last half group, 1dc in last tr. Turn.
3rd row Ss to first tr, 3ch, 1tr into each of next 4tr, work in patt to last tr panel, 1tr into each of 5tr. Turn.
Complete next 3rd patt row.

Divide for centre back

Work 1 row tr to one st before centre st, working 1tr into each tr, 3tr into ch sps and 1tr into dc. Turn. 38tr.
Work 1 row tr.
Continue in patt on these sts, beg at armhole edge.
1st row 2ch, 1tr, *miss 3 sts, work 1 group in next st, miss 3 sts, 1tr, rep from * ending with 1 group, miss 3 sts, 1tr into each of next 5tr. Turn.

2nd row 2ch, 1tr into each of next 4tr, *4ch, 1dc in centre of group, 4ch, 1tr in tr, rep from * ending with 2tr. Turn.
3rd row 2ch, 1tr, *1 group in dc, 1tr in tr, rep from * ending with 5tr. Turn.
Rep 2nd and 3rd rows 3 times more, then 2nd row once.

Shape neck and shoulder

Continue in patt working 1tr only at neck edge on next row and half a group less at same edge until 3 groups rem. Work next 2nd row to give straight edge. Finish off.
Complete other side to correspond, reversing shaping.

Front

Work as given for Back until 1st row of tr for yoke is completed, omitting back opening. 77tr.
Work 1 row tr, dec 1tr at each end of row.
Continue in patt as given for Back yoke, beg and ending each row with 2 tr.
Continue until 5 group rows have been completed. Work one 2nd row.

Shape neck

Work in patt to centre 3 groups, turn.
Complete shoulder on these sts.
Continue in patt, dec 1tr at neck edge on next row only, (3 groups rem), until armhole measures same as Back to shoulder. Finish off.
Rejoin yarn to other side of 3 central groups and work other side to correspond.

To make up

DO NOT PRESS.
Join side and shoulder seams.
Armbands Work 2 rows dc round each armhole. Finish off.
Neckband Work 2 rows dc round neck and edge of back opening. Make button loop at top of opening. Sew on button to other side of opening.

◄ *Close up detail of treble panel*
Simply styled and simply pretty ►

Killarney cloaks

Once regarded as evening wear, cloaks nowadays have taken on a new importance in fashion for wearing with longer skirts and trousers. Warmly practical and yet immensely glamorous, these hooded cloaks are comparatively simple to crochet on a basic square motif, plus a triangular motif to give shape to the cloak and the hood. In two colours or a single colour, the instructions are for both women's and children's sizes.

Sizes
To fit 22-32 [36-40]in chest/bust
Length at centre back, 22 [42]in, adjustable
The figures in brackets [ ] refer to the 36–40in size.

Tension for this design
Each square measures 3½in x 3½in worked on No.3·50 (ISR) crochet hook.

Materials shown here
Mahony Killowen Extra Double Knitting
One-colour version.
13 [30] 50g balls
Two-colour version. 7[16] 50g balls of main shade, A
8[17] 50g balls of contrast, B
One No.3·50 (ISR) crochet hook
One No.5·00 (ISR) crochet hook
3½ [6½] yd ½in wide velvet ribbon
2 [3] button links or frog fastenings
Reel shirring elastic
274

Basic Wardrobe Crochet

Note
One 50g ball makes approximately 9 squares in one colour;
or 18 squares using A for first 3 rounds;
or completes 20 squares using B for last round.

Cape

Square motif
Using No.3·50 (ISR) hook and A, make 5ch. Join into a circle with ss to first ch.
1st round. With A work 3ch, 14tr into circle. Join with ss to 3rd of first 3ch.
2nd round With A work 6ch, *miss 1tr, 1dc into next tr, 4ch, rep from * 6 times more. Join with ss to 2nd of first 6ch.
3rd round With A work 3ch, 2tr into first ch sp, * 1ch, into next ch sp work 3tr, 2ch, 3tr—called work corner —1ch, 3tr into next ch sp, rep from * twice more, 1ch, work corner into next ch sp, 1ch. Join with ss to 3rd of first 3 ch, leaving 2 loops on hook.
4th round Complete with A or break off A and join in B, pull through 2 loops on hook, 2ch, 3 tr into 1ch sp, 1ch, *work corner into 2ch sp between tr, (1ch, 3tr into 1ch sp) twice, 1ch, rep from * twice more, work corner into 2ch sp, 1ch, 3 tr into last 1ch sp. Join with ss to 2nd of first 2ch. Fasten off. Darn in all ends.
Make 66[211] more squares in the same way; allowing 15[21] squares for each row subtracted or added to alter length.

Triangle motif
Using No.3·50 (ISR) hook and A make 4ch. Join into circle with ss to first ch.
1st round With A work 3ch, 10 tr into circle. Join with ss to 3rd of first 3ch.
2nd round As 2nd round of square, rep from * 4 times.
3rd round As 3rd round of square, rep from * once.
4th round As 4th round of square, rep from * once. Fasten off. Darn in all ends. Make 10[15] more triangles in same way.

Hood
Work 18[33] square motifs as given for Cape.
Work 5[6] triangle motifs as given for Cape.

To make up
Press each motif under a damp cloth with a warm iron. Using colour worked on last round join motifs tog with blunt ended wool needle or crochet hook and dc.

Cape
Points of all triangle motifs should be placed towards neck edge.
1st row (neck edge) Beg with a square, join 1 square to 1 triangle using a total of 4[5] squares and 3[4] triangles, ending with 1 square.

Stitch detail of the square motif ▼

2nd row Join 1[2] squares, 1 triangle, 1 square, 1 triangle, 3 squares, 1 triangle, 1 square, 1 triangle, 1[2] squares.
3rd row Join 2[3] squares, 1 triangle, 1 square, 1 triangle, 5 squares, 1 triangle, 1 square, 1 triangle, 2[3] squares.

Small size only
4th row (arm slits) Join 2 squares and leave, join 11 squares, join 2 squares and leave.
5th and 6th rows Join 15 squares.

Large size only
4th row Join 4 squares, 1 triangle, 1 square, 1 triangle, 7 squares, 1 triangle, 1 square, 1 triangle, 4 squares.
5th row (arm slits) Join 3 squares and leave, join 15 squares, join 3 squares and leave.
6th row As 5th.
7th-12th rows Join 21 squares. Join all rows tog leaving arm-slits 2[3] squares in from front edge on 4th [5th-6th] rows.

Hood
1st row (neck edge) as Cape.
2nd row Join 7[9] squares. Rep 2nd row once more for large size only.
Next row (crown edge) Join 2[3] squares, 1 triangle with point to crown, 1 square,

1 triangle with point to crown, 2[3] squares.
Next row (crown) Join 2[3] squares and insert into crown edge row to close hood. Press all seams. Join neck edge of hood to neck edge of cape. With RS work facing, No.3·50 (ISR) hook and colour used on last round, beg at neck edge of hood and work ribbon slot edging as follows:
Next round 7ch, *1dtr into ch sp, 3ch, rep from * all round edge of hood and cape, working 3dtr with 3ch between in corners. Join with ss to 4th of first 7ch. Fasten off. Thread ribbon through slots, easing fullness round face edge of hood. Sew ribbon ends tog. Work edging along inside edge of arm slits in same way. Thread with ribbon. Sew down ends.

Alternative picot edging
Join in yarn as given for ribbon slot edging.
1st round 1ch, work 1dc in each tr and 1ch sp round all edges, working 3dc in each corner sp. Join with ss to first ch.
2nd round 2ch, work 1dc in each dc, making a picot of 4ch with ss to first ch on top of every 17th dc, and working 1dc, 1dc with picot, 1dc into each corner dc. Join with ss to 2nd of first 2 ch. Fasten off. Darn in ends. Work 2 rows along arm slits in same way.

To make frog fastening
Using No.5·00 (ISR) hook and 3 strands of yarn work buttonloop fastening by making 80ch. Fasten off. Darn in ends. Twist into rings and stitch tog as illustrated. Make 1[2] more buttonloops in same way.
Make 2[3] button fastenings as given for buttonloops, working 70ch and omitting loop for button.
To work buttons see Crochet **Know-how Chapter 7.**
Weave 2 rows shirring elastic round neck edge on WS. Sew on button links or frog fastenings.

275

Elegant town coat

This slim and elegant butt-oned-through town coat is warm enough for early spring days yet, being unlined, is light enough to be indispensable to your summer wardrobe. The skirt and bodice are worked in an easy patterned stitch with simple trebles used for the yoke, sleeves, collar and pocket.

The coat illustrated is worked in shamrock green double crepe yarn, the collar, pocket and front edges being worked in sparkling white.

Sizes

To fit 34[36:38:40]in bust
36[38:40:42]in hips
Length from shoulder, 39 [39½:40:40½]in
Sleeve seam, 17in, adjustable
The figures in brackets [ ] refer to the 36, 38 and 40in sizes respectively.

> **Tension for this design**
> 8tr to 2in in width worked on No.4.00 hook. 1 rep of patt in depth to measure 3½in worked on Nos.4.50 and 4.00 hooks.

Materials shown here

Robin Double Crepe 26[28:30:32]oz in main shade A,
1 oz in contrast shade, B
One No.4.50 (ISR) crochet hook
One No.4.00 (ISR) crochet hook
Seven buttons

Back

Using No. 4.00 (ISR) hook and A make 98[102:106:110] ch.

Base row Miss 2ch, work 1tr into each ch to end. Turn with 3ch. 97[101:105:109]tr.
Work 1 row tr.
Continue in patt.
1st row (right side) Using No.4.00 (ISR) hook work in tr to end. Turn with 2ch.
2nd row Using No.4.50 (ISR) hook, work in dc to end. Turn with 2ch.
3rd row *Miss 1dc, 1tr into each of next 3dc, put hook in front of last 3tr and into missed dc, yrh, draw through long loop, yrh, draw through 2 loops on hook, rep from * to last st, 1dc into last st. Turn with 1ch.
4th row Work 1dc into each st to end. Turn with 2ch.
Rep 3rd and 4th rows once more.
7th row Using No.4.00 (ISR) hook, work 1tr into each st to end. Turn with 2ch.
Rep 7th row 4 times more, ending last row by turning with 1ch.
Rows 2–11 form patt.
Rep rows 2–11 once more. **
Rep 2–11 patt rows 5 times more, dec 8sts evenly across the first row of 1st, 3rd and 5th patt rep. 73[77:81:85]sts.
Rep 2–11 patt rows twice more, inc 4sts evenly across the first row of 1st and 2nd patt rep. 81[85:89:93]sts.
Continue working each row in tr only until work measures 31in from beg, or required length to underarm ending with a WS row. Omit turning ch at end of last row.

Shape armholes

Next row Ss over 9[10:11:12] sts, work in tr to last 9[10:11: 12]sts. Turn with 2ch. 63[65:67:69]sts.
Continue without shaping until armholes measure 8[8½:9:9½]in, ending with a WS row.

Shape shoulders

Next row Ss over 6[6:7:7] sts, work in tr to last 6[6:7:7] sts. Turn. Rep last row once more.
Next row Ss over 7[7:6:6] sts, work in tr to last 7[7:6:6] sts. Fasten off.

Right front

Using No.4.00 (ISR) hook and A, make 50[54:58:62]ch. Work as given for Back to **. 49[53:57:61]sts.
Rep 2–11 patt rows 5 times more, dec 4sts evenly across the first row of 1st, 3rd and 5th patt rep. 37[41:45:49]sts.
Rep 2–11 patt rows twice more, inc 4sts evenly across the first row of 1st patt rep. 41[45:49:53]sts.

1st and 2nd sizes only

Work 1 row tr inc 3[1]sts across the row. 44[46]sts.

3rd and 4th sizes only

Work 1 row tr dec 1[3]sts across the row. 48[50]sts.

All sizes

Continue working in tr until work measures same as Back to underarm, ending at armhole edge.

Shape armhole

Next row Ss over 9[10:11:12] sts, work in tr to end. 35[36: 37:38]sts.
Continue without shaping until armhole measures 5 rows less than Back to shoulder, ending at armhole edge.

Shape neck

Next row Work in tr to last 10 sts. Turn.
Continue in tr, dec one st at neck edge on next 4 rows.

Shape shoulder

Next row Dec one st, work in tr to last 6[6:7:7]sts. Turn.
Next row Ss over 6[6:7:7]sts, work in tr to last 2sts, dec one st. Fasten off.

Left front

Work as given for Right front, reversing all shapings.

Sleeves (two alike)

Using No.4.00 (ISR) hook and A, make 35[37:41:41]ch. Work Base row as given for Back, then work in tr for 2in.
Continue in tr, inc one st at each end of next and every alt row until there are 70[72:76:76]sts.
Continue without shaping until work measures 17in from beg, or required underarm length. Place coloured marker at each end of last row. Work a further 2in for top of sleeve, which is set into armhole. Fasten off.

Collar

Join shoulder seams.
Using No.4.00 (ISR) hook and A and with WS of work facing, work in tr over centre 8sts of Back neck, ss over all sts to end of Back neck. Turn with 3ch.
Work in tr over all sts of

Sparkling white on shamrock green ►
Pattern stitch and pocket detail ▼

Back neck, work in tr over 7sts of Left front neck. Turn with 3ch.

Work in tr to right shoulder, work in tr over 7sts of Right front neck. Turn with 3ch. Continue working in tr across all neck sts, inc one st at each end of every alt row and *at the same time* inc 4sts evenly across the next 3 alt rows. Fasten off.

Pocket flaps (2 alike)

Using No. 4·00 (ISR) hook and A, make 12 ch.
Work 5 rows tr. Fasten off.
Rejoin yarn to side edge and work 1 row tr round 3 sides of pocket, working 2sts in each corner st. Break off A and join in B. Work 1 row tr as before. Fasten off.

To make up

Press all pieces lightly on WS under a damp cloth with a warm iron. Join side seams. Join sleeve seams as far as markers. Set in sleeves, sewing top of sleeves from markers to cast off sts at underarms.

Edging

Using No.4·00 (ISR) hook and A and with RS facing, rejoin yarn to lower edge of Right front and work 1 row tr along Right front edge, working 7 buttonholes evenly spaced by missing the length of the button required and working 3ch, the 1st buttonhole to come 9in above lower edge and the last 8in from neck shaping; continue in tr round revers and collar working twice into corner sts, and down Left front. Break off A. Join in B and with RS facing beg at side seam and work 1 row tr evenly all round edges of Coat, working twice into corner sts. Fasten off.
Using No.4·00 (ISR) hook and B work 1 row tr round cuffs.
Fasten off.
Press all seams.
Sew on pocket flaps.
Sew on buttons.

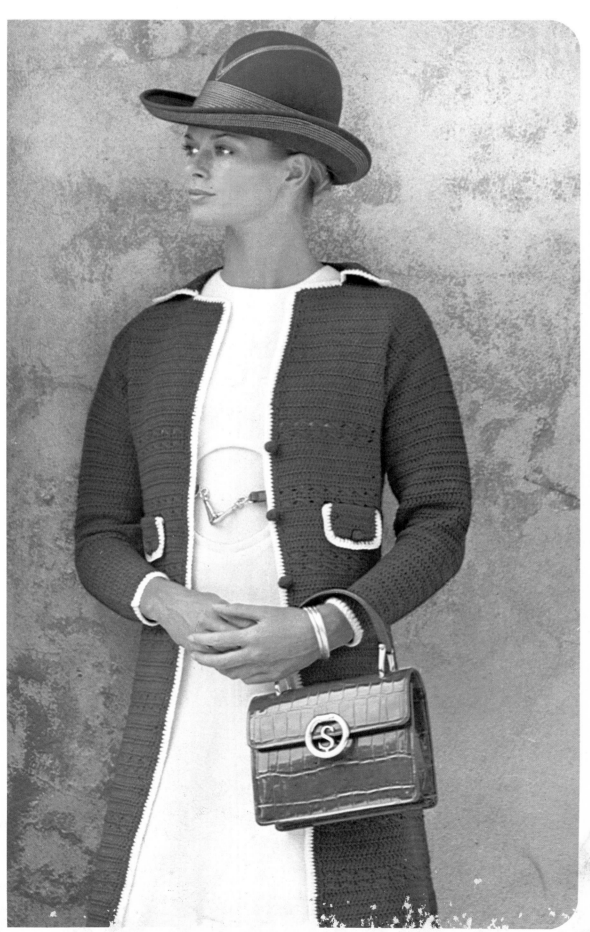

Silver evening bolero

As an example of how a motif design can be lifted into the couture class, this brief bolero has been worked in silver yarn. The charm of this particular design is that as each motif is worked, it is joined to the last motif completed as part of the final round of crochet, thus avoiding the necessity of sewing motifs together. This method of working also produces a lighter and more flexible fabric.

Glamorous worn on its own with a long skirt or harem pants, the bolero also looks good worn over a full-sleeved blouse or a plain dress.

Size
To fit a 34-36in bust
Length at centre back, $13\frac{3}{4}$in

> **Tension for this design**
> Motif measures $4\frac{1}{4}$in sq when pressed

Materials shown here
4 25g balls Twilley's Goldfingering
One No.4·50 (ISR) crochet hook
Six small buttons

1st motif

Using No.4·50 (ISR) hook make 8ch. Join with ss to first ch to form circle.
1st round 2ch, work 15dc into circle. Join with ss to 2nd of first 2ch.
2nd round 5ch, *miss 1dc, 1htr into next dc, 3ch, rep from * 6 times. Join with ss to 2nd of first 5ch.
3rd round Work 1dc, 1htr,

3tr, 1htr, 1dc into each ch sp. Join with ss to first dc. (8 petals).
4th round 2ch, *3ch, 1dc into top of next petal, 6ch, 1dc into top of next petal, 3ch, 1htr into sp before dc at beg of next petal, 3ch, 1htr into same sp, rep from * twice, 3ch, 1dc into top of next petal, 6ch, 1dc into top of next petal, 3ch, 1htr into sp before dc at beg of next petal, 3ch. Join with ss to 1st of first 3ch.
5th round *4ch, into 6ch sp work 3tr, 3ch, 3tr, 4ch, 1dc into htr, 1dc into 3ch sp, 1dc into htr, rep from * to end. Join with ss to 1st of first 4ch.
6th round *5ch, 1tr into each of next 3tr, 5ch, insert hook into 3rd ch from hook and work 1dc to form picot, 2ch, 1tr into each of next 3tr, 5ch, ss into next dc, 4ch, insert hook into 3rd ch from hook and work 1dc to form picot, 1ch, miss 1dc, ss into next dc, rep from * to end. Join with ss to 1st of first 5ch.
Fasten off.

2nd motif

Work as given for 1st motif until 5th round has been completed.
6th round 5ch, 1tr into each of next 3tr, 2ch, 1dc into corner picot of 1st motif, 2ch, 1tr into each of next 3tr on 2nd motif, ss into 1st of 5ch after tr of 1st motif, 4ch, ss into next dc of 2nd motif, 1ch, 1dc into centre side picot of 1st motif, 1ch, miss 1dc on 2nd motif, ss into next dc, 4ch, ss into ch before next 3tr on 1st motif, 1 tr into each of next 3tr on 2nd motif, 2ch, ss into

picot at end of 1st motif, 2ch, now complete this round as given for 1st motif.
Work 20 more motifs in same way, joining 8 to form first row.
On next row, join 2 motifs on 2 sides to form right front, 4 motifs to next 4 motifs for centre back and 2 motifs to last 2 motifs for left front.
On next row, miss first motif of right front and join 1 motif to next motif, 4 motifs to next 4 motifs and 1 motif to next motif for left front, joining shoulder seams at same time.
Fasten off. Darn in all ends.

Edging

Beg at centre back of lower edge and into each ch sp and picot work 1dc, 1tr, 3ch, 1tr, 1dc, around all edges, ss to first dc. Fasten off. Darn in ends.
Work round armholes in same way ss along underarm.
Sew on 6 buttons evenly spaced to left front to correspond with 3ch between trs on right front.
Press lightly under a damp cloth with a warm iron.

The button fastening can be worn at either the front or the back

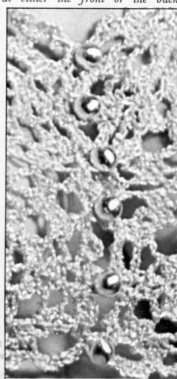

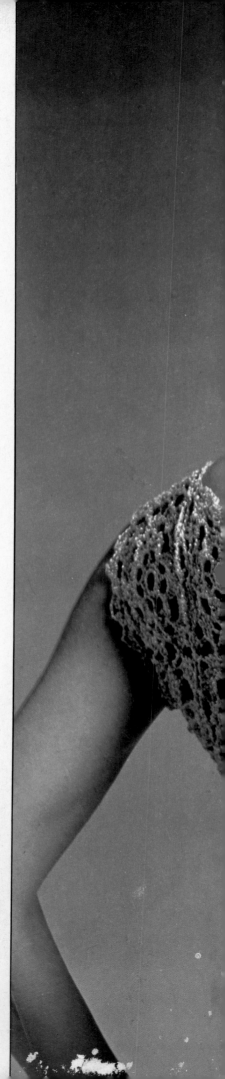

Gold & silver evening blouse

Versatile addition to your late-day wardrobe, here's a blouse that doubles as a lacy jacket. Wear it with your favourite evening skirt or over a plain sleeveless dress. Pick a thread with a lovely subtle sparkle — glowing gold, shimmering silver, gleaming bronze or lustrous copper. Combine two tones or use any one of them.

Sizes

To fit a 34 [36:38] in bust.
Length at centre Back, About 18¼ [19:19½] in.
The figures given in brackets [ ] refer to the 36 and 38in sizes respectively.

Tension
3 clusters to 1in.
3 rows to 1¼in.

Materials shown here

7[7:8] 25g balls of Twilley's Goldfingering in silver
5 [6:6] balls in gold
No.3·50 (ISR) crochet hook
4 small buttons (optional)

Abbreviations

See Crochet Know-how 1

Back

Using gold work 102 [108: 114] ch.

1st row Work 3tr into 3rd ch from hook leaving last loop of each tr on hook (4 loops on hook), yrh, draw through all loops to form 1 cluster (abbrev. cl), 1ch, miss 1ch, *1cl into next ch, 1ch, miss 1ch, rep from * to end working 1tr into last ch.

Turn.
2nd row Using silver, join with ss, 2ch, *1cl into next ch sp, 1ch, rep from *, ending with 1tr.
Leave the silver.
Continue working as for 2nd row alt using gold and silver and working from the end where the required colour has been left to avoid joining.
To start a new row work a long loop and ss into edge of last row, work 2ch and continue in patt.
Work until 11 [11¼:11½] in from start.

Shape armholes

Keeping patt correct work 4cl less at each end of next row, and 1cl less at each end of following row.
Work without further shaping until armholes measure 6¼ [6½:6¾] in.

Shape shoulder

Work 4cl less at armhole edges and omit 1ch after last cl, 1tr into next ch sp. Turn.
Next row Work 3cl, omit 1ch after last cl, 1tr into next ch sp.
Break yarn.
Work other shoulder in same way.

Left front

Using gold work 44 [48:52] ch.
Work in patt as given for Back until work measures same to armhole.

Shape armhole

Work 4 cl less at side edge.
Work without shaping until centre Front edge measures 14 [4½:4¾] in.

Shape neck

1st row Work 5cl less at centre Front, work to end. Turn.
2nd row Patt to last ch sp, omit 1ch after last cl, 1tr into edge. Turn.
3rd row Work cl into first ch sp, patt to end. Turn.
4th row As 2nd row.
Continue without further shaping until armhole measures same as Back to shoulder.

Shape shoulder

Work as given for Back shoulder.
Finish off.

Right front

Work in same way as for Left front.

Sleeves

Using gold work 68 [70:72] ch.
Work in patt for 6 [7:8] rows.

Shape top

Work 3cl less at each end of next row.
Work 1cl less at each end of next 13 [13:14] rows.
Break yarn and finish off.

To make up

Sew shoulder and side seams.

Border

Using silver work sleeve borders.

1st row *1dc into each of next 4ch, dec in next 2ch by inserting hook into next ch, yrh and draw through ch, insert hook into next ch, yrh and draw through ch, yrh and draw through all loops, rep from * to end. Turn.
2nd row 2ch, *yrh, insert hook into next dc (yrh and draw through a long loop) 4 times in the same st, yrh and draw through all loops on hook to make 1 puff, 1ch, miss 1ch, rep from * to end. Turn.
3rd row 2ch, 1dc into the top of each puff and each ch to end of row. Turn.
4th row *3ch, 1tr into next dc, miss 1dc, 1dc into next dc, rep from * to end of row.

Finish off

Work other sleeve border in the same way.
Work border around jacket in same way starting at side seam and working 1dc into each ch along lower edge, 1dc, 2ch, 1dc into corner st, 2dc into each row up front edges, and dec twice on curves at Front neck and once on either curve at Back as given for sleeve. On the following row work 2ch between the puffs at the corners.
Sew sleeve seams and set in sleeves.
Sew on buttons if required with the spaces between the puffs acting as button-holes.

The pattern and edging of the gold and silver blouse

280

Glamorous evening tunic

A glamorous long tunic for wining and dining, crocheted in a simple stitch which has a see-through look without being too open. Wear it over trousers or as it is.

Sizes
To fit 34-36in bust, 36-38in hips
Length at centre back, 57in
Sleeve seam, 17½in

Tension for this design
6 stitches and 3 rows to one inch worked over pattern on No.3·50 (ISR) crochet hook

Materials shown here
Listers Crisp Crepe 4 ply 32oz
One No.3·50 (ISR) crochet hook
6in zip fastener

Back

Using No.3·50 (ISR) hook make 138ch.
1st row 1tr into 3rd ch from hook, 1tr into each ch to end Turn. 136 sts.
2nd row 5ch, *miss 2tr, 1tr into next tr, 2ch, rep from * to end, working 1tr into turning ch. Turn.
3rd row 5ch, *1tr into next tr, (2 tr into 2ch sp, 1tr into next tr) 3 times, 2ch, rep from * to end, working 1tr into turning ch. Turn.
4th row 5ch, *1tr into each of next 4tr, 2ch, miss 2tr, 1tr into each of next 4tr, 2ch, rep from * to end, working 1tr into turning ch. Turn.
5th row 5ch, *1tr into each of next 4tr, 2tr in 2ch sp, 1tr into each of next 4tr, 2ch, rep from * to end, working 1tr into turning ch. Turn.
6th row 5ch, *1tr into next tr, (2ch, miss 2 tr, 1tr into next tr) 3 times, 2ch, rep from * to end, working 1tr into turning ch. Turn.
Rep rows 3—6 inclusive 14 times more, 62 rows in all, then work should measure approximately 20½in from beginning.

Make side slits
Next row 5ch, 1tr into 1st and 2nd of these 5ch, 1tr into turning ch tr of previous row, 2ch, 1tr into next tr, patt to end.
Next row As last row. 142 sts.
Continue in patt, dec one st at each end of every 4th row until 112 sts rem.
Continue without shaping until work measures 50in from beg, or required length to underarm.

Shape armholes
Next row Ss over first 6 sts, patt to last 6 sts, turn.
Dec one st at each end of next 6 rows. 88 sts.
Continue without shaping until armholes measure 3in from beg, ending WS row.

Divide for back opening
Next row Patt over first 43 sts, turn.
Continue in patt until armhole measures 7in from beg, ending at centre edge.

Shape shoulder
Next row Patt to last 8 sts, turn.

Next row Ss over first 8 sts, patt next 8 sts. Fasten off.
With RS of work facing miss next 2 sts for centre back, rejoin yarn to rem sts and patt to end. Complete to match first side.

Front
Work as given for Back until armhole shaping is completed. Continue without shaping until armholes measure 5 rows less than Back, ending WS row.

Shape neck
Next row Patt over first 35 sts, turn.
Next row Ss over first 3 sts, patt to end. Turn.
Next row Patt to last 3 sts, turn.
Next row Ss over first 3 sts, patt to end. Turn.
Next row Patt to last 2 sts, turn.
Next row Patt to last 8 sts, turn.
Next row Ss over first 8 sts, patt to end. Fasten off.
With RS of work facing miss next 18sts for centre neck, rejoin yarn to rem sts and patt to end. Complete to match first side.

Sleeves

Using No.3·50 (ISR) hook make 54 ch.
Work in patt as given for Back, (52 sts), for 6 rows.
Continue in patt, inc one st at each end of next and every following 4th row until there are 76 sts.
Continue without shaping until sleeve measures 17½in from beg, or required length to underarm.

Shape top
Next row Ss over first 6 sts, patt to last 6 sts, turn.
Dec one st at each end of next 6 rows.
Next row Patt to last 4sts. Turn.
Rep last row 9 times more. Finish off.

To make up

Press each piece under a damp cloth with a warm iron. Join shoulder and sleeve seams. Join side seams as far as side slits.
Collar. Using No.3·50 (ISR) hook make 90ch. Work in patt as given for Back, (88sts), for 10 rows. Finish off.
Slit edges. Using No.3·50 (ISR) hook and with RS of work facing, rejoin yarn to lower edge and work 1 row of tr to where extra sts were cast on, working 2tr into each row. Finish off.
Set in sleeves. Sew on collar. Work 2 rows dc along sides of collar and back opening. Sew in zip. Press seams.

Cord belt

Using No.3·50 (ISR) hook and yarn double throughout, make 2ch. Insert hook into first ch, *yrh, draw through a loop, yrh, draw through both loops on hook*, insert hook into the left of these 2 loops and work from * to * for required length. Finish off.

▼ *Stitch detail*   *Tunic with a metal link belt* ►

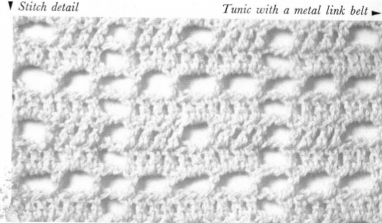

Plaid crochet pullover for a man

Fun to make for someone you love—a man's pullover in an unusual plaid effect crochet stitch with the armholes and neckline worked in plain double crochet.

Sizes
To fit 38[40:42]in chest
The figures in brackets [] refer to the 40 and 42in sizes respectively

Tension for this design
5 vertical stripes to 2in

Materials shown here
Templeton's H and O Shetland Fleece
8 1oz balls brown
6 1oz balls camel
2 1oz balls natural
One No.3·50 (ISR) Aero crochet hook
One No.5·00 (ISR) Aero crochet hook
NB This garment is worked in 2 stages—the net background is worked first and the vertical stripes worked in afterwards, using yarn double throughout.

Front

Using No.3·50 hook and single camel yarn, work 102[106: 110] ch.
1st row Into 6th ch from hook work 1tr, *1ch, miss 1ch, 1tr in next ch, rep from * to end.
Turn. 49[51:53] sp.
2nd row 4ch, miss first tr and 1ch, *1tr in next tr, 1ch, miss 1ch, rep from * ending with 1tr in turning ch.
The 2nd row forms the patt

284

and is rep throughout changing colour as required.
Work 4 rows camel and 2 rows brown throughout.
Work without shaping until 7th camel stripe is complete.

Shape armholes
1st row Miss 2 sp and join brown into next tr, 4ch, patt over 45[47:49] sp, ending with 1tr and leaving 2 sp at end unworked. Turn.
2nd row Ss to 2nd tr, 4ch, patt over 43[45:47] sp, ending with 1tr. Fasten off. Turn.
3rd row Miss first sp and rejoin camel into 2nd tr, 4ch, patt over 41[43:45] sp. Turn.
This completes armhole shaping and sides are now kept straight.

Shape neck, left side
1st row 4ch, patt over 19[20: 21] sp, 1tr. Turn.
2nd row 4ch, work in patt to end. Turn.
3rd row 4ch, patt over 18[19:20]sp, ending with 1tr. Turn.
4th row Using brown, 4ch, patt to end. Turn.
Continue dec 1 sp at neck edge every alt row until 12 sp rem, keeping stripes correct.
Work without shaping until 2nd row of 5th camel stripe has been completed. Fasten off.

Shape neck, right side
1st row Miss 1 sp at neck edge, join camel into next tr, patt over 19[20:21] sp ending with 1 tr. Turn.
2nd row 4ch, patt over 8 [19:20] sp, 4ch, miss 1ch an

work 1dc in next tr.
Continue shaping in this way until shoulder corresponds with other side. Fasten off.

Back

Work as given for Front until armhole shaping is complete. Continue in patt without shaping until armholes measure same as Front to shoulder, ending with 2 rows camel. Fasten off.

Work vertical stripes

Using No.5·00 hook and double camel, begin at base of centre Front sp.
Make a slip loop. Holding right side of net ground facing, insert hook into loop and work with yarn kept at back of work (see Crochet Know-how Chapter 13). Work up to top edge keeping work to the correct measurement.
Work other stripes to side edges in the following order:
*2 brown, 1 camel, 1 brown, 3 natural, 1 brown, 1 camel, 2 brown, 1 natural, rep from * to side edges.
Work Back in same way.

To make up

Darn in all ends.
Block and press each piece to correct size.

Welt
Using No.3·50 hook and single brown, work 99[103: 107] dc along lower edge of Front.
1st row 1ch, *1dc into next dc, rep from * to end. Turn.
Rep 1st row until welt measures 2½in, ending with a RS row.
Finish off.
Work Back in same way.
Join shoulder seams.

Armbands
Using No.3·50 hook and brown, with RS facing work 118dc evenly around armhole. Work in rows of dc as for welt for 4 rows more. Finish off.
Work second armhole in same way.

Neckband
Using No.3·50 hook and brown, with RS facing join yarn at left shoulder seam.
1st row Work 47dc to centre Front, 47dc to right shoulder seam and 43dc across Back neck.
Work 6 rows dc as given for welt dec 1 st at each side of centre Front on every row, and 1 st at each shoulder seam on every RS row only.
Finish off.
Join neckband seam.
Sew side seams.
Press as required.

▼ *Detail of plaid effect stitch*

Simple yet effective plaid crochet ►

INDEX